Reexamining the Federal Role in Higher Education

Reexamining the Federal Role in Higher Education

Politics and Policymaking in the Postsecondary Sector

Rebecca S. Natow

TEACHERS COLLEGE PRESS
TEACHERS COLLEGE | COLUMBIA UNIVERSITY
NEW YORK AND LONDON

Published by Teachers College Press,® 1234 Amsterdam Avenue, New York, NY 10027

Copyright © 2022 by Teachers College, Columbia University

Front cover photo courtesy of Peter Schultz via a Creative Commons license.

All rights reserved. No part of this publication may be reproduced or transmitted in any form or by any means, electronic or mechanical, including photocopy, or any information storage and retrieval system, without permission from the publisher. For reprint permission and other subsidiary rights requests, please contact Teachers College Press, Rights Dept.: tcpressrights@tc.columbia.edu

Library of Congress Cataloging-in-Publication Data is available at loc.gov

ISBN 978-0-8077-6676-7 (paper)
ISBN 978-0-8077-6677-4 (hardcover)
ISBN 978-0-8077-8093-0 (ebook)

Printed on acid-free paper
Manufactured in the United States of America

Contents

Acknowledgments	ix
Introduction	1
Federal Higher Education Policy Areas	3
Guiding Questions, Perspectives, and Methods	8
Preview of the Remainder of the Book	12
1. The Federal Structure and Higher Education Policy	**15**
Federalism in the United States	15
Federal Powers and Politics	20
Constitutional Provisions and Policy Instruments	25
Summary and Conclusion	31
2. The History of the Federal Government's Role in Higher Education	**33**
Higher Education's Early Expansion: 1780s–1920s	34
The Post–World War I Era, Great Depression, and New Deal: 1920s–1940s	38
Higher Education and the National Defense: 1940s–1950s	39
The Civil Rights Movement and Steps Toward Equity: 1930s–1970s	42
Consumerism and Accountability: 1970s–2020s	48
Summary and Conclusion	51
3. Congress's Roles in Higher Education	**53**
Structure of Congress	54
Congress's Legislative Power	59
Congressional Oversight Powers	64

	Senate Confirmation Power	66
	The Congressional "Bully Pulpit"	67
	Congressional Power Case Study: The CARES Act	69
	Summary and Conclusion	69
4.	**The President's Power and Influence Over Higher Education**	**71**
	Overview of the Presidency and Executive Branch	72
	The President's Legislative Role in Higher Education Policymaking	73
	Executive Action	75
	Using the "Bully Pulpit" and Presidential Messaging	80
	Policymaking in the White House	81
	Presidential Power Case Study: International Students and Scholars	88
	Summary and Conclusion	89
5.	**Federal Administrative Agencies and Higher Education**	**91**
	Overview of Federal Administrative Agencies	92
	Policy Powers of Federal Agencies	94
	Federal Agencies Influencing Higher Education	101
	Agency Power Case Study: Borrower Defense to Repayment	110
	Summary and Conclusion	111
6.	**Higher Education and the Federal Courts**	**113**
	Overview of the Federal Court System	114
	Federal Courts' Jurisdiction and Powers	117
	Key Higher Education Policy Areas Affected by the Federal Judiciary	119
	Judicial Power Case Study: Bankruptcy Courts	125
	Summary and Conclusion	126
7.	**Nonfederal Actors' Influence on Federal Higher Education Policy**	**127**
	Interest Groups	128
	State and Local Governments	134

Accreditors	138
News Media	140
Other Nonfederal Actors	141
Summary and Conclusion	144

8. Reexamining the Federal Role in Higher Education — 147
    Returning to the Guiding Questions — 148
    Revisiting Perspectives on the Size of Government — 159
    Summary and Conclusion — 161

Methodological Appendix — 163
    Interview Data — 163
    Documentary Data — 165

Notes — 167

References — 171

Index — 221

About the Author — 245

Acknowledgments

This work is the product of many years of considering and studying how federal policy shapes higher education, how the U.S. government derives its authority to regulate higher education, and why the federal government plays a ubiquitous role in higher education despite the fact that education is not once mentioned in the U.S. Constitution. At a time when higher education stakeholders of all kinds are in great need of federal support and interventions, my hope is that this book will provide students, leaders, and advocates with a detailed understanding of how federal policy processes work in the higher education space, and that with this knowledge, stakeholders will be well positioned to advocate for themselves and their organizations for the federal support they require.

I gratefully acknowledge the many individuals who helped me think through these topics and provided advice, perspectives, and support while I completed the manuscript. First, I owe great thanks to Brian Ellerbeck and the team at Teachers College Press. Thank you for taking an interest in this project and for your excellent work in moving the book toward publication.

Thank you to the dozens of policy actors in the higher education community who generously gave their time and insights to this effort when I interviewed them as part of the research on which this book is based. I am honored that these experts provided so much valuable data that will help higher education scholars, leaders, and advocates to learn more about the "inside baseball" of the federal higher education policy arena.

I owe enormous thanks to many friends and colleagues who read early drafts of one or more chapters of this book and provided valuable feedback. Thank you to Dominique Baker, Meena Bose, Matthew Camp, Rosemary Carolan, Kevin Dougherty, Sean Fanelli, Alison Griffin, Sosanya Jones, Robert Kelchen, Jacklyn Kuehn, Amy Laitinen, Clare McCann, Carina McCormick, H. Kenny Nienhusser, Rosanna Perotti, Clifford Pincus, Vikash Reddy, Holly Seirup, Sandra Stacki, Amy Stein, Laura Sulem, Eustace Thompson, and two Teachers College Press anonymous reviewers.

I am also immensely grateful to the Rockefeller Institute of Government, which did me the honor of selecting me as a Richard P. Nathan Public Policy Fellow for 2020–2021. During my fellowship year, I had the opportunity to meet and work with the Institute's impressive team of researchers, fellows, and staff, as well as a great cohort of Nathan Fellows. The Institute posted and promoted my analyses of federal higher education policy issues, and I received valuable feedback on early drafts of those writings from Laura Schultz, Brian Backstrom, Laura Rabinow, Nicholas Simons, and Heather Trela.

I would not have been able to complete this work or any other without the valuable support from the people who provide me with childcare, housekeeping, and administrative assistance. I very much appreciate your excellent and essential work. I also thank my extended family for their many years of constant support.

Some of the research underlying this book was funded by the Hofstra College of Liberal Arts and Sciences Faculty Research and Development Grant and the Hofstra University Presidential Research Award Program. I gratefully acknowledge this financial support.

Finally, I thank and dedicate this volume to my spouse Steven Natow and my children Adam and Charlotte Natow. I love you, now and always, more than words could ever express.

—RSN

Introduction

The United States Constitution provides no enumerated power regarding educating the populace to any branch of the federal government. The words "educate" and "education" do not appear in the text of the Constitution at all—not in the original document, and not in any of its 27 amendments. The Tenth Amendment to the Constitution states that "powers not delegated to the United States by the Constitution, nor prohibited by it to the States, are reserved to the States respectively, or to the people." It would therefore seem that the role of regulating higher education, which has not been specifically assigned to any branch of the federal government, should be the exclusive responsibility of the states (Mumper et al., 2016; Williams, 1991; Zumeta, 2005).

But that is not the case. The federal government inarguably plays an extensive and important role in the financing and regulation of higher education. In recent years, the federal government has spent more than $75 billion annually on higher education (Pew Charitable Trusts, 2019). As of 2018–2019, approximately 85% of first-time, full-time students at 4-year colleges and 79% of first-time, full-time students at 2-year colleges received some form of federal financial aid (U.S. Department of Education, 2021b). The federal government has encouraged innovation in higher education and sponsored an untold number of research and development breakthroughs via grant funding to universities, their employees, and their partnerships (Brint, 2019; Pew Charitable Trusts, 2019). With this federal funding come conditions and regulations to which colleges and universities must adhere, including requirements to meet accreditation standards, to maintain students' privacy, to report incidents of crime on or near campus, and to provide accommodations for persons with disabilities, among other mandates (Feder, 2012; Kaplin et al., 2020; Kelchen, 2018; U.S. Department of Education, 2016b). The federal government also enforces civil rights by investigating and penalizing colleges and universities that violate these federal laws (Kaplin et al., 2020; Wolanin, 2003). The U.S. Department of Education continuously develops and revises regulations and federal guidance regarding for-profit and career-focused higher education, and devises policy on how institutions should handle allegations of sexual harassment and assault under Title IX (Kreighbaum, 2018a, 2018b; Natow, 2017). Federal laws and regulations from intellectual property protections to immigration policies to the federal tax code all have relevance to higher education (Kaplin et al., 2020).

The federal government's policymaking has influenced the lives of untold millions, including people who have paid tuition prices at colleges and universities, work in educational institutions, conduct or benefit from university-based research and development, and countless others. For example, federal student financial aid policies affect the personal finances of millions of people, and those finances have ripple effects across the broader economy. Each of those millions is an individual, with their own life, dreams, and loved ones. They are, as the *Washington Post* has reported, the 28-year-old whose postsecondary art school lost accreditation, the couple who incurred six figures in debt to pay for their children to attend college, the Ivy League doctoral graduate with more than $300,000 in student loans, and many more (Douglas-Gabriel & Harden, 2021). The reach of federal higher education policy is at once wide and deeply personal.

Why does the federal government play such a central role in higher education in the United States, when the Constitution is completely silent on the issue of education? The answer to this question, which is explored throughout this book, involves a complex interplay of historical context, economic pressure, and the push and pull of political power—all against the restraining, but changing, structure of the U.S. government. Colleges and universities receive funding from the federal government in amounts that sometimes constitute up to 90% of institutional revenues (Lee & Looney, 2019). By providing student loans on a vast scale and enforcing civil rights laws to counter segregation and discrimination, the federal government has played an essential role in broadening access to higher education (Fuller, 2014; Harper et al., 2009; Thelin, 2011; Wolanin, 2003). Indeed, the federal government's role in the historical growth and trajectory of higher education has been enormous.

This book provides a comprehensive account of the federal government's role in higher education and how that role came to be so large over time. Policymakers who have vocally decried federal overreach—such as President Ronald Reagan in the 1980s and Republicans who controlled all branches of the federal government during President Donald Trump's administration—have, at one time or another, been in a position to curtail federal involvement in higher education. Yet the federal role in this sector has not only persisted, but has expanded over time. The U.S. Department of Education, for whose elimination policymakers have perennially called (Stallings, 2002), still exists and is arguably more powerful than ever. Recent reauthorizations of the Higher Education Act—the most comprehensive federal higher education statute—have involved several hundred pages of legislation (e.g., Higher Education Opportunity Act, 2008).

There are few books uniquely dedicated to exploring the U.S. government's role in regulating, financing, and otherwise influencing higher education. An exception is Michael Parsons' thorough and well-researched book, *Power and Politics: Federal Higher Education Policymaking in the 1990s* (1997). Parsons' excellent work provides a detailed account of federal higher education policymaking around the time of the 1992 Higher Education Act reauthorization. But much has changed in the higher education policy community in the decades since Parsons' book was published, including multiple Higher Education Act reauthorizations, and several swings in party control of Congress and the White House. Increased political polarization in the federal government in recent decades has resulted in greater division between the two major parties about many policy issues, including education (Harbridge, 2015). The United States has also experienced numerous high-profile events that affected policymaking for higher education and beyond, including economic recessions, natural disasters, and a global pandemic. Given the changes in government and political context that have taken place since Parsons' book was published, a more up-to-date, comprehensive analysis of the federal government's role in higher education is important to help higher education leaders, researchers, policymakers, and writers understand how the federal government has been involved in this sector and how policymaking for higher education occurs at the federal level. This book provides such an analysis. The chapters that follow include examinations of the federal role's evolution over time, the activities of specific governmental branches and agencies that affect higher education, the nature of the federal government's role in higher education today, and the prospects for the future of federal involvement in higher education.

FEDERAL HIGHER EDUCATION POLICY AREAS

As Chapter 1 explains in more detail, all branches of the federal government play major roles in higher education policymaking and implementation, using a variety of policy instruments and their own constitutional authorities to do so. Substantive federal policies involving higher education have been vast and extensive as well. This section spotlights some of the most prominent federal policy areas affecting higher education, although there are many others, as virtually all areas of federal law and policy affect higher education in some way.

Nondiscrimination and Civil Rights

An important responsibility of the federal government is to ensure civil rights in higher education and to prohibit unlawful discrimination in educational programming (Center on Education Policy, 1999; Wolanin, 2003). To this end, the federal government has created nondiscrimination policies and ordered the racial desegregation of colleges and universities (Bagenstos, 2008; Epperson, 2017; Kaplin et al., 2020; Mumper et al., 2016; Pelsue, 2017). The federal government has also used its taxing and spending powers to enforce nondiscrimination and civil rights laws. For example, the Internal Revenue Service may deny tax-exempt status to higher education institutions that discriminate on the basis of race (Kaplin et al., 2020; U.S. Department of the Treasury, 2021). The federal government can also deny funding to institutions that illegally discriminate under a variety of federal statutes (Kaplin et al., 2020). These include Title VI of the Civil Rights Act of 1964 (prohibiting race, color, and national origin discrimination in federally funded programs), and Title IX of the Education Amendments of 1972 (prohibiting sex, sexual orientation, and gender identity discrimination) (Bagenstos, 2008; Kaplin et al., 2020; Mumper et al., 2016; Pasachoff, 2013; Wolanin, 2003). Moreover, two federal laws—the Americans with Disabilities Act and Section 504 of the Rehabilitation Act—prohibit unlawful discrimination based on disability and require institutions to provide reasonable accommodations for individuals with disabilities so they may study, work, and visit on campus (Kaplin et al., 2020; Konur, 2000; Wolanin, 2003).

Student Financial Aid

Federal policy has also directed billions of dollars to higher education students and institutions through student financial aid, which helps students and their families pay tuition, fees, and other expenses. Particularly since the passage of the Higher Education Act in 1965, the federal government has played a major role in providing financial aid to help students afford college (Brint & Clotfelter, 2016; Fuller, 2014; Mumper et al., 2016; Wolanin, 2003). Today, federal spending on student financial aid, which tops $100 billion and reaches nearly 11 million recipients (Federal Student Aid, 2020a), is a crucial vehicle for higher education access for millions of postsecondary students. Federal student aid takes many forms, including grants (which need not be repaid), loans to both students and parents (which must be repaid), and work study (which provides funding for student work opportunities on campus) (Baker, 2019; Dynarski & Scott-Clayton, 2013; Federal Student Aid, 2020a; Scott-Clayton, 2017; Scott-Clayton & Zhou, 2017; Zumeta & Kinne, 2011). A massive shift in the federal government's role in student loans occurred beginning in 2010, when the Department of Education became the direct lender for all federal student loans; before then, largely private banks had been the lenders, with the Department of Education as a guarantor (Dortch et al., 2010; Dynarski, 2014; Mumper et al., 2016; New America, n.d.). Another important form of financial aid is the subsidy provided by the federal government to students and their families through tax benefits (Dill,

1997; Internal Revenue Service, 2019; Kelchen, 2018; Maag et al., 2007; Mumper et al., 2016; Scott-Clayton, 2017; Wolanin, 2003).

Higher Education Quality and Accountability

The federal government also uses policy to promote educational quality and student success in higher education. One way the government has done this is to attach certain accountability requirements to institutions' ability to receive federal student aid funding. One such requirement is that institutions receiving federal student aid must be accredited by an approved accrediting body (Eaton, 2003; Kelchen, 2018). Another accountability requirement is that institutions must maintain low rates of student loan default (Itzkowitz, 2017; Kelchen, 2018). Moreover, the federal government requires colleges and universities that participate in the student aid programs to receive authorization from their state government to operate legally as a provider of postsecondary education. Title IV of the Higher Education Act provides that states, accrediting agencies, and the Department of Education compose the Program Integrity Triad and oversee higher education institutions that receive federal student aid in order to ensure the institutions are meeting minimal standards of educational quality (McCann & Laitinen, 2019; Natow et al., 2021; Tandberg et al., 2019; Tandberg & Martin, 2019).

Also to promote postsecondary student success, the federal government funds a number of programs designed to help college students succeed. For example, TRIO programs—called "TRIO" because there were originally three of them, though there are currently eight—provide services and programming for historically underserved students, to enhance college preparation and to increase higher education access and success (Pitre & Pitre, 2009; U.S. Department of Education, n.d.-d, 2008). Other federal programs aimed at improving student success have been authorized over the years, although many have not been consistently funded (Hegji, 2018). An example of such a program is the Centers of Excellence for Veteran Student Success, which was authorized under the Higher Education Act and funded through the Department of Education (Rose & Stuckey, 2012; U.S. Department of Education, n.d.-b). This program has provided student services for veterans with the goal of increasing their success in higher education; however, it was not funded from 2016 through 2019 (Hegji, 2018; U.S. Department of Education, n.d.-b).

Campus Crime

The federal government has also created policies aimed at increasing safety and reducing crime on college campuses. The primary federal statute on this topic is the Jeanne Clery Disclosure of Campus Security Policy and Campus Crime Statistics Act, better known as the Clery Act. Named after a college student who was the victim of violent crime on her campus, the Clery Act requires higher education institutions to track and report data regarding crimes occurring on or near campus (Clery Center, n.d.-b; Fisher et al., 2002; Lee, 2017). The federal government maintains a database of campus crime and fire data, compiled by the Department of Education based on the Clery Act's required disclosures (U.S. Department of Education, n.d.-a).

Apart from the Clery Act, the federal government has issued other policies relating to postsecondary campus safety. Title IX of the Education Amendments of 1972 is one such policy. As stated above, Title IX prohibits unlawful discrimination on the basis of sex, sexual orientation, or gender identity in educational programming. As part of that prohibition, Title IX requires higher education institutions to work toward ending sexual harassment and assault on campus (Clery Center, n.d.-a; Koss et al., 2014). Moreover, under the Drug-Free Schools and Communities Act, colleges and universities must take steps to prevent and investigate unlawful drug use on the part of campus affiliates (Clery Center, n.d.-a; Custer & Kent, 2018).

Research and Development

Higher education institutions benefit from federal funding for research through several federal agencies (Brint, 2019; Brint & Clotfelter, 2016; Hearn et al., 2013; Mumper et al., 2016; Sargent et al., 2020; Wolanin, 2003). The Department of Education, unsurprisingly, provides grants for educational research (U.S. Department of Education, 2015; Weiner, 2009); but many other agencies also provide funding for research and development to university-based researchers. These include the National Science Foundation, the Environmental Protection Agency, and the Departments of Agriculture, Health and Human Services, Defense, and Energy, among many others (Mumper et al., 2016; Pece, 2019).

Additionally, the federal government regulates ethics in research with human and animal subjects. The Department of Health and Human Services' *Common Rule* requires organizations that receive federal funding (such as higher education institutions) to adhere to regulations designed to protect individuals who participate as subjects in biomedical, social, and behavioral research (Fiske & Hauser, 2014; Hudson & Collins, 2015; Korenman, 2006). These regulations include, among other things, that Institutional Review Boards overseeing ethics compliance meet certain requirements about board composition and function, that human subjects give informed consent to participate in research, and that certain vulnerable populations—such as prisoners, minors, and pregnant individuals—receive some additional protections (Korenman, 2006). Federal law also governs research with animal subjects, including a requirement that an Institutional Animal Care and Use Committee (IACUC) reviews proposed research involving animals for ethical compliance and conducts semiannual inspections of research facilities involving animals (National Institutes of Health, 2018; National Research Council, 2004).

Intellectual Property

Federal policies on copyrights, trademarks, and patents have implications for higher education as well. Copyrights protect the intellectual property rights of authors and artists, enabling them to prevent, or to receive a benefit from, their works being copied (Rooksby & Hayter, 2019; U.S. Patent & Trademark Office, n.d.). As organizations who count writers, artists, librarians, and scientists among their affiliates, higher education institutions are both producers and users of copyrighted materials (Cate et al., 1998). Patents protect the intellectual property of inventors with regard to the use, sale, or engineering of their creations. As explained above, many universities receive federal funding for research and development, and sometimes those projects result in patentable inventions. Since Congress enacted the Bayh-Dole Act in 1980, inventions developed with federal funding can be patented by a university as creator of the invention (Kenney & Patton, 2009). A trademark is defined by the U.S. Patent and Trademark Office (2019) as "a word, phrase, symbol, or design, or a combination thereof, that identifies and distinguishes the source of the goods of one party from those of others" (p. 2). Trademarks are used in a variety of ways in higher education, including as logos or slogans for institutions and their programs (Rooksby & Collins, 2016).

Student Privacy

Federal policy protects the privacy of higher education student information. Since 1974, the Family Educational Rights and Privacy Act (FERPA) has protected students' academic and identifying information from disclosure to other parties without the student's consent (Parks, 2017). Although there are some exemptions (such as in emergency situations), FERPA applies fairly broadly to a wide range of academic records (Parks, 2017; U.S. Department of Education, 2019a).

Other Federal Policies

Numerous other federal policies influence higher education and impact students, their families, institutions, faculty, administrators, executives, other staff, state-level officers, and the many others for whom higher education is an important aspect of life. Such policies include human resources policies such as the Family and Medical Leave Act, labor policies such as National

Labor Relations Board rules, and environmental health and safety policies with which higher education institutions must comply (Environmental Protection Agency, 2007; Flaherty, 2019; Thornton & Westcott, 2013; Wolanin, 2003). Immigration policies are relevant to higher education institutions that enroll immigrant and international students (Darolia & Potochnik, 2015; Nienhusser, 2015; Redden, 2019; Wolanin, 2003). Federal policies also directly affect military veterans in higher education. When it was first enacted in 1944, the GI Bill of Rights increased access to higher education for military and veteran students (Wolanin, 2003). More recent versions of the GI Bill have expanded higher education access even further, including the "Forever GI Bill," which eliminated the time limit for veterans to make use of the bill's benefits (Dortch, 2017). Like other organizations, colleges and universities are subject to the federal tax code, anti-corruption policies, wage-hour laws, and many other regulations (Higher Education Compliance Alliance, n.d.). Given the many federal policies that affect higher education on an everyday basis, it is no surprise that a considerable higher education lobby has grown, with Washington, D.C.–based associations representing all types of colleges and universities, attempting to influence federal policy on Capitol Hill and beyond (Camp, 2021; Cook, 1998; Marsicano, 2019; Marsicano & Brooks, 2020; Natow, 2015; Parsons, 1997).

GUIDING QUESTIONS, PERSPECTIVES, AND METHODS

Questions

As these many examples illustrate, the federal government influences higher education a great deal, and has not completely ceded the authority to regulate higher education to the states. A key assumption of this book is that higher education policy and policymaking must be understood within the context of the structures, processes, and politics of the federal government. It is important for higher education leaders and advocates to have a solid understanding of federal policymaking processes and influences, as colleges and universities continue to face dwindling resources and turn to government for support. Scholars of higher education must also understand the constitutional, legal, and political contexts of federal policymaking to fully engage with the ways that policy affecting higher education is made and implemented. Therefore, this book provides a detailed description and analysis of the federal government's role in higher education, including how that role has evolved over time and how constitutional structures, politics, and various economic and social contexts have helped to influence the federal role as it expanded to become massive and virtually indispensable. Questions that this volume addresses include the following:

1. How have the constitutional, political, and administrative structures of the U.S. government shaped the nature of the federal government's role in higher education policymaking?
2. How have the federal government's regulation and funding of higher education evolved over time?
3. What do higher education policy actors and observers perceive to be the most important federal higher education policy issues, both currently and in the near future?

Perspectives

The federal government's role in many aspects of life has expanded throughout U.S. history, including its involvement in higher education. Political science and public administration scholars have developed a number of theories regarding government growth in general and why the federal government's role has become so large (Holcombe, 2005; Legrenzi & Milas, 2002). Some theories focus on the people employed by the government, positing that the size of government expands as agency personnel actively seek to increase their relevance and resources. These theories conceptualize government employees as self-interested actors who seek to enlarge their budgets and powers, and in doing so, maintain the large role and size of government (Holcombe, 2005; Legrenzi & Milas, 2002; Miller & Moe, 1983; Niskanen, 1968, 1971). From this perspective, it is the actions of federal employees working with higher education issues that has led the federal role in higher education to become so large.

A different perspective focuses on how government tends to grow in times of crisis but not recede back to its previous, smaller size once the crisis is over (Bellante & Porter, 1998; Holcombe, 2005). During wars, economic recessions, and similar critical events, new government programs are created, and existing programs expand to deal with the emergency. But when the period of crisis ends, largely due to "status-quo bias" (Holcombe, 2005, p. 102), government size may recede a little, but not return to its previous size (Bellante & Porter, 1998; Holcombe, 2005). Adherents to this perspective would argue that federal involvement in higher education increased during times of prominent national need, such as when the Soviet Union's launch of the Sputnik satellite in 1957 led to fears that the United States was falling behind its rival nation in terms of scientific and military capabilities. As a result, the federal government greatly increased spending on research and development and passed the National Defense Education Act to promote the study of science and foreign relations in higher education. The launch of Sputnik was decades ago, and the Cold War has long since ended. However, many of the agencies, policies, and regulatory apparatuses created during the Cold War remained active long after its close (Cross, 2014; Geiger, 1997; Labaree, 2016).

Yet another perspective holds that government size is related to the emergence of interest groups and other nongovernmental organizations that exist to lobby government, obtain benefits from it, and work in policy development and implementation (Lu & Xu, 2018; Mueller & Murrell, 1986). As economists Thomas Garrett and Russell Rhine (2006) have explained, interest groups increase the size of government by putting pressure on public officials to provide benefits for the group. In turn, a large government provides incentives for the development of new interest groups, which are created in response to the existence of government policies and programs (Leech et al., 2005). From this perspective, the emergence of higher education interest groups, particularly in the late 20th century (Cook, 1998; Parsons, 1997), has helped to keep the federal government's role in higher education large, and the large federal government has in turn helped the higher education lobby to thrive.

Because governments and government agencies are organizations, organizational theory may also shed light on why the scope of the federal government's role in higher education is so expansive. Some such theories conceive of organizations as organic, similar to living creatures that grow, feel, and have needs that must be met. Organizations also tend to respond to their surrounding environments, become ill, and even die (Morgan, 1997; Oliver, 2002). Governments that grow and expand in response to environmental stimuli, and to obtain more resources for themselves, often fit these descriptions of organic organizations. Indeed, there have been a number of metaphors for the United States government as organic, including "Uncle Sam," "Big Brother" (Langford, 2015, p. 3), and "Leviathan" (Brennan & Buchanan, 1980, p. 16). The Constitution itself has also been described as "living," meaning its interpretation can evolve over time as its contexts and environments change (Langford, 2015). Thus, the federal government itself—and the individual agencies within it—can be conceived as living creatures prioritizing their own growth, comfort, and longevity.

It is unlikely that any one theory holds the sole explanation for the federal government's expansive role. Indeed, government growth is likely owed to a combination of factors, including, along with the ones discussed above, international pressures, equity concerns, and the preferences of powerful entities (Huang & McDonnell, 1997; Lewis-Beck & Rice, 1985).

There are also differing opinions as to whether a large federal role in higher education is desirable (Baum et al., 2017). Some argue that this federal role has become too large and burdensome. The late Thomas Wolanin, who had served as a Department of Education official, congressional staffer, and senior associate at the Institute for Higher Education Policy, wrote in 2003 that the large federal role in higher education has produced some "risk," in that increased government involvement "might stifle the freedom and autonomy of higher education" (Wolanin, 2003, p. 49). Others, according to the Center on Education Policy (1999), "question whether the federal government should be involved in education at all" (p. 3). However, still others recognize that federal involvement in—and funding for—higher education has led to many benefits for institutions, individuals, and society. To this point, Wolanin (2003) also noted:

> Federal support helped to create the best research universities in the world. It also helped to create the world's largest system of higher education—an example of how an open and diverse system provides opportunities to a high percentage of students able to benefit from advanced education. (p. 49)

Proponents for a continued robust federal role in higher education argue that such a role is necessary in a diverse society, in which meeting the educational needs of society's most underserved populations is an imperative, and for which economic stability and educational quality are priorities (Center on Education Policy, 1999). The federal government has also played an essential historical role in efforts to desegregate and enforce civil rights in higher education (Alexander et al., 2021; Hinrichs, 2015). As the Center on Education Policy (1999) has noted, "the federal government is uniquely positioned to mobilize a national effort and encourage state and local action whenever a critical educational need arises" (p. 15).

Whether viewed as generally positive or negative, the federal role in higher education today is massive and complicated. It is therefore crucial for anyone with an interest or stake in U.S. higher education to understand this role.

Methods

This volume draws on a variety of sources to construct a detailed depiction of how the federal government creates and implements policy in the higher education space. These sources include the following:

- **Law and policy documents** such as current and historical statutes, constitutional provisions, executive orders, case law, regulatory policies, legislative history, and other documents produced by the federal government relating to higher education policy.
- **Published reports** of research regarding the federal government and higher education, whether produced by government or nongovernment researchers, using a variety of methodologies. This includes academic literature that discusses the federal government's involvement with or regulation of higher education, as well as Congressional Research Service and other government agency reports.
- **News media** articles regarding federal higher education laws and policymaking, which provide a useful resource for facts and context, both historically and in contemporary times.

- *Original interviews* with dozens of policy actors and other stakeholders in federal higher education policy to provide information about stakeholder experiences with and perceptions of the various policies and processes described in this book. Much of the nuance and "inside baseball" that occurs in the federal higher education policy arena cannot be understood by analyzing documents alone. Interview data provide context and explanation for the phenomena reflected in documents, reports, and previous literature. Higher education policy insiders' perspectives about the roles of various federal institutions in higher education policy, including how the mechanisms of federal policy development and implementation work in practice and what the future is likely to hold for the federal role in higher education, provide great insight into how government institutions, interest groups, and sociopolitical contexts influence higher education policy.

More details about these methods are included in the Methodological Appendix.

PREVIEW OF THE REMAINDER OF THE BOOK

Following this Introduction, the first chapter discusses the structure of the federal government and its authority to regulate higher education. The chapter includes a discussion of federalism and an overview of the three branches of the federal government, with examples of how each branch influences higher education policy. Also discussed are the separation and sharing of powers within the federal government and the role that partisan politics plays in federal policymaking. The first chapter concludes with a discussion of policy instruments, including an examination of how the federal government exerts much of its regulatory and oversight powers over higher education by attaching conditions to the receipt of federal funding.

Chapter 2 summarizes the history of the U.S. government's role in higher education, noting how particular spans of time took on a specific character. For example, in the late eighteenth century and throughout the nineteenth century, the federal role in higher education gradually expanded (Thelin, 2011). During the New Deal era, the federal government invested in the construction of educational buildings as well as youth and workforce training (Loss, 2012). The federal role in 20th-century war efforts and the Cold War expanded federal funding for higher education research and other programs in the 1940s and 1950s (Geiger, 1997; Loss, 2012; Thelin, 2011). During the 1930s through 1970s, the federal government worked to increase equity in higher education through civil rights enforcement, broad legislation, and increased funding for student financial aid (Cervantes et al., 2005). The

1970s and particularly the 1980s ushered in an era of consumerism and accountability that continues through today (Kelchen, 2018; Labaree, 2016). The second chapter of this book describes these historical eras in detail, and also examines how higher education was involved in the federal government's historical roles in colonialism, racial injustice, and other inequities (Lee & Ahtone, 2020; Wheatle, 2019).

Chapters 3 through 6 individually examine different institutions of the federal government: Congress, the presidency, federal administrative agencies, and the federal courts. Each of these chapters begins with an overview of that sector of government, including its structure, authority, and policymaking powers. The third chapter explains Congress's structure and constitutional authority over higher education, including a discussion of congressional powers and major higher education legislation. Chapter 4 provides an overview of U.S. presidents as policymakers, beginning with a description of presidential policymaking powers and an explanation of how those powers have generally been used to influence higher education policy. The fourth chapter also explains the role of certain White House offices—such as the Office of Management and Budget and the Office of Science and Technology Policy—in higher education policy. Chapter 5 describes the role that federal administrative agencies have played in regulating higher education. The federal agency that has the most relevance to this topic is the Department of Education, which produces the largest volume of policies and decisions that directly affect higher education. However, the chapter also discusses a variety of other federal agencies that influence higher education, including the Departments of Labor, the Treasury, and Homeland Security, and the Consumer Financial Protection Bureau, among others. Chapter 6 explains the role that federal courts have played in influencing federal higher education policy, including important and influential judicial decisions. That chapter discusses the constitutional foundation and structure of the federal judicial system as well as the jurisdiction, powers, and limitations of the federal courts. Chapters 3 through 6 also contain case studies examining the power of each of these federal institutions within the context of a particular higher education issue. As these case studies demonstrate, federal policy processes can have profound effects on the everyday lives of students, families, and others.

Chapter 7 provides an overview of various nonfederal policy actors who influence higher education policy. These include interest groups, states, the media, accreditors, foundations, and other nongovernmental organizations. The eighth and final chapter of the book summarizes the current status and character of federal involvement in higher education. The chapter also provides an outlook for the future of the federal role in this sector.

In sum, the chapters that follow provide detailed explanations of the federal government's relationship with higher education, supported by research, policy documents, and insiders' perspectives on government and policy matters of importance to the higher education community. Readers of this volume will gain knowledge regarding numerous aspects of the federal government that pertain to higher education and a fuller understanding of the politics, constitutional structures, and nuanced contexts that have shaped the federal higher education policy landscape.

CHAPTER 1

The Federal Structure and Higher Education Policy

As explained in the Introduction, the federal government's role in higher education has been prominent and expansive, affecting numerous substantive policy areas. Over the years, federal policy has contributed to mass access to higher education via civil rights, nondiscrimination, student financial aid, and other policies (Goldin, 1999; Longanecker, 2008). Today, each branch of the federal government as well as the federal bureaucracy are so entwined with higher education that it is likely impossible to rescind this involvement, and even to greatly restrict the federal government's role would be highly disruptive (Wolanin, 2003).

The structure of the federal government and the ways in which various federal institutions exercise power in the higher education policy arena contribute to this strong and pervasive federal role. The federal structure also influences the political, economic, and social environments in which higher education institutions and their stakeholders exist and behave (Dill, 1997). This chapter describes that federal structure, beginning with the Constitution and the powers it confers on different branches of government, and ending with the mechanisms that lawmakers use to put their policies into action, in order to contextualize how the federal government exerts power over higher education.

FEDERALISM IN THE UNITED STATES

Levels of Government

The form and structure of federalist governments vary around the globe, but have in common (and are defined by) different levels of government that are somewhat autonomous but also somewhat interdependent (Gamper, 2005). Milakovich and Gordon's (2013) definition of federalism as "a constitutional division of governmental power between a central or national government and regional governmental units (such as states), with each having some independent authority over its citizens" (p. 100), describes the U.S. situation quite well. In the United States, there are three levels of government: the federal government, which oversees the entire country; the state governments, which have jurisdiction within their own state borders; and local or municipal governments, which are themselves often split into multiple regional jurisdictions, such as when cities, hamlets, or villages exist with their own municipal governments within larger counties or townships (Bowman, 2017; Grissom & Herrington, 2012; White House, n.d.-a).[1]

To make matters more complex, the structure and relative power of state and local governments vary widely. Federal systems of government tend to separate power into three separate branches at both the subnational and national levels, as is the case with the federal and state governments in the United States (Cameron & Falleti, 2005). The breakdown of governmental units into levels (federal, state, and local) and branches (executive, legislative, and judiciary) is depicted in Table 1.1. All 50 states have executive and

Table 1.1. Levels and Branches of Government in the United States

Executive Branch	Legislative Branch	Judicial Branch
FEDERAL GOVERNMENT		
President	Congress	Supreme Court
Vice president	• Senate	Federal Courts of Appeals (circuit courts)
Cabinet and other executive branch agencies (e.g., U.S. Department of Education)	• House of Representatives	
	Legislative agencies (e.g., Congressional Budget Office)	Federal District Courts (trial courts)
	Legislative courts ("Article I" courts)	Judicial agencies (e.g., Federal Judicial Center)
STATE GOVERNMENT		
Governor	State legislature (name, structure, and powers vary by state)	State courts (name, structure, and jurisdiction vary by state)
Lieutenant governor or equivalent		
Executive-level state agencies (vary by state)	State-level legislative agencies (vary by state)	State-level judicial agencies (vary by state)
LOCAL GOVERNMENT		
Local executive (e.g., Mayor, County Executive)	Local legislature (name, structure, and powers vary by locality)	Local/municipal courts (name, structure, and jurisdiction vary by locality)
Deputy local executive, if any (e.g., Deputy Mayor)		
Local/municipal agencies, if any (vary by locality)	Local legislative agencies, if any (vary by locality)	Local judicial agencies, if any (vary by locality)

Sources: U.S. Const.; U.S. Courts, n.d.; White House, n.d.-a

legislative branches of government; however, the structure and organization of these branches in each state are unique (White House, n.d.-a). For example, all states except Nebraska have two legislative chambers (similar to the U.S. Congress), but how frequently legislative elections occur and the names of the chambers vary by state (Nebraska Legislature, n.d.; White House, n.d.-a). State legislatures also vary in the level of "professionalization" of their legislatures, with some state legislative positions resembling a full-time job with regard to legislator compensation and time commitments (highly professionalized), and others resembling a part-time job for citizens with other careers (less professionalized "citizen" legislatures) (Lax & Phillips, 2012, p. 158). Similarly, state judiciary systems typically have one highest court and several lower courts, but certain characteristics—such as the structure of state court systems, whether judges are elected or appointed, and what the courts are named—differ from state to state (U.S. Courts, n.d.; White House, n.d.-a).

Separate branches of government are often found at the local level as well. Many local governments include an executive branch (e.g., mayor, deputy mayor, county executive, etc.), a legislative branch (e.g., city or town council, county legislature, etc.), and a judicial branch (e.g., municipal or village courts) (White House n.d.-a). Within states, the number, structure, and powers of local governments vary widely (Bowman, 2017). Local governments include counties, cities, towns, villages, school districts, "and other special districts with their own governing bodies" (Stone, 2014, ¶ 1). These localities are "overlapping" in that residents often live within the jurisdiction of multiple local governments (Stone, 2014). For example, in New York State alone, there are multiple different types of local governments—including cities, counties, towns, and villages—some of which physically overlap with each other (New York State Department of State, 2018).

Another important aspect of federalism is the concept of relative sovereignty (Bowman, 2017; Gamper, 2005). Each state or local government holds a certain amount of autonomy; but to borrow public law professor Anna Gamper's (2005) words, "no constituent unit may enjoy full external sovereignty" (p. 1302). Under the doctrine of *preemption*, federal laws that were issued under the federal government's due authority preempt the ability of state or local governments to legislate in that area and also render state or local laws that conflict with federal laws invalid (Kaplin et al., 2020; O'Reilly, 2006). A federal law may also preempt the *application* of an otherwise valid state law if the state law, as applied, conflicts with federal law. An example of this latter type of preemption occurred in the *Adams v. Pennsylvania Higher Education Assistance Agency* (2016) case, in which the Supreme Court of Appeals of West Virginia held that the application of a state-level fair debt collection practices law was preempted where applying the state law would have resulted in conflicts with federal regulations issued under the authority of the Higher Education Act. Just as federal laws can preempt state ones, state-level governmental actions can preempt local laws and actions because a local government's power exists only due to the state having delegated some of its own power to the local government (Bowman, 2017).

Over the years, scholars have developed a variety of metaphors for U.S. federalism, none of which fully capture the concept, which is characterized by complexity, competition, collaboration, and even coercion (Grissom & Herrington, 2012; Hills, 1998; Lieberman, 1988; Volden, 2005). Some early metaphors invoked the imagery of various kinds of cake, most notably the layer cake and marble cake analogies created in the 1960s by political science scholar Morton Grodzins (1966; see also Grissom & Herrington, 2012; Herian, 2012; Posner, 2007; Volden, 2005). In Grodzins' analogies, the layer cake was held up as a faulty metaphor, because each layer in the cake is neatly separated and clearly defined, which is not how federalism in the United States works. Instead, Grodzins proposed that federalism was more like a marble cake, the "intermingling layers" of which more accurately characterize the "pattern of power, resources and authority across the three levels of government" (Grissom & Herrington, 2012, p. 5; see also Grodzins, 1966; Volden, 2005). The marble cake analogy describes "cooperative federalism," which is characterized by collaboration between the various levels of government on the implementation and administration of federal policies and programs (Hills, 1998, p. 815; Lieberman, 1988, p. 287). Another cake metaphor for the U.S. federalist system is that of a fruitcake because it is "dense and unmanageable" (Grissom & Herrington, 2012, p. 5).[2] Moving away from cake metaphors, federalism in the United States has also been described as akin to a picket fence, with the creation and implementation of various policies cutting across the different levels of government (Grissom & Herrington, 2012; Thompson, 2013). Ultimately, U.S. federalism may be too complicated and politicized to be condensed into any useful metaphor (Thompson, 2013). As Grissom and Herrington (2012) observed, "the patterns of distribution across the three levels are difficult to predict or explain with simple principles" (p. 6).

Federalism and Higher Education Policy

Sociologist Martin Trow (1993) once wrote, "Federalism in the United States can be seen as the major determinant of the governance and finance of the nation's system of higher education" (p. 39). The federal, state, and local governments all play some role in regulating and funding certain aspects of higher education, but each level's role is distinct, and the extent to which a government has authority over a college or university often depends on institution-specific factors, such as whether it is public or private, the sources from which it receives funding, and whether it is religiously affiliated (Kaplin et al., 2020; Trow, 1993). As discussed later in this chapter, the federal government's authority over higher education is often derived from tying conditions and mandates to the receipt of federal funding. Federal funding includes not only research funding but also financial aid that students receive to cover tuition and other expenses at the institution. Some institutions, such as Historically Black Colleges and Universities (HBCUs) and those designated as Minority-Serving Institutions, also receive some direct appropriations from the federal government under the Higher Education Act (2018; see also Cunningham et al., 2014; Wolanin, 2003).

State governments' role in funding and regulating higher education is more direct, although the extent and structures of state-level governance over higher education are quite inconsistent across states. Some state constitutions (including those of Florida, California, Michigan, North Dakota, and others) specifically mention the creation or funding of public higher education institutions as a function of state government (National Conference of State Legislatures, n.d.; Trow, 1993). Moreover, state government entities often govern or coordinate public higher education within their state, but the forms and powers of those entities also vary widely by state (e.g., Education Commission of the States, 2007). Boards of trustees oversee the governance of public institutions, which may provide "a buffer against direct state management" (Trow, 1993, p. 40). But often, members of those boards are appointed or overseen by state-level public officials, such as the governor or legislature (Lingenfelter, 2004). Public institutions of higher education receive state-level student financial aid as well as financial appropriations from their state governments (State Higher Education Executive Officers Association, 2018; Taylor et al., 2016). Private institutions do not receive as much financial support or management from the state as public institutions. However, states must authorize higher education institutions (including private ones) to provide educational services within the state—a process that, once again, varies by state (Harnisch et al., 2016; Tandberg et al., 2019). Some states also offer a limited amount of direct funding to private colleges and universities, such as New York's unrestricted "Bundy Aid" funding for nonprofit private institutions within the state (Yokoyama, 2011, p. 268).

Local governments are also involved in the governance and funding of some public institutions, particularly community colleges (Tollefson, 2009). As of 2016–2017, local governments provided a total of more than $11 billion in appropriations to community colleges (Bombardieri, 2020). Additionally, in some states, local governments appoint individuals to community college governing boards, and some local boards determine community college tuition (McGuinness, 2014; Zinth & Smith, 2012). Although state laws govern the election or appointment of community college trustees, those trustees are sometimes elected by, and often required to be residents of, the local community (Association of Community College Trustees, n.d.-a). Local governments have also been involved in implementing some federal higher education programs, such as the U.S. Department of Agriculture's extension programs with land-grant colleges and universities (Croft, 2019).

The federalist concept of different levels of government working together to implement federal programs has been reflected in the higher education policy arena throughout U.S. history. During the New Deal era, for example, federal work-study programs that helped students pay for higher education were administered by both state-level public officials and institution-level higher education administrators (Loss, 2012). The federal government has also provided incentives for states to fund higher education by attaching maintenance-of-effort (MOE) requirements to federal funding for states. For example, following the Great Recession of 2007–2009, Congress passed the American Recovery and Reinvestment Act (ARRA) as a financial stimulus. Included in this Act was an MOE requirement that states maintain certain levels of funding for education (including higher education) as a condition of receiving ARRA funding (Alexander et al., 2010; Harnisch, 2012). The American Rescue Plan, a massive coronavirus stimulus bill passed in 2021, also contained an MOE provision (Natow, 2021c). By attaching requirements for states to take certain actions in order to receive federal funding, the federal government helps to ensure state activity will further federal goals, such as maintaining a certain amount of state-level funding for higher education.

Another example of federalism in higher education is reflected in the administration of federal student financial aid programs under Title IV of the Higher Education Act. This title authorizes the use of federal funding in the form of grants, loans, and work-study jobs to assist students and their families with paying for postsecondary education (Hannah, 2010; Natow, 2017). Multiple levels of government are involved in implementing these programs. The federal government provides the funding and establishes the regulations to which institutions must adhere to remain eligible to receive this funding (Cellini et al., 2016). State governments provide the authority for institutions to exist and officially operate as educational providers, thereby granting eligibility for federal student financial aid. Individual institutions administer their own students' financial aid packages and work to comply with accreditation requirements and federal regulations that help to ensure their continued ability to receive Title IV funds (Hannah, 2010; Harnisch et al., 2016; Kelchen, 2018; Taylor et al., 2016). These examples demonstrate how the structures of U.S. federalism and the federal government's lack of much direct constitutional authority to regulate higher education results in the active role of multiple levels of government in the implementation of federal higher education policy.

FEDERAL POWERS AND POLITICS

Branches of Government

In addition to the different levels of government, there are also different branches of government: legislative, executive, and judicial. Basic descriptions of the separation of powers typically state that the primary function of each governmental branch is as follows: The legislative branch *creates* the law, the executive branch *enforces* the law, and the judicial branch *interprets* the law (e.g., Krent, 2005; Oleszek, 2014; Sundquist, 2010). This separation of powers, it is theorized, is designed so that each branch may serve as a check on the power of another branch. Vesting different kinds of authority in each branch helps to avoid concentrating power too heavily within any one governmental institution (Oleszek, 2014). But the powers prescribed to the branches by the Constitution do not actually provide for a clear separation of powers (Oleszek, 2014; Selin & Lewis, 2018), and governmental institutions are far more complex than these relatively simple concepts imply (Cameron & Falleti, 2005; McCarthy, 2015).

Legislative Branch. Congress is the federal government's legislative body, consisting of two chambers: the Senate (upper chamber) and the House of Representatives (lower chamber) (U.S. Const. art. I, § 1; see also Ashbee, 2004; Dauster, 2016). Congress's most prominent policymaking function is through the creation of legislation, and Congress has enacted higher education–related legislation throughout U.S. history. The Higher Education Act, Title IX of the Education Amendments of 1972, and the Clery Act are all examples of enacted legislation affecting higher education.[3] As explained in Chapter 3, Congress holds additional power as well, including the power to oversee and investigate other branches of government (Davis et al., 2021; Relyea & Tatelman, 2007).

Executive Branch. Article II of the Constitution establishes the federal executive branch and states, "The executive Power shall be vested in a President of the United States of America" (U.S. Const. art. II, § 1). Presidents have influence over higher education policy in a number of ways. The president may sign legislation passed by Congress, including bills to reauthorize the Higher Education Act and other education-related legislation (Krent, 2005). The president may also choose to veto legislation. Moreover, presidents may issue executive orders, which are binding mandates to regulate aspects of the executive branch of government (Mayer, 1999). The power to appoint the leaders of executive-level agencies and federal judges (U.S. Const. art. II, § 2; see also Wilson et al., 2016) gives the president far-ranging power. Presidents can also influence policy discussions simply because the power and stature of the office command a great deal of attention. Thus, the president is a powerful influencer of policy agendas (Lee, 2009), including agendas affecting higher education.

In addition to the president and vice president, the executive branch includes a number of administrative agencies.[4] The U.S. Department of Education is one such agency, and the secretary of education is a member of the president's cabinet. This agency is tasked with implementing provisions of the Higher Education Act, among other administrative and policy functions (Natow, 2017). As representatives of the president's administration, political appointees in the Department of Education have been quite influential over federal higher education policy. Recent decades have demonstrated the extent to which policy can vary depending on the political leadership of the Department of Education. During President Barack Obama's administration, the department issued rules and guidance that scrutinized for-profit higher education, provided enhanced protections for student loan borrowers, and extended Title IX nondiscrimination policies to transgender students (Anderson, 2020; Chen, 2020; Kreighbaum, 2016b; Mettler, 2014; Natow, 2017; Student Assistance General Provisions, 2016). When conservative businesswoman Betsy DeVos served as secretary of education under President Donald Trump, the department withdrew, repealed, or otherwise curtailed these policies (Chen, 2020; Fain, 2017; Harris & Kelderman, 2017; Kreighbaum, 2017a, 2017b, 2017d, 2019c; Program Integrity, 2019; Student Assistance General Provisions, 2019). Then during the early months of President Joe Biden's administration, the Department of Education took steps to change these policies once again, moving back in the direction of Obama-era policies on for-profit higher education, student-loan borrowers, and Title IX (Natow, 2021c). Such swift and drastic redirections of policy from one presidential administration to the next illustrate how a change in the presidency and political leadership of federal agencies can suddenly and dramatically affect higher education policy.

Judicial Branch. The federal judicial branch was established by Article III of the Constitution (U.S. Const. art. III). There are three levels of the federal judiciary: district courts at the trial level, circuit courts at the appellate level, and the United States Supreme Court, which is the most powerful court in the country. Federal courts have decided a number of cases affecting higher education over the years, ranging from landmark Supreme Court decisions on desegregation and race-conscious college admissions (Kaplin et al., 2020), to a federal district court invalidating part of a U.S. Department of Education regulation of the for-profit higher education sector (Natow, 2017), to various federal courts making decisions about the applicability of civil rights and intellectual property laws, among many other matters (Kaplin et al., 2020).

Separating and Sharing Powers

The Constitution provides specific powers that each branch of the federal government holds. Section 8 of Article I lists 18 specific powers of Congress, and Section 2 of Article II sets forth several powers of the president. Apart from these "enumerated" powers, branches of the federal government hold "implied" powers as well. For example, the presidential power to remove the leaders of some executive departments is not specifically listed in the

Constitution, but it is a power the president has been presumed to hold (Fisher, 2015). Moreover, under the power of judicial review, which is also not expressly mentioned in the Constitution, federal courts have the authority to strike down laws created by other branches and to overrule decisions made by lower courts (Administrative Office of the U.S. Courts, 2016; Chemerinsky, 2016; Federal Judicial Center, n.d.; Whittington, 2015).

As government researcher Walter Oleszek (2014) has observed, "The Constitution creates a system not of separate institutions performing separate functions but of separate institutions sharing functions," and the powers of the three federal branches "overlap" one another in significant ways (p. 4). It is through not just the separation of powers, but also the sharing of them, that the different branches of government are able to check one another. As explained above, Congress is the branch primarily responsible for legislating, but the president has legislative powers as well via the presidential authority to sign or veto legislation (U.S. Const. art. I, § 7). Congress may check a presidential veto of a popular bill by overriding the veto with a supermajority vote. In another example of sharing powers, the executive branch is not the only federal branch permitted to enforce the law and investigate possible transgressions; Congress also has enforcement powers of oversight and investigation (Kriner & Schickler, 2014; Wilson et al., 2016). Although the president nominates Supreme Court justices and other federal judges, the Senate has a hand in the appointment process by either approving or disapproving the president's nominees (Black et al., 2011). Exercising judicial power outside the court system, executive branch agencies perform adjudications (Chemerinsky, 2016), such as when the U.S. Department of Education's Office of Hearings and Appeals adjudicates disputes regarding institutional eligibility to participate in Title IV student financial aid programs (Natow, 2017). Additionally, Congress may create new federal courts and establish non-Article III courts that exercise judicial functions, including federal bankruptcy courts (Administrative Office of the U.S. Courts, 2016; Chemerinsky, 2016; Federal Judicial Center, n.d.). However, those courts' rulings may sometimes be appealed to the traditional "Article III" federal courts (Administrative Office of the U.S. Courts, 2016, p. 3).

Partisan Politics and Federal Higher Education Policy

Political partisanship across the branches of government affects the inclination of one branch to use its power to check another. In recent decades, the two major political parties in the United States (Republicans and Democrats) have become more internally unified and "ideologically distinct" from each other (Wilson et al., 2016, p. 263; see also Parker & Dull, 2009). In an era when political polarization runs high, the willingness of one branch of government to oppose the actions of another branch often hinges on whether the coequal branches are in ideological agreement on the policy matter in question. It is therefore unsurprising that Congress and the president would be more likely to serve as a check on each other during periods of "divided" government, when the executive branch is controlled by a president from one political party and at least one house of Congress is controlled by another political party (Epstein & O'Halloran, 1996; Levinson & Pildes, 2006; Parker & Dull, 2009). This phenomenon is what legal scholars Daryl Levinson and Richard Pildes called a "separation of parties, not powers," which was the title of their 2006 *Harvard Law Review* article on the subject. As Levinson and Pildes (2006) wrote, "The degree and kind of competition between the legislative and executive branches vary significantly, and all but disappear, depending on whether the House, Senate, and presidency are divided or unified by political party" (p. 2315). A higher education advocate interviewed for my research characterized the separation-of-parties phenomenon this way when explaining the politics surrounding the Coronavirus Aid, Relief, and Economic Security Act (CARES Act), an emergency stimulus bill that was enacted during the early weeks of the COVID-19 pandemic. Before the CARES Act passed Congress, reports surfaced indicating that the bill was being blocked by congressional Democrats (Werner et al., 2020). My interviewee characterized the Democrats' moves as a strategic check on Republican influence over the bill. This interviewee said:

> I think it's a good example of how checks and balances work. The Dems were holding it up because [they believed] some of the stuff that [Republicans] were trying to push through was not going to be helpful for the average American citizen. And so what that did is, it forced a certain amount of checks and balances and accountability amongst all of the different groups.

Despite the partisanship that can result in policy standstills during eras of divided party control, most reauthorizations of the Higher Education Act occurred during times when different political parties controlled Congress and the presidency. Although the Higher Education Act of 1965 was initially enacted during a period of united Democratic party control of the federal government, it has since been reauthorized eight times, and only two of those reauthorizations (1968 and 1980) occurred during periods of united party control of the federal government (both Democratic). Four of the reauthorizations (1972, 1976, 1992, and 2008) occurred when Congress was controlled by Democrats during Republican presidencies, one (1998) occurred when Congress was controlled by Republicans during a Democratic presidency, and one (1986) occurred when the two houses of Congress were controlled by different parties and the president was a Republican.[5]

Although support for higher education in general may receive bipartisan support, the perspectives and policies promoted by the two parties tend to be quite different. Since the early 1990s there has been considerably less bipartisan agreement on higher education matters (Parsons, 1997). In fact, political scientist Laurel Harbridge (2015) observed that education is one of the least bipartisan substantive policy areas, just above labor and civil rights and just below social welfare and community development (p. 121). Conspicuous party divisions are apparent on a number of high-profile higher education policy issues. Republicans tend to favor policies that are believed to promote efficiency in higher education (Doyle, 2007, 2010), including market-oriented incentive programs such as funding institutions based on desired outcomes rather than enrollments (Dougherty & Natow, 2015; McLendon et al., 2006; see also Hearn & Ness, 2017). Democrats tend to promote policies designed to broaden access to higher education (Doyle, 2007, 2010).

With regard to federal policy specifically, partisan divisions appear in both proposed and enacted higher education policies. The content of regulations that administer Title IV financial aid programs varies depending on whether the presidential administration is controlled by a Democrat or a Republican. For example, the U.S. Department of Education's regulatory policies took a more consumer protectionist stance during the Obama and Biden administrations and a more pro-business stance (i.e., one that was more favorable to for-profit higher education) during the Bush and Trump administrations (Fain, 2018; Kreighbaum, 2019c; Natow, 2017, 2021c). Moreover, the fact that reauthorizations of the Higher Education Act have been few and far between may reflect the reality that there is not enough bipartisan consensus on higher education policy to attain sufficient votes to enact such comprehensive legislation (Natow, 2021b).[6] The years-long stalemate on a Higher Education Act reauthorization illustrates that partisan differences may be responsible for the inaction of policymaking as well as for the content of higher education policies that reflect the controlling party's ideology.

CONSTITUTIONAL PROVISIONS AND POLICY INSTRUMENTS

As indicated in the Introduction, power over education is not specifically granted to any branch of the federal government by the Constitution (Williams, 1991; Zumeta, 2005). Yet the federal government has created higher education policy since the 1700s, and the federal role has only expanded since. What, then, is the constitutional basis for the federal government to regulate higher education? In fact, several constitutional provisions give justification for the federal government's authority over higher education. Depending on the type of authority the Constitution grants, the federal government has made use of various policy instruments—that is, methods or tools used by government to effectuate policies (Bengston et al., 2004; Dill, 1997; Dill & Beerkens, 2010, 2013; McDonnell & Ellmore, 1987; Park, 2015; Stone, 2012). Some categories of policy instruments include:

- *Rules* (sometimes called *regulations*), defined as requirements to act (or not to act) in a particular manner (Bengston et al., 2004; Dill & Beerkens, 2013; Park, 2015; Stone, 2012). These instruments "command and control" certain behavior (Dill, 1997, p. 178; Dill & Beerkens, 2010, p. 7). Governments may also *deregulate* by lessening requirements (Dill, 1997).
- *Capacity-building*, through which the government provides resources to increase the capabilities of policy targets to engage in particular desired behavior (Dougherty et al., 2016; Park, 2015).
- *Information*, referring to the government either providing information to the public or requiring policy targets to provide information to the government (Bengston et al., 2004; Dill, 1997; Dill & Beerkens, 2013; Dougherty et al., 2016; Park, 2015).
- *Incentives*, which are a system of rewards and punishments—commonly called "carrots and sticks"—intended to prompt policy targets to engage in certain behaviors or avoid others (Stone, 2012, p. 271; see also Bengston et al., 2004; Dill, 1997; Dill & Beerkens, 2013; Dougherty et al., 2016; Park, 2015). These instruments often make use of "market mechanisms" to prompt or discourage behavior (Dill, 1997, p. 178; see also Dougherty et al., 2016).
- *Self-regulation*, which refers to adherence to professional norms, peer review, or other standards within the field or profession (Dill & Beerkens, 2013). This policy instrument is sometimes exercised in coordination with government (Dill & Beerkens, 2013), and sometimes exists largely or entirely apart from governmental control (Hearn & Ness, 2017).

Policies are often designed to employ combinations or "hybrids" of multiple policy instruments together, and the combined use of different types of policy instruments can be quite effective (Dill & Beerkens, 2013, p. 344). The subsections below describe the specific constitutional provisions through which the U.S. government acts to control and influence higher education and the types and combinations of policy instruments the government has employed with regard to each of its constitutional powers.

Taxing and Spending Clause

Article I, Section 8 of the Constitution gives Congress broad powers to legislate, including the ability to impose taxes and spend federal funds "for the common defense and general welfare of the United States" (U.S. Const. art. I, § 8; see also Center on Education Policy, 1999; Mumper et al., 2016). Much of the expansive role the federal government has played in regulating and influencing higher education is attributable largely to its power to tax and spend. Through this power, Congress has been able to incentivize students and families to invest in higher education by providing tax benefits via deductions and credits (Dill, 1997; Internal Revenue Service, 2019; Maag et al., 2007; Scott-Clayton, 2017). Federal tax laws serve as regulations and incentives for colleges and universities as well. For example, the Internal Revenue Service may deny tax-exempt status to higher education institutions that discriminate on the basis of race (Kaplin et al., 2020; U.S. Department of the Treasury, 2021). Tax advantages also incentivize charitable giving to colleges and universities when donors can receive tax deductions for the donations (Dill, 1997). These tax incentives involve a combination of *rules* and *incentives*—both "carrots" and "sticks"—as policy instruments (Stone, 2012, p. 271): To benefit from tax deductions, credits, or exemptions (the incentives), taxpayers must abide by the Internal Revenue Code and related regulations (the rules).

Congress's spending power, known as "the power of the purse" (e.g., Stith, 1988), gives it a great deal of influence over many aspects of higher education. This is largely due to a policy tool called *conditional spending*. Conditional spending refers to tying regulations and requirements to the receipt of federal funding and making compliance with those mandates a condition for receiving funding. This enables the federal government to exercise great power in policy areas that it may not have much authority to regulate directly, including education (Bagenstos, 2014; Haney, 2013). Like the tax policies described above, conditional spending involves a combination of *rules* and *incentives*. The "carrots" (Stone, 2012, p. 271) of conditional spending are funding or other resources provided by the federal government. Currently, the federal government spends tens of billions of dollars every year on higher education (Pew Charitable Trusts, 2019; U.S. Department of Education, n.d.-c), and higher education institutions have come to rely on that funding year after year. Federal dollars enable university-based researchers to pursue extensive, multiyear research projects with coverage for staff, state-of-the-art technology, and long-distance travel. But this funding is conditional—it must be used in conjunction with the specific research commissioned by the government, and recipient institutions must comply with certain mandates, including nondiscrimination and other rules (e.g., National Institutes of Health, 2021).

Federal funding includes not only research funding but also federal student financial aid, which makes up a substantial portion of revenues for many colleges and universities. In fact, the federal government has become a larger source of student financial aid than state governments (Scott-Clayton, 2017). For some higher education institutions, as much as 85 to 90% of their revenues derive from federal funds (Smith, 2019). Given such heavy reliance by higher education on federal funding, this incentive is not just a very attractive "carrot," but a necessary one. Indeed, the "carrot" of eligibility to receive federal funds is virtually indistinguishable from the "sticks" (Stone, 2012, p. 271) associated with losing that revenue if institutions fail to comply with federal laws, regulations, and standards.

The incentives of federal funding combine with another type of policy instrument: *rules* (Stone, 2012). Numerous federal laws and regulations apply only to higher education institutions that receive federal funds (Kaplin et al., 2020). For example, the obligations and penalties under FERPA apply to educational institutions receiving federal funding (Ritvo, 2016), as do the obligations and penalties under the Clery Act (Clery Center, n.d.-b; U.S. Department of Education, 2016b). A variety of federal nondiscrimination laws—including Title VI of the Civil Rights Act of 1964 (prohibiting race, color, and national origin discrimination), Title IX of the Education Amendments of 1972 (prohibiting sex and gender identity discrimination), and Section 504 of the Rehabilitation Act of 1973 (prohibiting discrimination against persons with disabilities)—use conditional spending as the method for putting their policy goals into action, by threatening an institution's federal funding if the institution is found to be violating one of those statutes (Cross, 2014; Feder, 2012; U.S. Department of Justice, n.d.-b). Similarly, a number of regulations issued by the U.S. Department of Education impose requirements on colleges and universities as a condition of eligibility to receive federal student financial aid under Title IV of the Higher Education Act (Kelchen, 2018; Natow, 2017). If institutions do not comply with the regulations, they risk becoming ineligible to receive those funds.

The threat of losing federal funds is substantial enough to give conditional spending policies tremendous force. One of my study's interviewees who worked on behalf of state government officials explained the federal government's conditional spending power over higher education as follows:

> If you were an institution, what is more devastating to you, what's going to cause you to shut down: If the state pulls their funding, or if the federal government disqualifies you from receiving and having students attend your institutions that receive Title IV financial aid, whether that be Pell Grants or student loans? There are some institutions that would have to close down without state support, but by far, if you are an institution of higher education and you lose [federal] Title IV eligibility, it is a death knell, unless you're . . . someone that has a massive endowment. For the broad, overwhelming majority of institutions, federal money is more important than state money.

Other categories of policy instruments also combine with rules and incentives in higher education conditional spending policies. Some federal spending programs employ the policy instrument of *capacity building* in addition to rules and incentives when grants are provided to higher education institutions to enhance their operations. Examples of such grants include the Department of Agriculture's Capacity Building Grants Program for HBCUs, the Department of Education's FIPSE grant, and various federal programs that have existed over the years to enhance the quality of teacher education

(Cohen-Vogel, 2005; Matthews, 2008; Miller, 2002; Wolanin, 2003). In a combination of *rules*, *incentives*, and *self-regulation* policy instruments (Dill, 1997; Dill & Beerkens, 2013), institutions must be accredited by a federally approved accrediting body in order to be eligible to receive Title IV funds (Eaton, 2003; Kelchen, 2018). Some federal laws also require higher education institutions that receive federal funding to report certain information to the federal government, their students, and/or the general public (Dill, 1997; Kelchen, 2018). One example is the requirement for institutions receiving Title IV funds to annually provide the federal government with a large amount of data about the institution for use in a publicly available large-scale dataset known as the Integrated Postsecondary Education Data System (IPEDS) (Kelchen, 2018). Institutions must also provide information to their students who receive federal student loans in the form of entrance and exit counseling (Baker, 2019; Counseling Borrowers, 2020). Additionally, since 2008, institutions that participate in Title IV financial aid programs must post consumer-relevant information on the institutional website, including information about the price of attendance (Anthony et al., 2016; Kelchen, 2018). These policies make use of a combination of *incentives*, *rules*, and *information* as policy instruments by making it a requirement (rule) to provide certain data (information) if an institution receives Title IV funding (incentive).

Equal Protection Clause

The Fourteenth Amendment of the Constitution provides the federal government with direct power to make and enforce new laws. A post–Civil War addition to the Constitution, the Fourteenth Amendment places restrictions on states and empowers the federal government to enforce those restrictions "by appropriate legislation" (U.S. Const. amend. XIV, § 5). This includes, among other provisions, the Equal Protection Clause, which declares: "No state shall make or enforce any law which shall . . . deny to any person within its jurisdiction the equal protection of the laws" (U.S. Const. amend. XIV, § 1; see also Center on Education Policy, 1999; Kaplin et al., 2020). Thus, under the Fourteenth Amendment, the federal government has the power to create and enforce civil rights laws, including requirements (from the *rules* category of policy instruments) regarding racial desegregation in educational institutions and nondiscrimination laws for higher education and other organizations (Epperson, 2017).

Public colleges and universities, as agents of their state government, may not abridge any individual's constitutional rights, and are subject to the requirement to provide equal protection of the laws under the Fourteenth Amendment. Individuals who believe they have been denied equal protection of the laws from a public higher education institution may file a lawsuit for money damages or a court order requiring the organization to cease denying equal protection (Kaplin et al., 2020). Although the Equal Protection Clause does not apply to nonstate actors such as private institutions, a federal civil rights law known as "Section 1981"[7] applies to both public and private institutions and does not require the institution to receive federal funding for the law to apply. Section 1981 forbids race discrimination in contract agreements and permits an aggrieved party to sue another party in a court of law for such discrimination (Feder, 2012; Kaplin et al., 2020). This statute may apply in the higher education context with regard to race discrimination claims in the creation of employment, admissions, and financial aid contracts (Kaplin et al., 2020).

Patent and Copyright Clause

Another direct federal power that affects higher education comes from the Constitution's Patent and Copyright Clause in Article I, Section 8. This clause gives Congress the authority "to promote the progress of science and the useful arts, by securing for limited times to authors and inventors the exclusive right to their respective writings and discoveries" (U.S. Const. art. I, § 8; see also Cate et al., 1998). Via this power, Congress has enacted statutes giving writers, scientists, artists, musicians, and other creators of art or scientific works intellectual property protection in the form of patents and copyrights (Rooksby & Hayter, 2019; U.S. Patent & Trademark Office, n.d.). Because universities are so often the site of research, development, writing, and the creation of works of art, patent and copyright policies have numerous implications for these institutions (Kaplin et al., 2020). Depending on the policy, federal intellectual property laws make use of a variety of policy instruments, including *rules, information,* and *incentives*. Rules include requirements not to copy protected works without receiving appropriate permission or else face civil or criminal penalties (Yeh, 2007). Examples of the use of *information* as a policy instrument include the requirement of inventors to provide information about an invention to the federal government in order to obtain a patent (Lerner & Seru, 2017). Finally, the Bayh-Dole Act of 1980—because of which universities may hold patents for inventions developed at their institutions with the use of federal funds (Kenney & Patton, 2009)—demonstrates how the federal government has made use of *incentives* via its patent power to encourage the production of research and development at higher education institutions.

Executive Action

As vague and indirect as Congress's constitutional authority over higher education is, the president's is even more so. Article II of the Constitution vests certain powers in the president, and much of this relates to foreign policy and the appointment power. Otherwise, the president's Article II powers are quite general in nature. For example, the first section of this article states that the president "shall take Care that the Laws be faithfully executed" (U.S. Const. art. II §§ 1, 3). As explained in Chapter 4, Article II implicitly grants the president direct policymaking power through the use of executive actions such as executive orders; however, the power to issue executive orders does not specifically appear in the text of the Constitution (Contrubis, 1999). The president may also exercise power by approving or vetoing legislation passed by Congress, a policy tool that is unique to chief executives (Krent, 2005).

Article II also states that the president "shall from time to time give to Congress information on the State of the Union, and recommend to their consideration such measures as he shall judge necessary and expedient" (U.S. Const. art II § 3). This clause gives the president the ability to provide a regular "State of the Union" address as well as to make recommendations about legislation to Congress (Coven, 2020; Light, 1999; Oliver et al., 2011). Through both of those powers, the president has the ability to use *information* as a policy instrument by providing information about policy preferences with the goal of generating widespread support for a policy proposal (Altikriti, 2016; Kesavan & Sidak, 2002).[8] An example of this was when President Barack Obama, in his 2015 State of the Union address, discussed the possibility of making community college tuition-free (Field, 2015; Stratford, 2015b). Both before and after this announcement, Obama toured the country to promote this proposal, and he created a federal advisory board to gather and provide information in support of tuition-free community college (Smith, 2015; Stratford, 2015a). This is another example of employing information as a policy tool: even without a nationally televised address, simply making public statements about a policy matter may result in influence by the president. As Chapter 4 explains in more detail, the presidential "bully pulpit" has been an important policy instrument of presidents for generations (Goodwin, 2013; Greenberg, 2011; Shaw, 2017) and certainly constitutes a form of persuasive communication.

SUMMARY AND CONCLUSION

This chapter has described the structure of the U.S. federal government and explained how this structure contributes to the manner and methods through which the government creates and implements federal higher education policy. All three levels of government—federal, state, and local—are involved in creating and implementing higher education policy in some way, with at least two different levels of government often playing distinct roles in administering a single policy. Similarly, all three branches of the federal government—legislative, executive, and judicial—influence higher education policy. While federal powers are separated across the different branches of government, these branches often work together in higher education policymaking, as when Congress passes a bill related to higher education and the president signs it into law. The different branches may also serve as checks against each other, as when the president vetoes a bill or when a federal court invalidates a governmental action. Typically, the extent to which each branch is willing to serve as a check on another reflects the degree of partisan or ideological agreement between the branches.

Two of the most prominent policy instruments the federal government uses to regulate higher education are *rules* and *incentives* (Stone, 2012), particularly with regard to tax benefits and the conditional spending power. By using its constitutional authority to spend federal funds, Congress and the federal agencies tie conditions to the receipt of those funds, and higher education institutions must comply with those conditions or risk losing the funding. Because of the large number of colleges and universities that receive federal funds by participating in Title IV financial aid programs (in addition to those institutions that receive federal research and other funds), the federal government has wide latitude to regulate higher education despite the fact that education is not mentioned at all in the U.S. Constitution. The federal government also regulates higher education by creating and enforcing civil rights laws; but again, some of these laws (such as Title VI of the Civil Rights Act and Title IX of the Education Amendments of 1972) are often enforced via conditional spending (Kaplin et al., 2020).

The legal and constitutional structure of the federal government as described in this chapter tells only part of the story as to why the federal role in higher education is so vast. The next chapter provides another component of this story: a historical analysis of federal involvement in higher education from the late 18th century through the early 21st century. This history illustrates the evolving political, social, and economic contexts that—together with the federal structure described in this chapter—explain how and why the federal government's involvement with higher education has become so prominent and important over time.

CHAPTER 2

The History of the Federal Government's Role in Higher Education

The federal government has been involved in higher education since the nation's earliest years (Cervantes et al., 2005; Johnson, 2014). Indeed, education was identified as a priority of the federal government in some of its earliest legislation. The Northwest Ordinance of 1787, for example, contained a provision that read, "Religion, morality, and knowledge, being necessary to good government and the happiness of mankind, schools and the means of education shall forever be encouraged" (U.S. National Archives & Records Administration, n.d.). Moreover, following the Civil War, the federal government required some states that had seceded from the union to adopt state constitutional guarantees of education as a condition to rejoin the United States (Riley, 1997). Also, as has been the case with many aspects of U.S. history, federal policy on higher education was often involved with inequity, colonialism, and other forms of oppression (Lee & Ahtone, 2020; Wheatle, 2019).

This chapter provides a historical overview of the U.S. government's involvement with higher education for the purpose of situating the federal role in its historical context and explaining how that role evolved and expanded over time. The federal government's relationship with higher education has taken on distinctive characteristics during different, sometimes overlapping eras in United States history. These eras are: higher education's early expansion (1780s–1920s); post–World War I, the Great Depression, and the New Deal (1920s–1940s); the federal government's prominent partnership with higher education during World War II and the early Cold War years (1940s–1950s); the federal role in expanding access to higher education and the civil rights movement (1930s–1970s); and the era of consumerism and accountability, which continues to this day (1970s–2020s). The chapter concludes with a summary of this history, as well as a brief assessment of the current state and likely future directions for higher education and the federal government.

HIGHER EDUCATION'S EARLY EXPANSION: 1780s–1920s

Federal higher education policy from the late 18th century through the early 20th century was characterized primarily by expansion—that is, the federal government encouraged the development of new colleges and universities as well as the expansion of higher education institutions across the growing territories of the United States. But as this section explains, both governmental incentives and the desires driving expansion were often steeped in oppression and inequity (Harper et al., 2009; Kelchen, 2018; Lee & Ahtone, 2020; Wheatle, 2019).

Federal Land Grants for Higher Education

As educational historian John R. Thelin (2011) has observed, the earliest days of the United States as its own independent nation were characterized by "the widespread distrust of a strong national government" (p. 42). Therefore, when prominent national figures such as George Washington and James Madison proposed the creation of a national higher education institution, those proposals were rejected by policymakers. In the 1800s, Congress would charter national military institutions and two D.C.-based private institutions—Howard University (a Historically Black University) and Gallaudet University (a bilingual institution serving hearing impaired students) (Parsons, 1997; Shohfi, 2020; Thelin, 2011). But by and large, chartering new higher education institutions would remain the responsibility of the states (Kelchen, 2018; Thelin, 2011).

Despite the early distrust of national government, the federal role in education dates back centuries, even before the Constitution was ratified. The Northwest Ordinance of 1787 provided for the sale of land in midwestern territories, the proceeds of which were to be used for, among other things, funding schools and colleges (Carleton, 2002; Center on Education Policy, 1999; Cervantes et al., 2005; Putansu, 2020; Riley, 1997). The federal government continued to pass land-grant legislation during the early 19th century, providing land to states in the Western, Midwestern, and Southern United States, with the resources derived from those lands being used to develop schools and, in some cases, higher education institutions (Thelin, 2011). Although early land-grant policies had the effect of expanding higher education, this was not the policies' primary purpose. Rather, the land grants were part of a larger federal plan to encourage westward settlement and to enable the formation of new states (Onuf, 2019; Parsons, 1997). In the case of the Northwest Ordinance, an additional purpose was to repay debts incurred during the Revolutionary War (Loss, 2012).

During the Civil War, many colleges in the southern U.S. ceased providing instruction, particularly during the war's later years. Postsecondary military academies saw increases in their enrollments during this time (Thelin, 2011).

It was also during the Civil War that Congress passed the first Morrill Land Grant Act, in 1862. Similar legislation had been stymied in 1859 by federal policymakers who opposed an expansive federal role in education, including southern Democrats and President James Buchannan, who had vetoed the bill. But by the time the 1862 bill was considered, southern states had seceded from the United States, leaving less opposition to land-grant legislation in Congress. The bill was sponsored by and named for Representative Justin Morrill from Vermont, who had long supported land-grant legislation, and the Act was signed into law by President Abraham Lincoln (Croft, 2019; Florer, 1968; Mercier & Halbrook, 2020; Thelin, 2011).

Under the 1862 Morrill Act, the federal government designated land for the purpose of states obtaining funding from the sale or other use of that land to develop one or more postsecondary institutions in each state. These institutions would be dedicated to the study of agriculture, mechanics, and military studies as well as arts and sciences. A goal of the policy was to provide greater access to higher education for individuals who were not part of the higher socioeconomic classes that had historically been the clientele of colleges and universities. Another goal of the Morrill Act was to promote the study of agriculture and technical fields (Gavazzi & Gee, 2018; Martin & Hipp, 2016; Moore, 2017b; National Research Council, 1995; Neiberg, 2000).

Land-grant institutions received more support from the federal government in 1887, when Congress passed the Hatch Agricultural Experiment Station Act (often called the Hatch Act), which spawned agricultural experiment stations and funded agricultural research taking place at land-grant institutions (Cash, 2001; Croft, 2019; Futrell & Stout, 1965; Gavazzi & Gee, 2018; Hillison, 1996; Parsons, 1997; Weeks, 1989; Wheatle, 2019). Then in 1890, the second Morrill Act was enacted. Aimed particularly at southern states that had seceded prior to the Civil War, the 1890 Act provided states with funding for the purpose of creating new land-grant institutions dedicated to serving Black students in higher education (Gavazzi & Gee, 2018; Wheatle, 2019). This Act produced 19 land-grant institutions, which are now designated as Historically Black Colleges and Universities (HBCUs) (Association of Public and Land-Grant Universities, n.d.; Croft, 2019).[1]

In addition to enabling the expansion of higher education across the United States and promoting the study of agriculture and mechanics, federal land-grant policies are also part of the nation's painful history of land expropriation and racial segregation. Scholars and journalists have documented how land taken by the government from Indigenous people, for vastly inadequate or no compensation, was used to provide states with funding for land-grant colleges (Lee & Ahtone, 2020; Martin & Hipp, 2016; Nash, 2019). Investigative reporters Robert Lee and Tristan Ahtone (2020) wrote that the federal government paid very little and "often paid nothing at all" to obtain the Indigenous lands that funded institutions through the Morrill Act

(¶ 7). As education professor Margaret Nash (2019) has noted, it is important to recognize the colonizing and expropriating functions of the 1862 policy, as well as the compelled removal of Native Americans from their land to facilitate the land grants, even as the Morrill Act has "long been lauded for democratizing higher education" by making college more accessible to students outside elite social classes (p. 437). More than 130 years after the passage of the first Morrill Act, the federal government designated Native American Tribal Colleges and Universities as land-grant institutions in 1994; however, funding inequities prevented 1994 land-grant colleges from receiving many resources to which 1862 land-grant institutions were entitled (Croft, 2019).

Similarly, the 1890 Morrill Act—which has been commended for expanding access to higher education for Black students mainly in the southern United States—helped to further racial segregation in higher education (Harper et al., 2009; Wheatle, 2019). The 1890 Act permitted existing land-grant institutions to discriminate on the basis of race in student enrollment so long as the state also had a comparable land-grant institution that admitted Black students. These institutions were part of the nation's *de jure* racially segregated educational system prevalent in the United States under the "separate, but equal" standard, which would be endorsed by the Supreme Court's *Plessy vs. Ferguson* decision not long after the second Morrill Act was enacted (Cervantes et al., 2005; Harper et al., 2009; Gavazzi & Gee, 2018; Wheatle, 2019). Educational researcher Katherine Wheatle's (2019) analysis of the legislative history of the 1890 Act found that this policy was actively sought by leaders of predominantly White land-grant colleges to further their own interests and obtain additional resources for their institutions. Also, the 1890 Act's HBCUs were insufficiently funded and provided with fewer government resources than predominantly White land-grant colleges (Harper et al., 2009; Jones & Brown, 2020; Wheatle, 2019). It was not until *Brown v. Board of Education* in 1954—over 60 years later—that the Supreme Court recognized that racially segregated educational institutions violated the Fourteenth Amendment's Equal Protection Clause (Henderson, 2004).

The Supreme Court's Protection of Institutional Autonomy

Another important development for the expansion of higher education during the early 19th century was the *Trustees of Dartmouth College v. Woodward* (1819) Supreme Court decision. In that case, the Supreme Court rejected an attempt by the state of New Hampshire's government to assume state control over the private university. This landmark case distinguished between public and private colleges, the latter of which were to be subject to less state control than the former. But this case was also instrumental in establishing institutional autonomy for higher education more broadly, largely protecting colleges and universities, particularly in the private sector, from undue interference by the government (Kelchen, 2018; Labaree, 2016; Stith & Blumenthal, 2019; Thelin, 2011; Trow, 1988).

As legal scholars Kate Stith and Claire Blumenthal (2019) have observed, the *Dartmouth College* decision likely furthered higher education expansion in the 19th century by protecting private institutions from undue interference by the state. Numerous new private colleges were founded in the decades following the decision (Stith & Blumenthal, 2019; Trow, 1988). This included many private women's colleges, religious colleges, and HBCUs (Stith & Blumenthal, 2019).[2]

Higher Education Policy at the Turn of the Twentieth Century

The beginning of the 20th century brought more federal legislation that continued to expand higher education in the United States, often by strengthening land-grant institutions. For example, the Adams Act of 1906 provided additional funding for research at agricultural experiment stations, including those at land-grant universities (Futrell & Stout, 1965; Rosenberg, 1964). In 1914, Congress passed the Smith-Lever Act, which funded the U.S. Department of Agriculture's extension programs at land-grant institutions (DeLauder, 2013; Gavazzi & Gee, 2018; Loss, 2012; Parsons, 1997). Three years later, Congress passed the Smith-Hughes Act, which provided federal funding to states for the purpose of supporting vocational education, including agricultural education and teacher training programs (Moore, 2017a, 2017b; Putansu, 2020). The Purnell Act, which provided additional federal funding for research at experiment stations, was enacted in 1925 (Futrell & Stout, 1965).

The early 20th century also brought strengthened partnerships between higher education and the U.S. military. The United States was involved in World War I from April 1917 through the war's end, with the Armistice being signed in 1919 (Rockoff, 2004). Like institutions in the South during the Civil War, colleges and universities across the United States incurred steep enrollment declines during World War I due to a large segment of the male college-age population serving in the military (Loss, 2012). As a result, many institutions chose to partner with the U.S. Army to develop Student Army Training Corps programs on their campuses, which provided military deferments to postsecondary students enrolled in these military training programs (Leal, 2007; Loss, 2012; Neiberg, 2000; Thelin, 2011). Higher education institutions and the U.S. Army had partnered to provide military training, particularly at land-grant universities, prior to World War I, but those programs were greatly strengthened during the war (Neiberg, 2000; Parsons, 1997). These partnerships brought increased enrollments and resources to participating institutions (Loss, 2012; Neiberg, 2000). Apart from the war-induced lull in college enrollments, higher education continued to expand. In the decade after the war's end, enrollment in higher education institutions increased substantially, to the point that, as historian Christopher Loss (2012) observed, "a new college or university—or at least an institution that called itself by that name—opened every ten days" (p. 20).

THE POST-WORLD WAR I ERA, GREAT DEPRESSION, AND NEW DEAL: 1920s–1940s

Although enrollment in higher education surged following World War I, the federal government did not have much involvement with higher education during the 1920s. However, it was during this time that the current-day conceptualization of college student affairs first developed, with an emergent understanding that college students often benefited from administrative support and student services to be successful in their educational endeavors (Loss, 2012; Thelin, 2011). Within this context, associations of student affairs administrators—including the organizations that would eventually be known as ACPA (American College Personnel Association) and NASPA (National Association of Student Personnel Administrators)—were established (Hevel, 2016; Loss, 2012). Today, these and other higher education associations play a key role in training their membership about federal higher education policy and advocating for federal policies that are favorable to college students and student affairs professionals (e.g., ACPA, n.d.; NASPA, n.d.).

The end of the 1920s saw the onset of the Great Depression, heralded by stock market crashes in October and November 1929 (Mishkin & White, 2002), as well as a depression in farming and agriculture that predated the stock market crashes (Loss, 2012). By 1932, the economy was in a dismal state, and Franklin Delano Roosevelt was elected president after promising to provide a "new deal" to help the United States recover (Rauchway, 2008, p. 1). The federal government's response to the Great Depression—particularly President Roosevelt's New Deal—resulted in an expanded federal role in many aspects of society, including education. Although higher education was not a top priority of the New Deal, several of its programs involved higher education in some way (Fass, 1982; Kantor & Lowe, 1995).

One of the earliest New Deal programs that affected higher education was the Civil Works Administration (CWA), which lasted for only a few months (during the winter of 1933 into 1934) and employed over 4 million workers on approximately 180,000 government projects. The CWA included construction projects for educational institutions (such as the University of Pittsburgh), and an early form of work-study to provide jobs for college students with financial need (Walker & Brechin, 2010). Another New Deal initiative, the Civilian Conservation Corps (CCC) was an "exclusively youth-oriented" program (Fass, 1982, p. 45). The CCC lasted from 1933 until 1942, employed young men in federal conservation projects, and enrolled participants in educational programs, primarily in vocational studies (Fass, 1982; Loss, 2012; Walker & Brechin, 2010).

The Works Progress Administration (WPA), which existed from 1935 until 1943, was a successor to the CWA and provided jobs on a variety of federally funded projects. Among the WPA programs were construction projects (including construction for educational institutions), arts projects, sanitation work, and others (Campbell et al., 1939; Couch, 2008; Fass, 1982; Loss, 2012; Walker & Brechin, 2010). Within the WPA was a Division of Education Projects. An employee of the U.S. Office of Education—a predecessor to the U.S. Department of Education that was part of the Department of the Interior at the WPA's inception—was sent to work "on loan full time to the Works Progress Administration" to manage the agency's education programs (Campbell et al., 1939, p. 14). Programs in teacher, vocational, and arts education were included among the WPA's projects (Campbell et al., 1939; Fass, 1982). The WPA also housed the National Youth Administration (NYA), which was "an autonomous division within the WPA" that enabled college students to work part-time while attending school, sometimes in jobs at their institution, constituting another New Deal–era work-study program (Fass, 1982, p. 44; see also Loss, 2012; Walker & Brechin, 2010).[3]

Other federal policies of the Great Depression era that affected higher education involved land-grant institutions and agricultural extension programs. Land-grant institutions partnered with the Department of Agriculture to implement provisions of the Agricultural Adjustment Act, which was enacted in 1933 (Loss, 2012). Then in 1935, Congress passed the Bankhead-Jones Act, which provided additional federal monies for land-grant colleges' cooperative extension programs (Futrell & Stout, 1965; Loss, 2012). Loss (2012) reported that as of 1940 "the federal government's annual contribution for extension activities was . . . nearly 60 percent of the nation's total cooperative extension budget" (p. 66). Even more federal funding came in 1946, when the Research and Marketing Act amended the Bankhead-Jones Act to provide additional funds and to authorize new types of research, including agricultural marketing research (Bowers, 1982; Futrell & Stout, 1965). As these examples demonstrate, the federal government greatly expanded its presence and activities with regard to education—including higher education—via the New Deal, just as it had done with so many other aspects of life in response to the Great Depression (Loss, 2012; Putansu, 2020).

HIGHER EDUCATION AND THE NATIONAL DEFENSE: 1940s–1950s

The federal role in higher education continued to expand in the 1940s and 1950s. During this time period, higher education played a key role in the federal government's constitutional imperative to "provide for the common defense" (U.S. Const.). As a result, higher education was rewarded with new resources.

World War II and the GI Bill

World War II and the early Cold War years expanded the federal government's relationship with higher education. During the war, universities engaged in research relevant to national defense and military operations, with financial support from the federal government. World War II–era research included the Massachusetts Institute of Technology's Radiation Laboratory and the Manhattan Project (a nuclear weapons development initiative), which involved researchers from several universities across the country (Geiger, 2008; Hiltzik, 2015). In addition to research, higher education collaborated with the U.S. government to provide education to service members during the war (Loss, 2012).

Toward the end of World War II, policymakers grew concerned about possible implications for the economy once soldiers returned home. Specifically, there were worries about mass unemployment and other difficulties veterans could face as they returned to the civilian way of life (Loss, 2012; Olson, 1973). In 1943, President Roosevelt proposed that Congress develop a legislative program of support for veterans, including educational aid, unemployment insurance, and other benefits (Olson, 1973). In 1944, the Servicemen's Readjustment Act, also known as the GI Bill of Rights, was enacted (Cervantes et al., 2005; Labaree, 2016; Loss, 2012; Olson, 1973; Strach, 2009; Thelin, 2011). The GI Bill provided veterans with funding for college tuition, fees, and supplies, plus a "subsistence allowance" for up to four years, depending on how long the veteran had served (Thelin, 2011, p. 263). Other benefits provided by the bill included counseling services, unemployment insurance, and loans with low interest rates that could be used for starting a business or buying a home (Loss, 2012). Despite predictions by some that the education benefits would not be popular among veterans, just six years after the GI Bill was enacted, 16% of eligible GIs—totaling over two million individuals—had enrolled in college (Thelin, 2011).

The GI Bill had a tremendous influence on higher education in several ways. First, it served as a precedent for other GI Bills adopted in later decades, including the post–Korean War GI Bill in the 1950s, the Montgomery GI Bill in the 1980s, and the post-9/11 "Forever GI Bill" in the 2000s (Dortch, 2017; Fuller, 2014; Keillor, 2009; Wolanin, 2003). Moreover, the original GI Bill greatly expanded enrollment in U.S. colleges and universities, and it provided access to college for a wider range of students, such as low-income students, the children of immigrants, those who were the first in their family to attend college, and students who were older than the traditional college-going age (Bound & Turner, 2002; Cervantes et al., 2005; Labaree, 2016; Thelin, 2011). As such, the policy enabled substantial growth of the U.S. middle class

(Cervantes et al., 2005). However, the direct benefits of the GI Bill accrued primarily to White men. As Loss (2012) wrote, "fewer than 3 percent of all female veterans actually made use of" the policy's benefits (p. 116). Also, there was no prohibition on racial discrimination in admissions on the part of institutions receiving GI Bill funding (Thelin, 2011). Racist lending practices and segregated educational institutions led to only a small number of Black veterans making use of the educational and loan benefits of the GI Bill (Cervantes et al., 2005; Herbold, 1994; Loss, 2012). Thus, while opening access to higher education for many veterans, nontraditional students, and others who might not otherwise have had an opportunity to attend college, the GI Bill did not dismantle race and gender inequities in higher education.

The GI Bill was also influential in the way it administered educational benefits. Student veterans were able to use their benefits at any institution at which they were able to enroll, provided that the college met certain quality standards. This "portable" financial aid would become the norm for federal student aid programs decades later (Strach, 2009, p. 69; Thelin, 2011, p. 264). Following the post–Korean War GI Bill, quality standards were determined by recognition from approved accreditors (Kelchen, 2017, 2018). The role accreditors played following this GI Bill foreshadowed the role accreditors currently play in helping to maintain quality control over higher education programs that receive federal student aid funds (Kelchen, 2017, 2018; Thelin, 2011).

Higher Education and 1950s National Defense Policy

In the late 1940s, federal officials wondered about the sustainability of research productivity in the United States following the conclusion of World War II. Such officials included the leader of the federal government's Office of Scientific Research and Development, Vannevar Bush (Labaree, 2016). Bush had envisioned a federal agency that would support scientific research in postwar times. The National Science Foundation (NSF) Act was enacted in 1950 to create an agency similar to what Bush had in mind. The purpose of the NSF was twofold: first, to fund and otherwise support research, and second, to create and coordinate the federal government's policy on science (Geiger, 1992; Kevles, 1977; Waterman, 1960).

Following the Korean War in the 1950s, the United States was in a relatively secure position as a *global power*, holding an edge over the Soviet Union with regard to nuclear development (Kay, 2013, p. 124). However, the Cold War between the United States and the Soviet Union, which began soon after World War II and would last for decades thereafter, resulted in an increased demand for military and other research related to national defense. This demand kept universities in partnership with the federal government and allowed for continuing federal support for university-based research (Geiger, 1992; Labaree, 2016). The flourishing postwar economy in the 1950s further helped to expand higher education's research agenda (Geiger, 1997). It was also during this time that the federal Office of Education received a promotion, as it was moved into the cabinet-level Department of Health, Education and Welfare (Loss, 2012).

Additional support for defense-related research emerged later in the 1950s. In October 1957 the Soviet Union's launch of Sputnik, which was the first satellite to successfully orbit the Earth, led to a policy environment that would bolster the higher education–federal government partnership even further by creating a sense of urgency around research and development to promote national defense. Many in the United States viewed the Sputnik launch as a preview of how the Soviet Union might outperform the United States with regard to science, technology, and—importantly—nuclear capability (Geiger, 1992, 1997; Kay, 2013; Labaree, 2016; Loss, 2012). Following Sputnik, President Dwight Eisenhower identified a need for the United States to support more scientific research. Eisenhower also viewed higher education as important for developing an informed citizenry of innovative and critical thinkers, which was likewise important for national security (Kay, 2013). In this context, the Sputnik launch prompted federal lawmakers to provide more research support to higher education (Labaree, 2016; Loss, 2012). This included the creation of the National Aeronautic and Space Administration (NASA), which has served as an additional source of funding for university-based research (Geiger, 1997; Kay, 2013).

The national response to Sputnik combined with preexisting concerns about the quality of education in the United States led to the enactment of the National Defense Education Act (NDEA) in 1958 (Cervantes et al., 2005; Cross, 2014; Kay, 2013; Loss, 2012; Parsons, 1997). This policy provided close to a billion dollars in funding for education from kindergarten through postgraduate programs, framing this as a much-needed investment in national security (Loss, 2012). Provisions of the NDEA directly relevant to higher education included funding for: postsecondary programs in languages, mathematics, international studies, and the sciences; the development of new educational technologies; fellowships and other incentives for students to pursue higher education in fields relevant to national defense and postsecondary teaching; a funding boost for the NSF to further support scientific research; and a low-interest student loan program that would come to reflect the current model of students taking out loans to pay for higher education (Cervantes et al., 2005; Kay, 2013; Loss, 2012; Putansu, 2020).

THE CIVIL RIGHTS MOVEMENT AND STEPS TOWARD EQUITY: 1930s–1970s

The civil rights movement brought massive change to social policy in the United States, including in the higher education sector. Although many new civil rights policies emerged during the 1960s, the civil rights movement actually began decades earlier (Epp, 1998; Valocchi, 1996). Events from the 1930s through the 1960s such as boycotts of segregated schools and public accommodations, protests of Jim Crow laws, and court cases alleging violations of the Equal Protection Clause helped to usher in an era of legislative, executive, and judicial policy change to protect civil rights (Cashin, 2005; Epp, 1998; Kantor & Lowe, 1995; Morris, 1984). A good number of civil rights demonstrations took place on college campuses or were organized by college students (Cervantes et al., 2005; Loss, 2012; Rhoads, 2016; Wheatle & Commodore, 2019). Federal civil rights and educational access policies that emerged during this era, as well as Supreme Court cases on desegregation and nondiscrimination, had profound effects on higher education in the United States.

The Truman Commission

As higher education enrollments were on the rise following the enactment of the GI Bill, President Harry Truman appointed a Commission on Higher Education, which would come to be known as the Truman Commission, to study pressing issues affecting higher education and to make recommendations for improvement (Cervantes et al., 2005; Fuller, 2014; Loss, 2012; Reuben & Perkins, 2007; Thelin, 2011). The Truman Commission's report, entitled *Higher Education for American Democracy*, consisted of six separate volumes released in 1947 and 1948 (Reuben & Perkins, 2007). This commission viewed access to higher education as imperative for achieving an equitable and democratic society (Gilbert & Heller, 2013; Loss, 2012). To attain the goal of having a well-educated populace by greatly increasing higher education enrollments, the report recommended that the federal government provide financial assistance to enable more students to attend college, in recognition that the price of higher education was prohibitive for many. The Commission proposed the expansion of community colleges, which would be instrumental for providing widespread, affordable access to higher education across the United States (Cervantes et al., 2005; Gilbert & Heller, 2013). The report also called for an end to racial segregation, racial and religious discrimination, and "antifeminism" in higher education (Gilbert & Heller, 2013, p. 420).

As many have since recognized, the Truman Commission was "prescient" with regard to a number of its recommendations (Reuben & Perkins, 2007, p. 265; see also Gilbert & Heller, 2013, p. 417). For example, the commission identified desegregation, mass higher education, and a significant federal role in promoting college affordability as important policy priorities. Over time, these matters would become policy objectives of the federal government. Not all of the commission's recommendations were ultimately adopted, and some reforms did not occur until decades later. Nonetheless, echoes of the

Truman Report can be seen in higher education policies to this day, particularly in federal student financial aid programs and nondiscrimination policies (Gilbert & Heller, 2013; Loss, 2012; Reuben & Perkins, 2007).

Judicial Decisions on Civil Rights

In the 1950s and 1960s, the federal judiciary—and in particular the Supreme Court, as the most powerful federal court—made decisions that set important precedents with regard to civil rights and liberties in education and beyond. Legal and political scholars have noted that this "rights revolution" (Dodd, 2018, p. 3; Epp, 1998, p. 2; Loss, 2012, p. 165) did not occur by accident, but resulted from a combination of legislative action, interest group advocacy, and accessibility of the federal court system (Epp, 1998; Kantor & Lowe, 1995; Scherer, 2017). Political scientist Charles Epp (1998) observed that through activism and expanding diversity in the legal profession in the early 20th century, a "support structure" was built for litigants who were not part of the political elite to gain access to federal courts (p. 18). These reforms led to enhanced resources for civil rights litigants, enabling the Supreme Court to render decisions that expanded protections for civil rights and liberties (Epp, 1998; Scherer, 2017).

Among the landmark Supreme Court cases issued during this era were some involving education. In *Brown v. Board of Education* (1954), the Supreme Court held that racially segregated public schools were unequal and violated the Fourteenth Amendment's Equal Protection Clause (McCarthy, 2015). *Brown* cited as precedent prior Supreme Court decisions, which had found racially segregated postsecondary education programs unconstitutional. One of those prior cases was *McLaurin v. Oklahoma State Regents* (1950), in which the Supreme Court held that Oklahoma's policy of racial segregation in graduate schools was a violation of the Fourteenth Amendment. Another case decided the same year as *McLaurin* was *Sweatt v. Painter* (1950), which similarly held that racially segregated law schools in Texas were unequal, and therefore violated the Equal Protection Clause (Kantor & Lowe, 1995; McCarthy, 2015).[4]

Race-conscious postsecondary admissions policies have also been scrutinized under the Equal Protection Clause. In *Regents of the University of California v. Bakke* (1978), the Supreme Court ruled that it was permissible for colleges to consider race as a factor in admissions in order to achieve diversity among the student body; however, the use of quotas in doing this would be unconstitutional. The *Bakke* decision set in place a framework—which would be affirmed decades later by other Supreme Court cases in the 2000s—for postsecondary institutions to consider race, ethnicity, and other factors in admissions decisions so long as the procedures for doing so were part of a holistic decision-making process and not overly mechanistic (Ancheta, 2008; Lehmuller & Gregory, 2005).

Executive and Legislative Actions on Civil Rights

The civil rights movement also led to important executive and legislative actions to recognize, enforce, and protect civil rights. Earlier in the twentieth century, presidents had used executive action to advance civil rights policies, such as President Franklin Roosevelt's executive action to create the Justice Department's Civil Rights Section, and President Harry Truman's order to desegregate the U.S. military (Cashin, 2005). Both Roosevelt and Truman also issued executive orders to enforce nondiscrimination policies among federal contractors (U.S. Department of Labor, n.d.-b). Law professor Sheryll Cashin (2005) observed that such executive actions had been encouraged by civil rights activists, demonstrating "that social movement pressure could yield policy gains" (p. 1034, n. 25).

Legislatively, President Eisenhower proposed a civil rights bill to Congress that became the Civil Rights Act of 1957. The bill, which provided protections for Black Americans' voting rights, was the first major federal civil rights legislation to pass Congress in more than 80 years. Another Civil Rights Act was enacted in 1960. However, both bills had been subjected to substantial opposition by lawmakers from some southern states and were weakened in order to gain sufficient votes to pass both chambers of Congress (Brown, 2014; Cashin, 2005; Scheb & Stephens, 2017).

Despite the Supreme Court's *Brown v. Board of Education* ruling in 1954, the desegregation of educational institutions was a process that lasted many years and was met with protests by segregationists. In June, 1963, Alabama Governor George Wallace protested desegregation of the University of Alabama by physically blocking the entrance to the campus building where two Black students were to register for classes. President John F. Kennedy issued a proclamation ordering the university to be integrated, and when the National Guard arrived on the scene, Wallace ceased blocking the entrance. That same evening, Kennedy gave an address to the nation, vowing to protect and enforce civil rights (Brown, 2014).

Following Kennedy's assassination in November, 1963, Lyndon Johnson, who had served as Kennedy's vice president, was sworn in as president. The Johnson administration presided over significant federal policy changes intended to promote civil rights and seek the eradication of poverty through a series of legislative and executive actions (Brown, 2014). Education played a major role in Johnson's "Great Society" agenda, as Johnson was a former school teacher and viewed education as an important means for ending poverty and promoting social equity (Goldstein, 2014; Kantor & Lowe, 1995). One of the first pieces of legislation that Johnson ushered through Congress was the Civil Rights Act of 1964, which prohibited race, color, and national origin discrimination in public accommodations, public facilities, employment, and programs receiving federal funding (Hersch & Shinall, 2015). Johnson pushed for the passage of this new Civil Rights Act from the beginning of his presidency, arguing that such legislation would honor the late President Kennedy. Johnson used his considerable knowledge of and clout with Congress to see that this law was enacted (Brown, 2014; Cross, 2014; Hersch & Shinall, 2015). The 1964 Act was considerably stronger than the other civil rights legislation passed just a few years earlier, and it contained protections for voting rights, penalties for discrimination, and requirements to desegregate public facilities and educational institutions (Brown, 2014).

In 1965, President Johnson signed Executive Order 11246, which gave the U.S. Department of Labor the power to enforce nondiscrimination policies among federal contractors (Farrell, 2020; Harper et al., 2009; U.S. Department of Labor, n.d.-b). This executive order built upon an earlier executive order signed by President Kennedy, which required not only that federal contractors not discriminate in employment, but also that contractors must "take affirmative action to ensure that applicants are employed, and that employees are treated during employment, without regard to their race, creed, color or national origin" (U.S. Department of Labor, n.d.-b, ¶ 10). Executive Order 11246 contained a similar provision that also included a prohibition on sex discrimination, making the order consistent with Title VII of the newly enacted Civil Rights Act (Farrell, 2020).[5]

Also in 1965, two landmark pieces of education legislation were enacted. The first was the Elementary and Secondary Education Act (ESEA), a comprehensive federal policy that still exists today, although it has been amended and reauthorized many times. The original ESEA provided federal funding to elementary and secondary schools, including $1 billion to schools that served large numbers of low-income students (Cervantes et al., 2005). The second was the Higher Education Act, another comprehensive statute that is still in place today and that has expanded considerably since it was first enacted. Title IV of the Higher Education Act included federal student financial aid programs, which would become increasingly important over time as the price of college climbed substantially. The original Act included need-based grants, a work-study program, and student loans that were guaranteed and subsidized by the federal government. The NDEA's National Defense Student Loan program also became part of the Higher Education Act.[6] The 1965 Act also contained financial assistance for libraries, Minority-Serving Institutions, community and technical colleges, teacher education programs, the three original TRIO student success programs, and new technologies to improve the quality of postsecondary teaching (Cervantes et al., 2005; Gándara & Jones, 2020; Johnson, 2014; Jones & Brown, 2020; Parsons, 1997; Strach, 2009; U.S. Department of Education, 2008, 2011b). As part of its first reauthorization in 1968, the Higher Education Act was amended to include "precollege encouragement programs" (Johnson, 2014, p. 561). Subsequent reauthorizations during the 1970s brought more student financial aid, for both low- and middle-income students. In 1972, the creation of the Basic Educational Opportunities Grant (BEOG) program—which would later be known as the Pell Grant program—and the Federal Supplemental Opportunity Grant provided portable federal grants to help low-income students pay for college (Fountain, 2018; Loss, 2012; Parsons, 1997; Strach, 2009). The 1978 reauthorization included low-interest federal student loans for middle-income students. These policies further expanded financial access to higher education (Johnson, 2014).

In addition to directly supporting colleges and students through its financial benefits, the Higher Education Act also provided incentives for institutions to comply with federal civil rights laws. The influx of additional funding to K–12 and higher education through the ESEA and the Higher Education Act would increase institutions' reliance on federal dollars, which could be lost if an institution failed to comply with Title VI of the Civil Rights Act (Kantor & Lowe, 1995). In the years that followed, institutions were similarly incentivized to comply with other conditional spending requirements—such as FERPA privacy protections, Clery Act reporting mandates, and others—as a result of institutional reliance on federal student aid funds. As such, the Higher Education Act was instrumental to expanding federal control over postsecondary education in the United States. In the words of Loss (2012), the Johnson-era policies "ushered in an unparalleled period of federal involvement with education policy" (p. 168).

The expanded role of the federal government in education became more visible in 1979, when the U.S. Department of Education became an independent, cabinet-level agency (Cross, 2014). Creation of this agency was strongly supported by a prominent teachers' union and President Jimmy Carter. Many Republicans opposed the agency, viewing it as excessive federal involvement in education (Cross, 2014).[7]

In addition to the policies described above, other federal nondiscrimination laws with relevance to higher education were created in the 1960s and 1970s. In 1967, President Johnson signed the Age Discrimination in Employment Act, which prohibited discrimination against older workers in hiring and employment (McCann, 2017). During Richard Nixon's presidency, the Education Amendments of 1972 were enacted. Title IX of that Act prohibited discrimination on the basis of sex in educational institutions, with threatened loss of federal funding as a consequence for violating this policy (Cross, 2014; Loss, 2012). Over time, some federal courts interpreted the scope of Title IX more broadly to include a private cause of action against the educational institution by the victim of sex discrimination (Zehrt, 2019).[8] Moreover, the Rehabilitation Act, which was enacted in 1973, prohibited disability discrimination and provided for the reasonable accommodation of individuals with disabilities in higher education institutions and other organizations that receive federal funding (Cook & Laski, 1980). In 1975, President Gerald Ford signed the Age Discrimination Act, which prohibited discrimination on the basis of age by organizations receiving federal funds, such as colleges and universities (Eglit, 1981). All of these policies are still in place today.

CONSUMERISM AND ACCOUNTABILITY: 1970s–2020s

The 1970s and 1980s ushered in a new era for higher education that still exists today: An era of consumerism and accountability. The 1970s saw the end of the war in Vietnam and the discontinuation of the U.S. military draft, and by the early 1990s, the Cold War was over (Labaree, 2016). Meanwhile, the financial value of a college degree more than tripled between 1980 and 2013, and college tuition prices increased substantially (Abel & Dietz, 2014; The College Board, 2020). Within this context, the view of higher education as important for national defense began to decline relative to the perception that higher education was useful and even necessary for high earnings and upward social mobility. During this era, higher education was largely conceptualized as a private good, and federal policies since the 1970s have reflected that conceptualization (Labaree, 2016).[9]

Beginning in 1972, federal student financial aid programs became more consumer-oriented with regard to the types of aid that were provided to students and the way that aid was administered. As explained above, the BEOG/Pell Grant program expanded financial access to higher education (Johnson, 2014). The program also made student aid portable. Adopting the GI Bill model, BEOG/Pell Grants channeled funding to eligible institutions indirectly, via the student recipients who could use the grants to attend the institution of their choice so long as the institution admitted them and met federal quality standards (Hegji, 2018; Strach, 2009). The distribution of student aid in this manner increased consumerism and competitive markets with regard to federal financial aid programs (Johnstone, 1995). Similarly, the expansion of student loans to middle-income students in 1978 likewise expanded access to higher education (Johnson, 2014). However, it also kicked off an era of increased borrowing to pay for college, and loans eclipsed grants soon thereafter as the primary source of federal student aid (Loss, 2012).

Moreover, the 1970s and 1980s were a time when U.S. tax policy began to change in a way that conceptualized taxpayers as consumers of public services. Education scholar David Labaree (2016) observed that an early "taxpayer revolt" occurred in California in 1978, when voters passed a limitation of property tax increases in the state (p. 113). These and other tax reform policies led to decreased per-student state appropriations for public higher education in California. Similar tax revolts led to cuts in higher education funding in other states as well. Beginning in the early 1980s, many state governments decreased financial support for higher education, and as a result, tuition and fees began to rise at colleges and universities to make up for receiving less revenue from state government funding (Labaree, 2016; Lopez, 2015). Ronald Reagan's presidency in the 1980s led to tax policy reform at the federal level as well. As Labaree (2016) has written, Reagan's election "meant that the push to lower taxes would become national policy" (p. 113).

Critical of the federal role in education, Reagan had campaigned on eliminating the Department of Education as a cabinet-level agency (Cross, 2014; Parsons, 1997). But in his first year, Reagan appointed Terrel Bell—a former school administrator who had previously argued in favor of the existence of the Department of Education—as the department's secretary (Mouat, 1981). Bell appointed the National Commission on Excellence in Education, which produced the landmark *A Nation at Risk* report in 1983. This report decried what it identified as "a rising tide of mediocrity" in the country's educational system that was leading the United States to fall behind competitor nations, suggesting this was a threat to economic growth and even national security (National Commission on Excellence in Education, 1983, p. 7). The report reinvigorated the argument in favor of a federal Department of Education (Cross, 2014; Parsons, 1997). The department survived Reagan's presidency and still exists today.

The 1980s also saw an increase in defaults on federal student loans, particularly by individuals who had attended for-profit colleges (Flores, 2018; Looney & Yannelis, 2015; McCann & Laitinen, 2019). Around this time, policies scrutinizing tax-funded programs, and educational programs in particular, emerged. At the state level, this included performance accountability policies for higher education. For example, some states began to require public reporting on student outcome measures from colleges and universities that received state dollars. Other state-level accountability policies based public institutions' appropriations at least partially on the institution's performance on outcome measures such as graduation and job placement rates (Burke & Associates, 2005; Dougherty & Natow, 2015; Dougherty et al., 2016; Kelchen 2018).

At the federal level, Congress used its conditional spending power to include accountability policies in the 1992 reauthorization of the Higher Education Act. For example, beginning with the 1992 Act, institutions receiving federal student aid funds have been required to report a great deal of information about themselves to the federal government. These requirements have continued and expanded over time, and include reporting on campus safety, student enrollments, graduation rates for Pell Grant recipients, and a myriad of other data (Kelchen, 2018). Also, although appropriate accreditation had been a requirement for institutions receiving federal student aid funds since the Higher Education Act was first enacted, the 1992 reauthorization provided a more specific role for accreditors, and it also enlisted state governments and the U.S. Department of Education as guardians of the quality of higher education through the Program Integrity

Triad. The 1992 Act also included some tighter requirements for for-profit higher education providers in an attempt to lower the sector's student loan default rates (Flores, 2018; Harnisch et al., 2016; Kelchen, 2018; McCann & Laitinen, 2019).

In the 1990s, the Department of Education began to take on features of a consumer-oriented business that would traditionally have been uncharacteristic of a bureaucratic public agency. During Bill Clinton's presidency, Vice President Al Gore led an effort called "Reinventing Government," which among other things recommended the creation of *performance-based organizations* within government for the purpose of streamlining agency operations and providing clients with more effective and satisfying services. The Office of Federal Student Aid within the Department of Education became the first of these organizations (Jackson, 2003). Also in the 1990s, the department got more involved in the student loan business with the creation of the William D. Ford Federal Direct Loan program, through which borrowers could receive student loans directly from the Department of Education. In 2009, Congress passed the Student Aid and Fiscal Responsibility Act (SAFRA), which would phase private lenders out of federal student loan programs, making the Department of Education the sole lender for such loans going forward (Dortch et al., 2010).

Federal policies continued to impose broader accountability measures through the 2000s. Margaret Spellings, who had served as secretary of education under President George W. Bush, led the Commission on the Future of Higher Education, which produced a report in 2006 recommending policy reforms to increase higher education accountability; however, those policies were not formally adopted (Kelchen, 2018; Lowry, 2009). Then, when President Barack Obama took office, his administration's Department of Education promptly began to develop regulations to hold accountable for-profit and other career-focused higher education institutions that received federal student aid funds. Among these regulations were restrictions on the manner in which colleges could pay their admissions and recruiting staff so as to discourage conflicts of interest. Another Obama-era accountability policy was the Gainful Employment Rule, which required certain disclosures of data and acceptable debt-to-income ratios for program graduates (Kelchen, 2018; Natow, 2017, 2020).[10] The Gainful Employment Rule was later repealed by the Trump administration (Natow, 2020), but other forms of higher education accountability and consumer protection remained. For example, the College Scorecard—a federal website and large database of consumer-relevant information about colleges—began during the Obama administration and was embraced by the Trump administration. The College Scorecard's website posts information about individual colleges, such as their graduates' debt and earnings, graduation rates, student loan repayment data, and tuition prices (Bauman & Thomason, 2019; Kelchen, 2018; Kyaw, 2021; Turner, 2015).

SUMMARY AND CONCLUSION

The history of the federal government's relationship with higher education dates back to the nation's earliest days. For more than a century following the ratification of the Constitution, the federal government's actions expanded higher education across the United States, often through grants of land expropriated from Native Americans (Lee & Ahtone, 2020). Moreover, higher education often served as a partner with the federal government on meeting the country's vital needs at various points in history. This has included providing research in agriculture, the sciences, and other areas relevant to national defense. In addition, the federal government has called on higher education to provide jobs, job-relevant training, and other educational opportunities during times of economic need (Loss, 2012). But the federal government has also used higher education to continue oppressive and inequitable practices that have characterized much of United States history, including racial segregation, colonization, and unequal access to higher education (Cervantes et al., 2005; Herbold, 1994; Lee & Ahtone, 2020; Loss, 2012; Thelin, 2011; Wheatle, 2019).

During the mid- to late 20th century, following pressure from the civil rights movement, the federal government developed nondiscrimination and other policies that would broaden access to higher education, end *de jure* racial segregation, and take steps in the direction of educational equity, although these measures took a long time to accomplish, and there still remains much room for improvement (Cervantes et al., 2005; Loss, 2012). As the 20th century progressed and the Cold War ended, the potential for higher education to play an active role in a potential war effort decreased (Labaree, 2016). At the same time, the need for higher education increased for those seeking economic security and social mobility. College tuition prices rose as well, as did federal student loan defaults (Lopez, 2015). Policymakers and the public became increasingly skeptical about the quality of education, and the national mood on government spending shifted to one of lower taxes and economic austerity. This ushered in an era of higher education consumerism and accountability that continues through today (Kelchen, 2018; Labaree, 2016).

In the year 2020, the emergence of COVID-19 led to widespread transitions of classes and other programming online to prevent the spread of the virus. Higher education institutions spent massive amounts of money on this transition, as well as on sanitizing campuses, refunding room and board payments, and defending lawsuits brought by students for tuition reimbursements due to in-person classes being canceled (Hubler, 2020; Mitchell, 2020, 2021; Robert, 2021). The federal government responded by providing tens of billions of dollars in funding for higher education (Natow, 2021c). The pandemic greatly transformed a number of aspects of higher education, perhaps permanently. As a policy consultant interviewed for my study reflected, "From retrofitting campuses for safety measures to just costs [institutions] incurred because of the shutdown . . . that's not going to go away quickly." Given these and other challenges facing the postsecondary sector, substantial federal support may be necessary to sustain many higher education institutions well into the future.

What else characterizes the current relationship between the federal government and higher education? Beginning in the 2010s, marked partisanship has led to legislative gridlock in the higher education space. Congress has become increasingly polarized in recent years (Harbridge, 2015). It has been quite difficult for the two main political parties to reach sufficient agreement to pass major higher education legislation (Natow, 2021b). As a result, recent decades have also seen a rise in federal higher education policymaking via executive action, whether by the president or executive branch agencies. The trend of partisan gridlock giving way to executive action has marked a turning point in the history of the federal government's role in higher education. The chapters that follow provide more details about this turn, as well as the legislative, executive, and judicial structures and politics that have enabled it.

CHAPTER 3

Congress's Roles in Higher Education

As the federal government's legislative body, Congress has passed legislation regarding higher education for centuries, and with particular significance since World War II (Labaree, 2016; Thelin, 2011). Recently, the passage of major higher education legislation has slowed, with Congress experiencing more partisan polarization, and Higher Education Act reauthorizations becoming less frequent (Gándara & Jones, 2020; Harbridge, 2015; Pogarcic, 2018). In addition to the power to legislate, Congress holds other authorities that can influence policy as well as other branches of government. The ability to investigate federal officials, including the president, is a powerful way for Congress to hold the executive branch accountable (Davis et al., 2021). Congress can also investigate alleged wrongdoings on the part of private entities (Sopko & O'Connor, 2009). The Senate's power to confirm or deny presidential appointments for federal agency personnel, and—perhaps more importantly, due to their lifetime tenure—federal judges, extends the reach of senators well beyond legislation.

Moreover, the majority party in Congress wields considerable power. This is because majority votes in each house of Congress select leadership for their respective chambers, and majority party members chair congressional committees. These leaders have the power to advance the policy agenda for the party (Caulfield, 2019; Harbridge, 2015; Heitshusen, 2019; Oleszek et al., 2019). If the president has a different political party affiliation than the majority party in a house in Congress, then that chamber's party leader holds power that can stifle the president's agenda. The party leader may also use that power to negotiate policies that are likely to receive bipartisan support. For this reason, political parties have a strong interest in obtaining majority-party status in each chamber of Congress (Lee, 2009).

As Congress holds *the power of the purse*—the power to levy taxes and determine federal spending—it has considerable power over higher education. As Chapter 1 showed, institutions of higher learning depend on federal funding through financial support via loans and grants to students. Congress can control the amount of such funding and the circumstances and conditions of its distribution. Other powers of Congress, including its ability to enforce civil rights laws and its power to regulate intellectual property protections, have likewise provided this body with a great deal of influence over higher education (U.S. Const. art. I, § 8, amend. XIV).

This chapter delineates Congress's constitutional authority over higher education. It begins with a description of the structure of Congress, followed by a discussion of Congress's legislative power. The chapter also explains Congress's oversight power and the Senate's role in confirming presidential nominations for federal posts. The chapter closes with a discussion of the ability of Congress members to draw attention to issues through public platforms that are analogous to the presidential "bully pulpit." Throughout the chapter, real-world examples and perspectives of policy actors illustrate how the various roles of Congress affect higher education in many important ways.

STRUCTURE OF CONGRESS

The Bicameral Legislature

Following its well-known "We the People" preamble, the second sentence of the U.S. Constitution establishes Congress as the federal government's legislative body, dividing the institution into two chambers: the Senate and the House of Representatives (U.S. Const. art. I, § 1). In the House, the number of representatives assigned to each state depends on the state's population, with each state having a minimum of one representative, and more populous states having more representatives. Drawing district boundaries for the House of Representatives—a process known as redistricting, which occurs every ten years (Eckman, 2021; Hebert & Jenkins, 2011; U.S. Census Bureau, n.d.)—is influenced by politics. This is because the drawing of district lines is conducted by political actors at the state level, who tend to draw boundaries that benefit their own electoral prospects. The politics of redistricting has the potential to dilute democratic representation in the House by giving one political party a disproportionate advantage, depending on how congressional district lines are drawn (Hebert & Jenkins, 2011). For its part, the Senate is even less democratically representative than the House, because each state has two U.S. senators regardless of the state's population. Therefore, states with smaller populations are overrepresented in the Senate in terms of the ratio of senators to state inhabitants (Dauster, 2016; Drutman, 2020; Stephens, 1996).[1]

Congressional Powers

The powers of Congress specifically provided in the Constitution are called *enumerated* powers, appearing in Article I (Johnson, 2005). Among other things, these include powers (U.S. Const. art. I, § 8):

- To tax and spend for the purpose of promoting national defense and the "general Welfare of the United States" (U.S. Const. art. I, § 8; see also Nolan & Glassman, 2016, p. 1).
- To regulate interstate and international commerce;[2]
- To provide intellectual property protections for inventors, writers, artists, and other innovators;
- To create federal courts below the Supreme Court;
- To create law for the District of Columbia; and
- "To make all laws which shall be necessary and proper for carrying into execution the foregoing powers, and all other powers vested by this Constitution in the government of the United States, or in any department or officer thereof" (cl. 18).

These enumerated powers have generally been interpreted broadly, and Congress also exercises unenumerated powers, such as the power to conduct investigations (Boudreaux, 2006; Johnson, 2005; Johnson et al., 1992).

Importantly, Article I vests federal spending authority in Congress (Saturno, 2020; U.S. Const. art. I §§ 8, 9). As explained in Chapter 1, conditional spending has served as a key policy instrument through which Congress regulates higher education. Thus, the spending power is a crucial force in federal higher education policymaking.

Constitutional amendments have also provided Congress with authority to legislate. Following the Civil War, the Thirteenth through Fifteenth Amendments granted Congress additional powers to enforce the terms of those amendments, including the protection of civil rights and liberties afforded by the Fourteenth Amendment's equal protection, due process, and privileges and immunities clauses (Alexander et al., 2021; Schmidt, 2018; U.S. Const. amend. XIII-XV).

In theory, congressional powers can serve as a check on the executive branch, including the president and the president's cabinet. For example, Congress can override a presidential veto of legislation. Congressional spending authority means that presidential budget proposals must meet with Congress's approval. Congress may also investigate alleged executive branch wrongdoing, and the chambers may vote to impeach (in the House) and remove (in the Senate) a wayward executive or judicial official (Johnson et al., 1992; Kriner & Schickler, 2014; Prakash, 2006). Also, thanks to the Congressional Review Act, Congress can pass a filibuster-proof resolution to repeal a recent agency regulation, and thereby ban the agency from ever issuing a "substantially similar" regulation in the future (Carey & Davis, 2020, p. 2).

But the structure of Congress can also lead some of its members to refuse to check the executive branch (Devins, 2018). This is because Congress is made up not only of two chambers but also of hundreds of individual members, who represent different states and regions of the country, different political parties and factions within those parties, and different ideologies. Individual members of Congress have vastly different demographic and professional backgrounds and hold their own areas of interest and expertise. As a result, individual Congress members seek to fulfill their own interests in addition to, and often instead of, the interests of Congress as an institution—a typical "collective action problem" (Devins, 2018, p. 57; see also Lee, 2009). Such collective action problems can lead to legislative inaction and gridlock (Teter, 2011). This phenomenon also helps to explain why Congress has struggled to pass a comprehensive Higher Education Act reauthorization in the polarized environment of recent decades: Congressional leaders and political parties have their own priorities that may not be conducive to bipartisan compromise on higher education legislation (Natow, 2021b).

Congressional Leadership and Committees

Congressional leadership and committees are fundamental to the operations of Congress, including its higher education policymaking, because much of the body's work occurs behind the scenes in committees or among congressional leaders (Parsons, 1997). Some chamber leadership, such as the Speaker of the House, is selected by a majority vote of congressional members. Other leaders (such as majority and minority party leaders) are selected by that party's members. The party that holds the most seats in a chamber receives more seats on committees than the minority party. Thus, because committees are able to advance or stall legislation, the political party that holds the majority of seats in each house of Congress is vested with considerable power to control the body's agenda (Caulfield, 2019; Eckman & Egar, 2019; Harbridge, 2015; Heitshusen, 2019; Lee, 2009; Oleszek, 2014; Oleszek et al., 2019; Schneider, 2006).[3]

Key congressional leaders for higher education issues include chamber, party, and committee leaders. The chamber leader of the House of Representatives is the Speaker of the House, who sets the chamber's legislative agenda (Caulfield, 2019; Heitshusen, 2017; Oleszek et al., 2019). The vice president serves as president of the Senate but does not vote on legislation other than in the case of a tie. The president pro tempore, elected by other senators, serves as president of the Senate in the absence of the vice president (U.S. const. Art. I § 3; see also Davis, 2015). But the leader who has the most power in the Senate is the majority party's leader, who holds roles and authorities similar to those of the Speaker of the House (Heitshusen, 2019; Oleszek et al., 2019).

Congressional committee leaders are the committee chairs and ranking members—that is, the majority-party and minority-party leader, respectively, on a given committee. Committee chairs in each chamber are selected according to party rules, which tend to involve some combination of seniority and preferences of the chamber's party leaders (Schneider, 2009, 2016). Committee chairs are able to advance or block legislation (and in the Senate, nominations by the president) within those committees. Congressional committees are instrumental in determining the contents of a bill and whether it will receive floor time (Gándara & Jones, 2020; Oleszek et al., 2019; Schneider, 2009, 2018).

Legislation introduced in a chamber of Congress is generally referred to the chamber's committee with jurisdiction over the bill—that is, the committee overseeing the bill's policy area (Oleszek, 2020). Congressional committees also have the ability to initiate new legislation (Heitshusen, 2020). The committee in the Senate that handles most bills related to higher education is the Health, Education, Labor, and Pensions (also known as "HELP") committee (U.S. Senate Committee on Health, Education, Labor, and Pensions, n.d.). The official name of the House of Representatives committee handling most education bills has varied depending on which political party has held the majority in that chamber, with the Democratic majority using "Education and Labor Committee" and the Republican majority using "Education and the Workforce Committee" (Barab, 2018; Education & Labor Committee, n.d.). Sometimes bills involve policy matters that are overseen by multiple committees. In those cases, a congressional committee may have secondary jurisdiction over the bill (Oleszek, 2020). Apart from education-specific committees, other congressional committees that handle higher education matters include the House and Senate Budget and Appropriations Committees, which deal with bills that provide and allocate federal funding, including for higher education (Heniff, 2012), and the Agriculture Committees, which may handle matters relating to land-grant colleges or agricultural research (Rawson, 2006). Bills regarding student loan debt have sometimes been sent to the Senate Finance Committee, the House Financial Services Committee, or the House Ways and Means Committee (American Association of College Registrars et al., 2018; Burns, 2019; U.S. House Committee on Financial Services, 2020).

Rules of Congress

Both the House and Senate have their own sets of complicated rules that govern the way they do business. These rules have been consequential for policy and governance, and some have made the difference in whether certain laws get enacted or presidential nominees get confirmed. In addition to the rules for each chamber of Congress, the different political parties have their own sets of rules to which their members must adhere (Oleszek et al., 2019; Schneider, 2009, 2016). For example, the Republican party has imposed term limits on congressional committee leadership, while the Democratic party has not (Schneider, 2009).

Rules and procedures can facilitate or hinder the progression of a bill through Congress. One procedural action that can expedite a bill's movement is "suspending the rules" in the House of Representatives (Oleszek et al., 2019, p. 14). When House leadership decides to suspend the rules on a bill, the time permitted to debate the bill is limited, and no floor amendments to the bill are allowed. This procedure is typically done only for uncontroversial matters, because a two-thirds majority vote is needed to pass a bill when the rules are suspended (Oleszek et al., 2019). Additionally, in the House of Representatives, the Rules Committee issues "special rules" to establish whether and how individual bills may be amended or debated on the floor (Harbridge, 2015, p. 80; see also Davis, 2019; Thorning, 2019).

An example of a chamber rule that can hinder the passage of legislation—and one that has had tremendous impact on the passage of legislation and the approval of federal appointments—is the Senate's filibuster rule. A filibuster refers to senators' activity that prevents a matter from being the subject of a vote, typically by declining to end debate on the matter. A vote of *cloture* ends debate for the purpose of bringing a matter to a vote, and consent from at least 60 senators—or a three-fifths supermajority of the chamber—is needed for cloture to occur (Dauster, 2016; Heitshusen & Beth, 2017; Oleszek et al., 2019). Thus, the existence of the filibuster and the requirement of a supermajority for cloture has resulted in the indefinite delay of voting on matters unable to gain a minimum of 60 senators' support (Cohen, 2020). Senate minority parties have filibustered legislation of all kinds, including higher education–related legislation, such as when a bill to lower interest rates on federal student loans was blocked by Senate Republicans in 2014, falling four votes short of the 60 needed to invoke cloture (Stratford, 2014). An interviewee for my research who used to work as a Senate staffer described the power of the filibuster to shape policymakers' thinking about legislation from the outset. This respondent said:

> The filibuster lives in the Senate in every moment. The filibuster doesn't just live when somebody goes to the floor and uses a filibuster. The filibuster is a mechanism by which you understand you can't get anything done without 60 votes.

Congressional rules may be changed by a cohesive majority party, which is a key reason why the party in control of Congress has substantial power. However, rules exist that govern how the rules may be changed, and some rules are easier to change than others. For example, although a rule change to eliminate filibusters entirely would require a supermajority of senators to agree (Davis, 2020; Reynolds, 2020), removing the ability to filibuster in limited circumstances via changing precedent requires only a simple majority vote (Reynolds, 2020; Wice, 2020). This is because Senate rules allow for parliamentary decisions to be overruled by a simple majority of senators.

Thus, if the Senate chair (i.e., the vice president or president pro tempore) holds that Senate precedent requires 60 votes to invoke cloture in particular cases—such as confirming presidential nominees—a senator may appeal that decision and ask the full Senate to vote on whether a simple majority would suffice. Should a majority of senators vote to overrule the chair's decision, then the procedure approved by a majority of senators would become the new precedent for handling similar Senate procedures in the future (Dauster, 2016). This very type of precedent-changing procedure was used by the Democratic Senate majority in 2013 to end the filibuster for presidential appointees to executive branch offices and federal courts other than the Supreme Court. This was also done by the Republican Senate majority for Supreme Court appointees during the early days of the Trump administration. In both cases, the majority party accomplished this change by setting a new precedent for how the cloture rule was interpreted when voting on a president's nominees—a precedent change that was limited in scope (Dauster, 2016; Reynolds, 2020; Wice, 2020). Given the power that the filibuster and other congressional rules have over Congress's operations, the majority coalition's ability to manipulate these rules is a powerful tool.[4]

CONGRESS'S LEGISLATIVE POWER

Enacting Legislation

The legislative process is perhaps the most recognizable and far-ranging method for developing higher education policy. Under regular order (which refers to the sequential procedure for moving legislation through Congress on its way to enactment), once a bill is introduced by a member of Congress, it is typically sent to the relevant congressional committee for consideration (Heitshusen, 2020; Oleszek et al., 2019). During a bill's markup process, the committee debates and votes on recommendations for amendment to the bill, and it is during this process that significant changes to a bill are often made (Gándara & Jones, 2020; Heitshusen, 2020; Schneider, 2009, 2018). Committees also sometimes hold hearings regarding a bill, sometimes as early as the drafting stage, to gather other information from stakeholders. Committees with jurisdiction over a bill may vote on whether to move the bill forward to the full chamber (Oleszek et al., 2019; Schneider, 2009, 2018). If the full chamber votes to pass the legislation, the bill is sent to the other chamber for consideration and a vote.

It is important to note that many bills do not follow this sequential path under regular order (Coval, 2015; Oleszek et al., 2019). For example, bills sometimes skip the committee process altogether or are otherwise rushed through the legislative process. This has happened more frequently in recent decades due to increased partisanship and the need for lawmakers to be able to point to legislative accomplishments on the campaign trail (Oleszek et al., 2019). Because the version of a bill introduced in one house of Congress is unlikely to be identical to the version passed by the other chamber, the chambers attempt to work out their differences or convene a conference committee to negotiate the language of a final bill, to be voted on by both chambers so that they pass identical legislation (Davis, 2019).

Legislation becomes enacted law when both houses of Congress pass the same bill and the president then signs the bill into law. The president may also veto a bill, which may then be overridden by two-thirds of the membership of both the House of Representatives and the Senate. Legislation may also be enacted (or rejected) in another way: If Congress presents a passed bill to the president and the bill is not signed within ten days while Congress is in session, then the bill becomes law; if Congress is not in session during that period, then the bill does not become law (U.S. Const. art. I, § 7). Because congressional terms last 2 years (from January 3 of one odd-numbered year to January 3 of the following odd-numbered year), bills introduced within a particular term that are not voted on when the term expires are effectively dead. Those bills must be reintroduced in a subsequent congressional term to receive further consideration (Oleszek et al., 2019). An example of a bill introduced in multiple congressional terms is the College Transparency Act, which would allow the U.S. Department of Education to maintain a student-level database of information (Miller, 2016; ProPublica, 2021).

Major Higher Education Legislation

Many kinds of federal legislation—such as laws governing labor and employment and laws protecting civil rights—are applicable to higher education just as they are to other fields more broadly. However, some legislation focuses specifically on higher education (Kaplin et al., 2020). The most prominent of these laws is the Higher Education Act, which is the basis for a substantial amount of federal higher education policy and spending (Gándara & Jones, 2020; Putansu, 2020). First enacted in 1965 as part of President Lyndon Johnson's Great Society initiatives, the Higher Education Act aimed to make postsecondary education more accessible for people for whom pursuing education past high school was not financially feasible. Since then, the Act has been reauthorized eight times (Johnson, 2014; Gándara & Jones, 2020; Natow, 2017). The Higher Education Act is a lengthy and comprehensive statute, whose major provisions include the following (Hegji, 2018; Higher Education Act, 2018; Natow, 2017; Parsons, 1997):

- Title I—General provisions and definitions
- Title II—Policies designed to enhance teacher preparation programs
- Title III—Support for Historically Black Colleges and Universities (HBCUs) and Minority-Serving Institutions

- Title IV—Federal student financial aid, TRIO, and GEAR UP programs as well as other grant programs aimed at student success
- Title V—Support for Hispanic-Serving Institutions
- Title VI—Support for international education
- Title VII—Funding to improve graduate and other postsecondary education
- Title VIII and beyond—A variety of additional programs, many of which are focused on improving higher education and supporting access to college and beyond (although as Hegji [2018] notes, "Most of these programs have not been funded" [p. 24])

Other examples of major higher education legislation include the GI Bill, the Clery Act, the Family Educational Rights and Privacy Act (FERPA), and the Higher Education Amendments of 1972, Title IX of which prohibits sex and gender identity discrimination in educational programming (Grissom & Herrington, 2012; Kaplin et al., 2020; NASPA, n.d.). Some legislation that primarily targets education outside the postsecondary sector also has implications for higher education. For example, the Elementary and Secondary Education Act and its reauthorizations have implications for college readiness and teacher preparation programs (Fránquiz & Ortiz, 2016; Klein, 2016). The Carl D. Perkins Career and Technical Education Act likewise influences preparation for education beyond high school by authorizing and providing funding for career and technical education programs (Granovskiy, 2016). The Farm Bill has provisions affecting higher education, including requirements for states to report their funding allocations for 1890 land-grant institutions, additional funding for HBCUs, and additional funding for research on food production and security (Kreighbaum, 2018c). Other legislation that has affected higher education includes the Workforce Innovation and Opportunity Act, the Civil Rights Act, the Americans with Disabilities Act, the Fair Labor Standards Act, the Copyright Act, and others (Boylan et al., 2018; Kaplin et al., 2020). As the case study near the end of this chapter explains, the CARES Act, which Congress passed in 2020 as its first major legislative response to the COVID-19 pandemic, contained billions of dollars' worth of funding for higher education, although only a small amount of that funding reached students (McLean, 2020; U.S. Government Accountability Office, 2021).

Congress and the "Power of the Purse"

An important way Congress uses its legislative power to influence higher education is by passing appropriations laws, also known as spending bills. This congressional power, dubbed the "power of the purse" (e.g., Desan & Peer, 2020, p. 1), has great influence over higher education. Conditional spending—funding that is contingent upon higher education institutions' compliance with certain rules and regulations (Bagenstos, 2014; Haney, 2013)—is a primary tool through which the federal government creates higher education policy. As discussed above, the Constitution gives Congress the power to spend the federal government's funds. However, the process through which this is done is governed by congressional rules and procedures (American Council on Education, n.d.-a; Heniff, 2012; Oleszek et al., 2019; Sablan & Hiestand, 2020; Saturno, 2020). Before funds can be appropriated, Congress must enact a substantive authorizing law, such as the Higher Education Act. This law creates (or, in the case of a reauthorization, continues) federal programs such as student financial aid, TRIO student success programs, and the many other programs authorized by the Higher Education Act. Such bills are called *authorizing legislation* because they establish federal programs and authorize the use of federal funds. Following authorization or reauthorization, Congress passes budget and appropriations legislation to allow for the programs and activities in the authorizing statute to be funded (Adler & Wilkerson, 2012; Heniff, 2012; Oleszek et al., 2019; Saturno, 2020; Saturno et al., 2016; Saturno & Yeh, 2016).[5]

Under regular order, the annual budget and appropriations process generally unfolds as follows (see Center on Budget & Policy Priorities, 2020; Committee for a Responsible Federal Budget, 2020; National Association of Student Financial Aid Administrators, n.d., 2018; Oleszek et al., 2019; Sablan & Hiestand, 2020; Saturno et al., 2016; Yourish & Stanton, n.d.). The process begins early in the year, initiated by the president's budget proposal, which is supposed to be submitted to Congress by the first Monday in the month of February, although this submission is often late.[6] Budget Committees in both houses of Congress then develop budgetary targets for the fiscal year and submit a resolution that must be voted on by each chamber. The differences between the two chambers' versions of the budget resolution are handled by a conference committee. Budget allocations are typically finalized by mid-April.

Next, both chambers' Appropriations Committees—which are separate from the Budget Committees—work within the Budget Committees' limits to determine how federal funding will be spent in the next fiscal year. This is done via the work of 12 subcommittees in each chamber that focus on a particular area of federal spending. There is a Subcommittee on Labor, Health and Human Services, Education, and related agencies in both the House and the Senate, and those subcommittees handle appropriations for the Department of Education, the Department of Labor, and other "related agencies" (House Committee on Appropriations, n.d.-a; U.S. Senate Committee on Appropriations, n.d.). These subcommittees are known as the "Labor-H" subcommittees, and the bills they put forward are called "Labor-H" bills (House Committee on Appropriations, 2020). Each of the 12 subcommittees sends a draft bill to the full Appropriations Committee, which may make changes and ultimately vote on the bills. In regular order, this would be 12 separate appropriations bills, one from each of the subcommittees (Committee for a Responsible Federal Budget, 2020). The versions passed by the Appropriations Committee then go to the full chamber for a vote. Differences between the House and Senate versions of the bills that ultimately pass are addressed by a conference committee, and the conference committee's final bills go back to each house of Congress to be voted on again (now as the same bill being voted on by both chambers). If the appropriations bills pass both houses, they are presented for the president's signature. Ideally, this process would be complete by October 1, when the fiscal year officially begins; however, it frequently gets delayed (Committee for a Responsible Federal Budget, 2020; National Association of Student Financial Aid Administrators, n.d., 2018; Oleszek et al., 2019; Saturno et al., 2016; Yourish & Stanton, n.d.). Although this multistep process is how budgets and appropriations are developed under regular order, this process is not typical of how the federal budget has been passed in recent years. In fact, since 1974, Congress has met the Spring deadline for passing the budget resolution only a handful of times (Pfiffner, 2020).

Sometimes higher education policy is made through a process known as budget reconciliation, which is an expedited process for the enactment of bills relating to fiscal policy (Griffin, 2021; Heniff, 2016; Oleszek et al., 2019; Reich & Kogan, 2021; Sablan & Hiestand, 2020; U.S. House of Representatives Committee on the Budget, 2018). These bills are labeled "reconciliation" because they are designed "to bring existing law into conformity with the current budget resolution," or in other words, to *reconcile* federal policy with the budget (Oleszek et al., 2019, p. 71). Congress creates a reconciliation by first passing a budget resolution that instructs particular committees in the House or Senate to alter "spending, revenues, or deficits by specific amounts" (U.S. House of Representatives Committee on the Budget, 2018, p. 1). The committees do so by drafting legislation, and the resulting legislation then receives a vote on the chamber's floor. Because Senate rules limit the time for debate on budget reconciliations, these bills cannot be filibustered, and only a simple majority vote is needed for such a bill to pass (Griffin, 2021; Heniff, 2016; Oleszek et al., 2019; Reich & Kogan, 2021; Sablan & Hiestand, 2020; U.S. House of Representatives Committee on the Budget, 2018). Due to the accelerated and filibuster-proof nature of reconciliation, this has been a useful tool for the majority party to advance its agenda on policy matters that meet the requirements to be addressed by this process (Griffin, 2021; Sablan & Hiestand, 2020).[7] As one of my respondents who worked as a policy director at a higher education association observed, "If you want to get something done relatively quickly . . . then the reconciliation bill has been the vehicle of choice for a long time."

Although reconciliations are budget bills, their reach can be wide. An example of a reconciliation bill that changed the substance of higher education policy was the Health Care and Education Reconciliation Act in 2010, which made changes to the Affordable Care Act (ACA), and also contained a provision, called the Student Aid and Fiscal Responsibility Act (SAFRA), that initiated the federal student loan programs' transition to entirely federal Direct Loans (American Council on Education, 2010; Dortch et al., 2010; Sablan & Hiestand, 2020).[8] However, not every policy can be passed as a reconciliation, even if it involves mandatory spending programs. Under the Byrd Rule (so called because it was originally championed by Senator Robert Byrd), senators may object to reconciliation bills that contain "extraneous matter" (Heniff, 2016, p. 4), such as items that do not have a "budgetary effect," or have such an effect that is only "incidental to the non-budgetary policy change" (U.S. House of Representatives Committee on the Budget, 2018, p. 4; see also Heniff, 2016). SAFRA passed as part of a budget reconciliation because of the large fiscal savings it was expected to provide, and such savings could be used to offset other costs, like increasing the size of the Pell Grant and helping to pay for the expensive ACA (American Council on Education, 2010).

The budget and appropriations process, an important legislative procedure for higher education policy, can be confusing to stakeholders outside the federal government, with its numerous committees and subcommittees, complicated rules, and infrequent use of regular order. However, the basic concepts of the budget and appropriations process are not too different from common household budgeting. One of my respondents who had worked on Capitol Hill compared the Budget and Appropriations Committees to having "a savings account and a checking account." This respondent said:

> The Budget Committee . . . sets the top line numbers, and it says, okay, you have X amount to spend. . . . And then the appropriators go in, and they're the ones who say, we want to put this much into Pell Grants, and this much into Title I, and this much into health care, and defense. . . . They go through their process to decide how to spend that money.

CONGRESSIONAL OVERSIGHT POWERS

Congress also holds powers of oversight and investigation. These powers play a key role in congressional checks and balances of the other federal branches (Davis et al., 2021; Kriner & Schickler, 2014; Marshall, 2004; Relyea & Tatelman, 2007; U.S. Const. art. II, § 4; Wilson et al., 2016). The Constitution provides an express power for Congress to penalize the president, vice president, federal judges, and other federal officials for "Treason, Bribery, or other high Crimes and Misdemeanors" with impeachment by majority vote in the House of Representatives and, following that, removal from office by a two-thirds vote of the Senate (U.S. Const. art. II, § 4; see also Davis et al., 2021). Congress has the power to launch other kinds of investigations as well, of both government and private entities (Davis et al., 2021; Sopko & O'Connor, 2009). According to the Congressional Research Service, Congress's power of oversight is "an implied power" that "helps to ensure a more responsible bureaucracy while supplying Congress with information needed to formulate new legislation" (Davis et al., 2021, p. 5). Congress may conduct investigations that are germane "to some legitimate legislative function" (Sopko & O'Connor, 2009, p. 234). Other reasons Congress may conduct investigations include evaluation of programs and federal financial decisions, examining potential executive branch overreach, protecting civil rights, reviewing agency procedures, and investigating "[i]nstances of fraud and other forms of corruption, wasteful expenditures, incompetent management, and the subversion of governmental processes" (Davis et al., 2021, p. 2).

Congressional investigations are not a small matter. Federal courts have typically allowed Congress a substantial amount of leeway to conduct investigations (Davis et al., 2021). Being subject to one can be costly both financially and reputationally (Sopko & O'Connor, 2009). For elected officials, congressional investigations can have a negative political effect in that they draw attention and scrutiny to real or perceived wrongdoings by those officials, and may also draw attention away from the officials' accomplishments and policy priorities (Marshall, 2004). Indeed, as a political tool, congressional investigations can be quite effective. Kriner and Schickler (2014) found that investigations of the executive branch have tended to negatively impact presidential approval ratings. Investigations are generally conducted by congressional committees, but sometimes individual Congress members launch investigations on their own. There is a range of methods congressional actors may use to obtain information in an investigation, including requests for documents or interviews, formal subpoenas to provide documents or testimony, and seeking information through congressional hearings (Davis et al., 2021; Schneider, 2009). Noncompliance with a congressional subpoena may result in a contempt of Congress citation, which may involve civil or criminal penalties (Davis et al., 2021; Sopko & O'Connor, 2009). However, the use and enforcement of subpoenas by congressional committees are rare (Garvey, 2019).

An example of a congressional investigation in the higher education space is the Senate HELP committee's investigation of the for-profit higher education sector in 2010 through 2012, launched by Democrats who controlled the committee at that time. The investigation involved six hearings, numerous interviews with for-profit higher education students and employees, expert opinions, and an analysis of relevant documents and other data (U.S. Senate Committee on Health, Education, Labor, & Pensions, 2012). One of my respondents who was familiar with this investigation reported that some of the evidence obtained by the HELP Committee "continue[d] to drive policy conversations" years later. This example illustrates how Congress's oversight authority can impact an entire sector of higher education.

Apart from investigations, Congress can exercise oversight powers in other ways. For example, a Congress member may send a letter seeking information from agencies or other organizations for the purpose of investigating the lawfulness of organizational practices, such as in early 2020, when two Democratic senators (Sherrod Brown and Elizabeth Warren) sent letters to online program management (OPM) companies seeking information about their tuition-sharing agreements with colleges and universities that received federal student aid funds (McKenzie, 2020). Moreover, Appropriations Committees regularly exercise oversight when reviewing agencies' budget requests to determine the extent to which these requests should be granted (Davis et al., 2021). Also, as will be discussed in the next section, the Senate's power to confirm presidential appointees involves an element of oversight. A former congressional staffer provided the following example: "The confirmation of nominees to Department of Education positions, [and] the opportunity through hearings and confirmations to drive certain things in that regard," can be a powerful form of congressional oversight in the higher education policy space.

SENATE CONFIRMATION POWER

The Constitution grants the Senate the power to provide "advice and consent" (that is, approval) for the president's appointments to federal posts, including high-level cabinet positions and lifetime appointments for Supreme Court justices and other federal judges (U.S. Const. art. II, § 2; see also Davis & Greene, 2017; Davis et al., 2021; Rybicki, 2019b; Wilson et al., 2016). The confirmation power is uniquely held by the Senate—the House of Representatives plays no formal role in confirming presidential nominees. Individuals nominated by the president for executive-level posts are generally first considered by the congressional committee or committees overseeing that agency's work. Nominations of high-level appointees to the U.S. Department of Education— including the secretary of education, under secretary, deputy and assistant secretaries, general counsel, and inspector general of the department—are all handled by the Senate HELP committee (Davis & Greene, 2017). Nominations to Article III judgeships, including the Supreme Court, are handled by the Senate Judiciary Committee. These committees review nominees' qualifications, background, policy positions, and other relevant information before voting on whether to advance a particular nominee for confirmation by the full chamber (Davis & Greene, 2017; Rybicki, 2019b). During the confirmation process, senators have the opportunity to obtain a great deal of information regarding nominees, including their qualifications, policy views, relevant writings and other communications, and personal information such as health and finances (Davis et al., 2021). Hearings are almost always held for agency heads, such as the secretary of education; however, due to time and resource constraints, committees often do not hold hearings for appointees to a number of other positions that require Senate approval (Rybicki, 2019b). A respondent who had worked as a Senate staffer said the following about confirmation hearings:

> There's always a hearing for the secretary. For every other role, [the committee] can choose to have a hearing or not. . . . If they're pretty clear that this [nominee] will drive things in a direction they're comfortable with, then they don't always bother to have a hearing.

The power to confirm executive and judicial appointments gives senators an indirect yet highly consequential power. Federal judges are given lifetime tenure to interpret the law, including laws affecting higher education. Supreme Court justices hold the unique and very powerful authority to give the final word on constitutional matters brought before the Court (Chemerinsky, 2016). Chapter 6 of this volume explains the great importance of the Supreme Court for higher education policy. For example, Supreme Court decisions on desegregation and race-conscious admissions have served to diversify and promote equity in access to higher education (Bowen & Bok, 1998; Kaplin et al., 2020). Moreover, as discussed in Chapter 5, the leaders of federal agencies are also quite consequential for policy outcomes, as these leaders have the power to create policy via agency guidance and rulemaking, as well as to influence policy narratives. The secretary of education and other political appointees to the Department of Education have the most direct relevance for higher education policy, but other agencies—including the Departments of Agriculture, Labor, Homeland Security, Treasury, Veterans Affairs, and several others—all create policies that influence higher education in some way. In light of the numerous federal posts that have wide-ranging impacts on higher education and other policy areas, senators who hold the power to confirm or deny confirmation of presidential nominees can influence the trajectory of federal policymaking for years or even generations.

THE CONGRESSIONAL "BULLY PULPIT"

As Chapter 4 explains, the president of the United States speaks from a platform that receives much attention and from which the president may exert substantial influence—known as the "bully pulpit," a term first coined by President Theodore Roosevelt (Goodwin, 2013; Greenberg, 2011; Shaw, 2017). But some have observed that members of Congress hold something of their own bully pulpit, by drawing attention to matters and priorities via the powers and platforms available to them (Grove, 2019; Zelizer, 2018). Because members of Congress, and particularly congressional leaders, hold positions of power and stature within the United States government, their activities are newsworthy and garner attention. Congress members can and do use this spotlight to draw attention to matters they believe are important and to promote their preferred policies. A former congressional staffer I interviewed explained that together with legislation, "the bully pulpit of influence" is one of the main ways members of Congress affect policy conversations. This interviewee said Congress members use their bully pulpit by determining "what hearings are called, what witnesses come to testify, [and] what voices are being elevated in the space to give solutions towards the federal legislation."

Announcing an investigation and particularly holding public hearings are ways members of Congress can draw awareness to an issue or bring negative attention to a public official or government agency (Davis et al., 2021; Grove, 2019; Kriner & Schickler, 2014). Several of my respondents identified the bully pulpit as one of the purposes of congressional hearings. For example, a representative of a higher education association said that "holding hearings to spotlight attention on issues" is a key way that members of Congress "influence or attempt to influence" policy. Another respondent agreed that congressional hearings are useful to draw attention to issues, stating that "if there are certain issues that [congressional committee members] want to focus the administration or the public on, they might choose to have a hearing and ask a bunch of questions."

However, formal hearings or investigations are not necessary for Congress members to make use of their bully pulpit. A respondent who worked for a D.C.-based higher education association described this phenomenon as follows:

> Congress influences higher education . . . simply by convening people around issues related to higher education. Lawmakers have a podium, and sometimes Washington is gridlocked, and things don't move very quickly here. But if a lawmaker who is well-known or popular, or holds a certain position of power, decides to have a conversation about free college, for example, or college and university endowments, they are shaping a public discussion about that issue and about higher education. It's not a legal, regulatory, or budgetary influence, but it is a behavioral influence that they have.

Another of my respondents agreed that much of Congress's power is "not really legislating at all. It's really using their government megaphones to have an impact [on what] they can't seem to get done legislatively."

CONGRESSIONAL POWER CASE STUDY: THE CARES ACT

Beginning in Spring 2020, COVID-19 presented a public health and economic emergency on a global scale. Higher education stakeholders incurred enormous costs as a result of the pandemic. Many college students—especially those from underserved communities—lost jobs, became ill, cared for ill relatives, could not access technology needed to attend online courses, had young children whose schools were closed, or otherwise experienced financial, physical, or emotional hardship (Harper, 2020; Hubler, 2020; Whistle & West, 2020).

To address the economic and public health crises posed by the pandemic, Congress passed the CARES Act, providing billions in funding for colleges and universities, including more than $6 billion to be used as student emergency relief funding (U.S. Government Accountability Office, 2021). The CARES Act legislation passed quickly in both chambers of Congress and was signed into law by President Donald Trump on March 27, 2020 (Taylor et al., 2020). CARES Act funding for higher education would later be supplemented by two additional coronavirus stimulus bills, enacted via the legislative process in late 2020 and early 2021 (Natow, 2021c).

The provision of CARES Act funding was rolled out unevenly across colleges, and the dollar amounts received by students were relatively small. Nevertheless, this federal funding benefited a large number of students in many ways (McLean, 2020; U.S. Government Accountability Office, 2021). For example, a college student from Oregon, who received more than $1,000 under the CARES Act, said the funding helped her to avoid working extra summer shifts (McLean, 2020). Meanwhile, a community college in Minnesota used funding from the CARES Act to provide laptop computers to students in need of the technology (Minnesota State Community & Technical College, 2020).

SUMMARY AND CONCLUSION

This chapter examined the various roles that Congress plays in influencing higher education policy. Most prominently, Congress does this via the passage of legislation, often through funding bills and reauthorizations or amendments of the Higher Education Act. But members of Congress influence policy in other ways as well, such as by conducting oversight and investigations, making use of the congressional bully pulpit, and—in the Senate—confirming (or not confirming) presidential appointments to influential government positions.

One takeaway from this analysis is that Congress is far from monolithic. Individual members of Congress have their own interests and viewpoints, and as the two main political parties become more cohesive and ideological (Devins, 2018), Congress is less likely to be able to pass major legislation (Jones, 2001). Individual members of Congress can have substantial influence on higher education both within and outside the legislative process. Leaders of each chamber and congressional committees can determine which matters will move forward to a floor vote and what issues or presidential nominees may be subject to public hearings. And individual Congress members may choose to make use of their bully pulpit to draw attention to issues that are important to them.

Higher education is one of the policy areas for which congressional gridlock and partisanship have stymied much legislative policymaking, with Higher Education Act reauthorizations becoming fewer and farther between as time goes on (Gándara & Jones, 2020; Pogarcic, 2018). Even bills with bipartisan support have had a difficult time getting enacted in recent years (e.g., Kreighbaum, 2019d; Natow, 2021b). With legislation generally stalling in Congress, policymaking in the executive branch—the subject of the next chapter—has become increasingly important (Foster, 2020). But ultimately, Congress's power of the purse provides the first branch of government with enormous influence over higher education, as the expansive federal role in higher education is based largely on colleges' and universities' increasing dependence on federal dollars.

CHAPTER 4

The President's Power and Influence Over Higher Education

The president of the United States is the most important figure in the federal government. As head of state, chief of the executive branch, commander-in-chief of the armed services, and political party leader, the president plays many roles and wields great influence over foreign and domestic policy (Lee, 2009; Rochelle, 1999; U.S. Const. art. II; Wilson et al., 2016). The president also holds much symbolic power, by assuming "the trappings and symbols of [the] office" (Mervin, 1995, p. 19).

Presidents' use of unilateral executive powers, such as executive orders and presidential proclamations, have increased over time (Foster, 2020; Howell, 2005; Woolley & Peters, 2017). Increased political polarization in recent decades has led to gridlock in legislation during periods of divided party control of the federal government, which has led presidents, frustrated in reaching their policy goals through legislative channels, to employ these executive tools (Burum, 2008; Carmines & Fowler, 2017). Though executive orders and proclamations are easy for a president to issue, they are also relatively easy for a later administration to reverse (Chu & Garvey, 2014).[1] The increased use of executive power underscores the importance of the president as an individual policy actor, as the president's ideology, values, and policy positions can have far-ranging consequences. Many of the policy tools available to the president—including executive action, legislative proposals, political appointments to key agency positions and the courts, and communicating priorities from a prominent stage—have been used in a variety of ways to influence higher education policy.

Recent shifts in federal policy between presidencies demonstrate the critical importance of the president for higher education. Federal policy regarding for-profit higher education provides a striking example of these shifts. The for-profit sector experienced deregulation under the George W. Bush and Trump administrations, and more restrictive regulatory policies during the Obama administration (Natow, 2017, 2020). Indeed, the politics and ideology of the president have been so influential in this area that during the 2020 campaign, the leader of a for-profit higher education advocacy group said that a Democratic victory in the presidential election that year would be "alarming" and "concerning" for for-profit education providers (Murakami, 2020c, ¶ 4).

This chapter examines the United States presidency's influence on higher education. The chapter begins with an overview of the U.S. presidency, including the powers conferred upon the president by the Constitution. The chapter then takes a closer look at how presidents have influenced higher education policy via legislative actions, executive actions, and presidential messaging. A number of White House offices also play a role in higher education policymaking, as described later in the chapter.

OVERVIEW OF THE PRESIDENCY AND EXECUTIVE BRANCH

Article II of the Constitution establishes the federal executive branch, stating: "The executive Power shall be vested in a President of the United States of America" (U.S. Const. art. II, § 1), and that the president "shall take Care that the Laws be faithfully executed" (§ 3). Section 2 of Article II lists specific powers granted to the president, such as service as the commander-in-chief of the U.S. military, the ability to create treaties (with Senate approval), and the ability to grant pardons on federal matters that do not involve impeachment. Moreover, the president has the power to appoint the leaders of executive branch agencies, ambassadors, and federal judges, with approval by the Senate (U.S. Const. art. II; see also Burum, 2008; Fisher, 2014; Wilson et al., 2016). The vice president is elected together with the president, as they run on the same ticket (U.S. Const. amend. XII).

In addition to the president and vice president, the federal government's executive branch includes a number of administrative agencies. The president appoints many of the leaders of federal agencies; some of these appointments require approval of the Senate (Davis & Greene, 2017; Fisher, 2014). The U.S. Department of Education is one such agency, and the secretary of education is a member of the president's cabinet. This agency is tasked with implementing provisions of the Higher Education Act, among many other administrative and policy functions. Other high-level Department of Education appointees require Senate approval as well, including the under secretary (who in recent administrations has overseen higher education policy), assistant secretaries (including those working in the Office of Postsecondary Education, the Office for Civil Rights, and others), the general counsel, the inspector general, and the director of the Institute of Education Sciences, among others (Davis & Greene, 2017). As explained later in this chapter, executive-level agencies housed within the White House, such as the Office of Management and Budget (OMB) and the Domestic Policy Council, also work on higher education policy matters.

THE PRESIDENT'S LEGISLATIVE ROLE IN HIGHER EDUCATION POLICYMAKING

Presidents have exercised legislative power in the higher education policy arena quite frequently. Although Congress is the federal government's legislative body, the president plays an important role in legislative policymaking. It is the president's responsibility to sign or veto legislation passed by Congress. Legislation signed by the president becomes law. Legislation that is vetoed does not become law unless the veto is overridden by a two-thirds supermajority of both chambers of Congress. The president issues a regular veto by returning the unsigned legislation and an explanation for the veto to the congressional chamber where the bill originated. The president may also issue a so-called *pocket veto*, which occurs when the president neither signs nor vetoes a bill, and Congress is not in session within ten days following the presentment of the bill to the president. Legislation subject to a pocket veto cannot be overridden by Congress (Cameron, 2000; Krent, 2005; Rybicki, 2019a; Stuessy, 2019; U.S. Const. art. I § 7). As law professor Harold J. Krent (2005) recognized, the president's ability to veto legislation is so powerful that the mere threat of a veto can shape congressional agendas and bill content. That is, if there is substantial likelihood of a veto and not enough bipartisan support to override it, Congress members may adjust proposed legislation to make a veto less likely, or even forgo plans to move a bill to the floor altogether. Thus the ability to issue vetoes provides the president with significant power to prevent acts of Congress from becoming law and to protect the president's policy agenda (Krent, 2005).

An example of using the veto power in the higher education context occurred upon President Donald Trump's veto of a resolution to repeal a rule, the Borrower Defense Rule, issued by his administration's Department of Education in 2019. This rule made it more difficult for student loan borrowers to have their debt discharged on the basis of fraud or misrepresentation on the part of their college or university. Despite the fierce partisanship and divided control of Congress that characterized the federal government at that time, both houses of Congress passed a Congressional Review Act resolution to revoke the rule.[2] However, President Trump vetoed the resolution (Friedman, 2020). Although the bill had some bipartisan support, it did not have enough to reach the two-thirds congressional vote requirement to override the president's veto. Thus, the Trump administration's Borrower Defense Rule remained in place (Douglas-Gabriel, 2020).

Another legislative role of the president is to propose legislation for consideration by Congress. To do this, the president works with members of Congress who support the president's policies to sponsor the legislation (Krent, 2005). For example, after President Barack Obama proposed making community colleges tuition-free, congressional Democrats introduced legislation for this proposal in both houses of Congress (Fain, 2015). Presidential proposals of legislation are often unsuccessful—indeed, President Obama's proposal for tuition-free community college did not gain traction—but such proposals do grab the attention of lawmakers. In his book about congressional agenda setting, political scientist John Kingdon (2003) quoted a lobbyist as saying, "When a president sends up a bill, it takes first place in the queue. All other bills take second place" (p. 23). Also, a president's legislative proposal may be influential simply by drawing attention to a policy issue and making it part of a national conversation. One of my study's respondents said of President Obama's tuition-free community college proposal, "Free community college was something that President Obama was talking about. Now . . . a lot of states have adopted free college policies." Then shortly after becoming president, Joe Biden (who had been Obama's vice president) sent a tuition-free community college proposal to Congress (Jaschik, 2021). This example illustrates how one president's policy proposals can be influential over other policymakers—including a future, like-minded president.

As Chapter 1 explained, conditional spending is a primary mechanism through which the federal government regulates higher education. Therefore, a legislative proposal that is particularly important for higher education is the president's budget proposal. By early February each year, the president is to submit a budget proposal to Congress, although this deadline is often not met. This document is developed in consultation with the OMB after receiving budget requests from executive branch agencies (Bose, 2020; Center on Budget & Policy Priorities, 2020; Christensen, 2012; Yinug & Burgat, 2016). The president's budget proposal is just that—a proposal. Budget bills must originate in the House of Representatives and be enacted via the legislative process (U.S. Const. art. I, § 7; see also Christensen, 2012). However, the president's proposed budget can be persuasive in that it "sets the terms of the debate" on how federal monies might be spent in the near future, particularly when the president's party controls Congress (Pasachoff, 2020, p. 72).

Several of my study's respondents indicated that the president's annual budget proposal has importance for federal higher education policy. A former White House staffer said that the president's budget proposal can prompt members of the president's party to promote the policy, citing the example of President Obama's proposal to phase out the Federal Family Education Loan (FFEL) program in favor of Direct Loans (Dortch et al., 2010). This phase-out had originated as part of the president's budget proposal (Drawbaugh, 2009). My respondent said, "President Obama put in his budget that he wanted to get rid of the FFEL program. If he hadn't done that, it would likely not have been a priority for the Senate or the House." In fact, Congress did enact the transition to Direct Loans and phasing out of FFEL via the Student Aid and Fiscal Responsibility Act in 2010 (Dortch et al., 2010).[3]

In addition to the phasing out of FFEL, presidents have embedded other policy priorities with respect to higher education in budget proposals.

President Trump, who prioritized career and technical education as well as apprenticeships and other job-training programs (Ujifusa, 2018), submitted budget proposals that sought additional funding for career-focused postsecondary education and extensions of the Pell Grant to short-term educational programs (Kreighbaum, 2019a; Murakami, 2020b; Office of Management & Budget, 2020). Trump also used his budget proposal to call for the elimination of the Public Service Loan Forgiveness program (Office of Management & Budget, 2020). President Obama, whose administration sought increased regulation of the for-profit sector since the beginning of his first term (Natow, 2017), submitted a budget proposal that excluded for-profit institutions from a proposed multi-billion dollar job training program (Nelson, 2012). As these examples demonstrate, presidential budget proposals are policy documents that reflect the administration's values, politics, and goals (Biden, 2007; Pasachoff, 2016). As one of my interviewees, a government relations staffer at a higher education association, explained:

> The annual release of the president's budget is a major policy position on higher education. Every year when the White House releases its budget request it often proposes changes to the Department of Education and student aid programs. . . . That's just a proposal; it's a suggestion to Congress. But it kick-starts a conversation. . . . The budget process is an opportunity to kick-start a policy conversation.

EXECUTIVE ACTION

The term *executive action* refers to actions taken by the president outside the legislative process to administer policy (Chen, 2017). Some scholars define executive action to include only unilateral actions—that is, those taken by the president without requiring the approval of other federal entities (Moe & Howell, 1999). Others use a more expansive definition, including some actions that involve participation by agencies or Congress, such as agency rulemaking or Senate approval of treaties (Gulasekaram & Ramakrishan, 2016; Rottinghaus & Warber, 2015). Each of these types of executive action has had relevance for higher education policy.

Unilateral Executive Action

Some executive actions are unilateral exercises of presidential power. Presidents can take such actions only when there is a constitutional or statutory basis for doing so (Chu & Garvey, 2014). An *executive order*, which is an order issued by the president that is binding on federal agencies, is a fairly common form of unilateral action (American Bar Association, 2018; Chen, 2017; Chu & Garvey, 2014; Contrubis, 1999; Fisher, 2014; Halstead, 2001;

Mayer, 1999, 2002; Thrower, 2017). Although executive orders are directed at government agencies, their effects often have a much wider reach (Mayer, 1999, 2002). For example, in 1965, President Lyndon Johnson issued an executive order requiring federal agencies to include nondiscrimination and affirmative action mandates in certain government contracts and gave the Department of Labor the power to enforce these policies (Executive Order No. 11246, 1965; Farrell, 2020; Harper et al., 2009; U.S. Department of Labor, n.d.-b). This order's instructions applied directly to government agencies, but its influence was much broader. The executive order has affected all contractors doing business with federal agencies, and in so doing, has influenced the employment practices of a large number of private organizations, including higher education institutions holding government contacts (Vetter, 1974).

In addition to issuing new executive orders, presidents can cause policy change by revoking or amending previous executive orders, particularly those of prior presidents whose ideologies and policy preferences were different (Chu & Garvey, 2014; Halstead, 2001; Thrower, 2017). An example of this occurred during the White House turnover from Republican President Donald Trump to Democratic President Joe Biden. Trump had issued an executive order near the end of his term prohibiting federal contractors—including higher education institutions—from providing certain kinds of diversity training (Mangan, 2020). But on the first day of his presidency, Biden issued his own executive order revoking Trump's order (Guynn, 2021).

Some executive orders have effectively broadened the scope of White House power over federal regulatory policy. Two prominent examples of such orders are President Ronald Reagan's Executive Order 12291 (1981), and President Bill Clinton's Executive Order 12866 (1993). Those orders had the effect of increasing White House control over agency regulations by requiring the OMB—which is housed in the Executive Office of the President—to review and oversee many proposed and final regulations (Contrubis, 1999; Kagan, 2001; Kerwin & Furlong, 2011; Krent, 2005; Thrower, 2017). Because regulations on higher education issues, including the federal government's enormous student financial aid programs, often have a substantial effect on the economy, such regulations are regularly subject to OMB review (Natow, 2017, 2020).

Although many executive orders such as those described above affect higher education in some way, a smaller number are targeted specifically at higher education institutions. One example was President Trump's executive order on "Improving Free Inquiry, Transparency, and Accountability at Colleges and Universities," issued in 2019. This order gained attention for its admonition for college campuses to promote free speech and debate, but it also contained provisions about publishing more information regarding student loans and institutional outcomes on the U.S. Department of Education's website (Executive Order No. 13864, 2019; Kreighbaum,

2019b). Presidents have also used executive orders to establish initiatives and councils relating to higher education, such as President Trump's White House Initiative on Historically Black Colleges and Universities (Executive Order No. 13779, 2017), and President Obama's White House Rural Council, which included higher education among its components (Executive Order No. 13575, 2011). The White House Rural Council was created to determine how the federal government could help generate economic growth in rural areas of the United States (White House Rural Council, 2011). One of the results of the council was a partnership between the U.S. Department of Agriculture and community colleges in rural areas for the purpose of increasing access to higher education and generating economic growth (U.S. Department of Agriculture, 2012).

Unlike executive orders, *presidential proclamations* (also called *executive proclamations*) tend to affect private entities rather than executive branch agencies (Contrubis, 1999; Halstead, 2001; Rottinghaus & Lim, 2009; Rottinghaus & Maier, 2007). Recent presidential proclamations involving higher education have tended to be ceremonial or honorary only and include the annual designation of National Historically Black Colleges and Universities Week (e.g., Proclamation Nos. 9172, 2014; 9326, 2015; 9527, 2016; 9642, 2017; 9786, 2018; 9922, 2019), Career and Technical Education Month (Proclamation No. 9986, 2020), and National College Application Month (Proclamation Nos. 9203, 2014; 9356, 2015).

Other forms of unilateral actions include presidential designations, letters, determinations, memoranda, and other documents issued by the president that do not always appear in the *Federal Register* (Cooper, 2001; Lowande, 2014; Woolley & Peters, 2017). Woolley and Peters (2017) used the phrase "memo orders" to categorize such actions (p. 380). An example of such a memorandum was issued by President Trump in 2019, directing the Departments of Education and Veterans Affairs to discharge the student loan debt of veterans who were "totally and permanently disabled" (Trump, 2019). In another example, President Obama issued a memorandum known as the Student Aid Bill of Rights. This memo order instructed the Department of Education and other agencies to take certain actions designed to assist student loan borrowers, including the development of a centralized system for receiving student complaints concerning federal financial aid (Obama, 2015).

Executive Action Via Federal Agencies

Executive agency action may also advance the president's policy agenda (Chen, 2017). Unlike the unilateral presidential actions described above, agency activity involves an additional layer of bureaucracy between the president and the action. This is particularly true of rulemaking (i.e., regulation-making), because the Administrative Procedure Act (APA) requires a number of steps, including public notice and an open comment period for most rules, before a final regulation may be issued (Kerwin & Furlong, 2011; Parrillo, 2019).[4] Nonetheless, due largely to presidential influence over top-level agency personnel, federal agencies have often been effective at promoting a president's policy preferences through agency activity (Chen, 2017; Krent, 2005). Indeed, research has shown that regulations issued by the U.S. Department of Education and other agencies tend to represent the politics and policies of the presidential administration under which the regulations were issued (Natow, 2017; Rudalevige, 2016).

Presidential influence via agency action may also occur through the issuance of sub-regulatory guidance. Because guidance documents do not have the same force of law as regulations, they need not follow APA procedures, and are therefore easier for agency leaders to issue (Chen, 2020; Parrillo, 2019). Although guidance is technically nonbinding,[5] regulated parties—including higher education institutions—often face great pressure to comply with guidance the same way that they would with regard to a duly issued regulation, which makes the guidance effectively binding (Parrillo, 2019).

A notable example of presidential policy advancement via guidance was the Obama administration's Deferred Action for Childhood Arrivals (DACA) program, through which the Department of Homeland Security deprioritized immigration enforcement actions against undocumented young people who have lived in the United States since arriving as minors (Chen, 2017, 2020; Johnson, 2020; Skrentny & López, 2013). The DACA policy was created through a three-page memo issued by the secretary of homeland security based on the department's "prosecutorial discretion" (Napolitano, 2012, p. 1). The memo set forth criteria and procedures through which individuals would qualify for DACA protection and other benefits such as work authorization (Batalova et al., 2014; *Department of Homeland Security v. Regents of the University of California*, 2020; Napolitano, 2012). When President Trump's secretary of homeland security issued a memo to rescind DACA a few years later (Duke, 2017), the University of California's Board of Regents and others sued the Trump administration to prevent that from happening. The Supreme Court ruled that the attempted rescission was improper because the Department of Homeland Security had neglected to consider alternatives to full rescission or the extent to which DACA beneficiaries had relied upon the existence of the policy (*Department of Homeland Security v. Regents of the University of California*, 2020; see also Johnson, 2020; Lee, 2020). Despite this Supreme Court ruling, Trump's Department of Homeland Security continued to limit the DACA program until the very end of Trump's term. But when President Biden took office in 2021, one of his first executive orders instructed the department to reaffirm DACA (Redden, 2021).

The President's Role in Federal Appointments

Presidents also influence policy via appointments to high-level federal posts. Many of these appointments must be made with "Advice and Consent of the Senate" (U.S. Const. art. II, § 2, cl. 2), such as appointments to federal judgeships (including the Supreme Court), ambassadorships, and cabinet-level agency leadership (Black et al., 2011; Krent, 2005). Other appointments, such as many positions in offices within the White House and other executive agency personnel, do not require Senate approval (Brown, 2018; White House, n.d.-b). While appointments to the cabinet or White House offices tend to last only as long as the president's term (and sometimes less), some appointments can have a long-term influence. This is particularly true of federal judgeships, which are lifetime appointments (McMillon, 2018).

Presidents tend to appoint individuals who share their ideological and policy views to important posts (McMillon, 2018). For example, during the 2016 presidential campaign, then-candidate Donald Trump—who had once operated the for-profit Trump University—said that as president, he would promote policies allowing federal funds to be spent on private, charter, and religious schools via voucher programs. Upon becoming president, Trump appointed Betsy DeVos, a strong proponent of educational privatization, as his secretary of education (Alcindor, 2017; Cohen, 2017). DeVos and other political appointees to the Department of Education worked to roll back regulations of for-profit higher education that were put in place during the Obama administration. DeVos and colleagues also promoted policies that benefited charter schools and religious institutions (Associated Press, 2018; Green, 2020; Modan, 2019; Stratford, 2018).

Because presidential nominations to high-level posts often require Senate approval, presidents generally do not have as much control over appointments as they do over other executive actions. This is especially true when the Senate is controlled by a party other than the president's. Political resistance to presidential nominees dates back to the early days of the United States, when the Senate declined to approve a Supreme Court nominee of President George Washington in 1795 (Krent, 2005; Strauss & Sunstein, 1992). A more recent, high-profile example of partisan differences stymieing a presidential nominee was when leadership in the Republican-controlled Senate denied a hearing to President Obama's choice to fill a Supreme Court vacancy in 2016 (Elving, 2018; Unah & Williams, 2019).

Presidents have considerably more control over presidential appointments that are made during times when Senate is not in session. Such appointments, known as recess appointments, permit the president to make short-term appointments to federal posts without Senate approval, even if such approval would be necessary if the Senate were in session (Black et al., 2011; Hogue,

2015; McMillon, 2018). Presidents may also appoint acting leaders to fill vacant agency posts temporarily without Senate approval (O'Connell, 2019). This has occurred, for example, in the U.S. Department of Education during the early months of new presidential administrations, when senior department officials have been appointed in an acting capacity without the need for immediate Senate confirmation (e.g., Kreighbaum, 2017c).

USING THE "BULLY PULPIT" AND PRESIDENTIAL MESSAGING

Even when the president does not directly make new policy, presidential communication and messaging can have a powerful impact. The term "bully pulpit" refers to the president's power to influence public opinion and national attention via speech and other public communications. President Theodore Roosevelt created the term to describe this unique influence of presidents (Goodwin, 2013; Greenberg, 2011; Shaw, 2017). Scholars have observed that presidential communications are influential in many ways, including on public opinion (Kiousis & Strömbäck, 2010; Oliver et al., 2011; Wood et al., 2005), international relations (Wood, 2009), news media coverage (Eshbaugh-Soha, 2013; Olds, 2013), financial markets (Eshbaugh-Soha, 2005; Wood, 2009; Wood et al., 2005), and even the courts (Shaw, 2017). Presidential statements and messaging about priorities can also influence the federal government's policy agenda (Light, 1999; Kingdon, 2003; Kiousis et al., 2016).

Several respondents in my study observed that presidents have made use of the bully pulpit to promote their higher education policy preferences. These respondents noted that when the president speaks, stakeholders pay attention. One interviewee who represented community colleges said the following of President Obama's messaging regarding such institutions:

> President Obama, in the first year of his office, made a bold speech around the role of community colleges, the American Graduation Initiative . . . and that basically became part of a reconciliation bill and also part of [the Student Aid and Fiscal Responsibility Act of 2009]. So the president does have a bully pulpit in that context of, [if] he wants to do something, things can happen.

This interviewee went on to contrast Obama's statements regarding community colleges with comments from President Trump, who had publicly expressed unfamiliarity with the institutions (see also Arnett, 2018).

An interviewee from a higher education association reiterated that presidential messaging can influence dialogue within the policy community. This respondent observed:

> If the president . . . calls attention to an issue . . . you start hearing legislators talk about that issue more . . . and the community talking about it more. And it's either consciously or [sub]consciously, because it's been raised by the president.

Presidential rhetoric can also influence the nation's political climate, which may in turn affect the recruitment of international students and scholars to U.S. higher education institutions. Immigration policy is an area over which presidents have held much power. That power, coupled with presidential rhetoric, can affect the policy climate even short of creating and enforcing actual policies. As the case study near the end of this chapter indicates, some international students felt relief following Joe Biden's victory in the 2020 presidential election, in light of critical statements and policies on immigration that had come from the Trump White House during the previous 4 years (Fischer, 2020).

Another important opportunity for the president to attract national attention to policy priorities is the State of the Union Address (Coven, 2020). The president's responsibility to provide this address is written into the Constitution, as Article II states that the president "shall from time to time give to the Congress information of the State of the Union, and recommend to their consideration such measures as he shall judge necessary and expedient" (U.S. Const. art. II, § 3). Since the early 20th century, the State of the Union address has been delivered in person to a joint session of Congress almost every year (U.S. House of Representatives, n.d.-a), and in recent decades, the speech has been televised live by major news outlets (Greenberg, 2018; Oliver et al., 2011). This address presents the president with an opportunity to speak to a broad, public audience about past accomplishments and a vision for the future, including the president's policy agenda (Light, 1999; Oliver et al., 2011; Pasachoff, 2020). Presidents have used this occasion to discuss their higher education policy agenda, such as when President Obama spoke about his proposal for tuition-free community college during his 2015 State of the Union Address (Field, 2015; Stratford, 2015b). The fact that the president spoke on this issue from such a prominent platform drew a great deal of attention to this proposal, and tuition-free college policies were increasingly discussed in the years that followed (Harris, 2018).

POLICYMAKING IN THE WHITE HOUSE

Bodies within the White House, most prominently the agencies and staff within the Executive Office of the President, have had influence on higher education policy. Vice presidents have also influenced these policies, but in a more limited way. The subsections below describe policy activity within the White House that has been relevant to higher education.

The Executive Office of the President

The most prominent of White House offices is the Executive Office of the President (EOP), which is composed of agencies that conduct analyses, make recommendations to the president, and take other actions that influence policy creation and implementation (Bose, 2020; Kingdon, 2003; Lewis, 2005; Relyea & Tatelman, 2007; Selin & Lewis, 2018). The EOP plays a key role in executive branch policymaking through its influence on other executive agencies and its alignment with the president's policy agenda (Washington & Hitter, 2020). The president has traditionally had a fair amount of leeway with regard to structuring the EOP, and several EOP agencies were created by presidential executive orders. EOP personnel are therefore typically viewed as representatives of the president on policy matters (Selin & Lewis, 2018). Several key EOP subagencies that affect higher education include the White House Office, the OMB, the Council of Economic Advisers, and the Office of Science and Technology Policy.

White House Office. The agency known as the White House Office is a relatively complex agency-within-an-agency in the EOP that houses several important councils and advisors to the president. These include the president's chief of staff, White House Counsel, the National Economic Council, the Domestic Policy Council, the Office of Communications, the White House press secretary, the Office of the First Lady, and various other offices and presidential advisors (Selin & Lewis, 2018; U.S. Government Printing Office, n.d.).

A number of subagencies within the White House Office have done work relevant to higher education policy. One such subagency is the National Economic Council (NEC). The NEC was formed via executive order by President Clinton in 1993 and advises the president regarding international and domestic economic matters. The NEC also coordinates White House policies to align with the president's agenda and oversees the implementation of the president's economic policies (Executive Order No. 12835, 1993; Wartell, 2009).

Another subagency that has handled higher education matters is the Domestic Policy Council. The Domestic Policy Council was first created by President Reagan in 1985 (Plott & Nicholas, 2019). President Clinton issued an executive order in 1993 establishing the council in its contemporary form (Executive Order No. 12859, 1993; Plott & Nicholas, 2019; Selin & Lewis, 2018). Per the Clinton executive order, the council would be chaired by the president, include heads of executive departments and some other EOP offices as members, and serve the following purposes:

(1) to coordinate the domestic policy-making process; (2) to coordinate domestic policy advice to the President; (3) to ensure that domestic policy decisions and programs are consistent with the President's stated goals, and to ensure that those goals are being effectively pursued; and (4) to monitor implementation of the President's domestic policy agenda. (Executive Order No. 12859, 1993, p. 44102)

A former White House and congressional staffer interviewed for my research explained that different presidents have tasked different councils with higher education policy issues during their terms. In the Clinton White House, this respondent said, higher education policy was largely handled by the NEC, whereas in the George W. Bush, Obama, and Trump White Houses, higher education policy was primarily handled by the Domestic Policy Council. The same respondent said that these councils within the White House Office can "have a great deal of influence in terms of things like [the] regulatory agenda, executive actions, [and] also agenda setting."

Some subunits of the White House Office handle external communications regarding White House policy. One is the Office of the White House Press Secretary. The press secretary provides briefings to the news media and publicly presents the president's perspective on policy matters and other issues of the day (Kumar, 2001). Among the matters about which the press secretary must answer questions and distribute press releases is higher education policy. The press secretary has circulated "fact sheets" relating to a president's higher education policy efforts, such as student financial aid (e.g., White House Office of the Press Secretary, 2015), and Historically Black Colleges and Universities (e.g., White House Office of the Press Secretary, 2018). The press secretary has also been known to weigh in on higher education matters, such as when then-press secretary Sean Spicer of the Trump White House told members of the press that Secretary of Education Betsy DeVos had been "'100 percent' supportive of Trump's decision" to withdraw guidance issued by the Obama administration regarding Title IX protections for transgender students (Kreighbaum, 2017a, ¶ 6). The Office of Communications is another subunit in the White House Office that promotes the president's policies to external stakeholders and otherwise handles public relations for the White House (Kumar, 2017). One of my interviewees, who had worked in the Obama White House, said the Office of Communications:

> would help shepherd us through the process of getting all the internal approval, which usually meant we had to get all the policy offices to approve any public-facing documents and . . . any fact sheets. . . . And then ultimately, they would be the ones to put it out on social media or connect with a media outlet, and basically run a communications plan.

Similarly, the Office of Digital Strategy handles promoting presidential messaging via online outreach (Clark, 2018). The same respondent who described the Office of Communications said that the Office of Digital Strategy helped the White House get the president's message "out to the public." This respondent also said that before external communications were released, the White House Counsel's office typically reviewed them to spot potential legal implications.

Finally, the Office of the First Lady, a White House Office subunit that handles matters regarding the president's spouse, has occasionally had involvement in the president's higher education policy agenda and priorities. For example, First Lady Michelle Obama's "Reach Higher" program promoted postsecondary education and other training, which aligned with President Obama's "goal of re-achieving the U.S.'s former status as having the highest proportion of college graduates in the world" (Meyers & Goman, 2017, p. 33 n.4). However, as a former White House staffer whom I interviewed explained, the Office of the First Lady "is much less involved on actual policymaking, but more [involved] on [questions such as,] How do we get the word out, or organize a convening, that can bring different thought leaders together, or help move a message?"

Office of Management and Budget. As the largest of the EOP agencies, the OMB is responsible for advising the president on budgetary matters (Bose, 2020). This includes assisting with the annual presidential budget proposal, reviewing new regulations that are projected to have a large economic impact, and working with federal agencies on budget requests and regulatory processes (Bose, 2020; Brass, 2006, 2008; Christensen, 2012; Executive Order No. 12866, 1993; Haeder & Yackee, 2015; Selin & Lewis, 2018). These responsibilities are not strictly about dollars and cents; the OMB also reviews legislative and regulatory materials "to ensure compliance with the President's policy agenda" (Brass, 2006, p. 2). The Department of Education is one of the federal agencies that submits its budget and new regulations to the OMB for review and approval (U.S. Department of Education, 2017). Other federal agencies must do the same (Bose, 2020; Brass, 2006). Political appointees in the OMB also provide input for the president's State of the Union address, because policies discussed in that address have budgetary consequences (Pasachoff, 2020).

The agency within the OMB responsible for reviewing significant proposed and final regulations is the Office of Information and Regulatory Affairs (OIRA) (Potter, 2020; Washington & Hitter, 2020). This review process gives the White House a heightened level of influence on agency policymaking. One of my study's interviewees, a policy director for a Washington-based higher education association, pointed out that a presidential administration issuing a new regulation via the rulemaking process also gets to review it via OIRA, effectively giving the White House two bites at the apple. This respondent said:

An administration has influence as it writes, say, new Department of Education regulations. Well, those regulations have to go through an OMB approval process before they are officially printed in the *Federal Register*. It is another layer, another way, that the administration can have a second look, or a second level of influence, on rulemaking.

Moreover, a consumer advocate whom I interviewed acknowledged that "OIRA is still a part of the administration, so they are beholden to the goals of the administration," and that if consumer advocates disappointed in a pending regulation are "looking at OIRA as the place that's going to be our hero here, we're going to be disappointed." In other words, to the extent a new regulation reflects the will of the presidential administration, OIRA is not likely to substantially change the contents of the rule at the regulatory review stage.

The OMB may also work with the president to develop a Statement of Administration Policy, which communicates to Congress the president's position on a bill, particularly when the president finds something objectionable about it (Stuessy, 2019). In the higher education context, President Clinton's administration sent a Statement of Administration Policy to Congress in 1998, objecting to some provisions of the bill to reauthorize the Higher Education Act, including a provision that would have defunded the National Board for Professional Teaching Standards (Executive Office of the President, 1998). When this reauthorization was ultimately enacted, it did not contain that defunding provision (Stedman, 1998).

Council of Economic Advisers. Created in 1946, the Council of Economic Advisers (CEA) is composed of economists who advise the president on economic matters (Porter, 1997; Selin & Lewis, 2018; Stiglitz, 1997). The CEA is different from the NEC (described above as part of the White House Office), in that the CEA is more oriented toward economic research, while the NEC is more concerned with economic policy coordination (Block, 2008). One of my respondents who had worked in the White House described the CEA as:

> an internal think tank[6] or research body within the White House. They were usually involved in a lot of conversations, but less so as the final decision maker. More so [regarding] what's the research on this, and how do we build out the evidence base?

The CEA sometimes weighs in on the economic implications of the president's policy agenda, including presidential priorities for higher education. This may be done in conjunction with other offices within the EOP. A former White House staffer provided the following example:

> When rules are submitted by the agencies, they go through OMB clearance, they go through OIRA. And different people in the White

House, on occasion, weigh in on those rules. And sometimes OIRA will reach out to CEA in particular to just get their take on different matters that are usually a little bit more technical or involved interpretations of economic research or estimates of costs and benefits, things of that nature.

The CEA was also involved in developing the College Scorecard, a public-facing dataset housed on the Department of Education's website that allows viewers to compare and contrast colleges on a range of consumer-focused variables, such as net price of attendance, graduates' earnings, and graduates' student loan debt (Council of Economic Advisers, 2017; Matsudaira, 2017).

Office of Science and Technology Policy. The Office of Science and Technology Policy (OSTP) advises the president on matters relating to science and technology and supports the federal government's research and development agenda. Consultation with university researchers, including university-based scientists, on some of the office's initiatives are part of the OSTP's role (Matthews et al., 2017; Sargent & Shea, 2020; Saxe, 2019; Wysession & Rowan, 2013). Sometimes these consultations may be significant. As one of my interviewees who was familiar with OSTP operations explained, some "OSTP directors rely very heavily on outside advisory committees that might be made up of university officials." In a move that was viewed as favorable toward university-based and other scientific research, President Biden raised the stature of OSTP by making this agency part of his cabinet in 2021. This move placed a research scientist affiliated with two prominent postsecondary institutions—Harvard University and the Massachusetts Institute of Technology—as one of the closest advisors to the president (Kaplan, 2021; Murakami, 2021).

The Vice President

The vice president plays a unique role in the federal government, positioned close to the president but holding few enumerated powers (Holzer, 2021). The Constitution provides that the vice president is the person who would assume the presidency in the event of the president's removal from office or incapacitation (U.S. Const. art. II, § 1; see also Baumgartner, 2015; Cohen, 2001). The vice president also serves as president of the Senate, although this role is mostly symbolic, other than when a tie-breaking vote is needed in that chamber (U.S. Const. art. I, § 3). Although such tie-breaking votes have not occurred frequently, one occasion was when Vice President Mike Pence cast the tiebreaking vote to confirm Betsy DeVos as President Trump's secretary of education in 2017 (Darville, 2017). Moreover, the vice president can have a profound effect on the Senate's leadership and policy agenda when party representation is split evenly in the Senate, and the vice president's tie-breaking role puts the president's political party in the chamber's majority, as was the case with Vice President Kamala Harris tipping the evenly split Senate into a Democratic majority in 2021. As explained in Chapter 3, the Senate majority leader and committee chairs hold substantial power to take up legislation, hearings, and presidential nominees within the chamber. Thus, the vice president's Senate tie-breaking role, although often inconsequential, can have a substantial effect on the chamber's activities when its partisan membership is evenly split (Natow, 2021a).

Vice presidents have played other roles in terms of policymaking and drawing attention to the administration's priorities. As political scientist Jody Baumgartner (2015) observed, the vice president serves as "an important assistant to the president . . . a presidential surrogate," and sometimes "the last person to talk to the president before a policy decision is made" (p. 4). Some of my study's respondents made similar comments regarding the vice president as a key promoter of the administration's agenda. A former White House staffer confirmed that the "vice president in many ways is also someone to get the word out and someone to draw attention to things" on behalf of the president. Vice presidents have done this by, for example, leading targeted White House initiatives, such as Vice President Al Gore's "reinventing government" initiative in the 1990s (Kamensky, 1996). One recommendation from Gore's National Partnership for Reinventing Government was to build performance-based organizations within the federal government. These are consumer-oriented government agencies given autonomy and incentives to operate similar to a private-sector business (Jackson, 2003; Miller & Delisle, 2019; Roberts, 1997). Following the Higher Education Act's 1998 amendments, the U.S. Department of Education's Office of Federal Student Aid became the first of these organizations in the federal government (Jackson, 2003; Miller & Delisle, 2019). In a more recent example of the vice president drawing attention to administration policies, when Joe Biden was vice president, he promoted the Obama administration's proposed College Completion Toolkit, which was intended to serve as a resource for state-level leaders to promote college completion in their state (U.S. Department of Education, 2011a).

The vice president may also initiate new White House posts (Baumgartner, 2015). An example of this was when then-Vice President Joe Biden appointed an advisor on violence against women in the Obama White House in 2009—the first time that role had been formally appointed. This appointment underscored the commitment of the president and vice president to this policy issue (Obama White House, n.d.). Biden consulted this advisor on, among other matters, Title IX policy prohibiting sex- and gender-identity-based discrimination and harassment in educational institutions (Wilson, 2017).

Vice presidents may also become involved with higher education issues when trying to build policy accomplishments for themselves if they have ambitions for higher office. A former White House staffer explained:

In election years that the vice president is running for the presidency . . . the president wants the vice president to be seen as leading on issues and to have "wins." So, if the vice president says, "Hey, what I really want to do is do something significant in higher ed," then the president will often try to make that happen.

This interviewee cited the example of Vice President Gore, who ran for president during Clinton's second term. Gore had worked to establish a track record for himself in education and other policy areas. During the Clinton administration, Gore had some of his own staffers work on education issues. Additionally, the Clinton White House touted Gore's contributions to higher education policy, including working "with President Clinton to open the doors of college to all students—with more Pell Grants, more student loans, and new HOPE scholarship tax cuts that help families pay for college tuition" (Vice President's Education Initiatives, n.d., ¶ 8).

Another way the vice president can influence higher education policy is by advocating for higher education priorities within the White House. Depending on the issue, the president, and the relationship between the president and vice president, such advocacy can have an effect on the president's messaging and policy preferences. For example, a former White House staffer interviewed for my research described Vice President Joe Biden as "a big advocate for" community colleges during the Obama presidency. Biden's support for community colleges was shared by his spouse, Dr. Jill Biden, who worked as a community college professor for many years. During the Obama administration, the vice president and second lady advocated for the president's tuition-free community college proposal after it had been introduced in Congress (Smith, 2016). Dr. Jill Biden and President Obama also hosted a White House Summit on Community Colleges in 2010 (Dr. Jill Biden, n.d.). The Bidens' example illustrates another way the Office of the Vice President can influence higher education policy: via the vice president's spouse. Another of my study's respondents said that in the Obama White House, Second Lady Dr. Jill Biden—a champion of community colleges—had her own office, but she sometimes worked with the vice president's staff on higher education policy matters.

PRESIDENTIAL POWER CASE STUDY: INTERNATIONAL STUDENTS AND SCHOLARS

One policy area over which presidents hold much power is immigration, and their administrations' immigration policies affect international students and scholars in U.S. higher education. During Donald Trump's presidency, his administration adopted restrictive immigration policies, such as making the process for obtaining visas more difficult, and attempting to rescind the

Obama-era DACA program (Johnson, 2020; Rampell, 2020a, 2020b). Trump also frequently argued in favor of a more stringent immigration system and spoke out fervently against unauthorized immigration (Hesson & Kahn, 2020; Rampell, 2020b). It was therefore unsurprising that international student enrollments in U.S. colleges and universities declined during Trump's term (Sanger & Bear, 2019).

As a presidential candidate, Joe Biden spoke favorably about immigration and vowed to rescind many of the Trump-era immigration policies (Bauer-Wolf, 2020). Many international scholars and students took note. Following Biden's victory on Election Day 2020, the *Chronicle of Higher Education* reported that international students and scholars spoke of being "relieved," with one writing on social media, "Now I can go back to focusing on my research without having to look behind my back for when I would be booted!" (Fischer, 2020, ¶ 18). As these examples reflect, presidential rhetoric as well as presidential policies are influential over the lives of students and the operations of institutions.

SUMMARY AND CONCLUSION

The president holds many levers of power over higher education policy. These include direct, unitary actions (such as executive orders and presidential memoranda), powers dependent on Congress (such as signing legislation and appointing personnel to federal posts), and indirect powers (such as raising awareness and attempting to gain support for policy priorities). As time has progressed, presidential powers have expanded (Howell, 2005; Woolley & Peters, 2017), and as this chapter has shown, presidential influence over higher education policy has been significant.

The president's impact on executive branch agencies provides another lever of power that has proven important for higher education. Executive-agency action is a power the president shares not with Congress but with executive agency personnel, many of whom the president has appointed and with whom the president shares policy priorities. The Department of Education's regulation and deregulation of for-profit higher education and the Department of Homeland Security's DACA program represent just some of the ways executive agencies have influenced policy change in alignment with the president's goals. A more in-depth analysis of the role of federal agencies in higher education policy is the subject of the next chapter.

CHAPTER 5

Federal Administrative Agencies and Higher Education

Administrative agencies comprise a substantial component of the federal government. Employing more than two million civil servants and several thousand politically appointed personnel, agencies conduct a large share of federal business and operations (Bur, 2019; Jennings & Nagel, 2020). Although agency personnel are not elected by voters, they are often able to exercise meaningful policymaking authority (Breger & Edles, 2000; Hill, 2020; Kerwin & Furlong, 2011). Federal administrative agencies are vitally important in the creation and implementation of higher education policy. Indeed, federal agencies are significant players across all sectors of federal policymaking. As political scientists William Howell and David Lewis (2002) have written, "To understand what the federal government does, one must understand the bureaucracy—which agencies constitute it, how these agencies are structured, and who controls them" (p. 1095).

The U.S. Department of Education is the executive agency that has the most extensive influence over higher education. Through its policy authority, the Department of Education has created accountability standards for certain higher education programs, forgiven student loan debt, and set standards for Title IX compliance, among numerous other impactful actions (Chen, 2020; Cowley, 2018; Natow, 2017, 2020). This department has also played an important role in policy implementation, such as by administering the federal government's massive student financial aid portfolio (U.S. Department of Education, 2019d). Beyond the Department of Education, numerous other agencies influence higher education as well, often in profound ways.

This chapter describes the roles federal administrative agencies have played in regulating, funding, and otherwise influencing higher education. This discussion follows the chapter on the presidency because many federal agencies and their leadership represent the viewpoint of the presidential administration. However, federal agencies often exercise a fair amount of autonomy, particularly independent agencies. Additionally, federal agencies are influenced by other branches of government, including Congress and the federal courts. Indeed, not every federal agency is an executive branch agency;

legislative and judicial agencies also exist (Jennings & Nagel, 2020). This chapter's discussion of the role of administrative agencies in higher education policy begins with an overview of these governmental organizations. The chapter also describes the policymaking powers of federal agencies. Finally, the chapter discusses many of the agencies that have involvement with regulating, funding, and otherwise influencing higher education.

OVERVIEW OF FEDERAL ADMINISTRATIVE AGENCIES

Defined broadly, federal agencies are organizations that exist within the federal government that are not Congress or a court (Administrative Procedure Act, 2018; Selin & Lewis, 2018). There are a number of different kinds of agencies in the federal government, including departments that are part of the president's cabinet, offices (such as the Executive Office of the President), councils (such as the Domestic Policy Council), and other units within the federal government (Selin & Lewis, 2018). Agencies may be created through legislation, by executive order, or by executive branch reorganization (Howell & Lewis, 2002; Selin & Lewis, 2018). Agencies created via executive action are often smaller than agencies created via the legislative process, but presidents tend to have more control over those that were created through executive action (Howell & Lewis, 2002). Federal agencies generally have their own areas of specialization, and thus, they often employ people who are recognized as experts in their field (Hill, 2020).

The majority of federal agencies reside in the executive branch; the chiefs of more than a dozen of these are part of the president's cabinet. The leaders of cabinet-level agencies, including the secretary of education, are close advisors of the president regarding policy issues related to the areas overseen by their agency (Relyea & Tatelman, 2007; Selin & Lewis, 2018; U.S. Government Printing Office, n.d.). Agencies exist within the other two branches of government as well (Selin & Lewis, 2018). There are also independent agencies, which generally exist outside the president's cabinet and executive office but can reside within the executive branch (Breger & Edles, 2015; Datla & Revesz, 2013; Selin & Lewis, 2018; U.S. Government Printing Office, n.d.; USA.gov, 2019). An example of such an agency is the National Science Foundation, which is part of the executive branch, but also "freestanding" because it is "not within an executive department" (Harris, 2021, p. 1). For some independent agencies, their leaders can be removed only "for cause," providing a modicum of job security and insulation from the president's political influence (Datla & Revesz, 2013, p. 772; Selin & Lewis, 2018, p. 43).

The president's cabinet has agencies focusing on education, labor, health, housing, foreign policy, energy, transportation, and commerce, among other areas. Beyond the cabinet, there are a voluminous number of boards, commissions, and other agencies that specialize in, create, and implement policy in a broad range of subject areas (Selin & Lewis, 2018; U.S. Government Printing Office, n.d.; USA.gov, 2019). Agencies often house offices, bureaus, or subagencies that specialize even further (USA.gov, 2019). Table 5.1 lists some of the most prominent federal agencies as well as those that have particular

Table 5.1. Examples of Prominent and Higher Education-Related Federal Agencies (Selected)

Legislative Branch Agencies	Executive Branch Agencies	Judicial Branch Agencies
Congressional Budget Office	Executive Office of the President	Administrative Office of U.S. Courts
Library of Congress	President's Cabinet	Federal Judicial Center
Government Accountability Office	• Department of Education • Department of Labor • Department of Justice • Department of Defense • Department of Veterans Affairs	U.S. Sentencing Commission
Government Publishing Office	• Department of Agriculture • Department of State • Department of Homeland Security	
Architect of the Capitol	• Department of the Treasury • Department of Housing and Urban Development	
United States Botanic Garden	• Department of Health and Human Services • Department of Commerce • Department of the Interior • Department of Transportation • Department of Energy	
	Independent Agencies Housed within the Executive Branch (Selected—there are many others in addition to those listed here)	
	• Administrative Conference of the United States • Commission on Civil Rights • Consumer Protection Financial Bureau • Environmental Protection Agency • Equal Employment Opportunity Commission • Federal Trade Commission • General Services Administration • National Endowment for the Humanities • National Labor Relations Board • National Science Foundation • Occupational Safety and Health Review Commission	

Sources: Selin & Lewis, 2018; U.S. Government Printing Office, n.d.; USA.gov, 2019.

relevance for higher education. Many more agencies exist than appear in the table. Please note that the executive branch houses numerous independent agencies, such as the National Science Foundation. Although housed within the executive branch, they are nonetheless independent because they do not fall under the purview of a department (e.g., Harris, 2021).

There are two main categories of agency employees: career employees and political appointees. Career employees are federal staffers who are not appointed by the president, although they may hold influential positions within agencies. Career staffers often work in their positions for many years, develop expertise in the work they do for the agency, and not infrequently, serve across multiple presidential administrations (Cohen, 1996; Davis & Greene, 2017; Matjie, 2018; Selin & Lewis, 2018). Political appointees are agency officials who are appointed by political actors, often the president, but also sometimes the vice president or an agency leader (Hegji & Hogue, 2019; U.S. Office of Government Ethics, 2021). The heads of cabinet-level and numerous other executive agencies are political appointees, as are some leaders and other personnel of sub-agencies. Cabinet-level departments tend to have a larger proportion of political appointees than other agencies. An example of an appointment made by an agency leader is the Chief Operating Officer of the Department of Education's Office of Federal Student Aid, who is appointed for a term of 3 to 5 years by the secretary of education (Hegji & Hogue, 2019). Political appointees generally represent the views of the political leader who appointed them, and some require approval by the Senate. These include, for example, the secretary of education, the undersecretary of education, and assistant secretaries of education (Davis & Greene, 2017).

Top political appointees, particularly cabinet heads, have something of a bully pulpit, from which they can grab headlines, draw attention to policy issues, and make statements regarding their agency's positions. For example, as a policy director at a D.C.-based association told me, the secretary of education has a "bullhorn" through which "they can influence policy, or . . . where folks think American higher education is, just by doing speeches or going to conferences or events, writing articles, or doing that sort of stumping around."

POLICY POWERS OF FEDERAL AGENCIES

Federal agencies' policy authority is substantial. Agencies have the power to create new rules, regulations, and funding priorities. Federal agencies are also responsible for policy implementation, which refers to actions taken to effectuate enacted policies. During policy implementation, there is often "[s]lippage between what politicians want and what administrative agencies actually deliver" (Gilmour & Lewis, 2006, p. 22). That space between policymakers' intent and implementers' actions creates another avenue for federal agency personnel to influence policy. Rules and guidance issued by the Department of Education have been making fairly significant policy changes and have often been marked by politics. Examples include Title IX policy and the regulation of for-profit higher education, which have experienced large substantive shifts between Republican and Democratic presidential administrations (Kreighbaum 2018a, 2018b; Natow, 2017, 2020).

There are several mechanisms through which federal agencies influence policy creation and implementation. As explained in the subsections that follow, the policy powers of federal agencies include rulemaking (i.e., regulatory policymaking), issuing sub-regulatory guidance, advising the president and Congress, conducting investigations and inspections, adjudicating disputed matters, providing funding, and exercising discretion in decision making.

Rulemaking

Rulemaking refers to the process of creating regulations within administrative agencies. There are both formal and informal rulemaking procedures. Formal rulemaking involves hearings, testimony, and other courtroom-like procedures in the creation of rules. More frequently, however, agencies engage in informal rulemaking, through which they develop and post a Notice of Proposed Rulemaking (NPRM), receive and review comments from stakeholders regarding the NPRM, and issue a final regulation in the *Federal Register*. For regulations that are expected to have a large financial impact or to change the law considerably, the OMB conducts an advance review of the NPRM and final regulation. Once published, the final regulation becomes binding law on its effective date (Anderson, 2015; Kerwin & Furlong, 2011; Lubbers, 1998; Natow, 2017; Nielson, 2014).

In the higher education policy arena, a step preceding the development of the NPRM called *negotiated rulemaking* often takes place. Negotiated rulemaking is a process through which the agency and a panel of negotiators, composed of potentially affected parties, meet to debate and attempt to agree upon the language of the NPRM (Kerwin & Furlong, 2011; Lubbers, 1998; Natow, 2017; Pelesh, 1994). Negotiated rulemaking occurs frequently in the Department of Education's Office of Postsecondary Education because the Higher Education Act requires negotiated rulemaking in the development of regulations of federal student financial aid programs (Higher Education Act, 2018). Because much of the rulemaking in the Office of Postsecondary Education involves student financial aid in some way, the Department of Education and higher education interest groups have had a great deal of experience with negotiated rulemaking (Natow, 2017).

An agency regulation may be overturned by a court; however, courts tend to grant deference to agencies when reviewing regulations (Walker, 2017). Nonetheless, courts do occasionally invalidate regulations, such as when a federal court in the District of Columbia overruled a key component of the Department of Education's first Gainful Employment Rule, which imposed disclosure and other requirements on career-focused postsecondary programs based on a procedural flaw in creating the regulation. The court found that the department did not have a sufficiently reasoned basis for including a key measure of accountability in the rule (Natow, 2017, 2020). Regulations can also be revoked by legislation or a future rulemaking (Kerwin & Furlong, 2011; Lubbers, 1998; Natow, 2017). These types of regulatory rescissions have occurred in the higher education context. For instance, Congress repealed an Obama-era regulation of teacher preparation programs via a Congressional Review Act resolution in 2017. An example of rescission via subsequent rulemaking was when the Trump-era Department of Education rescinded the Obama administration's second Gainful Employment Rule in 2019 (Natow, 2020).

Sub-Regulatory Guidance

Sub-regulatory guidance refers to statements issued by agencies regarding how a law should be interpreted or to clarify an aspect of a policy. Guidance may take the form of a Dear Colleague Letter, question-and-answer document, memorandum, or any other informal statement or interpretation of policy (Chen, 2020; Gersen, 2007; McKee, 2008; Natow, 2017; Parrillo, 2019; Potter, 2020). Guidance relating to higher education has been issued quite frequently. Examples include Dear Colleague Letters regarding Title IX (Chen, 2020), the Clery Act compliance manual (U.S. Department of Education, 2016b), and visa guidelines for international students (Treisman, 2020), among many other matters. Similar to the increased use of executive action in recent decades (as was explained in Chapter 4), the issuance of sub-regulatory guidance has also increased (McKee, 2008).

Guidance can be controversial, particularly when it does more than simply clarify something about existing law. This is because guidance documents are produced by agencies without going through the legal procedures required to create binding regulations, such as the public notice and comment period described above. Therefore, agency guidance is relatively easy to issue, though it is not binding law. But, functionally, regulated parties regard guidance as binding and take actions to comply with guidance just as they would a final regulation (Chen, 2020; Gersen, 2007; Parrillo, 2019). Sometimes agencies in a new presidential administration have issued guidance walking back or rescinding guidance provided by the previous administration, such as when President Donald Trump's Department of Education rescinded guidance that had been issued by President Barack Obama's administration with regard to Title IX policy on transgender student rights and disciplinary proceedings involving allegations of sexual harassment or assault (Battle & Wheeler, 2017; Chen, 2020; Jackson, 2017; Kreighbaum, 2017a, 2017d).

Advising and Assisting the President and Congress

Agencies also provide advice and assistance to the president and Congress with regard to policy matters. Members of the president's cabinet play an important role in advising the president (Moe, 2000; Relyea & Tatelman, 2007). Political scientist Ronald Moe (2000) observed that cabinet members' advice regarding executive branch operations can be particularly helpful to the president. On this advisory role, Moe wrote, "Cabinet meetings can facilitate the raising of critical issues and the resolution of those issues within an executive branch context" (p. 22). Agency leaders may also bring to the president's attention matters relating to department operations, resources, personnel, and other matters affecting policy implementation (Moe, 2000).

Another way that agencies advise the president is through having agency personnel participate in task forces or committees charged with examining a particular issue. Such groups often provide a detailed report and recommendations for policy change (Lowry, 2009; McCann & Laitinen, 2017; Natow, 2017). A prominent example of a commission that involved agency personnel studying and recommending policies regarding higher education was the George W. Bush administration's Commission on the Future of Higher Education—commonly known as the Spellings Commission, because it was commissioned by then-Secretary of Education Margaret Spellings. The Spellings Commission studied and made recommendations regarding accountability and accreditation in higher education, and although the Department of Education's rulemaking that followed the release of the commission's report did not come to fruition, the commission sparked an influential dialogue within the higher education policy community about the role the federal government should play in maintaining accountability in higher education (Lowry, 2009; McCann & Laitinen, 2017; Natow, 2017).

Additionally, agencies may assist the president with developing the details of legislative proposals (Shobe, 2017). A former White House staffer who participated in my research said that officials from federal agencies sometimes assist with developing the president's higher education policy proposals, and that experienced agency staff offer information about "technical details" that White House staffers might not otherwise know. This interviewee went on to say:

> At the agency level, we have a lot of people who have the best expertise and experience. A lot of people . . . have been there for over a decade, and they're able to offer institutional knowledge and history about the policy. . . . So, even though we were at the White House and working on a financial aid initiative, we would have to talk to folks at Federal Student Aid who have been working on this for 30 years.

Federal agencies also provide advice to Congress in the form of consulting on legislative matters and helping to draft legislation. Agencies frequently house an office dedicated to legislative affairs, the purpose of which is to coordinate the relationship between the agency and Congress (Shobe, 2017; Walker, 2017). An example of such an office is the Department of Education's Office of Legislation and Congressional Affairs, which is responsible for (among other things) monitoring legislation, communicating with Congress about the department's legislative priorities, and coordinating meetings between department and congressional officials (U.S. Department of Education, 2014b). Agency staff also lend their subject matter expertise to the president and Congress by assisting with technical matters, such as by reviewing drafts of bills or even writing legislation (Walker, 2017).

Investigations and Inspections

Another way that agencies influence policy is through the power of investigation and inspection. Indeed, "inspection is the most commonly used form of regulatory action" (Anderson, 2015, p. 263). Through their investigatory powers, agencies can gather information and determine whether regulated parties or units of government are adhering to regulations and other standards (Anderson, 2015; Council of the Inspectors General, 2014; Drews, 2010; Natow, 2017; Zornow & Strauber, 2019). Investigations and inspections may involve conducting interviews, visiting regulated parties' sites of operation, or issuing subpoenas to receive documents and other information. Agencies can also issue penalties for violations uncovered by these inspections and, depending on the agency and the magnitude of the violation, may bring civil or criminal charges against the investigated party (Drews, 2010; Zornow & Strauber, 2019).

Several federal agencies have jurisdiction to conduct inspections and investigations relating to higher education. For example, the Department of Education's Office of Inspector General investigates claims of "waste, fraud, and abuse" with regard to the department's programs (U.S. Department of Education, 2016a, p. 1). Other Department of Education sub-agencies that conduct investigations include the Office for Civil Rights (handling investigations of alleged civil rights violations in higher education institutions) and Federal Student Aid (handling investigations of alleged misconduct with regard to financial aid programs) (Natow, 2017). Moreover, one of my respondents reported that the Government Accountability Office (GAO) "quite frequently" reviews the "programs or activities" of the Department of Education and often makes recommendations for changes and improvements. The Department of Justice has also conducted higher education–related investigations, such as its investigation during the Trump administration of Yale University's race-conscious student admissions policy (U.S. Department of Justice, 2020).[1]

Agency investigations may be formal or informal. Formal investigations may involve the agency subpoenaing testimony or documentation from or about the investigated party. Less formal investigations may involve requests for voluntary compliance with investigators (Zornow & Strauber, 2019). For example, one of my interviewees, who had worked for the Department of Education, said that department personnel complied with GAO audits often "by responding to specific questions during their investigation, and then submitting a response to their findings."

Adjudication

Many agencies also have the ability to conduct adjudications. An administrative adjudication is a proceeding that takes place within an agency in which the agency's personnel make decisions regarding disputes involving a federal program (Asimow, 2019). There are many different kinds of adjudications, some of which involve hearing-like proceedings, some of which involve fact-finding by an administrative law judge, and some of which involve none of those things. Because adjudication procedures can vary widely depending on factors such as the agency, the issue, and the federal program, parties to an administrative adjudication should familiarize themselves with the rules that will be used at their type of proceeding (Asimow, 2019; Wiener, 2018). Adjudications make policy when agencies interpret or apply the law in a particular way when rendering a decision (Anderson, 2015). Under certain circumstances, agency adjudications are appealable to federal courts (Cole, 2016).

Many agency adjudications relate to higher education matters. Various suboffices within the Department of Education's Office of Hearings and Appeals handle disputes regarding federal student financial aid programs, making determinations about such matters as misuse of student aid funds and institutions' eligibility to participate in the programs (Natow, 2017). The Department of Justice's Executive Office for Immigration Review houses immigration courts, which may handle matters relating to undocumented college students (Asian Law Caucus et al., 2012; National Immigration Forum, 2018). The National Labor Relations Board has adjudicated issues regarding labor law on college campuses, such as whether graduate student assistants can unionize (Harvard Law Review, 2017). These are just a few examples of the many ways that administrative adjudications can affect higher education.

Funding

Federal agencies also influence higher education through funding policies and decisions. Funding is provided by agencies for a variety of purposes, and often, agencies set the standards and terms on which the funding is to be disbursed (Natow, 2017). Agency funding can take on a variety of forms, including grants, loans, loan forgiveness, and federal contracts. In the higher education context, agency funding is provided to support research, improve higher education programming, promote college access and student success, and incentivize college graduates to pursue certain in-demand careers, among other things (Anderson, 2015; Messer, 2018; Natow, 2017). Congress and the president can exert political control over agency funding in that statutes or executive orders can direct agencies to award or prohibit funding for a particular purpose, thereby removing the discretion agencies have in making decisions about funding. Examples of such control by the political branches include statutes directing grant funding to go to certain types of institutions or postsecondary training programs (see examples in Natow, 2017), or executive orders prohibiting federal grants and contracts being awarded to organizations that do not comply with certain mandates (see example in Mangan, 2020). Moreover, agency budgets are developed through the legislative budget and appropriations process, which also gives Congress some control over agencies' ability to provide funding (Center on Budget & Policy Priorities, 2020; Natow, 2017).

There are a number of mechanisms through which agencies may award funding and make decisions regarding how much and to whom funding should be awarded. In the higher education context, agency funding is frequently provided to universities via grants and contracts for research and development (Brint & Clotfelter, 2016; Hearn et al., 2013; Mumper et al., 2016; Pew Charitable Trusts, 2019; Sargent et al., 2020; Wolanin, 2003). The Department of Education also awards grants and other funding for, among other things, improving postsecondary education programs, building institutional capacity, and supporting programs that help students pay for and succeed in college (Natow, 2017). Because federal funding is something that higher education institutions desire and increasingly need, agency decisions about funding can be influential over the types of research they conduct (Sargent et al., 2020). The Department of Education also publishes federal funding "priorities" in the *Federal Register*. Priorities express the agency's "funding preferences for certain federal grant programs," and are often created via a notice-and-comment process similar to rulemaking (Natow, 2017, p. 15; see also National Research Council, 2012).[2]

Discretionary Decision Making

As law professor Nicholas Parrillo (2019) observed, "Despite being voluminous and complex, regulations leave numerous important decisions to the agency's discretion or interpretation" (p. 167). In other words, agencies often have the power to use discretion when deciding, for example, what language to include in a regulation, how to interpret the law when issuing guidance, and how to implement and administer federal programs. Agencies have also used discretion in determining whether to enforce regulations and guidance in certain circumstances, whether to conduct or close investigations, whether to pursue or appeal an adjudication, and which parties and projects will receive grant funding (Pierce, 2009; Ruhl & Robisch, 2016).

A number of my study's respondents discussed the ways agencies can exercise discretion in matters that influence higher education. A policy leader at a higher education advocacy group said that agency discretion in whether to pursue investigations has been noticeable. This respondent said, "You see it, for example, in the Office [for] Civil Rights, the cases that they decide to either investigate or not investigate, [or] are dismissed totally." Similarly, a former congressional staffer said of the Department of Education:

> You manage the entire student loan program. And you have a lot of say over institutions that get federal money, who gets investigated . . . and by investigated, I don't mean like through the Senate, I mean, when you look at program integrity, and you decide who to take a look at, you decide . . . where you've found abuse. There's a lot of power there too.

It is also important to note that agency discretion is useful and even necessary, because it would be impossible for policymakers to predict all potential scenarios and nuances in which agencies must make decisions about how to implement and administer policy. A leader of a D.C.-based association gave the following example regarding the importance of agency discretion for fair and effective policy implementation:

> Life isn't clean, and working on a college campus isn't clean either. All the rules and regulations that we create, it doesn't necessarily mean that it's as "cookie-cutter" when it gets onto a campus. . . . What happens for an institution that needs to shut down because of wildfires? What happens to institutions that have a hurricane and need to be closed for two weeks? What happens with disbursement of Title IV aid? . . . If you close classes because of a hurricane for two weeks and the student dropped the class, what happens there? There's a myriad of things, as we administer aid, that sometimes it's not as clean as we would like.

FEDERAL AGENCIES INFLUENCING HIGHER EDUCATION

As explained above, there are a number of mechanisms federal agencies may use to influence higher education. There are also numerous kinds of federal agencies that handle matters related to higher education. As the subsections that follow illustrate, the federal reach over higher education is broad as well as deep, with many agencies across the federal government playing important roles.

Department of Education

The Department of Education, now a cabinet-level executive agency, did not emerge in its current form and status until 1980 (Cross, 2014). However, the first federal Department of Education was created in 1867 for the purpose of gathering statistical data and other information to understand "the condition and progress of education" in the United States (Riley, 1997, p. 34; Robinson, 2016, p. 926). Shortly thereafter, the Department of Education was demoted to the Office of Education and reorganized as a subagency within the Department of the Interior. In 1939, the Office of Education was moved into the newly created Federal Security Agency, which became the cabinet-level Department of Health, Education, and Welfare in 1953 (Cuéllar, 2009; Riley, 1997; Robinson, 2016). President Jimmy Carter, whose election in 1976 was supported by a prominent teachers' union, pushed for the creation of a cabinet-level department dedicated to education. After some political wrangling in Congress, Carter signed the bill creating the Department of Education in 1979 (Cross, 2014). Since then, several prominent Republicans—from President Ronald Reagan to Senator Bob Dole to President Donald Trump—have called for the elimination of the Department of Education (Bauman & Read, 2018; Cross, 2014; Reichmann, 1996). But more than 4 decades after its inception, the cabinet-level Department of Education continues to thrive.

Many of the Education Department's subdivisions affect higher education in some way. The ones most directly involved with higher education are the offices of Postsecondary Education, Federal Student Aid, and Career, Technical, and Adult Education (U.S. Department of Education, 2019c). The Offices of Postsecondary Education and Federal Student Aid develop and implement policy regarding the federal government's student financial aid programs, which reach nearly 11 million recipients and total more than $100 billion annually (Federal Student Aid, 2020a). Beginning in 2010, the Department of Education has been the sole direct lender for new federal student loans, which had an outstanding balance of about $1.5 trillion as of 2020 (Dortch et al., 2010; Federal Student Aid, n.d.; Looney et al., 2020). Also, the Clery Act—which requires federally funded institutions to report information about crimes occurring on or near campus—is implemented by the Office of Federal Student Aid (Federal Student Aid, 2020b).

Other divisions of the Department of Education handle higher education matters as well. The department's Office for Civil Rights (OCR), for example, is involved with enforcement of civil rights laws and investigates allegations of civil rights violations by colleges and universities. Laws enforced by OCR include the Civil Rights Act, Title IX, and federal desegregation policies (Lewis et al., 2019). The Institute of Education Sciences (IES) affects higher education as well. IES is an independent body within the Department of Education that provides statistical and other data about education and houses the National Center for Education Statistics (NCES) (Institute of Education Sciences, 2017–2018). Among other responsibilities, NCES administers the Integrated Postsecondary Education Data System (IPEDS) survey as well as longitudinal and other surveys regarding education (National Center for Education Statistics, n.d.-a, n.d.-b). IES also provides grants for research about education (Institute of Education Sciences, 2017–2018). Thus, IES's influence on higher education is twofold: It funds studies conducted by university-based researchers, and it allows for research about higher education via its statistical databases. The department also has a general counsel's office that provides legal counsel to the department. The general counsel's office has participated in some aspects of negotiated rulemaking for higher education, including being present for negotiations and the regional meetings that precede negotiated rulemaking (Natow, 2017).

Although not a subdivision of the Department of Education, the National Advisory Committee on Institutional Quality and Integrity (NACIQI) is a federal advisory committee that makes recommendations to the secretary of education about higher education accreditation, including recognition of accreditors for participation in federal student aid programs (Eaton, 2010; Kelchen, 2017, 2018). Some NACIQI members are appointed by the secretary of education, and some are appointed by members of Congress (National Advisory Committee on Institutional Quality and Integrity, 2011; for more about NACIQI, see Chapter 7 on nonfederal policy actors).

Department of Labor and Other Employment-Related Agencies

Federal agencies that handle issues related to labor and employment influence higher education in several ways. Higher education and workforce training are often interconnected, and the White House under President Trump once proposed merging the Departments of Education and Labor into a new Department of Education and the Workforce (Bauman & Read, 2018; Nelson, 2018). That proposal did not pan out, but it illustrates the close links between education and workforce training in the minds of some policymakers. In the words of one of my interviewees, agencies such as these represent "the other side of the same coin for some folks, when they think of higher education to workforce. They play a role . . . positioning what education means, or how it should be consumed to get a career."

The Department of Labor sponsors programming and provides grant funding regarding workforce training involving postsecondary institutions

(U.S. Department of Labor, n.d.-a). An example of such a grant was the Trade Adjustment Assistance Community College and Career Training Grant, which provided almost $2 billion over a 4-year period in the 2010s for community colleges to train adult students to work in high-demand jobs (Mikelson et al., 2017). The Workforce Innovation and Opportunity Act, which is administered by the Department of Labor, provides funds to community colleges and other educational organizations for workforce education (Eyster et al., 2016). Also, the Bureau of Labor Statistics (BLS), a subdivision within the Department of Labor, maintains economic and workforce data and conducts economic and behavioral research (U.S. Bureau of Labor Statistics, 2009). BLS data have been used in the process of creating higher education regulations (Natow, 2020).

The National Labor Relations Board (NLRB) makes decisions regarding unionization and collective bargaining on college campuses (e.g., Flaherty, 2020; *National Labor Relations Board v. Yeshiva University*, 1980). NLRB members serve 5-year terms after appointment by the president and approval by the Senate (National Labor Relations Board, n.d.). The set terms and political appointments of NLRB staff have led to political influence on NLRB decisions. As such, NLRB rules and standards have swung back and forth between pro-union and anti-union positions somewhat frequently when the political party of the elected officials who appointed and approved NLRB staff has changed. For example, when controlled by Trump appointees, the NLRB ruled that it did not have jurisdiction to hear labor disputes regarding part-time faculty at religiously affiliated colleges (Flaherty, 2020). This decision reversed course from a ruling by the NLRB during the Obama administration, which held that part-time faculty at religious institutions could unionize if the teachers' specific roles were not to perform religious functions (Jaschik, 2015).

Department of Justice

As the chief law enforcement and legal representation arm of the federal government (U.S. Department of Justice, n.d.-a), the Department of Justice (DOJ) affects higher education through its civil and criminal law enforcement and investigative functions. Examples of investigations involving higher education institutions have included a civil rights inquiry into race-conscious admissions policies at universities such as Harvard and Yale (Caldera, 2019; Davidson, 2020), and an antitrust investigation into the ethical code of the National Association of College Admission Counseling (NACAC). The NACAC inquiry led the association to change its code of ethics to permit institutions to recruit students who have already committed to attend another college, to offer incentives for students to apply for early admission, and to recruit prospective transfer students from the previous year's applicant pool

(Jaschik, 2019b). DOJ criminal investigations involving higher education include the so-called "Varsity Blues" scandal that broke in 2019, which involved allegations of parents and institutional officials committing fraud to get students admitted to selective colleges (Jaschik, 2019a). The Department of Justice also houses immigration courts, which may handle matters relating to undocumented college students (Asian Law Caucus et al., 2012).

Notably, DOJ investigations need not result in a verdict against an entity in order to force changes in practice. As one of my respondents observed:

> If they investigate you and they decide you're in violation of this or that provision . . . you could take them to court, you could fight it if you want and if you have a lot of money. . . . Or you could essentially accede to their demand. You could say, okay, fine, we have really no choice.

In other words, even if an organization believes it has a decent chance of winning in court if sued by the DOJ, the costs of litigation may be so high that the organization may choose instead to settle with the DOJ and change its practices. In this way, DOJ activity can force changes in practice without changing official policy or even going to court.

Departments of Defense and Veterans Affairs

The Departments of Defense and Veterans Affairs, as agencies that handle matters relating to the military and veterans, influence higher education policy in multiple ways. One prominent way is through the administration of federal programs that provide financing for active-duty service members, veterans, and their family members to enroll in higher education. The GI Bill and other programs, which are administered by the Department of Veterans Affairs (VA), have helped members of the military and veterans pay for higher education for decades (U.S. Department of Veterans Affairs, 2021). Additionally, the Department of Defense (DOD) developed several programs for spouses of military members, known as the Spouse Education and Career Opportunities (SECO) programs. These include educational benefits such as the My Career Advancement Account Scholarship (known as MyCAA), which provides financial assistance to military spouses who pursue a license, certificate, or associate degree in fields such as education, aerospace, information technology, and more (Friedman et al., 2015; Military One Source, n.d.).

The DOD and the VA affect higher education institutions directly, as well. The DOD has received a large proportion of funding for research and development compared to other agencies, and in 2019, the DOD's share was "more than 41% of all federal research and development (R&D)

appropriations" (Sargent, 2020, p. 1). The Congressional Research Service (2021) has reported that almost half of the agency's budget for basic research has funded university research (see also Sargent et al., 2020). The DOD also provides grants for Minority-Serving Institutions and grants to build partnerships between universities and industries to develop innovations in the area of national security (Office of the Under Secretary of Defense for Research & Engineering, n.d.). Unlike the DOD, the VA does not provide research funding to higher education institutions "or any other non-VA entity" (U.S. Department of Veterans Affairs, 2018, p. 1). However, the VA operates teaching hospitals, which are affiliated with medical schools and provide education to medical students and residents (Association of American Medical Colleges, n.d.).

Department of Agriculture

The Department of Agriculture (USDA)'s relationship with higher education dates back to 1862, the year in which the agency was established and the first Morrill Act creating land-grant institutions was passed (Loss, 2012; Mercier & Halbrook, 2020). The original purpose of the USDA was "to support agricultural research in an expanding, agriculturally dependent country" (Sargent et al., 2020, p. 39). To this day, the USDA provides funding for agricultural research and other programming for grantees, including higher education institutions (Parker & Wagner, 2016; Sargent et al., 2020). The USDA's National Institute of Food and Agriculture (NIFA), for example, provides funding for "research, education, and extension projects" through partnerships with land-grant colleges and Minority-Serving Institutions, among other partners (Sargent et al., 2020, p. 41). NIFA also administers Higher Education Challenge Grants, which fund projects designed to enhance postsecondary education in agricultural sciences and related fields (Parker & Wagner, 2016; U.S. Department of Agriculture, 2020). In addition to grant funding, the USDA's Hispanic Serving Institutions National Program provides educational programming, professional development, and internship opportunities for affiliates of Hispanic-Serving Institutions (U.S. Department of Agriculture, n.d).

The USDA has also been a supporter of rural higher education. Following recommendations from President Obama's White House Rural Council, the USDA entered into a partnership with rural community colleges to improve access to higher education in rural areas (U.S. Department of Agriculture, 2012). The USDA has also provided loans to rural community colleges at a relatively low cost. These USDA loans are provided directly to the colleges—there is no bank lender involved. USDA loans can be used to fund, for example, new academic or cocurricular programs or to repay loans previously made from an institution's endowment (Seltzer, 2019).

Departments of State and Homeland Security

The Departments of State and Homeland Security are two other cabinet-level agencies that influence higher education. One of the more prominent influences is through the Department of Homeland Security (DHS)'s implementation of immigration policy. This includes the DACA program (described in Chapter 4), and immigration enforcement within the department's Immigration and Customs Enforcement (ICE) division. The DHS is also responsible for issuing visas to international students and scholars through the agency's Citizenship and Immigration Services division (U.S. Citizenship & Immigration Services, 2020).

For its part, the State Department supports international higher education principally through its Bureau of Educational and Cultural Affairs. That bureau partners with nonprofits and transnational organizations to run the Fulbright Grant programs, which enable scholars, students, teachers, and professionals to travel, study, and work abroad (U.S. Department of State, 2012). The State Department also awards grants to higher education institutions to enhance their capacity to provide study-abroad educational experiences (U.S. Department of State, n.d.). The department's Bureau of Educational and Cultural Affairs also houses "EducationUSA," an organized "network . . . of advising centers in nearly every country of the world," providing information and support to recruit international students to study at United States colleges and universities (U.S. Department of State, 2015, p. 2).

Department of the Treasury

The Department of the Treasury oversees the implementation of federal tax policy, including tax benefits for higher education. The Treasury Department houses the Internal Revenue Service (IRS), which administers federal tax benefits for education, including the Lifetime Learning Credit, the American Opportunity Credit, the Qualified Tuition Program, and tax deduction for student loan interest (Internal Revenue Service, 2019, 2020). The IRS also oversees compliance with tax-exempt status for the many colleges and universities that qualify under Section 501(c)(3) of the Internal Revenue Code (Association of American Universities, 2019; Kaplin et al., 2020; U.S. Department of the Treasury, 2021).

The Treasury Department has also partnered with the Department of Education on various higher education policy matters. In 2014, for example, these two agencies collaborated with a private company that produced tax return software "to raise awareness about income-driven repayment plans and other repayment options for federal student loan borrowers" (U.S. Department of Education, 2014a, ¶ 1). Also, the FUTURE Act (enacted in 2019) enabled tax information for some applicants to be shared automatically from the IRS to the Education Department as a mechanism for certifying income and simplifying the Free Application for Federal Student Aid (Kerr, 2020). Moreover, the Treasury Department has partnered with the Department of Education on studying such matters as whether the IRS could collect student loan repayments (U.S. Department of the Treasury & U.S. Department of Education, 1995), and piloting a defaulted student loan servicing program (Lebryk, 2016). One of my interviewees said that the Treasury and Education Departments have worked together to study "policy initiatives that were at the intersection of what you'd call tax policy and education policy . . . like income-based repayment, or modeling the tax consequences of changing the tax treatment of Pell Grants and student loan interest."

Legislative and Judicial Branch Agencies

Although federal agencies are generally thought of as being part of the executive branch, the legislative and judicial branches have agencies as well. Legislative agencies provide services to, and work on behalf of, Congress (Selin & Lewis, 2018). The GAO—discussed above as an agency that conducts investigations—also conducts research and audits for Congress, often of executive branch agencies (Brudnick, 2020; Kaiser, 2008). This research is conducted at the request of members of Congress. For example, in 2021, the GAO investigated companies that had assisted higher education institutions with developing and launching online programming. This research was undertaken at the request of Democratic senators (Lederman, 2021). The Congressional Budget Office (CBO) is another impactful legislative agency. This agency is responsible for estimating the cost of legislation and the president's annual budget proposal, and for projecting the federal government's costs and revenues for the next 10 years (Brudnick, 2020). The CBO has, for example, estimated the cost of expected student loan debt forgiveness for the federal government for the decade of the 2020s (Seltzer, 2020).

The role of federal judicial agencies is to "provide administrative support for the federal courts, offer basic management support for the court system, and supply education and research about the court system and sentencing principles and guidelines" (Selin & Lewis, 2018, p. 9). Judicial branch agencies include the Administrative Office of the United States Courts, the Federal Judicial Center, and the United States Sentencing Commission. These agencies tend to have less involvement with higher education, but there are occasions for judicial agencies to collaborate with postsecondary institutions. For example, the Federal Judicial Center has conducted an institute for law clerks in collaboration with Pepperdine University Law School (Pepperdine University, n.d.).

Other Federal Agencies

There are many other federal agencies that influence higher education. A good many federal agencies provide grant funding for higher education scholars to conduct research. Prominent examples of these agencies include the National Science Foundation, the National Institutes of Health, the Department of Energy, the National Endowment for the Humanities, and the National Aeronautic and Space Administration, among others (National Endowment for the Humanities, 2017; Sargent et al., 2020). By receiving this funding, colleges and universities not only become subject to the funding agencies' rules and conditions, but also become federal contractors, making them subject to some executive orders and other policies as well (e.g., Mangan, 2020; National Institutes of Health, 2021; Vetter, 1974).

The mission of the Department of Commerce is to "promote job creation and economic growth by ensuring fair trade, providing the data necessary to support commerce and constitutional democracy, and fostering innovation by setting standards and conducting foundational research and development" (U.S. Department of Commerce, n.d.-a). Within this mission, there is much room for involvement with higher education, from supporting university-based research and development to providing workforce and skills training. This agency has collaborated with other agencies on higher education issues when the secretaries of education, labor, and commerce joined a task force to examine apprenticeship expansion in 2017–2018 (McCarthy et al., 2018). Moreover, the Department of Commerce is the parent agency for a diverse range of subagencies, many of which have implications for higher education (U.S. Department of Commerce, n.d.-b). One is the Census Bureau, which has worked with higher education institutions to obtain population counts of residential students (Alger, 2020). The Census Bureau has also collected data on people's educational backgrounds that are useful for researchers conducting studies about higher education (e.g., U.S. Census Bureau, 2020). The U.S. Patent and Trademark Office, through which university-based researchers may patent their inventions and university leaders may trademark institutional logos (Kenney & Patton, 2009; Rooksby & Collins, 2016), is also housed within the Commerce Department (U.S. Department of Commerce, n.d.-b). The department's National Oceanic and Atmospheric Administration provides grant funding for higher education institutions, including the Sea Grant College Program, which funds universities' "scientific research and stakeholder engagement to identify and solve problems faced by coastal communities" (Sargent et al., 2020, p. 49).

Agencies that enforce consumer protection policies, including the Consumer Financial Protection Bureau (CFPB) and the Federal Trade Commission, conduct investigations, provide information, and otherwise implement policy regarding consumer protection in higher education (Bureau of Consumer Financial Protection, 2020; Chopra, 2015, 2019; Watson, 2019). The CFPB also regulates for-profit higher education providers (Kreighbaum, 2016a), although the effectiveness and resources of the CFPB have varied by presidential administration (Watson, 2019). The agency also has a "student-loan ombudsman," which has placed "student-borrowing issues front-and-center at the bureau" (Blumenstyk, 2017, ¶ 10).

Other important federal agencies include the Corporation for National and Community Service—an independent agency that runs AmeriCorps—which involves college students and others in civic engagement and community service (Dote et al., 2006). The Department of the Interior houses the Bureau of Indian Education, which provides Tribal Colleges and Universities and other Minority-Serving Institutions with funding. The Interior Department also funds college scholarships for Native American and Indigenous students (Bureau of Indian Affairs, n.d.; U.S. Department of the Interior Office of Civil Rights, n.d.). The Administrative Conference of the United States sponsors a fellowship program "for current or aspiring academics" (Administrative Conference of the United States, n.d., ¶ 1). Agencies that oversee healthcare and health policy, such as the Department of Health and Human Services (HHS), the Centers for Disease Control and Prevention (CDC), and the Occupational Safety and Health Administration, produce regulations and guidance regarding public health matters that apply to higher education. For example, HHS regulations mandate that, among other things, higher education institutions receiving federal funds must take steps to comply with regulations designed to protect human subjects in research projects (Henry, 2013). Moreover, during the COVID-19 pandemic, the CDC issued guidelines on how higher education institutions could safely offer in-person instruction (Centers for Disease Control & Prevention, 2020). Also related to healthcare policy, teaching hospitals that train medical residents often receive federal funding from Medicare and Medicaid as well as other federal agencies (Congressional Budget Office, 2018).

AGENCY POWER CASE STUDY: BORROWER DEFENSE TO REPAYMENT

The potentially large influence agency activity can have on the lives of individuals is reflected in the U.S. Department of Education's "Borrower Defense to Repayment" policy. This policy refers to regulations, guidance, and agency decisions regarding the discharge of student loan debt for individuals whose institutions are found to have defrauded them (Kreighbaum, 2016b). Borrower defense policies have varied from Democratic to Republican administrations, with the Obama and Biden administrations inclined to grant full debt relief to defrauded borrowers, and the Trump administration inclined to grant only partial relief (Cowley, 2021; U.S. Department of Education, 2021a).

The difference between full and partial relief—or whether student loan debt is discharged at all—can dramatically affect a student loan borrower's finances. For example, one graduate of a now-defunct for-profit photography school, which was found by its accreditor to have misled its students, incurred more than $100,000 in student loans (Cowley, 2021). Another former student who attended a now-bankrupt court reporting school borrowed more than $60,000 to pay the price of attendance, and ultimately dropped out without completing the program. The institution lost its license after the state found the school had engaged in misrepresentation regarding its program and had hired underqualified instructors (Keshner, 2019). In both cases, the borrowers filed lawsuits to prompt the Trump-era Department of Education to forgive the loans (Cowley, 2021; Keshner, 2019). The debtor who had attended court reporting school was successful in getting her loans discharged. She spoke to *MarketWatch* of how the debt forgiveness made a substantial difference, saying: "I am just overjoyed because I believe this allows me to have a life again" (Keshner, 2019, ¶ 4).

SUMMARY AND CONCLUSION

Administrative agencies comprise a substantial part of the federal government, with agencies located in all three branches, but primarily in the executive branch. Agencies are involved in many aspects of policy creation and implementation, including rulemaking, guidance, investigations, adjudication, and assisting Congress and the White House with policymaking. The closer an agency and its leaders are to the president, the more likely they are to be influenced by presidential politics. For example, cabinet heads and other high-ranking personnel of cabinet-level agencies are appointed by the president with approval of the Senate. These agency leaders often act in accordance with the president's viewpoint (Davis & Greene, 2017). However, other federal agencies, including some executive branch agencies, are independent and more removed from presidential influence (Breger & Edles, 2000, 2015).

Agency officials' policymaking and implementation actions can have a profound reach. Among federal agencies, the U.S. Department of Education has the most direct influence over higher education, but as this chapter has explained, numerous other agencies also influence higher education in a variety of important ways. Although they often do not receive the attention that the president and members of Congress do, agency personnel, whether politically appointed or career staffers, can make a substantial impact on higher education policy, and on the lives of students as well as on the operations of institutions. Discretionary decision making occurs across different agencies and agency functions. My study's respondents emphasized the power of agency discretion, which underscores the importance of individual decisionmakers within administrative agencies, as these policy actors can make a real difference with regard to regulation development, policy implementation, and law enforcement.

CHAPTER 6

Higher Education and the Federal Courts

From landmark Supreme Court cases on race-conscious college admissions to trial court decisions about the applicability of intellectual property laws, the judicial branch's interpretation of the law has charted new paths for higher education policy and beyond. Court decisions are not only binding law, but they also provide precedents and legal logic that influence future court cases and policy implementation (McCarthy, 2015). Federal judges' decisions can overturn or modify policies set by other branches of government, and policy actors have recognized the importance of court cases—especially those heard by the U.S. Supreme Court—for policy change (Collins, 2007, 2018). A court's interpretation of the law creates policy that must be respected as the law within that jurisdiction (Carp et al., 2010).

Some observers have called the federal courts apolitical, perhaps recognizing that courts that are too closely associated with politics may lose credibility as impartial decisionmakers in legal disputes (Barnes, 2019; Lampe, 2020; Pasachoff, 2020). But the political nature of the courts has become undeniable. In recent years, there have been increasing numbers of Supreme Court decisions that have split along a slim, 5-to-4 vote margin based largely on the political party affiliation of the president who appointed each justice, with one justice often acting as the "swing vote" (Kuhn, 2012, ¶ 7). Moreover, Senate confirmation hearings for federal judges—and particularly Supreme Court justices—have been heated and partisan (Johnson, 2011; Siddiqui, 2018). An example of a political Supreme Court nomination fight was one that involved no confirmation hearing at all: when Judge Merrick Garland was nominated for a Supreme Court seat by President Barack Obama in 2016. Republican Senators Mitch McConnell and Charles Grassley, who at the time were Senate Majority Leader and Judiciary Committee Chair respectively, refused to hold hearings to consider the confirmation of Garland to the Supreme Court, leaving the vacancy open for President Donald Trump to fill when he took office the following year (Elving, 2018; Unah & Williams, 2019). In recognition of the policy consequences of Supreme Court appointments, McConnell identified this move as "the most consequential thing I've ever done" (Homans, 2019).

This chapter describes the role that federal courts have played in the higher education policy arena. The chapter first provides an overview of the constitutional foundation and structure of the federal judicial system. The chapter then discusses federal courts' jurisdiction and the powers of federal judges. Specific cases and precedents affecting higher education are also examined in this chapter, to provide illustrative examples of the federal judiciary's influence over higher education.

OVERVIEW OF THE FEDERAL COURT SYSTEM

The federal judicial branch was created by Article III of the Constitution, which states: "The judicial Power of the United States, shall be vested in one supreme Court, and in such inferior Courts as the Congress may from time to time ordain and establish" (U.S. Const. art. III, § 1). Congress holds a great deal of power regarding the number and kind of federal courts that exist, and also over the number of justices serving on the Supreme Court (Lampe, 2020). As a long-time observer of and participant in the federal higher education policy community told me:

> The only thing the Constitution says about the judicial branch, which is one of the three coequal branches, is that there should be a Supreme Court. It doesn't even say how many people have to be on it. It says nothing about the rest of the federal court system. The entirety of our federal court system dates back to 1789, with regular ordinary acts of Congress.

There are three levels of the federal judiciary: federal district courts at the trial level, federal courts of appeals (also called circuit courts), and the United States Supreme Court, which is the country's highest court (Administrative Office of the U.S. Courts, 2016). Typically, federal cases begin at the district court level. A party who loses a case at that level may appeal the decision to the federal court of appeals that oversees the district court's region or, in the case of certain specialized claims such as patents and international trade, to the Court of Appeals for the Federal Circuit. Table 6.1 indicates the geographic regions that are under the purview of each federal court of appeals. Appeals are typically heard by a three-judge panel, and their decisions are sometimes further appealed to a larger panel (sometimes the full panel) of judges for the circuit, known as an *en banc* proceeding. From there, a party may try to appeal a loss at the circuit court level to the United States Supreme Court by filing for a writ of certiorari asking the Supreme Court to hear the case. Unlike the circuit courts, the Supreme Court is not required to hear any appeal, and in fact agrees to hear only a small number of cases. The cases for which a writ of certiorari is granted often involve a

Table 6.1. Geographic Jurisdictions of Federal Courts of Appeals

Circuit	Geographic Jurisdiction
First	Maine, Massachusetts, New Hampshire, Puerto Rico, Rhode Island
Second	Connecticut, New York, Vermont
Third	Delaware, New Jersey, Pennsylvania, Virgin Islands
Fourth	Maryland, North Carolina, South Carolina, Virginia, West Virginia
Fifth	Louisiana, Mississippi, Texas
Sixth	Kentucky, Michigan, Ohio, Tennessee
Seventh	Illinois, Indiana, Wisconsin
Eighth	Arkansas, Iowa, Minnesota, Missouri, Nebraska, North Dakota, South Dakota
Ninth	Alaska, Arizona, California, Guam, Hawaii, Idaho, Montana, Nevada, Northern Mariana Islands, Oregon, Washington
Tenth	Colorado, Kansas, New Mexico, Oklahoma, Utah, Wyoming
Eleventh	Alabama, Florida, Georgia
District of Columbia	District of Columbia
Federal	Nationwide for certain types of cases (e.g., patent, federal claims, and international trade cases)

Source: Administrative Office of the U.S. Courts, 2016

legal issue of current importance or one that has been decided differently among different circuit courts (Administrative Office of the U.S. Courts, 2016).

Federal judges and Supreme Court justices are appointed—not elected—to their positions. The appointment process for Article III judges involves the president nominating the judge or justice and the Senate voting to confirm the appointment, thus fulfilling its constitutional "advice and consent" role (U.S. Const. art. II, § 2; see also Administrative Office of the U.S. Courts, 2016; McCarthy, 2015; McMillon, 2018; Scherer, 2017). For court of appeals and district court judicial appointees, whose courts have jurisdiction over particular regional areas, the senators in affected states have traditionally played a role in the appointment process. These senators may weigh in with their opinions of prospective judges before the president nominates someone (Scherer, 2017). Also, a practice known as the "blue-slip veto" has enabled senators representing the home state of a judicial nominee to effectively block the nominee's appointment by either not returning or negatively responding to a blue form sent as a courtesy to those senators by the chair of the Senate Judiciary Committee (Unah & Williams, 2019). During confirmation hearings held in the Senate, senators consider a potential judge's or justice's likely positions on a wide range of issues, including their views on the constitutionality of race-conscious college admissions policies (e.g., Gresko, 2018).

Built into the Constitution are strong job protections for all Article III judges, who hold lifetime appointments (provided they remain in "good behavior") and will never see their salaries reduced while they remain in judicial office (U.S. Const. art. III, § 1). These protections are intended to reduce the likelihood that federal judges will be influenced by politics; after their nomination and confirmation, only impeachment, voluntary resignation, or incapacity would remove them from office. Thus, the reasoning goes, federal judges will be less susceptible to political influence (Chemerinsky, 2016). But it is not the case that the federal judiciary is apolitical. In recent years, the process of appointing federal judges has become more polarized and contentious (Scherer, 2017). On average, when the president's party affiliation differs from that of the Senate majority, the number of federal judges confirmed by the Senate has been lower than when the Senate and the White House are controlled by the same political party (McMillon, 2019).[1] In the not-too-distant past, even when the Senate was controlled by the same political party as the president, the minority party could stall judicial appointments by invoking the filibuster, which effectively requires an affirmative vote of 60 rather than a simple majority of senators to approve a bill or nomination.[2] The filibuster was increasingly used to block judicial appointments in recent presidencies (Scherer, 2017). It was used so frequently by Republicans during President Obama's terms that in 2013 Democrats changed Senate rules to prohibit use of the filibuster for votes to confirm presidential nominations other than Supreme Court Justices (Unah & Williams, 2019; Werner, 2017). When Republicans gained control of the Senate following the 2014 elections, the party continued to block President Obama's judicial nominees, including a nominee for the Supreme Court (Elving, 2018; Homans, 2019). Then in 2017, after the Republican party took control of both the Senate and the presidency, Senate Republicans changed the chamber's rules to remove filibuster use for Supreme Court appointments, so that President Trump's nominees could advance to the Supreme Court on a simple majority vote (Homans, 2019; Unah & Williams, 2019; Werner, 2017).

In addition to Article III courts—that is, those established under Article III of the Constitution—there are other federal courts that oversee particular kinds of claims and courts located in non-state U.S. territories (Case, 2005; Lederman, 2001). Unlike judges in Article III courts, non-Article III judges do not hold their offices for life, but for a set term (Chemerinsky, 2016). Some non-Article III courts are known as legislative courts—also called "Article I" courts, named for the part of the Constitution that established Congress—and include the federal tax court, the Court of Appeals for the Armed Forces, the Court of Appeals for Veterans Claims, and the Court of Federal Claims

(Administrative Office of the U.S. Courts, 2016; Case, 2005; Chemerinsky, 2016; Federal Bar Association, n.d.; Lederman, 2001; Tua, 2009). Courts that govern U.S. territories are known as Article IV courts because congressional power to establish those courts derives from the Territorial Clause found in Article IV of the Constitution (Tua, 2009; U.S. Const. art. IV, §3, cl. 2). Some courts—such as bankruptcy courts—are considered subdivisions of Article III courts, but their judges do not enjoy the lifetime tenure and salary protections reserved for Article III judges (Resnik, 1998). The decisions of non-Article III judges are sometimes appealable to Article III courts (Administrative Office of the U.S. Courts, 2016). Such courts are relevant to higher education, for example, when a student loan borrower asks a bankruptcy court to discharge their debt (e.g., Keller, 2017). This function of bankruptcy courts in the finances of student loan debtors is discussed further in the case study near the end of this chapter.

FEDERAL COURTS' JURISDICTION AND POWERS

The Constitution states that the federal courts have jurisdiction over "Cases" and "Controversies" (U.S. Const. art. III § 2, cl. 1). In civil cases, courts have interpreted this to mean that a litigant must have suffered some kind of "injury" that is "fairly traceable" to the conduct of the party against whom the lawsuit has been brought (Hessick, 2013, p. 419). The courts do not have the power to issue orders of their own accord before a case has been brought by an aggrieved litigant (Chemerinsky, 2016; McCarthy, 2015). Generally speaking, federal courts have jurisdiction over cases that arise under federal law, such as the U.S. Constitution, a treaty, or a federal statute or regulation. Federal courts also have the ability to hear cases for which "diversity jurisdiction" applies, referring to cases in which the opposing parties are citizens of different states and the "matter in controversy" is valued at more than $75,000 (Chemerinsky, 2016, p. 318; see also Hessick, 2013).

Federal courts also have the power of *judicial review*, meaning they can review the legality of an action or law, and may even declare a law unconstitutional and, thus, unenforceable (Administrative Office of the U.S. Courts, 2016; Carp et al., 2010; Chemerinsky, 2016; Federal Judicial Center, n.d.; Whittington, 2015). Judicial review provides courts with tremendous power because it gives the judicial branch—and ultimately the Supreme Court—the last word on whether an action or law will stand or fall (Carp et al., 2010; Chemerinsky, 2016). Thus, as a coequal branch of the federal government, the judiciary plays a role in checking and balancing Congress and the president by examining those branches' activities and halting or overruling them if the court deems those actions to be unlawful (McCarthy, 2015). An example of this in the higher education context was when a federal court in the District of Columbia invalidated parts of the

Gainful Employment Rule—an accountability policy targeting mostly forprofit colleges issued by President Obama's Department of Education—for not fulfilling the Administrative Procedure Act's requirements when developing a key aspect of the rule (Natow, 2017).

In interpreting the law, federal courts generally follow the doctrine of *stare decisis*, which means the court must look to precedent in previous court cases on similar matters within the court's jurisdiction or from a superior court (McCarthy, 2015; Re, 2014; Spriggs & Hansford, 2001). However, in doing so, courts may cite nuanced differences in previous cases to distinguish that precedent—that is, to explain how the current case differs from prior ones in some key way—as a reason for ruling differently (Bagenstos, 2008; Lindquist & Cross, 2005; Re, 2014). Sometimes, however, courts outright overrule their own prior decisions, thereby breaking with precedent (McCarthy, 2015; Re, 2014). Overruling a precedent is considered "drastic" and does not occur often (Re, 2014, p. 1862). However, some Supreme Court decisions that overruled precedent have had profound impacts on education policy. A powerful example is the *Brown v. Board of Education* case, in which the Supreme Court declared racial segregation in public schools to be a violation of the Fourteenth Amendment. In that case, the Court overruled the earlier *Plessy v. Ferguson* standard that had previously allowed "separate, but equal" public education (McCarthy, 2015, p. 150). When no binding legal precedent that would apply to the facts of a case exists—that is, when a case is one of "first impression"—the court has a greater ability to rule based on its judges' own views of the law (Lindquist & Cross, 2005, p. 1158).

The United States Supreme Court is the most powerful court in the nation. This is because, in the words of legal scholar Erwin Chemerinsky (2016), the Supreme Court "not only . . . gets a voice in evaluating the constitutionality of statutes but also . . . has the decisive say" (p. 18). When the Supreme Court issues a ruling, all lower courts must abide by that ruling, and its reasoning sets a precedent that lower courts must then apply in similar future cases. A Supreme Court ruling becomes binding law for the whole country and remains as such unless overruled by a future Supreme Court ruling, a constitutional amendment, or in some cases an act of Congress (McCarthy, 2015; Spriggs & Hansford, 2001). Given the lifetime tenure of Supreme Court Justices, the rarity of overruling prior decisions, and the supermajorities needed for a constitutional amendment, Supreme Court decisions are remarkably durable. As a result of this substantial power, the Supreme Court's influence on higher education policy has been strong. For example, the Court's rulings on desegregation, nondiscrimination policies, and race-conscious admissions have helped to broaden college access and diversify student bodies (Bowen & Bok, 1998). In the words of one of my interviewees who represented HBCUs, "the [Supreme] Court has a critical, vitally important role [in higher education policy]. They had one from the beginning, and they will continue to have it."

KEY HIGHER EDUCATION POLICY AREAS AFFECTED BY THE FEDERAL JUDICIARY

There are numerous policy areas affecting higher education that have been influenced, and continue to be influenced, by the federal judiciary. As new higher education–related laws are created, the potential for lawsuits is created as well. Meanwhile some policy matters—such as race-conscious admissions and free speech in academia—seem to find themselves perennially in court (Kaplin et al., 2020). The subsections that follow describe several important higher education policy areas that have been affected by the federal judiciary. This description is by no means exhaustive, as laws of just about every kind at different levels of government can affect higher education. However, the following subsections describe some of the main ways that federal courts have influenced higher education policy through their interpretation of federal laws and constitutional provisions.

Civil Rights, Racial Justice, and Nondiscrimination

One of the most significant ways federal courts have influenced higher education policy—and the influence mentioned most often when my study's respondents were asked about the federal judiciary's role in higher education—has been through its rulings on civil rights, racial justice, and nondiscrimination. During the mid- to late 20th century, the Supreme Court began to hear more cases regarding individual rights than it had before. As political scientist Charles Epp (1998) observed, in the mid-1930s not even 10% of the Supreme Court's rulings related to individual rights that were not property rights; however, that rate escalated to nearly 70% of the Court's rulings by the late 1960s. During this period, the Supreme Court identified and defended individual and civil rights in an expansive way (Dodd, 2018; Epp, 1998). As part of this "rights revolution" (Dodd, 2018, p. 3; Epp, 1998, p. 2), the Supreme Court ruled that racial segregation was unlawful as violative of the Fourteenth Amendment's Equal Protection Clause. As explained above, the Supreme Court's landmark 1954 *Brown v. Board of Education* case established that public schools cannot be racially segregated, and a number of Supreme Court cases both before and after *Brown* held that racial segregation in various higher education settings is likewise unconstitutional. Indeed, the pre-*Brown* postsecondary desegregation cases set legal precedents that the Supreme Court would later follow in *Brown*. These cases included *Sweatt v. Painter*, a 1950 case in which the Court rebuked racial segregation in graduate education on Equal Protection Clause grounds (Donahoo, 2006; Heilig et al., 2011; Henderson, 2004).

One of the post-*Brown* desegregation cases involving higher education was *United States v. Fordice* (1992). In that case, the Supreme Court ruled that if a state's existing policies are "traceable to" the state's historic systems of segregation, if the policies still "have segregative effects," if they do not possess a "sound educational justification," and if they "can be practicably eliminated," then the policies are noncompliant with the Fourteenth Amendment and thus unconstitutional (*United States v. Fordice*, 1992, p. 731). Decades later, some federal courts continued to oversee higher education desegregation matters, such as a case filed in 2006 regarding racially segregated higher education institutions and funding disparities for HBCUs in the state of Maryland (Hawkins, 2020). A representative of HBCUs interviewed for my study emphasized the importance of the Supreme Court in desegregating education in the United States. This interviewee said, "Every step that we've made forward in education, elementary and secondary and higher, has been with the intervention of the Court."

Federal courts have also played a substantial role in policy regarding affirmative action, race-conscious admissions, and student body diversity in higher education. In 1978, the Supreme Court issued a landmark decision in *University of California v. Bakke*, ruling that higher education institutions may take race into consideration as one among several factors in admission decisions because achieving diversity in the student body constitutes a compelling interest for the government. However, the *Bakke* ruling also held that using racial quotas in admissions is unacceptable (Bowen & Bok, 1998; Goldstein Hode & Meisenbach, 2017; Lehmuller & Gregory, 2005). Twenty-five years later, the Supreme Court took up the issue of race-conscious postsecondary admissions again with two cases based on the University of Michigan's admission procedures—one for its law school (*Grutter v. Bollinger*), and another for one of its undergraduate divisions (*Gratz v. Bollinger*). The University of Michigan cases confirmed *Bakke*'s holdings that attaining a diverse student body was a sufficiently compelling interest to survive an Equal Protection Clause challenge, and race could be used as one factor among several (as was done at Michigan's law school) in admissions determinations. However, an overly mechanistic procedure—such as the quota examined in *Bakke* or the formulaic "point system" at issue in *Gratz* (Ancheta, 2008, p. 33)—were not constitutionally permitted (Ancheta, 2008; *Gratz v. Bollinger*, 2003; Lehmuller & Gregory, 2005). The Supreme Court once again upheld the key holdings of *Bakke* and *Grutter* in the 2016 *Fisher v. University of Texas* case, but also reiterated the very high "strict scrutiny" standard that must be met for a race-conscious admissions policy to satisfy the Fourteenth Amendment's standard (Liptak, 2016; Ziegler, 2018). Moreover, the Supreme Court has held that states are permitted to ban the use of race-conscious admission policies (*Schuette v.*

Coalition to Defend Affirmative Action, 2014; Ziegler, 2018). Thus, while the Supreme Court has generally protected institutions that use race as one of several factors in admissions decisions, the Court has reiterated that the standard to pass constitutional muster is quite high, and that states and institutions are not required to consider race as a factor in college admissions.

Moreover, the *Fisher* case was decided by a narrow one-vote margin in favor of upholding the University of Texas's policy (Liptak, 2016; Sherman, 2016). Civil rights and student advocacy groups are aware that the makeup of the Supreme Court can lead to changes in jurisprudence on the constitutionality of affirmative action and other matters. For example, an interviewee in my research said that civil rights and student advocates were concerned that the legal standard could change soon, "because the Court's become more conservative."

Federal courts also interpret and apply various nondiscrimination statutes in higher education contexts. These statutes include the Civil Rights Act of 1964, which has been called "perhaps the most prominent civil rights legislation enacted in modern times" (Feder, 2012, p. 1). Title VI of the Civil Rights Act forbids discrimination based on "race, color, or national origin" in programs that receive federal funds (Civil Rights Act of 1964, 2018, § 2000d). Title VII of the Act targets discrimination in employment due to "race, color, religion, sex, or national origin" (§ 2000e). A 2020 Supreme Court decision clarified that discrimination on the basis of sexual orientation is also prohibited by Title VII (Barnes, 2020). Title IX of the Education Amendments of 1972 prohibits sex and gender identity discrimination in federally funded educational programs. Title IX has been applied in various contexts in higher education, including cases involving discrimination in college athletics as well as sexual harassment and assault (Cole & Back, 2019; Pullias Center for Higher Education, 2017). Other statutes that have led to federal nondiscrimination cases include the Americans with Disabilities Act and Section 504 of the Rehabilitation Act (disability discrimination), the Age Discrimination and Age Discrimination in Employment Acts (age discrimination), and others (Feder, 2012; Kaplin et al., 2020; Zehrt, 2019).

The First Amendment

Federal courts often decide First Amendment issues, which encompass individual rights of speech and expression, religion, the right to associate, and freedom of the press (U.S. Const. amend. I). Each of these components of the First Amendment is relevant in higher education. First Amendment free speech and expression rights may apply with regard to faculty, students, staff, and visitors (for example, invited speakers), but only at public higher education institutions—or in the limited cases in which private institutions are deemed state actors—due to the necessity of state action for there to be a constitutional violation (Cope, 2007; Kaplin et al., 2020).[3] First Amendment protections for the rights to peaceably assemble and to free expression apply to student organizations and to protests and demonstrations on public college campuses. Campus newspapers and other publications are also protected by First Amendment rights of free expression and free press against actions by the government, including administrators at public colleges and universities. Federal courts have heard disputes and issued rulings in numerous cases involving these types of First Amendment issues (Kaplin et al., 2020; Lowery, 2004).

Academic freedom, which is the right of scholars to pursue their academic work without undue interference from either the government or their institutions, has been identified by the Supreme Court as rooted in the First Amendment (American Association of University Professors, 2001; Cope, 2007; DeMitchell & Connelly, 2007; Griffin, 2013; Kaplin et al., 2020; Levinson, 2007). Protection of professors' academic freedom is a main argument in favor of granting faculty tenure, as the job protections that come with tenure allow a faculty member freedom to speak and write more freely about provocative issues, to engage in innovative teaching and research, and to criticize the government or their institutional leadership (American Association of University Professors, 2001; Cope, 2007; Fichtner & Simpson, 2015). Academic freedom is also based on contract law as well as long-held traditions in academia, making it a freedom that applies to many private as well as public institutions (Dougherty et al., 2017; Kaplin et al., 2020; Lee, 2015; Levinson, 2007). Although federal courts at all levels have heard cases involving academic freedom as a legal concept, academic freedom remains "murky" because the Supreme Court has not provided many details about the doctrine or elements of the concept (Cope, 2007, p. 336; see also DeMitchell & Connelly, 2007; Griffin, 2013; Levinson, 2007). To complicate matters, federal courts have also recognized the academic freedom of institutions of higher education, with some holding that academic freedom of the institution is prioritized (Kaplin et al., 2020; Lee, 2015). A concurring opinion written by Justice Felix Frankfurter in the *Sweezy v. New Hampshire* (1957) case is often referenced as a description of the academic freedom held by universities. Specifically, Frankfurter wrote about the "four essential freedoms" of an institution: to "determine for itself on academic grounds who may teach, what may be taught, how it shall be taught, and who may be admitted to study" (Griffin, 2013, p. 9). This language in Frankfurter's *Sweezy* concurrence has been cited in other higher education cases as the basis for granting quite a bit of deference to institutional decisions, including in disputes with students (*who may be admitted to study*) and faculty (*who may teach, what may be taught,* and *how it shall be taught*) (Hiers, 2002; Lee, 2015).

The religion clauses of the First Amendment also have great importance for higher education policy. The first religion clause, known as the Establishment Clause, prohibits the government from "respecting an establishment of religion"; the second religion clause, called the Free Exercise Clause, prevents government from "prohibiting the free exercise" of religion (U.S. Const. amend. I). Supreme Court holdings on the religion clauses have implications for different types of higher education institutions, depending on whether they are public or private, and whether they are religiously affiliated or secular. Under the Establishment Clause, public higher education institutions cannot endorse or coerce participation in religious activity, and cannot create too much of an "entanglement" between the institution and religion (Pihos, 2005, p. 1357; see also Kaplin et al., 2020). Under the Free Exercise Clause, public institutions cannot unduly burden affiliates from practicing their religion, nor can the government unduly inhibit free religious practices at religiously affiliated institutions (Kaplin et al., 2020; Lowery, 2004).

Due Process

Federal courts have overseen a number of cases involving due process issues in higher education. There are two due process clauses in the Constitution: The Fifth Amendment due process clause applies to the federal government, while the one in the Fourteenth Amendment applies to the states (Monk, 2015). As state actors, public colleges and universities can be charged with constitutional due process violations. Procedural due process under the Fourteenth Amendment requires public institutions to provide advance notice and a hearing at which the person subject to an adverse action will have the opportunity to present their side of the story (Dutile, 2001; Kaplin et al., 2020; Nisenson, 2016; Pavela & Pavela, 2012; U.S. Const. amend. XIV). While private institutions need not adhere to due process requirements under the Constitution, many private colleges have adopted policies that include procedures resembling constitutional due process, which can be binding against those institutions as contracts (Dougherty et al., 2017; Kaplin et al., 2020; Pavela & Pavela, 2012). Federal courts have fielded due process cases in a variety of areas involving higher education. For example, federal courts have held that public institutions must meet procedural due process standards for faculty tenure denials and dismissal of tenured faculty, as well as for issuing punishments in student disciplinary proceedings (Fichtner & Simpson, 2015; Kaplin et al., 2020).

Other Areas of Judicial Influence

Other areas in which the federal judiciary has influenced are legion. These include immigration matters, which affect immigrant and international students, faculty, and staff in higher education institutions. Immigration courts are not part of the federal judiciary—they are housed within the U.S. Department of Justice—but decisions of immigration courts are reviewable by

Article III courts in some circumstances (Kim, 2018; Lee, 2013). Immigration issues can reach Article III courts, and even the Supreme Court, in other ways as well. For example, presidential executive orders and federal agency actions affecting immigration may be challenged in Article III courts, as happened with executive actions issued by President Trump regarding refugee admissions and by Presidents Obama and Trump regarding DACA (Margulies, 2018; Mullen & Diamond, 2015; Redden, 2020; Totenberg, 2020).

Related to the Supreme Court's DACA ruling, which was decided on procedural grounds, is another somewhat common area of judicial influence over higher education: the proper use of government power. In the DACA case, the Court reasoned that the Trump administration's attempt to end the program was an "arbitrary and capricious" government action due to noncompliance with federal law on administrative procedures (Redden, 2020, ¶ 4). Federal courts have made similar rulings regarding other matters affecting higher education, such as when a federal court nullified parts of the Obama administration's Gainful Employment Rule, as explained above. One of my interviewees who worked in government relations for a higher education association observed that in an era characterized by legislative gridlock, executive agencies are likely to increase policymaking activity, which may generate lawsuits alleging executive branch overreach. This allows federal courts to play a larger role in defining the boundaries of government power. The interviewee said that some recent court cases have been

> trying to determine, Does the federal government have the power to regulate certain things? Did they go too far or overreach otherwise? So, the court is the mediator, ultimately, of overreach in a place where not much legislation is being put forth on higher education. But there is regulatory action over time, and in the absence of Congress sort of doing its duty, you have the courts effectively playing part of that role.

In the area of bankruptcy law, federal bankruptcy and other courts' determinations of whether student loan debt presents an "undue hardship" have serious implications for the extent to which such debt may be dischargeable through bankruptcy proceedings (Keller, 2017; Murakami, 2020a; Pardo & Lacey, 2005). An interviewee from a nonprofit organization working on higher education policy issues pointed out how this standard gives individual bankruptcy judges some discretion over whether student loan debt may be discharged. This interviewee said:

> It's just very much like a case-by-case basis. The judge has to make the decision to allow it. There's a lot of authority that goes to the person who is overseeing the case. So I think that obviously, at an individual level, that has an impact on students who are borrowers.

The case study presented at the end of this chapter further describes this power of bankruptcy courts.

Other areas of judicial influence on higher education policy include intellectual property and labor law. Regarding intellectual property, federal court decisions have addressed such issues as fair use in copyright law and ownership of patents on inventions created by university researchers (Kaplin et al., 2020; Rooksby, 2016). Federal courts have also made consequential decisions regarding labor law in the higher education context. In one prominent example—the *National Labor Relations Board v. Yeshiva University* (1980) case—the Supreme Court ruled that college faculty who have managerial roles at some private institutions cannot unionize under the National Labor Relations Act (see also Herbert & Apkarian, 2017; Julius & DiGiovanni, 2019; Kaplin et al., 2020). Similarly, the Supreme Court and other federal courts have issued rulings limiting the ability of faculty at religiously affiliated institutions to unionize (Herbert & Apkarian, 2017; Jaschik, 2020). In light of these and many other federal cases that affect higher education, it is plain that the federal judiciary plays an important and wide-ranging role in many areas of higher education policy.

JUDICIAL POWER CASE STUDY: BANKRUPTCY COURTS

Although not Article III courts, bankruptcy courts hold a great deal of power over the financial well-being of individuals, families, and organizations. For most student loan debtors, bankruptcy has not resulted in the forgiveness of student loan debt (Iuliano, 2012). That is because borrowers must meet an "undue hardship" standard in order for student loans to be discharged in bankruptcy, which requires the filing of another proceeding (in addition to the bankruptcy filing), and the need to meet a standard of proof about the burdensomeness of the debt. Whether an individual debtor meets that standard is open to interpretation by the bankruptcy judge, giving the judge a fair amount of power via the use of discretion (Helhoski, 2020; Taylor, 2012).

Despite the commonly held perception that federal student loans are highly unlikely to be discharged in bankruptcy proceedings, one study found that almost 40% of the time, debtors seeking federal student loan discharge in bankruptcy receive it (Iuliano, 2012). In recent years, news stories of bankruptcy courts allowing the discharge of six-figure student loan debts have been reported (Arnold, 2020; Helhoski, 2020). Observers have noted a trend in the direction of allowing more leeway for federal student loans to be discharged in bankruptcy (Arnold, 2020; Murakami, 2020a). These cases and trends highlight the power that bankruptcy courts hold to alleviate the debt burden for student borrowers whose financial situations have become untenable. Indeed, one bankruptcy judge—recognizing the "myths" about the impossibility of discharging student loan debt in bankruptcy—said, "This Court will not participate in perpetuating these myths" (Arnold, 2020, ¶ 14).

SUMMARY AND CONCLUSION

As this chapter has explained, the federal courts hold a great deal of influence over policy outcomes. This results largely from the courts' power of judicial review, through which the judicial branch can determine the validity and interpretation of laws and other actions. Although a court cannot act until a case or controversy brought by an appropriate party arrives on its docket, judicial review gives the judiciary—and particularly the Supreme Court—the power to determine whether government actions are constitutional and the ability to set precedents that, under the legal principle of *stare decisis*, must be followed within the court's jurisdiction. Another reason the courts are so powerful is because of the lifetime tenure of federal judges, who need not worry about future employment and could serve on the court for several decades. These factors combine to give the third branch of the federal government a substantial and long-lasting policy impact.

Although judges are not always perceived to be policymakers, the federal judiciary in fact has had a powerful impact on federal policy, including, relevant to higher education policy, the areas of civil rights, school desegregation, diversity on campus, due process, immigration, administrative procedure, intellectual property, and First Amendment issues, among many other important matters. As time goes on, new laws will be enacted, new jurists will be appointed to the federal bench, and the federal jurisprudence of higher education will continue to evolve, even if that evolution is gradual.

CHAPTER 7

Nonfederal Actors' Influence on Federal Higher Education Policy

The preceding chapters have described how various federal policy actors—Congress, the president, White House staff, federal agencies, and the courts—have influenced higher education policy. But policy actors unaffiliated with the federal government are also actively involved. Nonfederal actors' influence on higher education policy may fall before, while, or after a policy is effectuated.

At the policy development stage, actors may attempt to shape public opinion in favor of their policy positions, lobby lawmakers to adopt their favored policies, or even participate directly in policymaking, as nonfederal negotiators do in the Department of Education's rulemaking process (Natow, 2015, 2017). At the policy implementation stage, nonfederal actors often work to help policy targets comply with or receive benefits from federal programs (Anderson, 2015; You, 2017). They might also implement policy in a way that is inconsistent with policymakers' intent or resist implementing policies they disagree with or are unable to implement (Brower et al., 2017; Dahill-Brown & Lavery, 2012; Meyers et al., 2007). Once a policy takes effect, nonfederal actors who oppose the policy may file lawsuits alleging it is illegal or unconstitutional. This strategy has been used by the for-profit higher education sector—sometimes successfully—to challenge federal regulations that increased scrutiny and restricted some practices of for-profit institutions and other career-focused higher education providers (Natow, 2017).

This chapter describes nonfederal actors who have influenced federal higher education policy as well as the mechanisms and strategies through which they have done so. The most prominent of these are higher education interest groups, which have used a variety of strategies to advocate for their preferred policies. Many such interest groups represent colleges and universities; however, there are interest groups representing numerous other kinds of higher education stakeholders with regard to federal policy. Additional nonfederal actors discussed in this chapter include state and local governments, accreditors, the news media, higher education interstate compacts, the business community, students, and other nongovernmental entities.

INTEREST GROUPS

Higher Education Interest Groups in the Federal Policy Space

Broadly defined, an interest group is a nongovernmental organization that represents a particular interest and advocates for policies favorable to that interest (Garrett & Rhine, 2006; Petracca, 2018; Yoho, 1998). In the federal higher education policy space, there are many kinds of interest groups, ranging from large organizations that represent a wide variety of colleges and universities to smaller, specialized groups that focus on particular issues or stakeholders. The most prominent interest groups are the "Big Six Associations" (Cook, 1998, p. 11)—that is, six of the larger organizations that represent different kinds of higher education institutions in Washington, D.C. The American Council on Education (ACE), which is the largest of the Big Six, has existed for over a century and has been highly influential over higher education policy and practice (American Council on Education, n.d.-d; Parsons, 1997; Stone, 2016). ACE represents presidents of colleges and universities as well as other higher education associations (American Council on Education, n.d.-c; Cook, 1998). One of my interviewees who worked on policy matters for a D.C.-based association told me, "We very rarely don't agree with a policy stance that ACE would take. I think it provides us cover, that lots of other higher education associations are signing onto this, or standing in support of it."

Other members of the Big Six are the National Association of Independent Colleges and Universities (NAICU, representing private, nonprofit institutions), the American Association of Community Colleges (AACC, representing 2-year institutions), the Association of American Universities (AAU, representing research universities), the Association of Public and Land-grant Universities (APLU, representing public 4-year institutions), and the American Association of State Colleges and Universities (AASCU, representing public regional institutions) (Cook, 1998; Lowry, 2009). The power of the Big Six on behalf of colleges and universities has been documented in the scholarly literature (e.g., Cook, 1998; Natow, 2017; Stone, 2016), and some of my study's respondents confirmed the influence that these associations have. In the words of an advocate for higher education students whom I interviewed, "The institutions have a significant amount of power in especially higher ed policy. . . . It's the Big Six, and they have significant impact on federal policies."

In addition to the Big Six, there are numerous other higher education associations that serve as interest groups for their focal stakeholders. These include, but are not limited to, the American Association of Community College Trustees (representing community college trustees), the American Association of University Professors (representing college professors), the Association of American Medical Colleges (representing medical schools), the Association of Governing Boards of Universities and Colleges (representing governing boards), Career Education Colleges and Universities (representing for-profit higher education), the Council for Higher Education Accreditation (representing accrediting agencies), the Council of Independent Colleges (representing private institutions), the Hispanic Association of Colleges and Universities (representing Hispanic-Serving Institutions), NASPA—Student Affairs Administrators in Higher Education (historically called the National Association of Student Personnel Administrators; representing student affairs professionals), the National Association for College Admission Counseling (representing admissions personnel), the National Association for Equal Opportunity (representing Historically Black Colleges and Universities), the National Association of College and University Business Officers (representing business administrators), the National Association of Student Financial Aid Administrators (representing financial aid administrators), the State Higher Education Executive Officers Association (representing state-level higher education executives), the United States Student Association (representing postsecondary students), and many others (Cook, 1998; Fain, 2016; Kelchen, 2018; Lowry, 2009; Parsons, 1997; Revilla-Garcia, 2019; Washington Higher Education Secretariat, n.d.-b).

Many higher education interest groups, including ACE, have offices at the National Center for Higher Education, at the address of One Dupont Circle in Washington, D.C. Thus, the collective of higher education associations is sometimes referred to as "One Dupont Circle" (American Council on Education, n.d.-d; Cook, 1998; Natow, 2015; Parsons, 1997). Additionally, many leaders of Washington-area higher education associations comprise the Washington Higher Education Secretariat. Led by ACE, this group convenes on a regular basis "to review trends/challenges confronting higher education and to develop responses" to those trends and challenges, as well as "to learn from colleagues and external experts" about current issues affecting higher education (Washington Higher Education Secretariat, n.d.-a, ¶ 3). Higher education interest groups are not limited to the Washington, D.C., area. Indeed, organizations both large and small located far from D.C. also influence federal higher education policy.[1]

Higher education associations tend not to view each other as competition, but rather as allies. The associations have frequently worked together to advocate for policies that benefit higher education collectively. One of my interviewees who worked for a higher education association shared that "working in coalition with other organizations" was an important part of the job. A common example of such collaboration is when numerous higher education associations sign on to the same letter or policy statement to be presented to policymakers and the public. These efforts have often been led by ACE, as with the many letters the higher education associations sent to policymakers seeking emergency funding during the COVID-19 pandemic (e.g., Mitchell, 2020, 2021). Decades earlier, when congressional

Republicans led by Speaker of the House Newt Gingrich sought steep funding cuts for federal student aid in the 1990s, dozens of higher education associations joined forces to create the Student Aid Alliance, which lobbied forcefully—and successfully—to prevent the cuts from gaining approval (Blair, 1999; Cook, 1998). More recently, associations representing Minority-Serving Institutions joined forces—again, successfully—in 2019 to advocate for the passage of a bill to provide federal funding for such institutions under Title III of the Higher Education Act (Jones & Brown, 2020).

Apart from associations, many colleges and universities act as interest groups in their own right (Marsicano, 2019). It is not uncommon for individual institutions and higher education systems to engage in lobbying and to expend resources on advocacy activity (Camp, 2021; Marsicano & Brooks, 2020). One study found that about 37% of institutions conduct lobbying (Camp, 2021). Some institutions are large and powerful enough to exert influence with lawmakers by contacting their congressional representatives and engaging affiliates on the institution's behalf. As a former federal staffer told me:

> For a very long time, the higher education agenda in the United States was essentially set by the institutions themselves. And what was good for higher education was what was good for the institutions. And the more powerful the institution, the more influence they had, not only because they are massive employers in the state, massive influences in the state, very prestigious in the state, but also because almost everybody in Congress went to these institutions. . . . So when Princeton calls, they have 20 alums on Capitol Hill who are members of Congress, who they call and say, "Hey, we would like this policy to be this way, not that way." So the institutions of higher education and the influence they have on the higher education policy agenda in Congress is really significant.

Interest Group Strategies

Higher education interest groups use a variety of strategies to influence policy in all branches of the federal government and beyond. These strategies include lobbying Congress, meeting with executive branch officials, advising policymakers and candidates for public office, filing lawsuits and legal briefs with federal courts, educating stakeholders about policy issues, and attempting to sway public opinion.

Influencing Congress. One way interest groups influence Congress is by sending representatives to testify before congressional committees and subcommittees regarding higher education policy matters. An example of this was when a vice president of ACE gave testimony to the House Committee on Space, Science, and Technology regarding diversifying the workforce in science, technology, engineering, and mathematics (STEM) careers by providing additional funding for STEM education at Minority-Serving Institutions (American Council on Education, 2019). Interest group representatives also schedule meetings with congressional staff and send drafts of legislation to key members of Congress. For example, one of my respondents who worked on federal policy matters for a higher education association described an important part of that job as "going up to the Hill and talking with staff, and doing education around who the students are . . . and what are the real problems facing them." Another respondent who served as a vice president of an advocacy association described the organization's congressional advocacy efforts as follows:

> We meet with congressional staff, both in the House and . . . Senate . . . to share our agenda and then to also try to identify areas where there are members that would support our higher education agenda. . . . In addition to that, we have worked on bill language. Not only bill language that supports our agenda, but providing feedback to legislators on their bills.

The same respondent also said that in addition to direct lobbying, this group has hired a professional lobbyist to do additional advocacy work on behalf of the organization.

Some interest groups organize "lobby days" on Capitol Hill. These events involve bringing organizational members and other stakeholders to Washington, D.C., to meet with Congress members and staff, and to advocate for particular policies. Stakeholders who participate in lobby days include current college students in addition to faculty, staff, and other institutional affiliates (De Veau, 2018; NASPA, n.d.; Szlezinger, 2021). An interviewee who has participated in lobby days told me:

> At the end of the day, the students like to tell the story about what the dollars have done from their perspective, how they were enriched, how they had new laboratories, how they have dormitories, how they have science and research or whatever they're working on.

Aside from directly lobbying members of Congress, higher education interest groups have also tried to shape public opinion and encourage sympathetic stakeholders to make their positions known to lawmakers. This has been done by publishing opinion pieces in media outlets, posting information on an interest group's website, sending emails to their membership and others via listservs, organizing letter-writing and emailing campaigns to policymakers, and purchasing advertisements in print and other media to advocate for the interest group's message and preferred policy positions (Blair, 1999; Cook, 1998; Jones & Brown, 2020; Natow, 2017, 2020). Advocates who have access to journalists may pitch stories or provide quotes or context for news reports regarding policies or points of view. As a representative of an interest group told me during my earlier research on the higher education rulemaking process, "The press can carry your message" (Natow, 2017, p. 90).

Influencing the Executive Branch. Interest groups also work to shape policymaking in the executive branch. Sometimes groups will seek to influence the president directly, such as by sending an open letter to the president and making that letter available to the public. For example, in 2017, ACE on behalf of several hundred institutions sent a letter to President Donald Trump asking him to support DACA and provide protection from deportation for undocumented immigrants who came to the United States as children (American Council on Education, 2017). In another example, the president of the Council of Independent Colleges penned an open letter to President Barack Obama in *Inside Higher Education* in 2013, touting the role of private colleges in supporting access to higher education and social mobility for historically underserved student populations (Ekman, 2013). Interest groups have also pressured new presidential administrations to appoint cabinet members and other agency leaders with whom the interest groups agree on policy (e.g., Siddiqui & Andrews, 2020). Even before a candidate becomes president, some interest groups seek to influence the candidate's positions on higher education matters or help the candidate to develop policy proposals. These actions could prove highly influential if the candidate were to win election. As a leader of one advocacy group told me during the 2020 campaign, "We've provided feedback to some folks who are running in the presidential election, for example [on] debt forgiveness. . . . They don't always take our advice, but we're happy to provide it when they come to us."

Interest groups have also scheduled meetings with White House staff to discuss policy matters. For example, as explained in Chapter 4, when a forthcoming regulation is being reviewed by the OMB, stakeholders may schedule meetings with OMB staff to provide information relevant to the review (Sunstein, 2013). These meetings provide an opportunity for stakeholders to give information to OMB about a pending regulation. However, providing information at this stage of the rulemaking process is not likely to have a large impact on the content of regulations. A respondent in my research use study described these meetings as "purely listening sessions," without much interactive conversation between participants and OMB staff. Other offices within the Executive Office of the President hold meetings with policy stakeholders as well. One of my study's interviewees who had worked in the White House said that "meeting people when they requested to share their work or their research with us" was "a large part of our job."

This respondent went on to say that not just interest groups but "all sorts of folks reach out to the White House to lobby. . . . Even if that term might be a little bit more negative, but it was actually very helpful in helping us . . . understand what's actually going on."

Interest groups influence other executive branch agencies as well. For example, Department of Education regulations of the Higher Education Act's federal student aid programs are required to undergo a negotiated rulemaking process, in which stakeholders and agency representatives meet publicly to debate what language should appear in a proposed rule (Natow, 2015, 2017; Pelesh, 1994). Prior to negotiated rulemaking, Department of Education representatives gather information about the regulatory content area from stakeholders around the country via written communications and in-person regional meetings. Representatives from interest groups frequently serve as negotiators and speak at regional meetings. Another phase of the rulemaking process that provides opportunities for interest-group influence is the notice-and-comment period, during which the agency receives written comments from stakeholders about a proposed rule. Higher education interest groups have participated in this stage of agency rulemaking as well (Natow, 2017).

Influencing the Federal Judiciary. Interest groups have also attempted to influence policy via the judicial branch. As litigants, organizations representing particular interest groups or sectors of higher education have filed lawsuits in federal court. If such a suit succeeds, the court may strike down the law, narrow its application, or issue rulings that set precedents for future, similar cases. Such lawsuits have been filed in cases involving higher education policy, such as during the Obama administration, when the Association of Private Sector Colleges and Universities (which later became Career Education Colleges and Universities [Fain, 2016]) filed multiple lawsuits against federal regulations of for-profit higher education (Natow, 2017).

Even if not a party to a particular federal case, higher education interest groups often have an interest in the outcome of litigation, given that courts interpret laws and set precedents that everyone in the jurisdiction must follow. Therefore, interest groups often monitor the dockets of federal courts to understand what legal issues are being decided and what policy issues are likely to be affected (e.g., American Council on Education, n.d.-b). Another common way interest groups have attempted to influence judicial decisions has been to submit an *amicus curiae* brief, which translates to "friend of the court" brief (e.g., Gilfoyle & Dvoskin, 2017, p. 753). These are written legal arguments that an interested individual or group may file with a court regarding cases in which they have an interest in the outcome but are not a party (Collins, 2007; Gilfoyle & Dvoskin, 2017). Interest groups in the higher education space have filed numerous amicus briefs with federal courts and quasi-judicial boards. For example, the American Association of University Professors (AAUP) filed an amicus brief in support of faculty unionization rights in a National Labor Relations Board case in 2012 (American Association of University Professors, n.d.). Filing amicus briefs is one of the more common ways that interest groups attempt to influence the judicial branch, and there is some evidence that such briefs can be persuasive to judges (Collins, 2007, 2018; Collins et al., 2015). In addition to bringing lawsuits or otherwise supporting litigation, interest groups have also been observed to weigh in on judicial nominees or potential nominees before they are appointed (McMillon, 2018; Scherer, 2017). An example of such a statement in the higher education sector was when the AAUP posted a statement on its website that was critical of Justice Neil Gorsuch before his appointment to the Supreme Court was confirmed by the Senate (American Association of University Professors, 2017).

Public Communications and Education. Interest groups often engage in public communications to persuade the public and policymakers to favor the groups' preferred polices, and to educate the public about issues the groups consider important. As explained above, this is sometimes done through publishing opinion pieces or paid advertisements, or otherwise obtaining media attention for an interest group's message and argument (Blair, 1999; Cook, 1998; Natow, 2017, 2020). Advocates also use social media to disseminate their messages, arguments, and policy positions to a wide audience (Jones & Brown, 2020; Natow, 2017). For example, interest groups have used Twitter and other social media to advocate for and provide information about the Department of Education's regulations governing higher education (Natow, 2017).

Some interest groups take further steps to educate their membership and others about policy matters, why they are important, and how to advocate for policy change that benefits the group's interests (Jones & Brown, 2020). One way that associations do this is to reach out to government or external affairs staff at member organizations and train them on policy advocacy. For example, an interviewee who worked at a Big Six association told me that one of the association's roles involved "working very closely with the governmental affairs staff in [member] institutions and systems, to help them understand what is happening at the federal level in terms of policy, regulation, agency directives, and how [policy] affects them."

STATE AND LOCAL GOVERNMENTS

Subnational governments—that is, state and local governments—are substantially affected by federal policies regarding higher education. Not only do state and local governments play a role in implementing federal policy, but they are also sometimes the targets of federal policy. Part of the reason the federal government's role in higher education has become so expansive is because competing budget priorities have reduced state funding as a share of college and university revenues. Institutions have raised tuition to make up for this shortfall in revenue, thereby placing greater importance on federal student financial aid (Alexander et al., 2010; Bowen, 2014). With federal funding come conditions and requirements that increase federal control over higher education. As Chapter 1 explained, federalism in the United States often involves all levels of government working within a policy subsystem, performing their own distinct roles while also working together with other levels of government to create and implement policy (Hills, 1998; Thompson, 2013). Federal, state, and local governments are constantly involved in higher education policy in the United States, and the different levels of government frequently influence one another in the higher education space (Grissom & Herrington, 2012; Trow, 1993).

Subnational governments and organizations representing them often play a role similar to interest groups and individual institutions in federal higher education policymaking processes (Natow, 2021d). If a prospective federal policy is likely to affect states, then states are likely to weigh in on what the policy details should be, and state government representatives will make their perspectives known to federal lawmakers. Just as colleges and universities do, state and local officials often have associations representing their interests in the policy community and providing resources for state and local officials to learn about federal policy. Associations representing state officials that have been active in higher education policy include the State Higher Education Executive Officers Association (SHEEO), the National Governors Association, and the National Conference of State Legislatures (Griffin, 2019).

States often serve as partners to the federal government in creating or implementing higher education policy (Natow, 2021d). Sometimes these partnerships are cooperative, and the different levels of government work together to develop or implement policy. State government representatives, including state attorneys general and associations representing state officials (such as SHEEO) have worked with the Department of Education on developing regulations when state-level government interests are likely to be impacted (e.g., Desjean, 2019; Student Assistance General Provisions, 2015). Representatives of state officials have also testified before congressional committees on matters relating to higher education. For example, SHEEO representatives have testified before the Senate Health, Education, Labor, and Pensions Committee with regard to higher education affordability and accountability (U.S. Senate Committee on Health, Education, Labor, & Pensions, 2018, 2019). Sometimes federal officials receive information about how to develop policies through less formal discussions with state and local officials. One of my interviewees who had worked in the White House said that conversations with state and local officials can give rise to ideas for new policies or program designs that federal policymakers may later pursue. This interviewee said:

> A lot of federal policy relies on what's happening at the state and local level. Good examples are for [finding] convincing evidence that something's worth doing. . . . It's some states or schools or groups [that] are doing really great work, and that's worth replicating. And so our role could also be bringing attention to that and encouraging more scaling of an existing model [rather] than starting from scratch.

The federal government has also enlisted state and local governments to implement federal higher education policy and help the federal government to meet its own policy goals. Under Title IV of the Higher Education Act, Congress identified state governments as one of the pillars of the Program Integrity Triad—the other two pillars being accreditors and the Department of Education—charged with maintaining educational quality in colleges and universities participating in federal student financial aid programs. For their part of the triad, states are responsible for authorizing (i.e., licensing) colleges and universities to operate as postsecondary institutions within the state (Natow et al., 2021; Tandberg et al., 2019). The Higher Education Act requires all institutions that receive federal student aid dollars to be duly authorized to operate as a higher education institution. Although states' processes for authorizing institutions vary, Congress expects that institutions must meet state standards in order to receive authorization. Thus, by authorizing institutions, states help to ensure that programs receiving federal student aid meet at least minimum quality requirements (Harnisch et al., 2016; Tandberg & Martin, 2019). Local governments have also been involved in implementing federal higher education policies. For example, local governments have worked alongside their state and federal counterparts to implement the Cooperative Extension Service, which provides local agricultural education as part of the land-grant university system (Croft, 2019).

Maintenance-of-effort (MOE) policies have been an influential way for the federal government to prompt states to increase funding for higher education (Delaney, 2014). These policies require, as a condition for obtaining federal funding, that state governments must invest a particular amount of money in higher education within the state (Alexander et al., 2010). The American Recovery and Reinvestment Act, an economic stimulus bill passed in 2009, included an MOE requirement for higher education. This MOE provision has shown to be effective at maintaining state funding for postsecondary education at least at federally required levels (Alexander et al., 2010; Harnisch, 2012). The Coronavirus Aid, Relief, and Economic Security Act (CARES Act), passed in Spring 2020 during the COVID-19 pandemic, also contained MOE provisions requiring states to assure they would maintain financial support for K–12 and higher education (U.S. Department of Education, 2020a).

As these examples demonstrate, federal policymaking in the area of higher education has had a profound influence on states and has brought them into partnership with the federal government. But federal policymaking for higher education has also had meaningful indirect effects on states. For example, federal higher education policy aimed at institutions—and not at states—may nonetheless prompt states to act where they otherwise might not (Natow, 2021d). A case in point is the Department of Education's state authorization regulations, which require (among other things) that institutions be authorized to act as postsecondary providers by every state where they enroll students. The regulations are aimed at institutions, but because institutions that enroll a large number of online students across several states must ensure they are authorized by all relevant states, state governments have been pressured by institutions to join a state authorization reciprocity agreement, which allows participating institutions authorized in a state that is a signatory to the agreement to have that authorization recognized by all other states who are also signatories (Natow, 2021d; Natow et al., 2021).

Federal policy has also shaped and constrained how states create their own policies. For example, federal policy on the kinds of data the U.S. Department of Education may maintain has limited the ability of states to make policies based on comprehensive, national data about student outcomes and federal financial aid. Specifically, under the Higher Education Opportunity Act of 2008, the Department of Education was forbidden from maintaining a database of higher education student-level information. One of the arguments given by opponents of this prohibition has been that the existence of a federal student-level database would enable states to develop accountability and other policies for higher education based on more comprehensive data than states otherwise have (Miller, 2016). In another example of federal higher education policy constraining state governments, federal MOE provisions may force states to prioritize funding postsecondary education over other state needs, such as healthcare and public assistance programs, unless the federal government waives the MOE requirement (Alexander et al., 2010). This would be particularly challenging during economic downturns or for states with strained budgets. As one of my respondents who has advocated for state governments explained, "Many states, just given their current fiscal situation with their state budgets, could not afford to pay" the required amounts under some MOE policies. Because all levels of government in the United States play a meaningful role in funding and regulating higher education, there are likely to be conflicts as well as collaborations between the federal and subnational governments when policymaking at any level occurs.

Finally, federal oversight of state governments has been important for enforcing civil rights in higher education (Alexander et al., 2021; Hinrichs,

2015). Desegregation of colleges and universities has involved lengthy periods of federal oversight, with involvement of the federal judiciary, the Department of Education's Office for Civil Rights, and racial equity advocates outside of government (Hinrichs, 2015). An interviewee who represented HBCUs spoke of the federal courts' oversight of states whose financial investment in predominantly White institutions was disproportionately higher than their investment in HBCUs. The interviewee spoke of multiple federal lawsuits and the Department of Education's oversight role as being crucial for the desegregation of higher education.

ACCREDITORS

Higher education accreditors are nonprofit organizations that determine whether colleges and universities meet certain quality standards and provide an endorsement of those who do. Accreditation decisions are made following a detailed examination that typically involves a combination of peer review, self-study, and visits from representatives of the accrediting organization. Accreditation by a reputable accreditor signals to observers that an institution or program meets a certain quality standard. Because accreditation by an organization recognized by the Department of Education is required for institutions to participate in federal student aid programs, accreditation has become a fiscal necessity for many institutions—and yet another way for the federal government to regulate higher education (Council for Higher Education Accreditation, 2002; Eaton, 2010, 2015; Kelchen, 2018; Volkwein, 2010). Higher education accreditors and groups representing them have also influenced federal policy by testifying in Congress and participating in the Department of Education's rulemaking process (Abdul-Alim, 2017; Natow, 2017). Together with states and the Department of Education, accreditors are the third group of participants in the Program Integrity Triad under Title IV of the Higher Education Act, charged with maintaining educational quality for institutions receiving federal student aid funds (Harnisch et al., 2016; Tandberg & Martin, 2019).

Just as institutions must maintain their accreditors' quality standards to remain accredited, accrediting agencies must meet certain quality standards to maintain status in their own field (Kelchen, 2018). The Council for Higher Education Accreditation, which is "a national coordinating body for institutional and programmatic accreditation," recognizes accreditors that meet the council's standards (Eaton, 2015, p. 5). Moreover, accreditors seek to remain recognized by the Department of Education, because such recognition means institutions accredited by the agency can receive funds through federal student aid programs, and therefore institutions will seek accreditation from those agencies. To be recognized by the Department of Education, accreditors must receive approval from an advisory committee called the National Advisory Committee on Institutional Quality and Integrity (NACIQI) (Basken, 2021; Eaton, 2010, 2015; Kelchen, 2017, 2018).

Although NACIQI may make a recommendation for the Department of Education not to recognize a particular accreditor, discretion lies with the department as to whether to accept NACIQI's recommendation (Kelchen, 2018). As political leadership in the Department of Education has varied from one presidential administration to the next, the agency has vacillated between accepting and rejecting NACIQI's recommendation to recognize (or not) a controversial accreditor known as the Accrediting Council for Independent Colleges and Schools (ACICS). ACICS had accredited some high-profile for-profit institutions that subsequently closed, leaving thousands of students to seek debt relief through the Department of Education, and in 2016, the department accepted NACIQI's recommendation to cease recognizing ACICS (McKenzie, 2021; Miller & Flores, 2018). This move was in keeping with other actions taken by the Obama administration, which was in office at the time, to increase oversight and regulation of for-profit higher education (Natow, 2017). When President Trump's political leadership came into the department, the agency took steps to deregulate for-profit and other career-focused higher education (e.g., Fain, 2017; Harris & Kelderman, 2017; Kreighbaum, 2017b, 2017d, 2019c). In 2018, following a court ruling that the department "failed to consider key evidence before terminating recognition of ACICS," Trump's secretary of education, Betsy DeVos, determined that the department would recognize ACICS once again (McKenzie, 2021, ¶ 6). Then in 2021, during the first week of Joe Biden's presidency, Department of Education career staffers recommended that the decision made during the DeVos era be reconsidered (Camera, 2021). Shortly thereafter, NACIQI recommended that the department cease its recognition of ACICS (Basken, 2021).

With accreditation so closely linked to the receipt of federal student aid, it is no surprise that the politics of accreditation tends to mirror the politics of federal higher education more broadly, including the Department of Education's policies on accountability and for-profit higher education. Such politics may lead observers to become skeptical about accreditors and what it means for a college to be accredited. An interviewee who worked for a higher education association described accreditors' role as "gatekeepers to federal money even though they're not part of the federal government." This interviewee went on to say that this power raises questions about "the role of those accreditors, and how they even can be allowed to be accreditors and open that gate." With highly visible and partisan swings in accreditor recognition (as was the case with ACICS), stakeholders may wonder whether institutional accreditation and accreditor recognition—which, in theory, should be based on educational quality—is unduly influenced by politics and ideology.

NEWS MEDIA

The news media plays an important role in the federal higher education policy space. News organizations report on matters such as new policies, the process of developing policies, policymakers' actions and statements, and the actions and statements of interest groups. Media outlets that regularly cover federal higher education policy issues include the *Chronicle of Higher Education*, the *Hechinger Report*, *Higher Ed Dive*, *Inside Higher Education*, and major daily newspapers such as the *New York Times*, *Washington Post*, and *Wall Street Journal*.

Media attention can elevate an issue on policymakers' agenda and influence public opinion. Policymakers can also influence the media, causing the media to broadcast the messages policymakers want the public to know or believe (Barnes et al., 2008; Tan & Weaver, 2007). Moreover, as mentioned in the section above regarding interest groups, policy advocates can write opinion pieces, have conversations with journalists, and purchase advertisements in media for the purpose of influencing public opinion and advocating for certain policies (Blair, 1999; Cook, 1998; Jones & Brown, 2020; Natow, 2017, 2020). Indeed, the use of media to carry advocacy ads was a key component of the Student Aid Alliance's ultimately successful strategy to lobby Congress not to cut student financial aid funding in the 1990s (Blair, 1999; Cook, 1998).

Sometimes media attention can influence members of Congress to investigate a policy problem. An example of this occurred from investigative reporting by National Public Radio (NPR) about Teacher Education Assistance for College and Higher Education (TEACH) Grants. TEACH Grants provide financial assistance for college students who commit to pursuing a career in teaching in both "a high-need field" (such as science, math, or reading) and "a high-need school" (schools where more than 30% of students meet the criteria for living in poverty under the Elementary and Secondary Education Act), for a minimum of 4 years within an 8-year timeframe (Barkowski et al., 2018, p. 1). If a recipient of a TEACH Grant does not meet these mandates "or does not annually certify toward completing their service obligation, the grant converts to an unsubsidized loan" (p. 1). In 2018, NPR published a series of reports revealing that one-third of TEACH Grant recipients' grants had been converted into loans due to minor errors in paperwork, such as missing dates or signatures that were later corrected, or when the federal contractor managing TEACH Grants claimed it did not receive a teacher's paperwork on time (Turner & Arnold, 2018a; Turner et al., 2018). Following these reports, the Department of Education launched an investigation of the TEACH Grant program, and 19 members of the Senate wrote to the department asking it to rectify the grant program's problems, citing the NPR report in their letter (Turner & Arnold, 2018b). One of my respondents, a representative of a D.C.-based higher education association, told me that the NPR reports were instrumental in drawing policymakers' attention to the TEACH Grant problems. This interviewee said:

> NPR started doing a lot of investigations and articles and deep dives into different people who had been affected, what was happening, and that their investigations detailed some internal studies that the Department of Education had done.... And the results were pretty startling.... I think given the sympathetic audience, or group of people who were really in a bad position, being these teachers who are trying to work in schools that typically don't pay as much, on average, as higher income schools, it drove a lot of congressional attention to the issue.

Situations like this, where a policy problem gains media attention, can prompt policymakers to take action.

OTHER NONFEDERAL ACTORS

There are numerous other nonfederal actors who influence higher education policy in a variety of ways. Such nonfederal actors include think tanks, foundations, higher education interstate compacts, and other nonprofit organizations that have emerged to address or advocate for a policy issue. Some nongovernmental organizations serve as intermediaries between the federal government and some other actor or group of actors—such as higher education institutions, state governments, or research organizations—to perform a role in the policy creation or implementation process (Abrams et al., 2018; Frandsen & Johansen, 2015; Honig, 2004; Orphan et al., 2021; Wohlstetter et al., 2015). An example of this is the role that interstate higher education compacts have played to assist states and institutions to implement and comply with federal regulations. Higher education compacts are formal collaborations between states to coordinate and cooperate on higher education matters, such as finding ways to expand college access and improve student success. There are currently four regional higher education compacts that coordinate states in particular geographic areas in the United States: The Western Interstate Commission for Higher Education, the Southern Regional Education Board, the New England Board of Higher Education, and the Midwestern Higher Education Compact (Longanecker & Hill, 2014; NC-SARA, n.d.). Once the Department of Education issued the state authorization regulations described above, the four regional compacts worked with other higher education nonprofit organizations (including SHEEO and APLU) to develop the State Authorization Reciprocity Agreement, which enables member institutions in participating states to have their state's authorization accepted by other participating states (Longanecker & Hill, 2014; Natow, 2021d; Natow et al., 2021).

Some nongovernmental organizations serve as intermediaries between research and policy by bringing research to the attention of policymakers to use in evidence-based policymaking (Natow, 2020). A former Department of Education official interviewed for my study of research use in higher education rulemaking explained that "intermediaries help to draw the lines, to make the connections" between research and policy, which is useful for policymakers. Think tanks are one kind of organization that produce research that may be of interest to policymakers. These organizations may be nonpartisan or may promote policies and viewpoints that align with a particular political party or ideology. Research has shown that think tanks influence policymakers, as think tanks' work has been cited in congressional debates and federal regulations, including regulations of higher education (Lerner, 2018; Natow, 2020). Examples of think tanks and other policy-focused research centers include the American Enterprise Institute, the Brookings Institution, the Center for American Progress, the Center on Budget and Policy Priorities, the Century Foundation, the Fordham Institute, the Hoover Institute, the Institute for Higher Education Policy, the Manhattan Institute, Mathematica Policy Research Institute, New America, RAND Corporation, and the Urban Institute, among others (McDonald, 2014; McLean & Robin, 2017; Ness & Gándara, 2014).

Think tanks may promote their own or others' research to policymakers in an effort to prompt policy change (Natow, 2020; Ness & Gándara, 2014). Think tank representatives also influence policy discussions by testifying before congressional committees (e.g., American Enterprise Institute, n.d.), providing comments during agency rulemaking (e.g., McCann, 2018), and gaining media attention for their work (McDonald, 2014). According to an interviewee who worked for a higher education association, think tanks also work collaboratively with associations, business leaders, and others to develop federal policy proposals. Another interviewee indicated that think tanks sometimes work directly with federal policymakers to develop legislative text.

Foundations—nonprofit organizations that provide funding to support research, education, and other charitable purposes (Council on Foundations, n.d.)—also play a role in federal higher education policy. One important way foundations do so is through advocacy. Foundations can advocate directly for their favored positions and can also fund research and other advocacy bodies (Haddad & Reckhow, 2018; Hall, 2011). Representatives of foundations have also consulted with the federal government on policy matters identified as important to the foundation. For example, Lumina Foundation consulted with the Department of Education regarding college completion policies, which helped to inform the Obama administration's policy goals in this area (Haddad & Reckhow, 2018). Foundations also advocate for their policy priorities in similar ways as associations and other interest groups, such as by serving on federal commissions (Eaton, 2010), or testifying before congressional committees about issues affecting higher education (e.g., Gates, 2007).

One of my interviewees who had worked in the White House listed foundations among the groups that schedule meetings to discuss policy with White House staff. Another respondent, who had worked for a foundation, said that foundations fund projects that examine how a preferred policy may work in practice, and if the results are encouraging, foundation representatives would "share with senators and [the] Department of Ed and others, . . . Here's what we're learning. Here's what we're doing. If a federal law allowed this, there could be more of that."

Members of the business community also participate in the federal higher education policy arena. Groups of leaders in business and industry have formed coalitions and joined task forces to develop recommendations for federal policy in higher education, workforce development, and related areas. For example, during the early months of the Biden administration, a group of business, industry, labor, and community college leaders collaborated to make recommendations to federal lawmakers about workforce development policies (Selko, 2021). Members of the business community have also served on federal task forces and commissions, such as former Secretary of Education Margaret Spellings' Commission on the Future of Higher Education in 2005–2006 (Eaton, 2010), and a "Task Force on Apprenticeship Expansion" coordinated by the Departments of Labor, Education, and Commerce in 2017–2018 (McCarthy et al., 2018). Moreover, some of the Department of Education's negotiated rulemaking committees have included seats for negotiators representing "business and industry" (Program Integrity, 2018, p. 40169; Program Integrity & Improvement, 2016, p. 48601). The business community has also weighed in on federal regulations during the notice-and-comment phase of the rulemaking process. An example of this was when the U.S. Chamber of Commerce sent comments to the Department of Education criticizing the Obama administration's impending Gainful Employment Rule, which would more closely scrutinize and regulate for-profit and other career-focused higher education institutions (U.S. Chamber of Commerce, 2014). As mentioned above, business leaders also sometimes collaborate with think tanks, higher education associations, and others on developing policy proposals.

Higher education students also participate in federal policymaking processes and lobbying. Sometimes students participate in lobby day events (described above) with their institutions (Szlezinger, 2021). Some students are involved in advocacy both on their campuses and with national organizations that lobby the federal government. For example, the student-run newspaper of the University of California, Los Angeles reported about a student who was active both in that campus's student-veteran organization as well as the national Student Veterans Association, which lobbies the federal government for policies that benefit student veterans (Erlandson, 2008). Students also regularly participate in the Department of Education's rulemaking process; the Higher Education Act says the department must consult affected stakeholders, including students, when developing regulations of student financial aid programs (Natow, 2015, 2017). Thus, students have been involved in negotiated rulemaking and the regional meetings that precede those negotiations, often represented by student advocacy groups.

Finally, members of the general public participate in higher education policy processes by making their perspectives known to federal policymakers. The public may do this by sending correspondence or making phone calls to their congressional representatives, participating in protests or demonstrations, writing opinion pieces or letters to the editor that may be published by news outlets, or discussing policy matters on social media or other websites. There is space for the general public to participate in the Department of Education's rulemaking process as well: Members of the public may speak at regional meetings that precede negotiated rulemaking or at the close of a negotiated rulemaking session, and any interested party may send written comments to the department about proposed regulations (Natow, 2017). Members of the public may also reach out to White House offices to schedule meetings, such as when OMB staff meets with interested parties during periods of proposed and final regulatory review (Sunstein, 2013). However, individual members of the public are unlikely to be very influential when advocating for policy change on their own. A respondent who had worked in the White House told me that it can be "much harder" for members of the public to schedule meetings with White House staff without having "had a history of working with the White House or have connections" in some other way. Some respondents opined that policy actors would be better off joining forces with an association or otherwise collaborating with other, similarly interested parties to influence policy change for higher education. As summarized by an interviewee who represented state government officers, "a key strategy" of organized higher education interest groups is that "they band together, and they have a fair amount of lobbying clout." Members of the public, therefore, may find their strength in policymaking influence to be enhanced by joining and participating in interest groups that promote their favored policies for higher education.

SUMMARY AND CONCLUSION

Nonfederal actors of many kinds have been influential in federal higher education policy development and implementation. This is particularly true for organized interest groups, which advocate for their preferred policies using a variety of strategies in all branches of the federal government. The higher education associations known as the Big Six who, led by ACE, represent an array of institutional types, tend to be the most powerful in the higher education policy arena (Cook, 1998; Parsons, 1997). A variety of other interest groups representing all kinds of stakeholders—from students to institutions to state government officials and others—likewise play a role in influencing federal higher education policy.

Beyond interest groups, other nonfederal actors who are active in the higher education policy space include state and local governments, accreditors, the news media, interstate higher education compacts, think tanks, foundations, students, and the business community. Members of the public may also participate in federal higher education policy processes, but they can be more effective by joining forces with other policy actors, such as organized interest groups. States and local governments have also been involved in the development and implementation of federal higher education policy. However, the federal government's actions with regard to higher education can place restraints on what the states are able to do.

Additionally, some nonfederal actors serve as intermediaries between the government and other entities. This includes, for example, research groups and think tanks who provide federal policymakers with research evidence on which they may base policy (Natow, 2020). As this chapter has illustrated, just as the federal government has become expansive and influential over higher education, many nonfederal actors also have a large and important role to play with regard to federal higher education policy.

CHAPTER 8

Reexamining the Federal Role in Higher Education

This book has presented a detailed depiction of the federal government's role in higher education, explaining how the federal government has derived power to regulate higher education and how that role has evolved and expanded over time. Federal policy has addressed numerous matters of importance to postsecondary education in the United States, such as providing student financial aid to make college more affordable, enforcing civil rights laws to prohibit unlawful discrimination and deprivation of rights, protecting intellectual property, providing consumer protection, funding research and development, and many other examples. Although education is not mentioned in the U.S. Constitution and is therefore often assumed to be primarily the responsibility of the states, a federal role in higher education has existed since the country's earliest days. As explained in the previous chapters, the federal government has enlisted higher education as a partner in furthering national goals, from expanding U.S. territories, to assisting with national defense, to boosting the economy during times of recession or depression. The federal government has also employed higher education as a means for promoting racial and economic equity, required colleges and universities to recognize civil and educational rights, and scrutinized the ways higher education makes use of students' and taxpayers' money. All branches of government and a large number of federal agencies have exerted some power in the higher education policy arena, not infrequently as a result of the actions (or inactions) of interest groups, state governments, and other nonfederal actors.

This chapter returns to the guiding questions presented in the book's Introduction to summarize how the preceding chapters have addressed those questions. This includes consideration of the third guiding question by examining higher education policy issues that this study's respondents identified as being important areas for federal attention in the present and foreseeable future. The chapter concludes by examining how the findings presented in this book have provided support for the various perspectives of government growth and federal expansion discussed in the Introduction.

RETURNING TO THE GUIDING QUESTIONS

Guiding Question 1

This book's Introduction set forth guiding questions about the federal government's role in higher education. The first question asked: *How have the constitutional, political, and administrative structures of the U.S. government shaped the nature of the federal government's role in higher education policymaking?* As described in the preceding chapters, constitutional, political, and administrative structures have helped to determine the policy instruments that federal actors in all branches of government have used to create higher education policy and to exert control over colleges and universities. And as the case studies presented in Chapters 3 through 6 have shown, policy processes in all branches of the federal government can profoundly affect higher education students, institutions, and other stakeholders.

Congress. Constitutionally, Congress has quite effectively used its conditional spending power—that is, its power to attach mandates and prohibitions to the receipt of federal funds—to enact its higher education policy agenda. The conditional spending power comes from Article I, Section 8, of the Constitution, which provides Congress with the power (among other things) to spend federal monies and attach mandates and other conditions to the receipt of those funds (Bagenstos, 2014; Haney, 2013). Statutes such as the Clery Act, FERPA, Title VI of the Civil Rights Act, Title IX of the Education Amendments of 1972, and others have made use of this power to get colleges and universities who receive federal funds to comply with the statutes' provisions. Federal funding—particularly in the form of student financial aid, but also federal research support and other funding—has become increasingly important for higher education institutions in an era of decreased state appropriations and increased costs of doing business. Institutions comply with conditional spending requirements because they cannot afford to lose federal funding. Congress has also compelled compliance by state governments through conditional spending, such as in maintenance-of-effort provisions that require states to maintain a certain level of appropriations for higher education in order to receive federal funds (Alexander et al., 2010; Harnisch, 2012). Other powers Congress has used to create higher education policy include the powers to enforce civil rights, to regulate intellectual property, and to collect taxes.

Politics has influenced congressional actions on higher education in a variety of ways. The political party that controls a chamber of Congress has a great deal of power to determine which bills will be considered in committee or called to the floor for a vote (Oleszek et al., 2019). The majority party can also pass legislation like reconciliation bills with a simple majority vote, as Congress did during President Barack Obama's first term with the Student

Aid and Fiscal Responsibility Act (SAFRA), which eliminated private lenders from the federal student loan program (American Council on Education, 2010; Dortch et al., 2010; Herszenhorn & Pear, 2010). Moreover, a simple majority is all that is needed in the Senate to approve or disapprove a president's nominee for executive or judicial posts, meaning that top-ranking federal personnel decisions can be made along party lines. Indeed, Betsy DeVos was elevated to her position as President Donald Trump's secretary of education following a nearly party-line tie vote on her nomination, with the vote of Vice President Mike Pence breaking the tie (Darville, 2017).

When Congress is controlled by a different party than the president's, Congress is more likely to act as a check on the president's policy agenda (Levinson & Pildes, 2006; Parker & Dull, 2009). For example, SAFRA, which had been a first-term priority of President Obama's, was enacted along party lines by congressional Democrats via a filibuster-proof reconciliation bill (American Council on Education, 2010; Dortch et al., 2010; Herszenhorn & Pear, 2010). But during Obama's second term, when Republicans controlled Congress, his tuition-free community college plan—another presidential priority—did not gain any traction (Harris, 2018). As these examples illustrate, in politically polarized environments, different branches of government are more likely to serve as checks and balances when controlled by different political parties (Harbridge, 2015; Levinson & Pildes, 2006; Parker & Dull, 2009).

The White House. The president may employ executive powers to influence higher education policy. Politically polarized environments have led to more congressional gridlock and more unilateral executive action in recent times (Burum, 2008; Carmines & Fowler, 2017). Through the power to issue executive orders, the president can create mandates for federal agencies that may also apply to federal contractors and other organizations that receive federal funds. Since the presidency of Franklin Delano Roosevelt, executive orders have required federal contractors to comply with nondiscrimination policies (Cashin, 2005; U.S. Department of Labor, n.d.-b; Vetter, 1974). Presidents can also revoke a previous president's executive order if it does not align with the current president's policy agenda. For example, President Joe Biden revoked an executive order issued by his predecessor that prohibited certain kinds of diversity training at higher education institutions and other organizations that received federal contracts (Guynn, 2021).

Presidents may also draw attention to policy matters or create White House initiatives involving higher education by issuing presidential proclamations (e.g., Executive Order No. 13779, 2017). Additionally, the president holds political power through the "bully pulpit," which refers to the president's ability to draw widespread attention to policy matters and attempt to persuade policymakers and the public in favor of the president's policy agenda (Goodwin, 2013; Greenberg, 2011; Shaw, 2017). Presidents may use the State of the Union address as an opportunity to promote their higher education policy agenda, as President Obama did when he argued in favor of tuition-free community college in his 2015 address (Field, 2015; Stratford, 2015b).

Because many political leaders in executive branch agencies are appointed by the president and generally selected because they are expected to favor the president's policy positions, federal agency actions, such as new regulations or guidance, tend to reflect the influence and policy priorities of the president (Chen, 2017; Krent, 2005). For example, the U.S. Department of Education's regulations of for-profit higher education and Title IX changed substantially from Democratic President Obama's administration to Republican President Trump's administration, and then from Trump to Democratic President Biden's administration (Kreighbaum 2018a, 2018b; Natow, 2017, 2020). Similarly, as immigration ideology differed from the Obama to Trump to Biden administrations, so did the Department of Homeland Security's DACA program, which provided deportation protection and work authorization for some undocumented youth who arrived in the United States as children. DACA began during Obama's presidency. The Trump administration attempted to repeal the policy and then, when the Supreme Court said the repeal was invalid, declined to enforce it until the tail end of Trump's term (Chen, 2017, 2020; Redden, 2021). Then on Biden's first day in office, he issued an executive order "preserving and fortifying" the program (Redden, 2021, ¶ 2).

Apart from the president, other White House offices influence higher education policy as well. The Office of Management and Budget, which is located in the Executive Office of the President and generally seeks to promote the president's policy priorities (Brass, 2006), advises the president on budgetary matters (including the Department of Education's budget and other budgets relating to higher education), assists with the development of the State of the Union address, and reviews significant regulations before they become final (Bose, 2020; Natow, 2017; Pasachoff, 2020; Potter, 2020; Washington & Hitter, 2020). Other White House offices that have involvement with higher education include the Council of Economic Advisers, the National Economic Council, the Office of Science and Technology Policy, and the Office of the Vice President. The spouses of the president and vice president have also influenced higher education matters, such as when First Lady Michelle Obama promoted postsecondary training through her "Reach Higher" initiative (Meyers & Goman, 2017, p. 33), and when then-Second Lady Dr. Jill Biden co-hosted (with President Obama) a White House Summit on Community Colleges (Dr. Jill Biden, n.d.).

Administrative Agencies. Like Congress, administrative agencies have made substantial use of conditional spending to control higher education. For example, agencies providing research funding require grantees to comply with agency rules (e.g., National Institutes of Health, 2021). Moreover, the U.S.

Department of Education's regulations govern eligibility for institutions to participate in federal student financial aid programs. Because nearly 80% of 2-year college students and more than 80% of 4-year college students receive some form of federal student aid (U.S. Department of Education, 2019b, 2020b, 2021b), remaining eligible to participate in these programs provides a strong incentive for institutions to comply with Department of Education regulations. Agencies also issue sub-regulatory guidance, which refers to statements of interpretation of the law or instructions for complying with regulations (Chen, 2020; Natow, 2017). As sub-regulatory guidance is technically nonbinding, agencies need not follow complicated rulemaking processes to release it, thereby making guidance somewhat easy for agencies to issue. However, stakeholders, such as college student affairs administrators trying to determine how to implement Title IX on their campuses, generally treat guidance as binding, because it has been issued by the same agency that created and that enforces the regulations (Chen, 2020; Gersen, 2007; Natow, 2017; Parrillo, 2019). Agencies may also affect higher education by conducting investigations (for example, of institutional use of federal student aid funds) and adjudications (for example, of disputes about institutional eligibility to participate in Title IV student aid programs), making decisions about funding (for example, whether to fund particular research projects), and advising the president and Congress on matters involving higher education (Anderson, 2015; Moe, 2000; Natow, 2017; Relyea & Tatelman, 2007).

Federal Courts. The federal courts—and most considerably the Supreme Court—have also shaped higher education policy. Often, courts do this by defining the scope of civil rights and liberties that the government must respect. In the mid-20th century, federal courts recognized that racially segregated educational institutions were fundamentally unequal and violated the Fourteenth Amendment's Equal Protection Clause (*Brown v. Board of Education*, 1954; Donahoo, 2006; *Sweatt v. Painter*, 1950). The Supreme Court has repeatedly upheld the constitutionality of race-conscious postsecondary admissions policies for the purpose of maintaining a diverse student body, provided the policy is part of a holistic evaluation (*Fisher v. University of Texas*, 2016; *Grutter v. Bollinger*, 2003; *Regents of the University of California v. Bakke*, 1978). Courts have also defined First Amendment protections for free speech on college campuses, outlined necessary elements for sufficient due process in public institutions' student and employee discipline proceedings, and determined whether public colleges' actions regarding religious practice violates the Constitution's Establishment Clause (Kaplin et al., 2020). Federal courts have also struck down policies made by other branches of government when those branches have not complied with appropriate procedures for creating the policies. For example, during the Trump administration, the Supreme Court ruled that the Department of Homeland

Security's attempt to rescind DACA was improper because the agency did not follow required procedures (Redden, 2020; Totenberg, 2020). As these examples show, the reach of the federal courts can be considerable, even when only determining the soundness of procedural processes.

Many consider the courts to be apolitical, or at least believe that an apolitical judiciary is important to perform its role in government with legitimacy and respect (Barnes, 2019; Lampe, 2020; Pasachoff, 2020). But the federal courts are, in fact, political. Federal judges and Supreme Court justices are appointed and approved by political actors (the president and senators) who nominate and confirm individuals they expect will support certain policy positions. In recent decades, increased polarization in the United States combined with the political nature of the courts has become more obvious, with increased 5-to-4 Supreme Court decisions along ideological lines, and judicial confirmation hearings that have been argumentative and partisan (Johnson, 2011; Kuhn, 2012; Siddiqui, 2018).

Nonfederal Actors. There are numerous nonfederal actors that influence federal higher education policy in a variety of ways. Interest groups of various kinds advocate in all branches of government for policies that favor their stakeholders. Advocacy tactics include meeting with members of Congress or White House staff, participating in rulemaking proceedings in federal agencies, and filing amicus briefs in federal courts, among other actions (American Association of University Professors, n.d.; Cook, 1998; Natow, 2017; Parsons, 1997; Sunstein, 2013). Interest groups also attempt to sway public opinion through communications and outreach efforts. Higher education interest groups, particularly the "Big Six" D.C.-based associations, have had success influencing federal policy, as evidenced by the hundreds of billions of dollars per year of federal funding that goes toward higher education (Marcus, 2014). State and local governments also influence, and are influenced by, federal policy. Sometimes subnational governments serve as implementers of federal policies and programs. This occurred when state governments changed their own policies and procedures to accommodate institutions following the U.S. Department of Education's issuance of state authorization regulations, which required institutions to have authorization in all states where they enrolled students in distance learning programs (Natow et al., 2021). Also, local governments have worked in partnership with states to implement agricultural education through the federal Cooperative Extension Service (Croft, 2019). The news media has also influenced the federal higher education policy community, such as when National Public Radio's investigation of TEACH Grants being converted into loans led to attention from senators and a federal investigation of the situation (Turner & Arnold, 2018b). Other nonfederal actors that have been involved and influential in the federal higher education policy space include accreditors, think tanks, foundations, the business community, students, and members of the general public.

Guiding Question 2

The second guiding question asked: *How has the federal government's regulation and funding of higher education evolved over time?* Chapter 2, which outlined the history of the federal government's role in higher education, demonstrated that this role has not only expanded over time, but has also changed in terms of the nature of federal policies and types of funding for higher education, depending on the national needs prevalent at a given moment in history.

Although the drafters of the Constitution did not write about education anywhere in the document (and in fact were skeptical of a strong national government with powers to intervene local matters), education played a prominent role in some of the country's earliest federal policies. The Northwest Ordinance, which was enacted two years before the Constitution was ratified, cited the importance of education and provided land grants for the development of schools and colleges (Carleton, 2002; Center on Education Policy, 1999; Cervantes et al., 2005; Putansu, 2020; Riley, 1997; Thelin, 2011). Early federal policies used higher education as one of many mechanisms to achieve westward expansion and to promote the study of agriculture and other fields deemed to be high-need. The expansion of higher education across the United States continued through the end of the 19th century, helped along by federal policies that protected private institutions from undue state interference (*Trustees of Dartmouth College v. Woodward*, 1819), and additional land-grant legislation, the most prominent of which were the Morrill Acts of 1862 and 1890 (Gavazzi & Gee, 2018; Martin & Hipp, 2016; Stith & Blumenthal, 2019; Thelin, 2011; Trow, 1988; Wheatle, 2019). At the same time, as explained in Chapter 2, the federal government's engagement with higher education contributed to land expropriation of Native Americans and racial segregation in higher education through the land-grant policies (Lee & Ahtone, 2020; Wheatle, 2019).

Throughout the 20th century, the federal role in higher education evolved as the government's needs and priorities shifted and as social movements and advocates drew attention to the potential for higher education to address social inequities. Higher education was enlisted in federal programs to help boost the economy during the Great Depression (Cervantes et al., 2005; Fass, 1982; Loss, 2012; Walker & Brechin, 2010). Also in the 20th century, higher education partnered with the federal government to provide research and education that was seen as useful in various war efforts and in enhancing national defense during World War II and the Cold War.

The federal government provided funding for research and development in areas important to national defense, financial aid for students to study scientific and other subjects deemed in need of additional research, and higher education benefits for veterans and active-duty military through several GI Bills (Cervantes et al., 2005; Labaree, 2016; Loss, 2013; Parsons, 1997; Strach, 2009; Thelin, 2011). During and after the civil rights movement, federal higher education policy aimed to protect civil rights by desegregating educational institutions, prohibiting various kinds of discrimination, and providing financial assistance to help students pay for college (Cervantes et al., 2005; Johnson, 2014; Kantor & Lowe, 1995; Loss, 2012; Strach, 2009).

The end of the Cold War in the late 20th century coincided with college prices increasing substantially and the need for a college degree becoming more necessary for obtaining a well-paying job (Abel & Dietz, 2014; Labaree, 2016). The federal government's relationship with higher education shifted once again. Beginning in the 1970s and continuing through the present, the federal government sought accountability from higher education to demonstrate that students were receiving a worthwhile return on their increasingly larger investments, and that taxpayers—in the emerging antitax political climate—did not view government investment in higher education as a waste of money (Labaree, 2016; Lopez, 2015). Federal policies that emerged in this era included additional requirements for reporting institutional outcomes, tighter regulations of for-profit higher education, and efforts to strengthen the states' role in upholding the quality of postsecondary programs (Flores, 2018; Harnisch et al., 2016; Kelchen, 2018; McCann & Laitinen, 2019; Natow, 2017; Tandberg et al., 2019).

In sum, the federal government throughout history has used higher education to further its own needs and priorities. As the government's policy goals changed over time, so did federal policy and support for higher education. Additionally, higher education has repeatedly played a role in the country's painful history of colonialism, land expropriation, racial segregation, and discrimination (Lee & Ahtone, 2020; Martin & Hipp, 2016; Nash, 2019; Wheatle, 2019). It is also important to recognize that higher education has helped many students through the years to attain upward social mobility and other financial and nonfinancial benefits, such as better health outcomes, more job satisfaction, and greater civic awareness (e.g., Chan, 2016; Ma et al., 2019; Mayhew et al., 2016). The federal government has supported higher education when the sector was deemed important to achieve national policy objectives. To the extent that having a well-informed populace and providing broad access to education and opportunity for social mobility are part of the federal government's goals, federal support for higher education should continue—and even increase—because the sector has a fundamental role to play in achieving those objectives.

Guiding Question 3

The third guiding question asked: *What do higher education policy actors and observers perceive to be the most important federal higher education policy issues, both currently and in the near future?* Though federal higher education policy can encompass a large number of issues and address numerous policy problems, this study's respondents consistently identified a few areas on which federal policy attention is likely to focus in the foreseeable future.

Affordability. When asked about what they expected to be the top federal higher education policy issues now and in the near future, the most common response by far among this study's respondents was college affordability. This is unsurprising, given that the federal role in higher education is largely tied to funding (and, more specifically, to research and development as well as student financial aid), and that the price of college has increased considerably in recent decades (The College Board, 2020). But respondents' perceptions about how the issue of affordability should be handled by the federal government, and about other policy problems that have arisen as a result of college becoming less affordable, indicate that addressing the affordability issue will not be a simple matter. In the words of one interviewee, who was a higher education policy analyst at a nonprofit organization, if affordability issues are not addressed through federal policy,

> It's going to be really challenging to keep the system going. It's just going to continue to be having low- and middle-income families and students go increasingly into debt at even higher levels than they are now. And then how will these families be able to afford college?

It is also important for policymakers to recognize that the total cost of college attendance must be considered in setting financial aid policies. A former White House staffer interviewed for this study explained that some "college costs . . . aren't necessarily related to tuition and fees." Specifically, this respondent observed that the "increasing cost [of attendance] comes from living expenses or housing," and therefore federal policymakers should become "more aware of students' needs in that area," and consider enacting policies that will help college students pay for the cost of food, clothing, and other expenses.

According to some policy actors, the affordability issue would best be addressed by making college tuition-free. A representative of a Big Six association said that tuition-free college plans can be easy for policymakers to embrace at first, as "free college is as simple a message as one can get." However, the details of such policies can be complicated because perceptions about "what free college means" vary widely. This interviewee said that some questions to consider when designing a free-college policy are "whether it's at the community college level" exclusively, or whether it's "only for Americans who make up to a certain amount of money." Indeed, a variety of conceptualizations of tuition-free college have emerged at both the state and federal levels in the early 21st century. Some plans provide free community college only, and others extend tuition waivers to 4-year institutions as well (Perna & Leigh, 2018). There are also differences in policy details in terms of what students must do to obtain free tuition (e.g., remain in-state for a certain period of time following graduation, or enroll for a minimum number of credits while in college), and whether the tuition-free scholarship covers expenses in addition to tuition and fees (Association of Community College Trustees, n.d.-b; Perna & Leigh, 2018; Pierce & Siraco, 2018).

Another important component of college affordability is student loan debt, which was a topic also identified by many respondents as a critical federal higher education policy matter in the present and the near future. As of 2020, outstanding student loan debt totaled approximately $1.5 trillion (Federal Student Aid, n.d.; Looney et al., 2020). Apart from mortgages, student loans comprise the largest type of household debt. To help relieve the student debt burden for borrowers, some policymakers and advocates have called on the federal government to forgive at least some of the student loan debt for which the Department of Education is the direct lender (Looney et al., 2020). Like tuition-free college policies, student loan cancellation can take on different forms. For example, Department of Education regulations provide student loan forgiveness for debtors whose institutions were found to have "engaged in certain misconduct" (U.S. Department of Education, 2021a, ¶ 3). Other kinds of loan management policies include income-based loan repayment and public service loan forgiveness plans, although such policies have previously encountered problems in terms of their complexity and sometimes ineffective implementation (Looney et al., 2020; Turner & Arnold, 2018a, 2018b; Turner et al., 2018).

Accountability. Several respondents also identified accountability for higher education as an issue that is likely to remain a major policy concern for the federal government into the foreseeable future. As a federal education policy consultant explained:

> The issue of higher education quality and the degree to which programs are actually yielding outcomes that students need, and particularly related to the student experience, is something that's getting more and more play—the issues of the low completion [rates] of higher education degrees.

Accountability for higher education at the federal level has generally taken the form of increased regulation of for-profit and other career-focused postsecondary programs, as well as requiring state authorization for colleges and universities receiving federal funds through the Higher Education Act's financial aid programs (Kelchen, 2018; McCann & Laitinen, 2019; Natow, 2017; Tandberg et al., 2019). One of my respondents believed that the details of federal accountability polices are likely to be contested going forward. This interviewee said:

> Democrats think we should have significant accountability measures for for-profits but leave [non-profit] higher ed institutions alone. And I would say that there is not a lot of agreement on what is accountability for higher ed. Is cohort default rate the right mechanism? And so I think that that will continue to be a conversation.

The same respondent pointed out that "tied to" issues of accountability are the pervasive problems of "affordability, and what we do about the $1.5 trillion in debt that we have in the United States around higher education."

Along similar lines, a different respondent told me that the general public's diminishing respect and trust for higher education is tied to both affordability concerns and the push for higher education accountability. This interviewee said:

> Affordability within higher education is a major conversation piece. Also within that context though, I think public opinion on higher education is diminishing because of the incessant conversations around student loans and the $1.5 trillion . . . in student loan debt. All have a corrosive effect on people's perspective, perceptions of higher education.

In other words, when public and policymakers' trust in higher education decreases in the face of escalating prices and concerns about quality, it is easy to see how accountability policies that seek to ensure students and taxpayers are getting their money's worth are likely to emerge.

Equity. Another important policy issue for the federal government is equity in higher education access, experiences, and outcomes. In a country as diverse as the United States, and with its history of colonialism, racism, and other forms of oppression and discrimination, there is a need for federal policy that redresses past wrongs, enforces civil rights, and works to ensure an equitable society (Perry & Hamilton, 2021). An important component of this is working to attain equity in higher education. Several of my respondents identified equity as an important policy issue and discussed how federal policymakers can take steps to advance equity in higher education.

One way the federal government can promote equity is to strengthen funding for Minority-Serving Institutions (MSIs). For example, an interviewee who represented Historically Black Colleges and Universities told me that "Congress . . . can legislate, and they can appropriate, and that's very important." But this interviewee went on to emphasize that federal policymakers "can also validate the issues of importance to their members, to their stakeholders, their constituents." As explained in Chapters 3 and 4, members of Congress and the president have a bully pulpit from which they can draw attention to an issue and demonstrate their support. The same respondent argued that policymakers can take steps to promote equity in higher education by using their high-profile platform to show support for MSIs and students from historically underserved communities.

Some respondents observed that higher education student bodies are becoming increasingly diverse, and federal funding and regulations can help institutions to transform in ways that would better serve a more diverse student population. Federal actions that could enhance equity in higher education include immigration reform, enforcing federal civil rights and nondiscrimination policies, recognizing gender identity and sexual orientation as protected groups under Title IX, and providing additional funding for student financial aid, support services, and diversity, equity, and inclusion programming. Federal funding and incentives can help institutions meet the needs of underserved student populations. One interviewee, an advocate for student veterans, said the following about serving nontraditional students:

> When you're seeing a larger adult population start going back to school . . . how are we changing the way in which we do higher education to meet the needs of that population that we've kind of failed to fully meet, since they've shifted from your traditional undergraduate student to either working adults that have kids, [and] all of these different things? How are institutions of higher learning meeting those needs and demands? What does childcare look like? How are we addressing food insecurity for families and not just individuals? Those are the things, I think, that you'll also see coming up.

As the previous quote illustrates, just as issues of student loan debt and accountability are related to college affordability, so are issues of educational equity. A representative of a higher education association explained that issues of equity and college affordability are related, in that resolving issues of affordability would make higher education more broadly accessible, which can increase equity in higher education enrollment. This interviewee was quick to point out that equity and affordability were not synonymous and that these policy issues "both have distinct . . . contours." The respondent believed that both equity and affordability are important issues that policy discussions in "the foreseeable future [will be] all about."

REVISITING PERSPECTIVES ON THE SIZE OF GOVERNMENT

As explained in the Introduction, theoretical perspectives from political science, public administration, and organizational theory may help to explain why the role of the federal government has become so large in the higher education space. Considering the descriptions and analyses presented throughout this book, it is apparent that no single theory fully explains the expansion of the federal role in higher education. Rather, multiple factors have contributed to it.

According to one perspective, government becomes large because the people who work in government seek to maximize their resources and maintain the relevancy and importance of their agencies (Miller & Moe, 1983; Niskanen, 1968, 1971). Chapter 5 described the myriad federal agencies that influence higher education in some way, and how those agencies have developed and implemented new policies that have provided the federal government with greater control over higher education. The agency with the most direct influence over higher education is the U.S. Department of Education, a relatively young cabinet-level department, though the federal government has had an office of education within other departments since 1867 (Riley, 1997; Robinson, 2016). The creation of the Department of Education in 1979 was not without controversy, and for decades afterward, Republican policymakers have called for the agency's elimination (Bauman & Read, 2018; Cross, 2014; Reichmann, 1996). But the department still exists at the cabinet level, and its policy development and implementation have had a powerful influence over higher education (Natow, 2017, 2020). One of the reasons the department still exists is due to the actions of President Ronald Reagan's secretary of education, Terrel Bell. Bell, who had been a proponent of a federal agency overseeing education, was appointed to lead the department by a president who was famously opposed to the agency's existence. Rather than taking steps to dismantle the Department of Education, Bell acted to strengthen the department's relevance, ultimately bringing it additional resources. This is largely because Bell's appointment of the National Commission on Excellence in Education resulted in the publication of *A Nation at Risk* in 1983, a report that underscored the importance of investing in education by instilling national anxiety around the fact that U.S. students were failing to compete academically with students in several other countries (Cross, 2014; National Commission on Excellence in Education, 1983; Parsons, 1997). More than 40 years after its inception, the Department of Education is still standing, thanks in no small part to an agency policy actor who took action to maximize the department's relevance.

Another perspective argues that the federal role is large because in times of great national need, government expands by developing new policies, agencies, and programs to address the immediate crisis, but then does not fully recede to its prior, smaller size once the crisis has ended (Bellante & Porter,

1998; Holcombe, 2005). As demonstrated in Chapter 2, the federal government frequently involves higher education in policies to address emergency situations and other instances of large national need. Higher education played a role in the New Deal, for example in work-study programs as part of the Civil Works Administration and the Works Progress Administration, to help pull the country out of the massive economic crisis that was the Great Depression (Fass, 1982; Loss, 2012; Walker & Brechin, 2010). For much of the 20th century, the federal government provided substantial funding to higher education to conduct research and development that would be useful for national defense. The Soviet Union's launch of the Sputnik satellite and other occurrences during the Cold War prompted the U.S. government to invest heavily in scientific and technological research and development, as well as higher education training programs in fields deemed important to national defense (Brint, 2019; Cervantes et al., 2005; Cross, 2014; Geiger, 1997; Kay, 2013; Labaree, 2016; Loss, 2012; Parsons, 1997). In the 1960s, President Lyndon Johnson saw the potential for education, including higher education, to serve a crucial function in diminishing poverty and promoting civil rights (Cervantes et al., 2005; Johnson, 2014; Loss, 2012). The federal government's conditional spending power—which was greatly enhanced in postsecondary education following the enactment of the Higher Education Act, one of Johnson's Great Society policies (Johnson, 2014)—proved to be a powerful means not only to enforce federal nondiscrimination policies (Kantor & Lowe, 1995), but also to prompt additional kinds of action from higher education institutions, such as reporting mandates that would later become central to federal accountability policies designed to improve the quality of higher education (Kelchen, 2018). These policy changes, preceded by crises or other urgent situations, effectively expanded the federal role in higher education. Although shifts in federal priorities and some streamlining of federal funding and programs have occurred, the federal government's role in higher education has never greatly declined after a crisis has been resolved or a policy problem has receded from public attention.

A third perspective on government size argues that interest groups and other nongovernmental organizations that play a role in policy creation and implementation keep the federal government large. According to this theory, interest groups and other nongovernmental organizations often arise due to the existence of new government programs, and also serve to maintain and even grow the size of government by putting pressure on government to provide more and additional resources (Garrett & Rhine, 2006; Lu & Xu, 2018; Mueller & Murrell, 1986). Chapter 7 described the vast number of nonfederal actors who influence federal higher education policy, including the large higher education lobby, which has had some notable successes in influencing higher education policy (Blair, 1999; Cook, 1998; Marcus, 2014). Numerous other interest groups representing a variety of stakeholders across higher education also attempt to influence the federal government, as Chapter 7 explained. Constance Ewing Cook's (1998) research on the higher education lobby documented how this policy community grew and its strategies expanded when it feared losing federal support and favorable federal programs; as a result of these interest groups' lobbying efforts, the federal programs continued and even expanded. Federal higher education programs that had been slated for elimination were maintained, and funding for research and development increased (Cook, 1998). Thus, as predicted by this perspective, interest groups in the higher education policy arena advocated for continued support from the federal government, and as a result of the groups' lobbying efforts, government programs expanded.

Like other types of organizations, government institutions and agencies behave as a living being, with instincts to survive, grow, and gather resources while avoiding its own harm and destruction (Morgan, 1997; Oliver, 2002). For example, when it was threatened with extinction, the Department of Education produced *A Nation at Risk*, which started a national conversation about the importance of quality education and justified the agency's existence (Cross, 2014). As state-level funding continued to make up an increasingly smaller share of college and university revenues, the federal government reacted by stepping in to fill the void with student financial aid and other forms of federal funding, thereby gaining itself more control over higher education and, hence, additional power and other resources. Conceptualized as "living" organizations (Oliver, 2002, p. 8), government agencies have an interest in their own survival and take steps to respond to happenings in their environments while also attempting to maximize their own comfort and longevity, as has happened throughout history in the higher education policy space.

SUMMARY AND CONCLUSION

This book has demonstrated how, despite early distrust of a strong national government and no mention of education in the Constitution, the United States government influences higher education in myriad ways. Although some policymakers have argued against this extensive involvement, the federal role has only expanded over time. As this volume has shown, policy instruments at the federal government's disposal have been used throughout history to promote different kinds of policies depending on the prevailing political, economic, and social contexts as well as the federal government's own needs. At times, the U.S. government has promoted equity in access to higher education through desegregation, affirmative action, and student financial aid policies (Loss, 2012; Kelchen, 2018; Thelin, 2011). Other times, the federal government has played a role in using higher education to further colonialism, segregation, and the reproduction of unearned privilege (Harper et al., 2009; Lee & Ahtone, 2020; Nash, 2019; Wheatle, 2019).

Political polarization has affected how higher education policy is made, with increased congressional gridlock leading to more executive branch policymaking, as has been observed in other policy arenas as well (Burum, 2008; Carmines & Fowler, 2017).

As this book has explained, constitutional, political, social, economic, and legal structures and contexts influence the federal government in the higher education policy arena. Higher education stakeholders of all kinds may use this information to develop strategies for seeking policy change that furthers their objectives. As explained earlier in this book, there exists a considerable higher education lobby, and advocacy groups of different kinds have had some success in influencing federal higher education policy. From civil rights advocates beginning in the early 20th century to higher education associations beginning in the late 20th century, interest groups have influenced federal policies following strong advocacy campaigns (Cashin, 2005; Cook, 1998).

The coming decades of the 21st century will be a critical time for redefining higher education's role in the United States. This is especially true in light of changes in the sector resulting from the global coronavirus pandemic, and changes that are still to come with emerging technological breakthroughs, growing skepticism of the value of higher education, and a decreasing number of traditional college-going-age individuals in the U.S. population (e.g., Gallup, n.d.; Grawe, 2018). In short, higher education in the United States is likely to face many challenges in the years ahead. Armed with a thorough understanding of how and why the federal government makes policy, higher education advocates can be well positioned to make a strong case for federal support and the adoption of policies that will benefit college students, faculty, staff, and other stakeholders.

Methodological Appendix

The purpose of this research was to develop a comprehensive description and analysis of the federal government's role in higher education. Data were drawn from a variety of sources identified as likely to provide information that would be useful in achieving this study's objectives. These data sources included: (1) interviews with a wide range of policy actors who have worked on federal higher education policy matters; and (2) documents reflecting federal institutions, laws, processes, politics, and policies.

INTERVIEW DATA

In-depth, semistructured interviews were conducted with a range of higher education policy actors, who provided information about their perceptions, experiences, and knowledge about the inner workings of policymaking for higher education at the federal level. Interviewees were purposefully sampled based on their current and/or previous professional positions that enabled them to serve as key informants in this research (Owen-Smith & Coast, 2017).

Two studies I conducted contributed to this interview dataset. The study that was the main source of interview data for this book (the Federal Higher Education Study) included 28 policy actors who have been active in federal higher education policy work. Many interviewees have held multiple positions relevant to federal higher education policy (e.g., a former congressional staffer who currently works at a higher education association, or a former White House advisor who had also worked as a congressional staffer and policy consultant). These interviews were conducted between January and October 2020.

The secondary set of interviews was taken in an earlier study of how research has been used in the higher education rulemaking process (Natow, 2020). Respondents for that study (the Research Use Study) were purposefully selected based on their status as participants in or observers of higher education rulemaking. A total of 34 policy actors were interviewed for that study. Interviewees for the rulemaking study included various kinds of policy actors, many of whom held multiple relevant positions within the higher education policy community. In addition to describing the rulemaking process, all respondents in the Research Use Study also described other aspects of the federal government's role in higher education that were relevant to this book. Interviews for the research use study were conducted between May and November 2018.

Across both studies, I conducted a total of 62 interviews with a total of 61 individuals (one individual was interviewed for both studies). Table A.1 displays the professional positions held by interviewees in both studies. Some interviewees held multiple positions (current and/or former) that were relevant to the federal government's role in higher education policy. Table A.1 reflects all such positions, and therefore the total number of positions shown in the table is greater than the total number of individuals interviewed.

Table A.1. Interview Participants' Professional Positions

Professional Position	Number of Interviewees in Federal Higher Education Study Who Held That Position	Number of Interviewees in Research Use Study Who Held That Position
Congressional Staff	10	1
White House Staff	4	3
Department of Education Staff	4	7
Other Federal Agency Staff	3	5
Federal Advisory Board/Commission	2	0
State-Level Government/Association Representative	4	2
Higher Education Institution/Association Representative	16	14
Financial Aid Administrator/Association Representative	1	5
Student Loan Industry/Association Representative	0	3
Accreditor/Association Representative	0	2
Student/Consumer/ Equity-in-Education Advocate/Legal Aid Representative	5	6
Think Tank Staff	3	4
Foundation Staff	2	0
Higher Education Policy Consultant/Lawyer	4	0

Interviews for both studies were audio-recorded with the consent of participants. Audio recordings were transcribed into Word documents, and transcripts were analyzed in multiple cycles. For interviews in the Federal Higher Education Study, in the first cycle of data analysis, I coded data as relevant to the following aspects of the federal government's role in higher education: (1) Congress; (2) Federal Higher Education Statutes; (3) President/White House; (4) Department of Education; (5) Other Federal Agencies; (6) Judiciary; (7) Nonfederal Actors; (8) Other/Miscellaneous. In the next cycle, I created eight separate spreadsheets for all data coded for each of the above codes, and I analyzed all excerpts in each spreadsheet together to identify themes, data patterns, and factual assertions about the federal government's role in higher education.

For interviews in the Research Use Study, in the process of coding data according to that study's research questions and coding scheme (see Natow, 2020), I separately labeled data relevant to the federal government's role in higher education. I then exported all data labeled as such into a spreadsheet and further analyzed those excerpts to identify themes, data patterns, and factual assertions about the federal government's role in higher education.

DOCUMENTARY DATA

Documentary data analyzed in this study included:

- *Law and policy documents,* including the U.S. Constitution, federal higher education statutes and bills, executive orders, presidential proclamations and memoranda, court opinions, federal regulations, agency guidance documents, information on federal websites including the White House, congressional committees and subcommittees, and federal agencies, interest group policy statements, and the websites of interest groups and other nongovernmental organizations.
- *Research reports,* including those published in academic journals, books, working papers, federal agency reports (including the Congressional Research Service and reports of federal commissions), law review articles, and nonprofit research organizations. Reports were identified via keyword searches in Internet search engines and databases of academic literature (EBSCO, Google Scholar, and Hein Online).
- *News media articles,* including reports in national and local newspapers, magazines, and news websites as well as reports in specialized higher education news, such as the *Chronicle of Higher Education*, *Higher Ed Dive*, and *Inside Higher Education*.

Documentary data were analyzed with an eye toward identifying details about each of the federal institutions, laws, processes, politics, and policies described in each of the chapters of this book. Multiple data sources were used to verify facts asserted in both interview and documentary data.

Notes

Chapter 1

1. There are also additional United States jurisdictions and territories that are not states. These include the District of Columbia, an entity known as a "federal district," which houses the physical centers of the federal government: the Capitol, the White House, and the Supreme Court (Harris, 2000). There exist a number of U.S. territories as well, including Puerto Rico, Guam, and the U.S. Virgin Islands (U.S. Citizenship & Immigration Services, n.d.). None of these nonstate jurisdictions has voting members in Congress.

2. Lieberman (1988) stated that the fruitcake analogy was applicable because U.S. federalism had become "thick, impenetrable, and too cumbersome for digestion" (p. 287). Both he and Grissom and Herrington (2012) attributed the analogy to Wildavsky.

3. For more information about these laws, see, e.g., Forseth et al. (1995), Gardner (2015), Hannah (1996, 2010), and Janosik and Gregory (2003).

4. As explained in Chapter 5, not all federal agencies are part of the executive branch. Some are legislative or judicial agencies, and some executive-branch agencies have a fair amount of independence from the president (Breger & Edles, 2015; USA.gov, 2019).

5. See information about Higher Education Act reauthorization years in Fuller (2014), and information about party control of Congress in U.S. House of Representatives (n.d.-b) and U.S. Senate (n.d.).

6. See also Cross (2014), discussing a similar phenomenon regarding the Elementary and Secondary Education Act.

7. This refers to the section of the 42nd volume of the United States Code at which this statute was codified (see 42 U.S.C. § 1981).

8. For more information about the use of such "persuasive communication" as a policy instrument, see Dougherty et al. (2016) regarding its use in the implementation of higher education performance-based funding policies at the state level.

Chapter 2

1. The federal government passed additional land-grant legislation well into the 20th century, with the University of the District of Columbia becoming a land-grant institution in 1967, and a number of Tribal Colleges and Universities as well as institutions in U.S. territories receiving land-grant status in 1994. As recently as 2014, Ohio's Central State University received land-grant status (Croft, 2019; Gavazzi & Gee, 2018).

2. The fact that 1890 Act colleges were substantially underfunded by state governments was an additional factor contributing to the growth of private HBCUs (Jones & Brown, 2020).

3. Among the notable people involved with the NYA were Lyndon Johnson and Richard Nixon, both of whom would later oversee major federal policy change for higher education as president (Cervantes et al., 2005).

4. Then-attorney Thurgood Marshall successfully argued these and other desegregation cases. Marshall was later appointed as a Justice of the Supreme Court by President Lyndon Johnson in 1967 (Administrative Office of the U.S. Courts, n.d.).

5. In 2014, President Barack Obama amended this executive order to also prohibit discrimination by federal contractors based on sexual orientation and gender identity (U.S. Department of Labor, n.d.-b).

6. The National Defense Student Loan program would be renamed the Perkins Loan program in 1986, after Representative Carl Perkins from Kentucky, who had been a champion of federal education policy programs to help underserved students (Cervantes et al., 2005). The Perkins Loan program was discontinued in 2017 (Hutchins, 2019).

7. Some Republicans still call for the elimination of the Department of Education (e.g., Bauman & Read, 2018).

8. Decades later, during the Obama and Biden administrations, the Department of Education would interpret Title IX to include gender identity and sexual orientation as protected under this law. The department's interpretation of Title IX did not include these groups during the Trump administration (Anderson, 2021; Executive Order 13988, 2021; Kreighbaum, 2017a).

9. The neoliberal turn in higher education practice and policy, which views students as consumers and crafts policies to make use of market forces, has been well documented in the scholarly literature (e.g., Dougherty & Natow, 2020; Slaughter & Rhoades, 2004).

10. The Obama administration also considered adopting a college ratings system, but following advocacy against such a system by the higher education lobby, the administration declined to adopt it (Bui, 2015; Marcus, 2014). The influence of higher education interest groups is discussed further in Chapter 7.

Chapter 3

1. A constitutional structure that favors a less representative legislative body is unusual among democratic societies (Dauster, 2016). As William Dauster (2016), a lawyer and educator who had served as chief of staff to former Senate Majority Leader Harry Reid, wrote in a law review article, the U.S. constitutional structure "preserves a less representative structure than almost all developed democracies" (p. 636).

2. This clause is known as the "Commerce Clause" and has historically justified a great deal of congressional legislation (Boudreaux, 2006; Johnson, 2005); however, Congress's power to regulate interstate commerce was restricted by a 1995 Supreme Court decision (*United States v. Lopez*, 1995).

3. When a chamber is evenly divided as to representation by political party, the chamber may enter into a power-sharing agreement to divide power between the two parties more evenly than if one party were to hold a clear majority. This occurred in the 107th Congress in 2001, in which the Senate had 50–50 representation between

Democrats and Republicans, with the Republican vice president's tie-breaking vote providing a slim majority for that party (Rybicki, 2021). A similar arrangement was made in the 117th Congress in 2021, when Senate seats were evenly divided among the parties, and a Democratic vice president served as the tie-breaking vote in favor of that party (Armstrong & Wooten, 2021).

4. Dauster (2016) identified another way to change the filibuster rule: by arguing that a Senate majority may adopt entirely new chamber rules at the start of a new Congress. Although there have been attempts to change Senate rules using this argument, these attempts have so far not been successful (Dauster, 2016).

5. The annual appropriations process applies to discretionary spending programs that Congress is not required to fund. Examples of discretionary higher education spending include the TRIO student success programs and federal work-study (Dortch, 2018; Hegji et al., 2018; House Committee on Appropriations, n.d.-b; Griffin, 2021; Sablan & Hiestand, 2020; Shohfi & Tollestrup, 2019). Federal student loans and some loan forgiveness programs are mandatory-spending entitlement programs. Pell Grants have been called "quasi-mandatory" spending, "because the student eligibility benefits are like a mandatory entitlement program, but the program is constrained by . . . the discretionary spending limits of the Appropriations Committee" (Sablan & Hiestand, 2020, p. 6; see also Shohfi & Tollestrup, 2019).

6. Reasons for delay in the president's budget proposal include a new presidential administration entering just a few weeks before the proposal is due, or a late budget process from the preceding year (Center on Budget & Policy Priorities, 2020).

7. Reconciliation bills are for mandatory spending programs only (Griffin, 2021; Sablan & Hiestand, 2020). Thus, the many higher education discretionary-spending programs—such as work-study, TRIO, and some aspects of the Pell Grant programs—cannot be handled via reconciliation (Griffin, 2021).

8. The transition to fully direct lending by the U.S. Department of Education was a policy priority of President Barack Obama, whose support was instrumental to the eventual adoption of this policy (Natow, 2021b).

Chapter 4

1. The vice president's role in policymaking has expanded as well, with vice presidents increasingly taking on active roles in decision making and serving among the president's main policy advisors (Baumgartner, 2015; Cohen, 2001; Goldstein, 2010).

2. The Congressional Review Act permits Congress to overturn a rule if a resolution to overturn it is approved by a simple majority of both chambers and signed by the president. The resolution must be submitted in Congress within 60 days of the publication of the rule, provided Congress is continuously in session during that time (Carey & Davis, 2020).

3. It is important to note that this occurred during a period when the president's party also controlled Congress, and it was done via budget reconciliation, which could not be filibustered under Senate rules. Had these conditions been different, that bill likely would not have passed, regardless of presidential priority (Natow, 2021b).

4. According to the Congressional Research Service, amendments of federal regulations must follow APA procedures. Presidents may issue executive orders

directing agencies to begin the process for amending regulations. But typically, agencies must follow the APA's procedural requirements when doing so, unless the president has statutory authority to make the regulatory change directly (Brannon, 2018).

5. To reiterate this point, a Trump-era executive order required agency guidance to "clearly state that it does not bind the public, except as authorized by law or as incorporated into a contract" (Executive Order No. 13891, 2019, p. 55237).

6. National Public Radio similarly referred to the CEA as "a sort of mini White House think tank" (Block, 2008, ¶ 2).

Chapter 5

1. This investigation was promptly discontinued when the Biden administration took office (Higgins, 2021).

2. The National Research Council (2012) provides a detailed description of the priority-setting process in the Department of Education's National Institute on Disability and Rehabilitation Research.

Chapter 6

1. These are median statistics reported by the Congressional Research Service based on data regarding federal judicial nominations and appointments from 1977 through 2018 (McMillon, 2019).

2. The filibuster and its importance in higher education policymaking are discussed in Chapter 3 of this volume.

3. However, to the extent that private institutions have policies that promote freedom of expression and prohibit viewpoint discrimination, those policies will often be interpreted by courts as binding contracts, making private institutions subject to constraints similar to those to which public institutions are bound by the First Amendment (Kaplin et al., 2020).

Chapter 7

1. For example, the Commission on Independent Colleges and Universities represents the interests of private, nonprofit colleges in New York state and does policy advocacy at the state and federal levels (Commission on Independent Colleges & Universities, n.d.).

References

Abdul-Alim, J. (2017, April 27). Stakeholders divided over accreditation reform. *Diverse: Issues in Higher Education.* https://www.diverseeducation.com/institutions/community-colleges/article/15100417/stakeholders-divided-over-accreditation-reform

Abel, J. R., & Dietz, R. (2014, September 2). The value of a college degree. *Liberty Street Economics.* Federal Reserve Bank of New York.

Abrams, J., Wollstein, K., & Davis, E. J. (2018). State lines, fire lines, and lines of authority: Rangeland fire management and bottom-up cooperative federalism. *Land Use Policy, 75,* 252–259.

ACPA. (n.d.). *ACPA speaks up!* https://www.myacpa.org/ACPA-speaks-up

Adams v. Pennsylvania Higher Education Assistance Agency, No. 15-0524 (S. Ct. App. W. Va., June 3, 2016).

Adler, E. S., & Wilkerson, J. D. (2012). *Congress and the politics of problem solving.* Cambridge University Press.

Administrative Conference of the United States. (n.d.). *Williams Fellowship.* https://www.acus.gov/williams-fellowship

Administrative Office of the U.S. Courts. (n.d.). *Justice Thurgood Marshall profile—Brown v. Board of Education reenactment.* https://www.uscourts.gov/educational-resources/educational-activities/justice-thurgood-marshall-profile-brown-v-board

Administrative Office of the U.S. Courts. (2016). *Understanding the federal courts.* https://www.uscourts.gov/sites/default/files/understanding-federal-courts.pdf

Administrative Procedure Act, 5 United State Code §§ 500 et seq. (2018).

Alcindor, Y. (2017, March 1). Trump's call for school vouchers is a return to a campaign pledge. *New York Times.*

Alexander, F. K., Harnisch, T., Hurley, D., & Moran, R. (2010). Maintenance of effort: An evolving federal-state policy approach to ensuring college affordability. *Journal of Education Finance, 36*(1), 76–87.

Alexander, K., Alexander, K. W., & Alexander, M. D. (2021). *University law.* West Academic.

Alger, J. R. (2020, April 13). Now more than ever: Higher education's civic responsibility. *Inside Higher Education.* https://www.insidehighered.com/views/2020/04/13/colleges-should-play-important-role-us-census-even-and-especially-light-pandemic

Altikriti, S. (2016). Persuasive speech acts in Barack Obama's inaugural speeches (2009, 2013) and the last State of the Union address (2016). *International Journal of Linguistics, 8*(2), 47–66.

American Association of College Registrars et al. (2018, August 27). [Letter to the Hon. Kevin Brady and the Hon. Richard Neal.] https://www.nacubo.org/-/media/Nacubo/Documents/127Davissupport.ashx?la=en&hash=86BB2C9751EB0CBD0F71D8AB4C72339B3C75C4AD

American Association of University Professors. (n.d.). *Point Park University v. Newspaper Guild of Pittsburgh/Communication Workers of America Local 38061, AFL-CIO, CLC, N.L.R.B. Case No.: 06-RC-012276 (Private Institute Faculty Organizing)*. https://www.aaup.org/brief/point-park-university-v-newspaper-guild-pittsburghcommunication-workers-america-local-38061

American Association of University Professors. (2001). *Policy documents and reports* (9th ed.). American Association of University Professors. https://www.aaup.org

American Association of University Professors. (2017, March 17). *Gorsuch poses threat to civil rights, workers rights*. https://www.aaup.org/news/gorsuch-poses-threat-civil-rights-workers-rights#.XwNcfeWSmUk

American Bar Association. (2018, November 27). *What is an executive order?* https://www.americanbar.org/groups/public_education/publications/teaching-legal-docs/what-is-an-executive-order-/

American Council on Education. (n.d.-a). *A brief guide to the federal budget and appropriations process*. https://www.acenet.edu/Policy-Advocacy/Pages/Budget-Appropriations/Brief-Guide-to-Budget-Appropriations.aspx

American Council on Education. (n.d.-b). *Law and the courts*. https://www.acenet.edu/Policy-Advocacy/Pages/Law-Courts/Law-Courts.aspx

American Council on Education. (n.d.-c). *Leadership & advocacy*. https://www.acenet.edu/Documents/General-Brochure.pdf

American Council on Education. (n.d.-d). *Our history*. https://www.acenet.edu/About/Pages/history.aspx

American Council on Education. (2010). *Summary of education provisions in the Health Care and Education Reconciliation Act of 2010*. https://www.acenet.edu/Documents/Education-Provisions-in-the-Health-Care-and-Education-Reconciliation-Act-of-2010.pdf

American Council on Education. (2017, March 17). *Letter to President Donald Trump*. https://www.acenet.edu/Documents/Letter-From-Institutions-to-President-Trump-on-Dreamers.pdf

American Council on Education. (2019, May 9). *House committee hears testimony on pursuing a diverse STEM workforce*. https://www.acenet.edu/News-Room/Pages/House-Committee-Hears-Testimony-on-Pursuing-a-Diverse-STEM-Workforce.aspx

American Enterprise Institute. (n.d.). *Testimonies*. https://www.aei.org/research-products/testimonies/

Ancheta, A. (2008). Bakke, antidiscrimination jurisprudence, and the trajectory of affirmative action law. In P. Marin & C. L. Horn (eds.), *Realizing Bakke's legacy: Affirmative action, equal opportunity, and access to higher education* (pp. 15–40). Stylus.

Anderson, G. (2020, May 7). U.S. publishes new regulations on campus sexual assault. *Inside Higher Education*. https://www.insidehighered.com/news/2020/05/07/education-department-releases-final-title-ix-regulations

References

Anderson, G. (2021, January 12). Dept. of Ed says Title IX does not apply to LGBTQ discrimination. *Inside Higher Education.* https://www.insidehighered.com/quicktakes/2021/01/12/dept-ed-says-title-ix-does-not-apply-lgbtq-discrimination

Anderson, J. E. (2015). *Public policymaking* (8th ed.). Cengage Learning.

Anthony, A. M., Page, L. C., & Seldin, A. (2016). In the right ballpark? Assessing the accuracy of net price calculators. *Journal of Student Financial Aid, 46*(2), 25–50.

Armstrong, C. J., & Wooten, T. (2021, February 9). The Senate power-sharing agreement for the 117th Congress. *Holland & Knight Alert.* https://www.hklaw.com/en/insights/publications/2021/02/the-senate-power-sharing-agreement-for-the-117th-congress

Arnett, A. A. (2018, April 2). Trump says he "doesn't know what a community college means." *Higher Ed Dive.* https://www.highereddive.com/news/trump-says-he-doesnt-know-what-a-community-college-means/520367/

Arnold, C. (2020, January 22). Myth busted: Turns out bankruptcy can wipe out student loan debt after all. *National Public Radio.* https://www.npr.org/2020/01/22/797330613/myth-busted-turns-out-bankruptcy-can-wipe-out-student-loan-debt-after-all

Ashbee, E. (2004). *U.S. politics today* (2nd ed.). Manchester University Press.

Asian Law Caucus, Educators for Fair Consideration, DreamActivist.org, & National Immigrant Youth Alliance. (2012). *Education not deportation: A guide for undocumented youth in removal proceedings.* https://www.advancingjustice-alc.org/wp-content/uploads/2012/11/Education-Not-Deportation-A-Guide-for-Undocumented-Youth-in-Removal-Proceedings-2.pdf

Asimow, M. (2019). *Federal administrative adjudication outside of the Administrative Procedure Act.* Administrative Conference of the United States.

Associated Press. (2018, April 7). For-profit colleges struggle despite assist from Betsy DeVos. *NBC News.* https://www.nbcnews.com/news/education/profit-colleges-struggle-despite-assist-betsy-devos-n863641

Association of American Medical Colleges. (n.d.). *Block 3 of instruction: The role and missions of teaching hospitals and Veterans Affairs medical centers.* https://www.aamc.org/media/19306/download

Association of American Universities. (2019, February). *Tax-exempt status of universities and colleges.* https://www.aau.edu/sites/default/files/AAU-Files/Key-Issues/Taxation-Finance/Tax-Exempt-Status-Universities-post-TCJA.pdf

Association of Community College Trustees. (n.d.-a). *A guide to the election and appointment of community college trustees.* https://www.acct.org/article/guide-election-and-appointment-community-college-trustees

Association of Community College Trustees. (n.d.-b). *First-dollar versus last-dollar promise models.* https://www.acct.org/page/first-dollar-vs-last-dollar-promise-models

Association of Public and Land-Grant Universities. (n.d.). *Council of 1890s Institutions.* https://www.aplu.org/members/councils/1890-universities/council-of-1890s-institutions.html

Bagenstos, S. R. (2008). Spending Clause litigation in the Roberts Court. *Duke Law Journal,* 345–410.

Bagenstos, S. R. (2014). Viva conditional federal spending! *Harvard Journal of Law & Public Policy, 37*(1), 93–99.
Baker, D. J. (2019). A case study of undergraduate debt, repayment plans, and post-baccalaureate decision-making among Black students at HBCUs. *Journal of Student Financial Aid, 48*(2), 1.
Barab, J. (2018, December 14). *What's in a name? House Labor Committee reborn.* DCReport.org. https://www.dcreport.org/2018/12/14/whats-in-a-name-house-labor-committee-reborn/
Barkowski, E., Nielsen, E., Noel, H., Dodson, M., Sonnenfeld, K., Ye, C., DeMonte, E., Monahan, B., & Eccleston, M. (2018, March). *Study of the Teacher Education Assistance for College and Higher Education (TEACH) Grant Program* (Final Report). U.S. Department of Education.
Barnes, R. (2019, June 16). Chief justice tries to assure the Supreme Court is apolitical, but term's biggest cases present partisan challenges; John Roberts fills pivotal role in politically fraught decisions on census, gerrymandering. *Washington Post Blogs.* Nexis Uni.
Barnes, R. (2020, June 15). Supreme Court says gay, transgender workers protected by federal law forbidding discrimination. *Washington Post.*
Barnes, M. D., Hanson, C. L., Novilla, L. M., Meacham, A. T., McIntyre, E., & Erickson, B. C. (2008). Analysis of media agenda setting during and after Hurricane Katrina: Implications for emergency preparedness, disaster response, and disaster policy. *American Journal of Public Health, 98*(4), 604–610.
Basken, P. (2021, March 8). U.S. accrediting agency rejected as wider battles lie ahead. *Times Higher Education.*
Batalova, J., Hooker, S., & Capps, R. (2014). *DACA at the Two-Year Mark: A National and State Profile of Youth Eligible and Applying for Deferred Action.* Migration Policy Institute.
Battle, S., & Wheeler, T. E. (2017, February 22). *Dear Colleague.* https://www2.ed.gov/about/offices/list/ocr/letters/colleague-201702-title-ix.pdf
Bauer-Wolf, J. (2020, October 30). How would Biden's immigration proposals affect international students. *Higher Ed Dive.* https://www.highereddive.com/news/how-would-bidens-immigration-proposals-affect-international-students/588092/
Baum, S., Harris, D. N., Kelly, A., & Mitchell, T. (2017). *A principled federal role in higher education.* Urban Institute Education Policy Program.
Bauman, D., & Read, B. (2018, June 21). A brief history of GOP attempts to kill the Education Dept. *The Chronicle of Higher Education.* https://www.chronicle.com/article/a-brief-history-of-gop-attempts-to-kill-the-education-dept/
Bauman, D., & Thomason, A. (2019, May 21). The College Scorecard just got bigger. Here are 4 factoids from the new data. *Chronicle of Higher Education.* https://www.chronicle.com/article/the-college-scorecard-just-got-bigger-here-are-4-factoids-from-the-new-data/
Baumgartner, J. C. (2015). *The American vice presidency: From the shadow to the spotlight.* Rowman & Littlefield.
Bellante, D., & Porter, P. (1998). Public and private employment over the business cycle: A ratchet theory of government growth. *Journal of Labor Research, 19*(4), 613–628.

Bengston, D. N., Fletcher, J. O., & Nelson, K. C. (2004). Public policies for managing urban growth and protecting open space: Policy instruments and lessons learned in the United States. *Landscape & Urban Planning*, 69, 271–286.

Biden, J. R. (2007, March 14). *Remarks at the International Association of Fire Fighters Bipartisan 2008 Presidential Forum*. CQ Transcriptions. Nexis Uni.

Black, R. C., Lynch, M. S., Madonna, A. J., & Owens, R. J. (2011). Assessing congressional responses to growing presidential powers: The case of recess appointments. *Presidential Studies Quarterly*, 41(3), 570–589.

Blair, J. (1999, May 26). Higher Education Alliance rallies for student-aid cause. *Education Week*. https://www.edweek.org/teaching-learning/higher-education-alliance-rallies-for-student-aid-cause/1999/05

Block, M. (2008, November 24). *Difference between NEC, CEA explained*. National Public Radio. https://www.npr.org/templates/story/story.php?storyId=97418915

Blumenstyk, G. (2017, March 16). An uncertain future for higher education's federal "cop on the beat." *The Chronicle of Higher Education*. https://www.chronicle.com/article/an-uncertain-future-for-higher-educations-federal-cop-on-the-beat/

Bombardieri, M. (2020, October 28). *Tapping local support to strengthen community colleges*. Center for American Progress. https://www.americanprogress.org/issues/education-postsecondary/reports/2020/10/28/491739/tapping-local-support-strengthen-community-colleges/

Bose, M. (2020). Understanding OMB's role in presidential policymaking. In M. Bose & A. Rudalevige (Eds.), *Executive policymaking: The role of the OMB in the presidency* (pp. 1–8). Brookings Institution Press.

Boudreaux, P. (2006). A Case for Recognizing Unenumerated Powers of Congress. *New York University Journal of Legislation & Public Policy*, 9, 551–585.

Bound, J., & Turner, S. (2002). Going to war and going to college: Did World War II and the GI Bill increase educational attainment for returning veterans? *Journal of Labor Economics*, 20(4), 784–815.

Bowen, J. (2014, November 24). Solutions to state higher ed. disinvestment are complicated but possible. *New America Ed Central*. https://www.newamerica.org/education-policy/edcentral/state-disinvestment/

Bowen, W. G., & Bok, D. (1998). *The shape of the river*. Princeton University Press.

Bowers, D. E. (1982). The Research and Marketing Act of 1946 and its effects on agricultural marketing research. *Agricultural History*, 56(1), 249–263.

Bowman, A. O. (2017). The state-local government(s) conundrum: Power and design. *The Journal of Politics*, 79(4), 1119–1129.

Boylan, H. R., Levine-Brown, P., Koricich, A., & Anthony, S. W. (2018). Education, the workforce, and developmental education: An interview with Congresswoman Virginia Foxx. *Journal of Developmental Education*, 42(1), 22–23.

Brannon, V. C. (2018, July 18). *Can a president amend regulations by executive order?* (CRS Report No. LSB10172). Library of Congress, Congressional Research Service.

Brass, C. T. (2006, March 31). *Office of Management and Budget: A brief overview* (CRS Report No. RS21665). Library of Congress, Congressional Research Center.

Brass, C. T. (2008, June 17). *The role of the Office of Management and Budget in Budget Development* (CRS Report No. RS20167). Library of Congress, Congressional Research Service.

Breger, M. J., & Edles, G. J. (2000). Established by practice: The theory and operation of independent federal agencies. *Administrative Law Review, 52*, 1111–1294.

Breger, M. J., & Edles, G. J. (2015). *Independent agencies in the United States: Law, structure, and politics*. Oxford University Press.

Brennan, G., & Buchanan, J. M. (1980). *The power to tax: Analytical foundations of a fiscal Constitution*. Cambridge University Press.

Brint, S. (2019). *Two cheers for higher education: Why American universities are stronger than ever—and how to meet the challenges they face*. Princeton University Press.

Brint, S., & Clotfelter, C. T. (2016). US higher education effectiveness. *RSF: The Russell Sage Foundation Journal of the Social Sciences, 2*(1), 2–37.

Brower, R., Bertrand Jones, T., Tandberg, D., Hu, S., & Park, T. (2017). Comprehensive developmental education reform in Florida: A policy implementation typology. *The Journal of Higher Education, 88*(6), 809–834.

Brown v. Board of Education of Topeka, 347 U.S. 483 (1954).

Brown, C. (2018, August 6). *Congressional Research Service Legal Sidebar: Advising the president: Rules governing access and accountability of presidential advisors* (CRS Report No. LSB10183). Library of Congress, Congressional Research Service.

Brown, P. (2014). The Civil Rights Act of 1964. *Washington University Law Review, 92*, 527–552.

Brudnick, I. A. (2020, June 23). *Support offices in the House of Representatives: Roles and authorities* (CRS Report No. RL33220). Library of Congress, Congressional Research Service.

Bui, Q. (2015, September 18). *Obama won't rate colleges, so we did*. National Public Radio, Planet Money. https://www.npr.org/sections/money/2015/09/18/440973097/obama-wont-rate-colleges-so-we-did

Bur, J. (2019, March 18). Is anyone actually tracking political appointee data? *Federal Times*. https://www.federaltimes.com/management/2019/03/18/is-anyone-actually-tracking-political-appointee-data/

Bureau of Consumer Financial Protection. (2020, October). *College credit card agreements: Annual report to Congress*. Bureau of Consumer Financial Protection. https://files.consumerfinance.gov/f/documents/cfpb_college-credit-card-agreements-report_2020-10.pdf

Bureau of Indian Affairs. (n.d.). *Bureau of Indian Education (BIE)*. https://www.bia.gov/bie

Burke, J. C., & Associates (Eds). (2005). *Achieving accountability in higher education: Balancing public, academic, and market demands*. Jossey-Bass.

Burns, J. (2019, September 22). Retirement reform in 2019. *The Burns Firm Blog*.

Burum, S. (2008). Constitutional theories of executive power: effects on current and future decision making in the executive branch and on the US Supreme Court. *National Social Science Journal, 33*(2), 28–34.

Caldera, C. G. (2019, December 18). Justice Department continues investigation into Harvard admissions. *The Harvard Crimson*. https://www.thecrimson.com/article/2019/12/18/foia-doj-continues-investigation/

Camera, L. (2021, January 25). Education Department recommends terminating for-profit accreditor. *U.S. News & World Report*. https://www.usnews.com/news/education-news/articles/2021-01-25/education-department-recommends-terminating-for-profit-accreditor

Cameron, C. M. (2000). *Veto bargaining: Presidents and the politics of negative power*. Cambridge University Press.

Cameron, M. A., & Falleti, T. G. (2005). Federalism and the subnational separation of powers. *Publius, 35*(2), 245–271.

Camp, M. J. (2021). *No longer exempt: Higher education's entrée into lobbying* [Doctoral dissertation]. Teachers College, Columbia University.

Campbell, D. S., Bair, F. H., & Harvey, O. L. (1939). *Educational activities of the Works Progress Administration* (No. 14). U.S. Government Printing Office.

Carey, M. P., & Davis, C. M. (2020, January 14). *The Congressional Review Act (CRA): Frequently asked questions* (CRS Report No. R43992). Library of Congress, Congressional Research Service.

Carleton, D. (2002). *Landmark congressional laws on education*. Greenwood Publishing Group.

Carmines, E. G., & Fowler, M. (2017). The temptation of executive authority: How increased polarization and the decline in legislative capacity have contributed to the expansion of presidential power. *Indiana Journal of Global Legal Studies, 24*(2), 369–398.

Carp, R. A., Stidham, R., & Manning, K. L. (2010). *The federal courts*. CQ Press.

Case, D. A. (2005). Article I courts, substantive rights, and remedies for government misconduct. *Northern Illinois University Law Review, 26*, 101–212.

Cash, D. W. (2001). "In order to aid in diffusing useful and practical information": Agricultural extension and boundary organizations. *Science, Technology, & Human Values, 26*(4), 431–453.

Cashin, S. D. (2005). The Civil Rights Act of 1964 and coalition politics. *Saint Louis University Law Journal, 49*, 1029–1046.

Cate, F. H., Gumport, P. J., Hauser, R. K., Richardson, J. T., Wexman, V., Alger, J. R., & Smith, M. F. (1998). Copyright issues in colleges and universities. *Academe, 84*(3), 39–45.

Caulfield, R. (2019, January 3). What does the Speaker of the House do? *The Conversation*. https://theconversation.com/what-does-the-speaker-of-the-house-do-94884

Cellini, S. R., Darolia, R., & Turner, L. J. (2016). *Where do students go when for-profit colleges lose federal aid?* (No. w22967). National Bureau of Economic Research.

Center on Budget & Policy Priorities. (2020, April 2). *Policy basics: Introduction to the federal budget process*. https://www.cbpp.org/sites/default/files/atoms/files/3-7-03bud.pdf

Center on Education Policy. (1999). *A brief history of the federal role in education: Why it began and why it's still needed*. Center on Education Policy.

Centers for Disease Control & Prevention. (2020). *Guidance for institutions of higher education*. https://www.cdc.gov/coronavirus/2019-ncov/community/colleges-universities/considerations.html

Cervantes, A., Creusere, M., McMillion, R., McQueen, C., Short, M., Steiner, M., & Webster, J. (2005). *Opening the doors to higher education: Perspectives on the Higher Education Act 40 years later*. TG (Texas Guaranteed Student Loan Corporation).

Chan, R. Y. (2016). Understanding the purpose of higher education: An analysis of the economic and social benefits for completing a college degree. *Journal of Education Policy, Planning and Administration*, 6(5), 1–40.

Chemerinsky, E. (2016). *Federal jurisdiction* (7th ed.). Wolters Klewer.

Chen, M. H. (2017). Administrator-in-Chief: The president and executive action in immigration law. *Administrative Law Review*, 69(2), 347–429.

Chen, M. H. (2020). How much procedure is needed for agencies to change "novel" regulatory policies? *Hastings Law Journal*, 71, 1127–1142.

Chopra, R. (2015, September 30). *Consumer protection & higher education financing alternatives*. Center for American Progress. https://www.jec.senate.gov/public/_cache/files/71c3008d-6ff2-4c2e-b46c-6e0b280aa163/testimony-of-rohit-chopra-before-the-joint-economic-committee---final.pdf

Chopra, R. (2019, December 10). *Statement of Commissioner Rohit Chopra*. Federal Trade Commission. https://www.ftc.gov/system/files/documents/public_statements/1557180/152_3231_statement_of_commissioner_rohit_chopra_0.pdf

Christensen, M. D. (2012, July 27). *The executive budget process: An overview*. Library of Congress, Congressional Research Service.

Chu, V. S., & Garvey, T. (2014, April 16). *Executive orders: Issuance, modification, and Revocation* (CRS Report No. RS20846). Library of Congress, Congressional Research Service.

Civil Rights Act of 1964, 42 U.S.C. §§ 1981 et seq. (2018).

Clark, C. S. (2018, April 27). Groups monitoring agency website changes see deeper Trump agenda. *Government Executive*. https://www.govexec.com/technology/2018/04/groups-monitoring-agency-website-changes-see-deeper-trump-agenda/147806/

Clery Center. (n.d.-a). *Overview of VAWA, DFSCA, & FERPA*. https://clerycenter.org/policy/vawa-dfsca-ferpa/

Clery Center. (n.d.-b). *Summary of the Jeanne Clery Act*. https://clerycenter.org/policy-resources/the-clery-act/

Cohen, D. M. (1996). *Amateur government: When political appointees manage federal bureaucracy* (CPM Working Paper 96-1). Brookings Institution.

Cohen, J. E. (2001). The polls: Popular views of the vice president: Vice presidential approval. *Presidential Studies Quarterly*, 31(1), 142–149.

Cohen, M. (2020, July 30). Obama calls for end of "Jim Crow relic" filibuster if it blocks voting reforms. *Politico*. https://www.politico.com/news/2020/07/30/barack-obama-john-lewis-filibuster-388600

Cohen, P. (2017, February 20). For-profit schools, an Obama target, see new day under Trump. *New York Times*.

Cohen-Vogel, L. (2005). Federal role in teacher quality: "Redefinition" or policy alignment? *Educational Policy*, 19(1), 18–43.

Cole, J. P. (2016, December 7). *An Introduction to Judicial Review of Federal Agency Action* (CRS Report No. R44699). Library of Congress, Congressional Research Service.

Cole, J. P., & Back, C. J. (2019, April 12). *Title IX and sexual harassment: Private rights of action, administrative enforcement, and proposed regulations* (CRS Report No. R45685). Library of Congress, Congressional Research Service.

The College Board. (2020). *Trends in college pricing*. The College Board. https://research.collegeboard.org/pdf/trends-college-pricing-student-aid-2020.pdf

Collins, P. M. (2007). Lobbyists before the US Supreme Court: Investigating the influence of amicus curiae briefs. *Political Research Quarterly*, 60(1), 55–70.

Collins, P. M. (2018). The use of amicus briefs. *Annual Review of Law and Social Science*, 14, 219–237.

Collins, P. M., Corley, P. C., & Hamner, J. (2015). The influence of amicus curiae briefs on US Supreme Court opinion content. *Law & Society Review*, 49(4), 917–944.

Commission on Independent Colleges & Universities. (n.d.). *About CICU*. https://cicu.org/about

Committee for a Responsible Federal Budget. (2020, July 8). *Appropriations 101*. Committee for a Responsible Federal Budget.

Congressional Budget Office. (2018, December 13). *Consolidate and reduce federal payments for graduate medical education at teaching hospitals*. https://www.cbo.gov/budget-options/54738

Congressional Research Service. (2021, June 14). *Defense primer: RDT&E* (CRS Report No. IF10553). Library of Congress, Congressional Research Service.

Contrubis, J. (1999, March 9). *CRS report for Congress: Executive orders and proclamations*. Library of Congress, Congressional Research Service.

Cook, C. E. (1998). *Lobbying for higher education: How colleges and universities influence federal policy*. Vanderbilt University Press.

Cook, T. M., & Laski, F. J. (1980). Beyond *Davis*: Equality of opportunity for higher education for disabled students under the Rehabilitation Act of 1973. *Harvard Civil Rights-Civil Liberties Law Review*, 15, 415–474.

Cooper, P. J. (2001). The Law: Presidential memoranda and executive orders: Of patchwork quilts, trump cards, and shell games. *Presidential Studies Quarterly*, 31(1), 126–141.

Cope, K. L. (2007). Defending the ivory tower: Twenty-first century approach to the *Pickering-Connick* doctrine and public higher education faculty after *Garcetti*. *Journal of College and University Law*, 33(2), 313–360.

Couch, J. (2008, March 16). Works Progress Administration. In R. Whaples (Ed.), *EH.net encyclopedia*. http://eh.net/encyclopedia/the-works-progress-administration

Council for Higher Education Accreditation. (2002, September). *The fundamentals of accreditation: What do you need to know?* Council for Higher Education Accreditation.

Council of Economic Advisers. (2017, January). *Using federal data to measure and improve the performance of U.S. institutions of higher education*. Executive Office of the President.

Council of the Inspectors General. (2014, July 14). *The inspectors general*. https://www.ignet.gov/sites/default/files/files/IG_Authorities_Paper_-_Final_6-11-14.pdf

Council on Foundations. (n.d.). *Foundation basics*. https://www.cof.org/content/foundation-basics

Counseling Borrowers, 34 C.F.R. § 685.304 (2020).

Coval, M. M. (2015). Reauthorization ready: How NASFAA influences the higher education policymaking process. *Journal of Student Financial Aid*, 45(3), 9.

Coven, M. B. (2020). OMB's role inside the White House. In M. Bose & A. Rudalevige (Eds.), *Executive policymaking: The role of the OMB in the presidency* (pp. 101–115). Brookings Institution Press.

Cowley, S. (2018, November 11). Borrowers face hazy path as program to forgive student loans stalls, under Betsy DeVos. *New York Times*.

Cowley, S. (2021, March 19). A DeVos system allowed 12 minutes to decide student loan forgiveness. *New York Times*.

Croft, G. K. (2019, August 29). *The U.S. land-grant university system: An overview* (CRS Report No. R45897). Library of Congress, Congressional Research Service.

Cross, C. T. (2014). *Political education: Setting the course for state and federal policy* (2nd ed). Teachers College Press.

Cuéllar, M. F. (2009). "Securing" the nation: Law, politics, and organization at the federal security agency, 1939–1953. *The University of Chicago Law Review*, 76, 587–718.

Cunningham, A., Park, E., & Engle, J. (2014, February). *Minority-serving institutions: Doing more with less* (Issue Brief). Institute for Higher Education Policy.

Custer, B. D., & Kent, R. T. (2018). Understanding the Drug-Free Schools and Communities Act, then and now. *Journal of College & University Law*, 44, 137–158.

Dahill-Brown, S. E., & Lavery, L. (2012). Implementing federal policy: Confronting state capacity and will. *Politics & Policy*, 40(4), 557–592.

Darolia, R., & Potochnick, S. (2015). Educational "when," "where," and "how" implications of in-state resident tuition policies for Latino undocumented immigrants. *The Review of Higher Education*, 38(4), 507–535.

Darville, S. (2017, February 7). It's official: Betsy DeVos wins confirmation after vice president's historic tie-breaker. *Chalkbeat*. https://www.chalkbeat.org/2017/2/7/21102906/it-s-official-betsy-devos-wins-confirmation-after-vice-president-s-historic-tie-breaker

Datla, K., & Revesz, R. L. (2013). Deconstructing independent agencies (and executive agencies). *Cornell Law Review*, 98, 769–843.

Dauster, W. G. (2016). The Senate in transition or how I learned to stop worrying and love the nuclear option. *New York University Journal of Legislation & Public Policy*, 19, 631–683.

Davidson, A. (2020, October 8). Justice Department sues Yale over alleged discrimination in admissions. *Yale Daily News*. https://yaledailynews.com/blog/2020/10/08/justice-department-sues-yale-over-alleged-discrimination-in-admissions/

Davis, C. M. (2015, September 16). *The president pro tempore of the Senate: History and authority of the office* (CRS Report No. RL30960). Library of Congress, Congressional Research Service.

Davis, C. M. (2019, May 20). *The legislative process on the House floor: An introduction* (CRS Report No. 95-563). Library of Congress, Congressional Research Service.

Davis, C. M. (2020, December 2). *CRS Insight: Eight mechanisms to enact procedural change in the U.S. Senate*. Library of Congress, Congressional Research Service.

Davis, C. M., & Greene, M. (2017, May 30). *Presidential appointee positions requiring Senate confirmation and committees handling nominations* (CRS Report RL30959). Library of Congress, Congressional Research Service.

Davis, C. M., Garvey, T., Wilhelm, B., Oleszek, W. J., Brass, C. T., Brudnick, I. A., Carey, M. P., Eckman, S. J., Egar, Oleszek, M. J., Petersen, R. E., Straus, J. R.,

Stuessy, M. M., & Riccard, T. N. (2021, March 31). *Congressional oversight manual* (CRS Report RL30240). Library of Congress, Congressional Research Service.

Delaney, J. A. (2014). The role of state policy in promoting college affordability. *The ANNALS of the American Academy of Political and Social Science, 655*(1), 56–78.

DeLauder, W. B. (2013). The USDA/1890 partnership: A model of success. In E. Fort (Ed.), *Survival of the Historically Black Colleges and Universities* (pp. 135–143). Lexington Books.

DeMitchell, T. A., & Connelly, V. J. (2007). Academic freedom and the public school teacher: An exploratory study of perceptions, policy, and the law. *Brigham Young University Education & Law Journal*, 83–117.

Department of Homeland Security v. Regents of the University of California, 591 U.S. ___ (2020) (Slip Opinion). https://www.supremecourt.gov/opinions/19pdf/18-587_5ifl.pdf

Desan, C., & Peer, N. O. (2020, June 10). *The Constitution and the Fed after the COVID-19 crisis* (University of Colorado Law, Legal Studies Research Paper No. 20-38). University of Colorado.

Desjean, J. (2019, June 20). *Analysis: Accreditation and Innovation Negotiated Rulemaking Committee NPRM summary of changes to state authorization*. National Association of Student Financial Aid Administrators. https://www.nasfaa.org/news-item/18577/Analysis_Accreditation_and_Innovation_Negotiated_Rulemaking_Committee_NPRM_Summary_of_Changes_to_State_Authorization

De Veau, L. A. (2018, July 31). Inaugural Hill Days: Observations from the steamy streets. *NASPA Blog*. https://www.naspa.org/blog/inaugural-hill-days-observations-from-the-steamy-streets

Devins, N. (2018). Congress, the courts, and party polarization: Why Congress rarely checks the president and why the courts should not take Congress's place. *Chapman Law Review, 21*(1), 55–81.

Dill, D. D. (1997). Higher education markets and public policy. *Higher Education Policy, 10*(3–4), 167–185.

Dill, D. D., & Beerkens, M. (2010). Introduction. In D. D. Dill, & M. Beerkens (Eds.), *Public policy for academic quality: Analyses of innovative policy instruments, Vol. 30* (pp. 1–13). Springer Science & Business Media.

Dill, D. D., & Beerkens, M. (2013). Designing the framework conditions for assuring academic standards: lessons learned about professional, market, and government regulation of academic quality. *Higher Education, 65*(3), 341–357.

Dodd, L. G. (2018). Reassessing the rights revolution. In Dodd, L. G. (Ed.), *The Rights revolution revisited: Institutional perspectives on the private enforcement of civil rights in the U.S.* (pp. 3–24). Cambridge University Press.

Donahoo, S. (2006). Derailing desegregation: Legal efforts to end racial segregation in higher education before and after Brown. *Equity & Excellence in Education, 39*(4), 291–301.

Dortch, C. (2017). *The Post-9/11 Veterans' Educational Assistance Act of 2008 (Post-9/11 GI Bill): A primer* (CRS Report No. R42755). Library of Congress, Congressional Research Service.

Dortch, C. (2018, March 16). *The TRIO programs: A primer* (CRS Report No. R42724). Library of Congress, Congressional Research Service.

Dortch, C., Smole, D. P., & Mahan, S. M. (2010, April 14). *The SAFRA Act: Education programs in the FY 2010 budget reconciliation* (CRS Report No. R41127). Library of Congress, Congressional Research Service.

Dote, L., Cramer, K., Dietz, N., & Grimm Jr, R. (2006). *College students helping America: Full report*. Corporation for National and Community Service. https://files.eric.ed.gov/fulltext/ED494174.pdf

Dougherty, K. A., Rhoades, G., & Smith, M. F. (2017). The "you're fired" era: Academic freedom, student complaints, and faculty discipline. In *The NEA 2017 Almanac of Higher Education* (pp. 35–460). National Education Association.

Dougherty, K. J., Jones, S. M., Lahr, H., Natow, R. S., Pheatt, L., & Reddy, V. (2016). *Performance funding for higher education*. Johns Hopkins University Press.

Dougherty, K. J., & Natow, R. S. (2015). *The politics of performance funding for higher education: Origins, discontinuations, and transformations*. Johns Hopkins University Press.

Dougherty, K. J., & Natow, R. S. (2020). Performance-based funding for higher education: how well does neoliberal theory capture neoliberal practice? *Higher Education*, 80, 457–478.

Douglas-Gabriel, D. (2020, May 29). Trump stands with DeVos, vetoes measure to overturn her controversial student loan forgiveness rule. *Washington Post*.

Douglas-Gabriel, D., & Harden, J. D. (2021, April 6). The faces of student loan debt. *Washington Post*.

Doyle, W. R. (2007). Public opinion, partisan identification, and higher education policy. *The Journal of Higher Education*, 78(4), 369–401.

Doyle, W. R. (2010). U.S. senator's ideal points for higher education: Documenting partisanship, 1965–2004. *The Journal of Higher Education*, 81(5), 619–644.

Dr. Jill Biden. (n.d.). https://obamawhitehouse.archives.gov/administration/jill-biden

Drawbaugh, K. (2009, February 26). Obama swings axe at private student lenders. *Reuters*. https://www.reuters.com/article/us-obama-budget-studentloans/obama-swings-axe-at-private-student-lenders-idUSTRE51P6K520090226

Drews, E. (2010). Agency investigations and enforcement proceedings. *Texas Tech Administrative Law Journal*, 12(1), 91–118.

Drutman, L. (2020, July 29). The Senate has always favored smaller states. It just didn't help Republicans until now. *FiveThirtyEight*. https://fivethirtyeight.com/features/the-senate-has-always-favored-smaller-states-it-just-didnt-help-republicans-until-now/

Duke, E. C. (2017, September 5). *Memorandum on Rescission of Deferred Action for Childhood Arrivals (DACA)*. https://www.dhs.gov/news/2017/09/05/memorandum-rescission-daca

Dutile, F. N. (2001). Students and due process in higher education: Of interests and procedures. *Florida Coastal Law Journal*, 2, 243–290.

Dynarski, S. (2014). *An economist's perspective on student loans in the United States* (Economic Studies Working Paper Series). Brookings Institution.

Dynarski, S., & Scott-Clayton, J. (2013). Financial Aid Policy: Lessons from Research. NBER Working Paper No. 18710. *National Bureau of Economic Research*.

Eaton, J. S. (2003). *Is accreditation accountable?: The continuing conversation between accreditation and the federal government*. Council for Higher Education Accreditation.

Eaton, J. S. (2010). Accreditation and the federal future of higher education. *Academe*, 96(5), 21–24.

Eaton, J. S. (2015, November). *An overview of U.S. accreditation*. Council for Higher Education Accreditation. https://files.eric.ed.gov/fulltext/ED569225.pdf

Eckman, S. J. (2021, April 27). Apportionment and redistricting following the 2020 census (CRS Report No. IN11360). Library of Congress, Congressional Research Service.

Eckman, S. J., & Egar, W. T. (2019, September 5). *House committee party ratios: 98th–116th Congresses* (CRS Report No. R40478). Library of Congress, Congressional Research Service.

Education & Labor Committee, U.S. House of Representatives. (n.d.). *History*. https://edlabor.house.gov/about/history

Education Commission of the States. (2007, October). *Postsecondary governance structures (archive)*. https://www.ecs.org/postsecondary-governance-structures-archive/

Eglit, H. (1981). The Age Discrimination Act of 1975, as amended: Genesis and selected problem areas. *Chicago-Kent Law Review*, 57, 915–968.

Ekman, R. (2013, August 12). Dear Mr. President . . . *Inside Higher Education*. https://www.insidehighered.com/views/2013/08/12/open-letter-president-obama-college-costs

Elving, R. (2018, June 29). What happened with Merrick Garland in 2016 and why it matters now. *National Public Radio*. https://www.npr.org/2018/06/29/624467256/what-happened-with-merrick-garland-in-2016-and-why-it-matters-now

Environmental Protection Agency. Office of Environmental Stewardship. (2007). *Environmental Management Guide for Colleges and Universities*. https://archive.epa.gov/region03/green/web/pdf/ems-guide-4-college-university-07.pdf

Epp, C. R. (1998). *The rights revolution: Lawyers, activists, and supreme courts in comparative perspective*. University of Chicago Press.

Epperson, L. (2017). Civil rights and remedies in higher education: Jurisprudential limitations and lost moments in time. *Washington & Lee Journal of Civil Rights & Social Justice*, 23(2), 343–381.

Epstein, D., & O'Halloran, S. (1996). Divided government and the design of administrative procedures: A formal model and empirical test. *The Journal of Politics*, 58(2), 373–397.

Erlandson, J. (2008, March 4). Student groups seek veteran aid. *Daily Bruin*. https://dailybruin.com/2008/03/04/student-groups-seek-veteran-aid

Eshbaugh-Soha, M. (2005). Presidential signaling in a market economy. *Presidential Studies Quarterly*, 35(4), 718–735.

Eshbaugh-Soha, M. (2013). Presidential influence of the news media: The case of the press conference. *Political Communication*, 30(4), 548–564.

Executive Office of the President. (1998, April 28). *Statement of Administration Policy: Reauthorization of the Higher Education Act*. https://www2.ed.gov/offices/OPE/PPI/Reauthor/hea_sap.html

Executive Order No. 11246: Equal Employment Opportunity. 30 Fed. Reg. 12319 (1965).

Executive Order No. 12291: Federal Regulation. 46 Fed. Reg. 13193 (1981).
Executive Order No. 12835: Establishment of the National Economic Council. 58 Fed. Reg. 6189 (1993).
Executive Order No. 12859: Establishment of the Domestic Policy Council. 58 Fed. Reg. 44101 (1993).
Executive Order No. 12866: Regulatory Planning and Review. 58 Fed. Reg. 51735 (1993).
Executive Order No. 13575: Establishment of White House Rural Council, 76 Fed. Reg. 34841 (2011).
Executive Order No. 13779: White House Initiative to Promote Excellence and Innovation at Historically Black Colleges and Universities. 82 Fed. Reg. 12499 (2017).
Executive Order No. 13864: Improving Free Inquiry, Transparency, and Accountability at Colleges and Universities. 84 Fed. Reg. 11401 (2019).
Executive Order No. 13891: Promoting the Rule of Law Through Improved Agency Guidance Documents, 84 Fed. Reg. 55235 (2019).
Executive Order No. 13988: Preventing and Combatting Discrimination on the Basis of Gender Identity or Sexual Orientation. 86 Fed. Reg. 7023 (2021).
Eyster, L., Durham, C., & Anderson, T. (2016). *Federal investments in job training at community colleges*. Urban Institute.
Fain, P. (2015, July 9). Free community college catches on. *Inside Higher Education*. https://www.insidehighered.com/news/2015/07/09/oregon-passes-free-community-college-bill-congressional-democrats-introduce-federal
Fain, P. (2016, June 7). For-profit college association changes name. *Inside Higher Education*. https://www.insidehighered.com/quicktakes/2016/06/07/profit-college-association-changes-name
Fain, P. (2017, March 7). Delay in gainful employment deadlines. *Inside Higher Education*. https://www.insidehighered.com/quicktakes/2017/03/07/delay-gainful-employment-deadlines
Fain, P. (2018, June 18). Gainful-employment disclosures delayed again. *Inside Higher Education*. https://www.insidehighered.com/news/2018/06/18/education-department-delays-disclosures-under-gainful-employment-while-working
Farrell, J. (2020). The Promise of Executive Order 11246: "Equality as a Fact and Equality as a Result." *DePaul Journal for Social Justice*, *13*(2), art. 4.
Fass, P. (1982). Without design: Education policy in the New Deal. *American Journal of Education*, *91*(1), 36–64.
Feder, J. (2012, March 26). *Federal civil rights statutes: A primer* (CRS Report No. RL33386). Library of Congress, Congressional Research Service.
Federal Bar Association. (n.d.). *Current non-Article III/Article I (also known as "legislative") courts*. https://www.fedbar.org/wp-content/uploads/2019/10/Current-non-Article-III-or-Article-I-Courts-pdf-1.pdf
Federal Judicial Center. (n.d.). *Courts: A brief overview*. https://www.fjc.gov/history/courts/courts-brief-overview
Federal Student Aid. (n.d.). *Federal Student Aid portfolio summary*. https://studentaid.gov/sites/default/files/fsawg/datacenter/library/PortfolioSummary.xls
Federal Student Aid. (2020a). *Annual report FY 2020*. U.S. Department of Education.
Federal Student Aid. (2020b, October). *Clery Act Appendix for FSA Handbook*. U.S. Department of Education.

Fichtner, J., & Simpson, L. (2015). Trimming the deadwood: Removing tenured faculty for cause. *Journal of College and University Law, 41*(1), 25–44.

Field, K. (2015, January 21). Obama presses for free community college and tax reform. *Chronicle of Higher Education.* https://www.chronicle.com/article/Obama-Presses-for-Free/151319

Fischer, K. (2020, November 10). Biden's victory has elated international students. But the road to lasting reform is long. *The Chronicle of Higher Education.* https://www.chronicle.com/article/bidens-victory-has-elated-international-students-but-the-road-to-lasting-reform-is-long

Fisher v. University of Texas, 579 U.S. ___ (2016).

Fisher, B. S., Hartman, J. L., Cullen, F. T., & Turner, M. G. (2002). Making campuses safer for students: The Clery Act as a symbolic legal reform. *Stetson Law Review, 32*, 61–89.

Fisher, L. (2014). *The law of the executive branch: Presidential power.* Oxford University Press.

Fisher, L. (2015). Presidential unilateral actions: Constitutional and political checks. *Congress & The Presidency, 42*, 293–316.

Fiske, S. T., & Hauser, R. M. (2014). Protecting human research participants in the age of big data. *Proceedings of the National Academy of Sciences of the United States of America.* https://www.pnas.org/content/111/38/13675

Flaherty, C. (2019, September 23). Ruling out grad unions. *Inside Higher Education.* https://www.insidehighered.com/news/2019/09/23/trump-labor-board-proposes-new-rule-against-grad-unions

Flaherty, C. (2020, June 11). No NLRB jurisdiction at religious colleges. *Inside Higher Education.* https://www.insidehighered.com/news/2020/06/11/no-nlrb-jurisdiction-religious-colleges

Florer, J. H. (1968). Major issues in the Congressional debate of the Morrill Act of 1862. *History of Education Quarterly, 8*(4), 459–478.

Flores, A. (2018, November 27). *Fact sheet: A legislative history of the federal government's reliance on accreditation.* Center for American Progress. https://www.americanprogress.org/issues/education-postsecondary/reports/2018/11/27/461451/fact-sheet-legislative-history-federal-governments-reliance-accreditation/

Forseth, R., Karam, J., & Sobocinski, E. J. (1995). Progress in gender equity? An overview of the history and future of Title IX of the Education Amendments of 1972. *Villanova Sports & Entertainment Law Forum, 2*(1), 51–98.

Foster, D. (2020, September). *Anticipating unilateralism.* http://www.wpsanet.org/papers/docs/2020-09-12%20Anticipating%20unilateralism.pdf

Fountain, J. H. (2018, February 20). *Campus-based student financial aid programs under the Higher Education Act* (CRS Report No. RL31618). Library of Congress, Congressional Research Service.

Frandsen, F., & Johansen, W. (2015). Organizations, stakeholders, and intermediaries: Towards a general theory. *International Journal of Strategic Communication, 9*(4), 253–271.

Fránquiz, M. E., & Ortiz, A. A. (2016). Co-editors' introduction: Every Student Succeeds Act—A policy shift. *Bilingual Research Journal, 39*(1), 1–3.

Friedman, E. M., Miller, L. L., & Evans, S. E. (2015). *Advancing the careers of military spouses: An assessment of education and employment goals and barriers facing military spouses eligible for MyCAA.* RAND Corporation.

Friedman, Z. (2020, May 30). Trump vetoes student loan forgiveness bill. *Forbes.* https://www.forbes.com/sites/zackfriedman/2020/05/29/trump-vetoes-student-loan-forgiveness-bill/#2f6323e488b1

Fuller, M. B. (2014). A history of financial aid to students. *Journal of Student Financial Aid, 44*(1), 42–68.

Futrell, G. A., & Stout, T. T. (1965, November). *Federally-supported research in agriculture at land grant colleges and universities and state experiment stations* (Agricultural Economics Series 391). The Ohio State University, Department of Agricultural Economics and Rural Sociology.

Gallup. (n.d.). *Education.* https://news.gallup.com/poll/1612/education.aspx

Gamper, A. (2005). A "global theory of federalism": The nature and challenges of a federal state. *German Law Journal, 6,* 1297–1318.

Gándara, D., & Jones, S. (2020). Who deserves benefits in higher education? A policy discourse analysis of a process surrounding reauthorization of the Higher Education Act. *The Review of Higher Education, 44*(1), 121–157.

Gardner, L. (2015, March 9). 25 years later, has Clery made campuses safer? *The Chronicle of Higher Education.* Nexis Uni.

Garrett, T. A., & Rhine, R. M. (2006). On the size and growth of government. *Federal Reserve Bank of St. Louis Review, 88,* 13–30.

Garvey, T. (2019, March 25). *Congressional subpoenas: Enforcing executive branch compliance* (CRS Report No. R45653). Library of Congress, Congressional Research Service.

Gates, B. (2007, March 7). *U.S. Senate committee hearing: Written testimony by Bill Gates, co-chair.* Gates Foundation. https://www.gatesfoundation.org/ideas/speeches/2007/03/bill-gates-us-senate-committee-hearing

Gavazzi, S. M., & Gee, E. G. (2018). *Land-grant universities for the future: Higher education for the public good.* Johns Hopkins University Press.

Geiger, R. L. (1992). Science, universities, and national defense, 1945–1970. *Osiris, 7,* 26–48.

Geiger, R. L. (1997). What happened after Sputnik? Shaping university research in the United States. *Minerva,* 349–367.

Geiger, R. L. (2008). *Research and relevant knowledge: American research universities since World War II.* Transaction Publishers.

Gersen, J. E. (2007). Legislative rules revisited. *University of Chicago Law Review, 74,* 1705–1722.

Gilbert, C. K., & Heller, D. E. (2013). Access, equity, and community colleges: The Truman Commission and federal higher education policy from 1947 to 2011. *The Journal of Higher Education, 84*(3), 417–443.

Gilfoyle, N., & Dvoskin, J. A. (2017). APA's amicus curiae program: Bringing psychological research to judicial decisions. *American Psychologist, 72*(8), 753–763.

Gilmour, J. B., & Lewis, D. E. (2006). Political appointees and the competence of federal program management. *American Politics Research, 34*(1), 22–50.

Goldin, C. (1999, August). *A brief history of education in the United States.* (NBER Working Paper Series on Historical Factors on Long Run Growth, Historical Paper 119). National Bureau of Economic Research.

Goldstein, D. (2014). *The teacher wars: A history of America's most embattled profession.* Anchor Books.

Goldstein, J. K. (2010). The contemporary presidency: Cheney, vice presidential power, and the war on terror. *Presidential Studies Quarterly, 40*(1), 102–139.

Goldstein Hode, M., & Meisenbach, R. J. (2017). Reproducing whiteness through diversity: A critical discourse analysis of the pro-affirmative action amicus briefs in the *Fisher* case. *Journal of Diversity in Higher Education, 10*(2), 162–180.

Goodwin, D. K. (2013). *The bully pulpit: Theodore Roosevelt, William Howard Taft, and the golden age of journalism*. Simon and Schuster.

Granovskiy, B. (2016, June 20). *Carl D. Perkins Career and Technical Education Act of 2006: An overview* (CRS Report No. R44542). Library of Congress, Congressional Research Service.

Gratz v. Bollinger, 359 U.S. 244 (2003).

Grawe, N. D. (2018). *Demographics and the demand for higher education*. Johns Hopkins University Press.

Green, E. L. (2020, May 20). DeVos funnels coronavirus relief funds to favored private and religious schools. *New York Times*.

Greenberg, D. (2011). Beyond the bully pulpit. *The Wilson Quarterly, 35*(3), 22–29.

Greenberg, D. (2018, January 30). TV gave us the modern State of the Union. Then it killed it. *Politico*. https://www.politico.com/magazine/story/2018/01/30/television-state-of-the-union-216548

Gresko, J. (2018, September 7). Senate concludes Kavanaugh hearing; confirmation likely. *Associated Press*. https://apnews.com/article/north-america-donald-trump-confirmation-hearings-ap-top-news-judiciary-0677a5d5bd4e4457b58f25fec805dc67

Griffin, A. (2019, May 6). Here's why Colorado is becoming 'One Dupont (West).' *Forbes*. https://www.forbes.com/sites/alisongriffin/2019/05/06/heres-why-colorado-is-becoming-one-dupont-west

Griffin, A. (2021, January 14). What is budget reconciliation anyway? *Forbes*. https://www.forbes.com/sites/alisongriffin/2021/01/14/what-is-budget-reconciliation-anyway

Griffin, O. R. (2013). Academic freedom and professional speech in the post-*Garcetti* world. *Seattle University Law Review, 37*, 1–54.

Grissom, J. A., & Herrington, C. D. (2012). Struggling for coherence and control: The new politics of intergovernmental relations in education. *Educational Policy, 26*(1), 3–14.

Grodzins, M. (1966). *The American system: A new view of government in the United States*. Rand McNally & Company.

Grove, T. L. (2019). Government Standing and the Fallacy of Institutional Injury. *University of Pennsylvania Law Review, 167*, 611–663.

Grutter v. Bollinger, 539 U.S. 306 (2003).

Gulasekaram, P., & Ramakrishnan, S. K. (2016). The President and immigration federalism. *Florida Law Review, 68*, 101–178.

Guynn, J. (2021, January 20). President Joe Biden rescinds Donald Trump ban on diversity training about systemic racism. *USA Today*. https://www.usatoday.com/story/money/2021/01/20/biden-executive-order-overturns-trump-diversity-training-ban/4236891001/

Haddad, N., & Reckhow, S. (2018). The shifting role of higher education philanthropy: A network analysis of philanthropic policy strategies. *Philanthropy & Education*, 2(1), 25–52.

Haeder, S. F., & Yackee, S. W. (2015). Influence and the administrative process: Lobbying the US president's Office of Management and Budget. *American Political Science Review*, 109(3), 507–522.

Hall, C. E. (2011). *'Advocacy philanthropy' and the public policy agenda: the role of modern foundations in American higher education* [Doctoral dissertation]. The Claremont Graduate University.

Halstead, T. J. (2001, March 19). *Executive orders: Issuance and revocation* (CRS Report No. RS20846). Library of Congress, Congressional Research Service.

Haney, P. (2013). Coercion by numbers: Conditional spending doctrine and the future of federal education spending. *Case Western Law Review*, 64(2), 577–617.

Hannah, S. B. (1996). The Higher Education Act of 1992: Skills, constraints, and the politics of higher education. *The Journal of Higher Education*, 67(5), 498–527.

Hannah, S. B. (2010, April). *Finding the balance: A political analysis of the 2008 reauthorization of the Higher Education Act*. Paper presented at the annual Midwest Political Science Association meeting, Chicago, IL. https://core.ac.uk/reader/47214720

Harbridge, L. (2015). *Is bipartisanship dead? Policy agreement and agenda setting in the House of Representatives*. Cambridge University Press.

Harnisch, T. (2012, July). *Update on the federal maintenance of effort provision: Reinforcing the state role in public higher education financing* [Policy brief]. American Association of State Colleges and Universities. https://www.aascu.org/policy/publications/policy-matters/2012/MaintenanceofEffort-II.pdf

Harnisch, T., Nassirian, B., Saddler, A., & Coleman, A. (2016, December). *Enhancing state authorization: The need for action by states as stewards of higher education performance*. Education Commission of the States.

Harper, S. R. (2020). COVID-19 and the racial equity implications of reopening college and university campuses. *American Journal of Education*, 127(1), 153–162.

Harper, S. R., Patton, L. D., & Wooden, O. S. (2009). Access and equity for African American students in higher education: A critical race historical analysis of policy efforts. *The Journal of Higher Education*, 80(4), 389–414.

Harris, A. (2018, September 11). America wakes up from its dream of free college. *The Atlantic*. https://www.theatlantic.com/education/archive/2018/09/where-did-americas-dream-of-free-college-go/569770/

Harris, C. M. (2000). Washington's "Federal City," Jefferson's "Federal Town." *Washington History*, 12(1), 49–53.

Harris, L. A. (2021, April 9). *The National Science Foundation: An overview* (CRS Report No. R46753). Library of Congress, Congressional Research Service.

Harris, A., & Kelderman, E. (2017, July 13). Who does DeVos's department really represent? *The Chronicle of Higher Education*. https://www.chronicle.com/article/Who-Does-DeVos-s-Department/240643

Harvard Law Review. (2017). Recent adjudications: Labor and employment law—National Labor Relations Act—NLRB holds that student assistants at colleges and universities are statutory employees covered by the NLRA. *Harvard Law Review*, 130, 1281–1288.

Hawkins, B. D. (2020, June 19). A coalition of Maryland HBCUs keeps the hope of a legal settlement alive. *Diverse: Issues in Higher Education*. https://diverseeducation.com/article/181481/

Hearn, J. C., McLendon, M. K., & Lacy, T. A. (2013). State-funded "Eminent Scholars" programs: University faculty recruitment as an emerging policy instrument. *The Journal of Higher Education*, 84(5), 601–639.

Hearn, J. C., & Ness, E. C. (2017). The ecology of state higher-education policymaking in the U.S. In D. Palfreyman, T. Tapper, S. Thomas (Eds.), *Towards the Private Funding of Higher Education* (pp. 19–47). Routledge.

Hebert, J. G., & Jenkins, M. K. (2011). The need for state redistricting reform to rein in partisan gerrymandering. *Yale Law & Policy Review*, 29, 543–558.

Hegji, A. (2018, October 24). *The Higher Education Act (HEA): A primer* (CRS Report No. R43351). Library of Congress, Congressional Research Service.

Hegji, A., Smole, D. P., & Heisler, E. J. (2018, November 20). *Federal student loan forgiveness and loan repayment programs* (CRS Report No. R43571). Library of Congress, Congressional Research Service.

Hegji, A., & Hogue, H. B. (2019, December 30). *The Office of Federal Student Aid as a performance-based organization* (CRS Report No. R46143). Library of Congress, Congressional Research Service.

Heilig, J. V., Reddick, R. J., Hamilton, C., & Dietz, L. (2011). Actuating equity: Historical and contemporary analyses of African American access to selective higher education from *Sweatt* to the top 10 percent law. *Harvard Journal of African American Public Policy*, 17(1), 11–28.

Heitshusen, V. (2017, May 16). *The Speaker of the House: House officer, party leader, and Representative* (CRS Report No. 97-780). Library of Congress, Congressional Research Service.

Heitshusen, V. (2019, September 4). *Party leaders in the United States Congress, 1789–2019* (CRS Report No. RL30567). Library of Congress, Congressional Research Service.

Heitshusen, V. (2020, November 24). *Introduction to the legislative process in the U.S. Congress* (CRS Report No. R42843). Library of Congress, Congressional Research Service.

Heitshusen, V., & Beth, R. S. (2017, April 17). *Filibusters and cloture in the Senate* (CRS Report No. RL30360). Library of Congress, Congressional Research Service.

Helhoski, A. (2020, October 22). Private student loans bankruptcy: Is it getting easier? *NerdWallet*. https://www.nerdwallet.com/article/loans/student-loans/student-loan-discharge-bankruptcy-getting-easier

Henderson, L. J. (2004). Brown v. Board of Education at 50: The multiple legacies for policy and administration. *Public Administration Review*, 64(3), 270–274.

Heniff, B. (2012, November 26). *Overview of the authorization-appropriations process* (CRS Report No. RS20371). Library of Congress, Congressional Research Service.

Heniff, B. (2016, November 22). *The budget reconciliation process: The Senate's "Byrd Rule"* (CRS Report No. RL30862). Library of Congress, Congressional Research Service.

Henry, L. M. (2013). Revising the common rule: prospects and challenges. *The Journal of Law, Medicine, & Ethics*, 41(2), 386–389.

Herbert, W. A., & Apkarian, J. (2017). Everything passes, everything changes: Unionization and collective bargaining in higher education. *Perspectives on Work*, 30–35.

Herbold, H. (1994). Never a level playing field: Blacks and the GI Bill. *The Journal of Blacks in Higher Education*, 6, 104–108.

Herian, M. N. (2012). The intergovernmental politics of Internet sales taxation in the United States. *Policy & Internet*, 4(1), 1–20.

Hersch, J., & Shinall, J. B. (2015). Fifty years later: The legacy of the Civil Rights Act of 1964. *Journal of Policy Analysis and Management*, 34(2), 424–456.

Herszenhorn, D. M., & Pear, R. (2010, March 26). Final votes in Congress cap battle over health. *New York Times*.

Hessick, F. A. (2013). Standing in Diversity. *Alabama Law Review*, 65(2), 417–433.

Hesson, T., & Kahn, C. (2020, August 14). Trump pushes anti-immigrant message even as coronavirus dominates campaign. *Reuters*. https://www.reuters.com/article/us-usa-election-immigration-insight/trump-pushes-anti-immigrant-message-even-as-coronavirus-dominates-campaign-idUSKCN25A18W

Hevel, M. S. (2016). Toward a history of student affairs: A synthesis of research, 1996–2015. *Journal of College Student Development*, 57(7), 844–862.

Hiers, R. H. (2002). Institutional academic freedom vs. faculty academic freedom in public colleges and universities: Dubious dichotomy. *Journal of College and University Law*, 29(1), 35–110.

Higgins, T. (2021, February 3). Justice Department drops suit accusing Yale of discriminating against white and Asian applicants, in reversal from Trump era. *CNBC*. https://www.cnbc.com/2021/02/03/doj-drops-suit-accusing-yale-of-discriminating-against-white-asian-students.html

Higher Education Act, 20 U.S. Code §§ 1001 et seq. (2018).

Higher Education Compliance Alliance. (n.d.). *Compliance matrix*. https://www.higheredcompliance.org/compliance-matrix/

Higher Education Opportunity Act, Pub. L. No. 110-315, 122 Stat. 3078 (2008).

Hill, F. (2020, May 27). Public service and the federal government. *Voter Vitals*. Brookings Institution. https://www.brookings.edu/policy2020/votervital/public-service-and-the-federal-government/

Hillison, J. (1996). The origins of agriscience: or where did all that scientific agriculture come from? *Journal of Agricultural Education*, 37, 8–13.

Hills, R. M. (1998). The political economy of cooperative federalism: Why state autonomy makes sense and "dual sovereignty" doesn't. *Michigan Law Review*, 96, 813–944.

Hiltzik, M. (2015). The origins of big science: And what comes next. *Boom: A Journal of California*, 5(3), 98–108.

Hinrichs, P. (2015). *An empirical analysis of racial segregation in higher education* (NBER Working Paper No. 21831). National Bureau of Economic Research.

Hogue, H. B. (2015, March 11). *Recess appointments: Frequently asked questions* (CRS Report No. RS21308). Library of Congress, Congressional Research Service.

Holcombe, R. G. (2005). Government growth in the twenty-first century. *Public Choice*, 124, 95–114.

Holzer, J. (2021, January 19). What does the vice president do? *The Conversation*. https://theconversation.com/what-does-the-vice-president-do-152467

Homans, C. (2019, January 22). Mitch McConnell got everything he wanted. But at what cost? *New York Times Magazine*.

Honig, M. I. (2004). The new middle management: Intermediary organizations in education policy implementation. *Educational Evaluation and Policy Analysis*, 26(1), 65–87

House Committee on Appropriations. (n.d.-a). *Labor, Health & Human Services, Education, & Related Agencies*. https://appropriations.house.gov/subcommittees/labor-health-and-human-services-education-and-related-agencies-116th-congress

House Committee on Appropriations. (n.d.-b). *Key terms*. https://appropriations.house.gov/about/key-terms

House Committee on Appropriations. (2020, July 7). *Chairwoman DeLauro statement at subcommittee markup of FY 2021 Labor-HHS-Education funding bill*. https://appropriations.house.gov/news/statements/chairwoman-delauro-statement-at-subcommittee-markup-of-fy-2021-labor-hhs-education

Howell, W. G. (2005). Introduction: Unilateral powers: A brief overview. *Presidential Studies Quarterly*, 35(3), 417–439.

Howell, W. G., & Lewis, D. E. (2002). Agencies by presidential design. *Journal of Politics*, 64(4), 1095–1114.

Huang, W. C., & McDonnell, G. (1997). Growth of government expenditure: the case of USA. *The Social Science Journal*, 34(3), 311–322.

Hubler, S. (2020, August 15). As colleges move classes online, families rebel against the cost. *New York Times*.

Hudson, K. L., & Collins, F. S. (2015). Bringing the common rule into the 21st century. *New England Journal of Medicine*, 373(24), 2293–2296.

Hutchins, A. (2019, July 24). What happened to the federal Perkins Loan? *USA Today*. https://www.usnews.com/education/blogs/student-loan-ranger/articles/2019-07-24/what-happened-to-the-federal-perkins-loan

Institute of Education Sciences. (2017–2018). *Director's biennial report to Congress: Fiscal years 2017 and 2018*. Institute for Education Sciences.

Internal Revenue Service. (2019). *Credits and deductions for individuals*. https://www.irs.gov/credits-deductions-for-individuals

Internal Revenue Service. (2020, January 17). *Publication 970: Tax benefits for education*. https://www.irs.gov/pub/irs-pdf/p970.pdf

Itzkowitz, M. (2017, October 3). *Measuring results: How does our higher education system use student outcomes?* Third Way. https://www.thirdway.org/memo/measuring-results-how-does-our-higher-education-system-use-student-outcomes

Iuliano, J. (2012). An empirical assessment of student loan discharges and the undue hardship standard. *American Bankruptcy Law Journal*, 86, 495–525.

Jackson, C. (2003, October 2). *The Office of Federal Student Aid: The federal government's first performance-based organization* (CRS Report No. RL32098). Library of Congress, Congressional Research Service.

Jackson, C. (2017, September 22). *Dear Colleague*. https://www2.ed.gov/about/offices/list/ocr/letters/colleague-title-ix-201709.pdf

Janosik, S. M., & Gregory, D. E. (2003). The Clery Act and its influence on campus law enforcement practices. *NASPA Journal*, 41(1), 182–199.

Jaschik, S. (2015, January 2). Big union win. *Inside Higher Education*. https://www.insidehighered.com/news/2015/01/02/nlrb-ruling-shifts-legal-ground-faculty-unions-private-colleges

Jaschik, S. (2019a, March 13). Massive admissions scandal. *Inside Higher Education*. https://www.insidehighered.com/admissions/article/2019/03/13/dozens-indicted-alleged-massive-case-admissions-fraud

Jaschik, S. (2019b, December 16). Justice Department sues, settles with NACAC. *Inside Higher Education*. https://www.insidehighered.com/admissions/article/2019/12/16/justice-department-sues-and-settles-college-admissions-group

Jaschik, S. (2020, January 29). Appeals court blocks adjunct union. *Inside Higher Education*. https://www.insidehighered.com/news/2020/01/29/federal-appeals-court-blocks-adjunct-union-duquesne

Jaschik, S. (2021, April 28). Biden proposes free community college, Pell expansion. *Inside Higher Education*. https://www.insidehighered.com/news/2021/04/28/biden-proposes-free-community-college-18-trillion-plan

Jennings, J., & Nagel, J. C. (2020, October 23). Federal workforce statistics sources: OMP and OMB (CRS Report No. R43590). Library of Congress, Congressional Research Service.

Johnson, C. H. (2005). The dubious enumerated power doctrine. *Constitutional Commentary*, 22, 25–96.

Johnson, K. R. (2011). An essay on the nomination and confirmation of the first Latina Justice on the U.S. Supreme Court: The assimilation demand at work. *Chicana/o-Latina/o Law Review*, 30, 97–162.

Johnson, K. R. (2020). DACA in three acts: Genesis, impacts, future [Policy brief]. UC Davis Global Migration Center. https://globalmigration.ucdavis.edu/sites/g/files/dgvnsk8181/files/inline-files/Policy%20Brief_DACA.pdf

Johnson, T. (2014). Going back to the drawing board: Re-entrenching the Higher Education Act to restore its historical policy of access. *University of Toledo Law Review*, 45, 545–578.

Johnson, L. K., Gelles, E., & Kuzenski, J. C. (1992). The study of congressional investigations: Research strategies. *Congress & the Presidency: A Journal of Capital Studies*, 19(2), 137–156.

Johnstone, D. B. (1995, October). Starting points: Fundamental assumptions underlying the principles and policies of federal financial aid to students. In U.S. Department of Education (Ed.), *Financing postsecondary education: The federal role* (pp. 79–83) U.S. Government Printing Office.

Jones, D. R. (2001). Party polarization and legislative gridlock. *Political Research Quarterly*, 54(1), 125–141.

Jones, S., & Brown, B. (2020). Changing the narrative: UNCF and its role in policy advocacy for Historically Black Colleges and Universities. *Interest Groups & Advocacy*, 9(4), 451–469.

Julius, D. J., & DiGiovanni, N. (2019). Academic collective bargaining: Status, process, and prospects. *Academic Labor: Research and Artistry*, 3(1), 127–183.

Kagan, E. (2001). Presidential administration. *Harvard Law Review*, 2245–2385.

Kaiser, F. M. (2008, September 10). GAO: Government Accountability Office and General Accounting Office (CRS Report No. RL30349). Library of Congress, Congressional Research Service.

Kamensky, J. M. (1996). Role of the "Reinventing Government" movement in federal management reform. *Public administration review*, 56(3), 247–255.

Kantor, H., & Lowe, R. (1995). Class, race, and the emergence of federal education policy: From the New Deal to the Great Society. *Educational Researcher*, 24(3), 4–21.

Kaplan, S. (2021, January 15). Biden will elevate White House science office to Cabinet-level. *Washington Post*.

Kaplin, W. A., Lee, B. A., Hutchens, N. H., & Rooksby, J. H. (2020). *The law of higher education: Student version* (6th ed.). John Wiley & Sons.

Kay, S. (2013). America's Sputnik moments. *Survival, 55*(2), 123–146.

Keillor, J. B. (2009). Veterans at the gates: Exploring the new GI Bill and its transformative possibilities. *Washington University Law Review, 87*, 175–201.

Kelchen, R. (2017). *Higher education accreditation and the federal government*. Urban Institute.

Kelchen, R. (2018). *Higher education accountability*. Johns Hopkins University Press.

Keller, R. (2017). The undue hardship test: The dangers of a subjective test in determining the dischargeability of student loan debt in bankruptcy. *Missouri Law Review, 82*, 211–239.

Kenney, M., & Patton, D. (2009). Reconsidering the Bayh-Dole Act and the current university invention ownership model. *Research Policy, 38*(9), 1407–1422.

Kerr, E. (2020, January 27). FUTURE Act: What students, borrowers should know. *U.S. News & World Report*. https://www.usnews.com/education/best-colleges/paying-for-college/articles/what-future-act-means-for-fafsa-income-driven-repayment

Kerwin, C. M., & Furlong, S. R. (2011). *Rulemaking: How government agencies write law and make policy* (4th ed.). CQ Press.

Kesavan, V., & Sidak, J. G. (2002). The Legislator-in-Chief. *William & Mary Law Review, 44*(1), 1–64.

Keshner, A. (2019, August 28). How one woman persuaded the government to forgive $63,000 in student-loan debt she incurred 15 years ago. *MarketWatch*. https://www.marketwatch.com/story/how-one-woman-persuaded-the-government-to-forgive-63000-in-student-loan-debt-she-incurred-15-years-ago-2019-08-23

Kevles, D. J. (1977). The National Science Foundation and the debate over postwar research policy, 1942–1945: A political interpretation of *Science—The endless frontier*. *Isis, 68*(1), 5–6.

Kim, C. Y. (2018). The President's immigration courts. *Emory Law Journal, 68*, 1–48.

Kingdon, J. W. (2003). *Agendas, alternatives, & public policies* (2nd ed.). Longman.

Kiousis, S., Ragas, M. W., Kim, J. Y., Schweickart, T., Neil, J., & Kochhar, S. (2016). Presidential agenda building and policymaking: Examining linkages across three levels. *International Journal of Strategic Communication, 10*(1), 1–17.

Kiousis, S., & Strömbäck, J. (2010). The White House and public relations: Examining the linkages between presidential communications and public opinion. *Public Relations Review, 36*(1), 7–14.

Klein, A. (2016, March 31). The Every Student Succeeds Act: An ESSA overview. *Education Week*. https://www.edweek.org/ew/issues/every-student-succeeds-act/index.html

Konur, O. (2000). Creating enforceable civil rights for disabled students in higher education: An institutional theory perspective. *Disability & Society, 15*(7), 1041–1063.

Korenman, S. G. (2006). *Teaching the responsible conduct of research in humans (RCRH)*. U.S. Department of Health & Human Services. https://ori.hhs.gov/education/products/ucla/default.htm

Koss, M. P., Wilgus, J. K., & Williamsen, K. M. (2014). Campus sexual misconduct: Restorative justice approaches to enhance compliance with Title IX guidance. *Trauma, Violence, & Abuse, 15*(3), 242–257.

Kreighbaum, A. (2016a, September 28). Small agency, big impact. *Inside Higher Education.* https://www.insidehighered.com/news/2016/09/28/consumer-financial-protection-bureau-plays-outsize-role-regulator-profits-and-loan

Kreighbaum, A. (2016b, October 28). Borrower defense rules finalized. *Inside Higher Education.* https://www.insidehighered.com/news/2016/10/28/education-dept-releases-final-version-defense-repayment-loan-rules

Kreighbaum, A. (2017a, February 23). Transgender protections withdrawn. *Inside Higher Education.* https://www.insidehighered.com/news/2017/02/23/trump-administration-reverses-title-ix-guidance-transgender-protections

Kreighbaum, A. (2017b, March 27). Long road for regulatory rollbacks. *Inside Higher Education.* https://www.insidehighered.com/news/2017/03/27/repeal-obamas-higher-education-regulations-wont-be-swift-process-gop

Kreighbaum, A. (2017c, April 13). The (temporary?) U.S. education team. *Inside Higher Education.* https://www.insidehighered.com/news/2017/04/13/department-education-makes-first-official-senior-hires

Kreighbaum, A. (2017d, June 15). Reset of rules aimed at for-profits begins. *Inside Higher Education.* https://www.insidehighered.com/news/2017/06/15/education-department-hit-pause-two-primary-obama-regulations-aimed-profits

Kreighbaum, A. (2018a, August 10). Education Department to repeal "Gainful" rules. *Inside Higher Education.* https://www.insidehighered.com/quicktakes/2018/08/10/education-dept-repeal-gainful-rules

Kreighbaum, A. (2018b, November 20). New uncertainty on Title IX. *Inside Higher Education.* https://www.insidehighered.com/news/2018/11/20/title-ix-rules-cross-examination-would-make-colleges-act-courts-lawyers-say

Kreighbaum, A. (2018c, December 14). Farm Bill includes wins for colleges. *Inside Higher Education.* https://www.insidehighered.com/quicktakes/2018/12/14/farm-bill-includes-wins-colleges

Kreighbaum, A. (2019a, March 12). Trump seeks billions in cuts. *Inside Higher Education.* https://www.insidehighered.com/news/2019/03/12/white-house-wants-12-percent-cut-education-spending

Kreighbaum, A. (2019b, March 22). Trump signs broad executive order. *Inside Higher Education.* https://www.insidehighered.com/news/2019/03/22/white-house-executive-order-prods-colleges-free-speech-program-level-data-and-risk

Kreighbaum, A. (2019c, July 2). DeVos issues final repeal of gainful employment. *Inside Higher Education.* https://www.insidehighered.com/quicktakes/2019/07/02/devos-issues-final-repeal-gainful-employment

Kreighbaum, A. (2019d, September 27). Alexander releases narrow higher ed package. *Inside Higher Education.* https://www.insidehighered.com/quicktakes/2019/09/27/alexander-releases-narrow-higher-ed-package

Krent, H. J. (2005). *Presidential powers.* NYU Press.

Kriner, D. L., & Schickler, E. (2014). Investigating the president: Committee probes and presidential approval, 1953–2006. *The Journal of Politics, 76*(2), 521–534.

Kuhn, D. P. (2012, June 29). The incredible polarization and politicization of the Supreme Court. *The Atlantic.* https://www.theatlantic.com/politics/archive

/2012/06/the-incredible-polarization-and-politicization-of-the-supreme-court/259155/
Kumar, M. J. (2001). The Office of the Press Secretary. *Presidential Studies Quarterly*, 31(2), 296–322.PE
Kumar, M. J. (2017). *The Office of Communications* (Baker Institute for Public Policy Report 2017—33). White House Transition Project. http://whitehousetransitionproject.org/wp-content/uploads/2016/03/WHTP2017-33-Communications.pdf
Kyaw, A. (2021, January 13). *U.S. Department of Education updates College Scorecard*. Diverse Issues in Higher Education. https://diverseeducation.com/article/200953/
Labaree, D. F. (2016). Learning to love the bomb: The Cold War brings the best of times to American higher education. In P. Smeyers & M. Depaepe, Eds., *Educational research: Discourses of change and changes of discourse* (pp. 101–117). Springer.
Lampe, J. R. (2020, December 14). *"Court packing": Legislative control over the size of the Supreme Court* (CRS Report No. LSB10562). Library of Congress, Congressional Research Service.
Langford, C. L. (2015). The Living Constitution: Origins and rhetorical implications of the Constitution as agent. *Communication Law Review*, 15(1), 1–33.
Lax, J. R., & Phillips, J. H. (2012). The democratic deficit in the states. *American Journal of Political Science*, 56(1), 148–166.
Leal, D. L. (2007). Students in uniform: ROTC, the citizen-soldier, and the civil-military gap. *PS: Political Science and Politics*, 40(3), 479–483.
Lebryk, D. (2016, July 1). An update on the Fiscal-Federal Student Aid pilot for servicing defaulted student loan debt. *Treasury Notes*. https://www.treasury.gov/connect/blog/pages/an-update-on-the-fiscal-federal-student-aid-pilot-for-servicing-defaulted-student-loan-debt.aspx
Lederman, L. (2001). Equity and the Article I Court: Is the Tax Court's exercise of equitable powers constitutional? *Florida Tax Review*, 5(5), 357–413.
Lederman, D. (2021, February 3). A federal look at managing online programs. *Inside Higher Education*. https://www.insidehighered.com/news/2021/02/03/government-accountability-office-exploring-landscape-companies-help-colleges-go
Lee, E. A. S. (2017). The Clery Act on campus: Status update and gender implications. *New Directions for Community Colleges*, 2017(179), 59–66.
Lee, F. E. (2009). *Beyond ideology: Politics, principles, and partisanship in the U.S. Senate*. University of Chicago Press.
Lee, M. M. (2013, September 11). *An overview of judicial review of immigration matters* (CRS Report No. R43226). Library of Congress, Congressional Research Service.
Lee, P. (2015). A contract theory of academic freedom. *Saint Louis University Law Journal*, 59(2), 461–530.
Lee, R., & Ahtone, T. (2020, March 30). Land-grab universities. *High Country News*. https://www.hcn.org/issues/52.4/indigenous-affairs-education-land-grab-universities
Lee, S. (2020, July 29). DACA and the limits of good governance. *The Regulatory Review*. https://www.theregreview.org/2020/07/29/lee-daca-good-governance/

Lee, V., & Looney, A. (2019, January). *Understanding the 90/10 Rule: How reliant are public, private, and for-profit institutions on federal aid?* Brookings Institution. https://www.brookings.edu/wp-content/uploads/2019/01/ES_20190116_Looney-90-10.pdf

Leech, B. L., Baumgartner, F. R., La Pira, T. M., & Semanko, N. A. (2005). Drawing lobbyists to Washington: Government activity and the demand for advocacy. *Political Research Quarterly, 58*(1), 19–30.

Legrenzi, G., & Milas, C. (2002). A multivariate approach to the growth of governments. *Public Finance Review, 30*(1), 56–76.

Lehmuller, P., & Gregory, D. E. (2005). Affirmative action: From before *Bakke* to after *Grutter*. *Journal of Student Affairs Research and Practice, 42*(4), 835–864.

Lerner, J. Y. (2018). Getting the message across: Evaluating think tank influence in Congress. *Public Choice, 175*(3), 347–366.

Lerner, J., & Seru, A. (2017). *The use and misuse of patent data: Issues for corporate finance and beyond* (NBER Working Paper No. 24053). National Bureau of Economic Research.

Levinson, R. (2007, July). *Academic freedom and the First Amendment*. American Association of University Professors. https://www.aaup.org/NR/rdonlyres/57BFFE5E-900F-4A2A-B399-033ECE9ECB34/0/AcademicfreedomandFirstAmenoutline0907doc.pdf

Levinson, D. J., & Pildes, R. H. (2006). Separation of parties, not powers. *Harvard Law Review, 119*(8), 2311–2386.

Lewis, D. E. (2005). Staffing alone: Unilateral action and the politicization of the Executive Office of the President, 1988–2004. *Presidential Studies Quarterly, 35*(3), 496–514.

Lewis, M. M., Garces, L. M., & Frankenberg, E. (2019). A comprehensive and practical approach to policy guidance: the office for civil rights' role in education during the Obama administration. *Educational Researcher, 48*(1), 51–60.

Lewis-Beck, M. S., & Rice, T. W. (1985). Government growth in the United States. *The Journal of Politics, 47*(1), 2–30.

Lieberman, J. I. (1988). Modern federalism: Altered states. *The Urban Lawyer, 20*(2), 285–299.

Light, P. (1999). *The president's agenda: Domestic policy choice from Kennedy to Clinton*. Johns Hopkins University Press.

Lindquist, S. A., & Cross, F. B. (2005). Empirically testing Dworkin's chain novel theory: Studying the path of precedent. *New York University Law Review, 80*(4), 1156–1206.

Lingenfelter, P. E. (2004). The state and higher education: An essential partnership. *New Directions for Higher Education, 127*, 47–59.

Liptak, A. (2016, June 24). Texas policy of race-based admissions is upheld: Supreme Court votes 4-3, paving way for continued use of affirmative action. *New York Times*.

Longanecker, D. A. (2008, November). *Getting what you pay for: What state policymakers should know about federal higher education policy* [Policy brief] National Council of State Legislatures and Western Interstate Commission for Higher Education.

Longanecker, D., & Hill, M. A. (2014). The State Authorization Reciprocity Agreement (SARA): A good idea whose time has come. *Change: The Magazine of Higher Learning, 46*(3), 45–52.

Looney, A., Wessel, D., & Yilla, K. (2020, January 28). Who owes all that student debt? And who'd benefit if it were forgiven? *Policy 2020 Brookings*. Brookings Institution. https://www.brookings.edu/policy2020/votervital/who-owes-all-that-student-debt-and-whod-benefit-if-it-were-forgiven/

Looney, A., & Yannelis, C. (2015). A crisis in student loans?: How changes in the characteristics of borrowers and in the institutions they attended contributed to rising loan defaults. *Brookings Papers on Economic Activity, 2015*, 2, 1–89.

Lopez, L. (2015, October 13). America's student debt nightmare actually started in the 1980s. *Business Insider.* https://www.businessinsider.com/student-debt-crisis-started-in-the-1980s-2015-10

Loss, C. P. (2012). *Between citizens and the state: The politics of American higher education in the 20th century*. Princeton University Press.

Lowande, K. S. (2014). The contemporary presidency after the orders: Presidential memoranda and unilateral action. *Presidential Studies Quarterly, 44*(4), 724–741.

Lowery, J. W. (2004). Understanding the legal protections and limitations upon religion and spiritual expression on campus. *College Student Affairs Journal, 23*(2), 146–157.

Lowry, R. C. (2009). Reauthorization of the federal Higher Education Act and accountability for student learning: The dog that didn't bark. *Publius: The Journal of Federalism, 39*(3), 506–526.

Lu, J., & Xu, C. (2018). Complementary or supplementary? The relationship between government size and nonprofit sector size. *VOLUNTAS: International Journal of Voluntary and Nonprofit Organizations, 29*(3), 454–469.

Lubbers, J. S. (1998). *A guide to federal agency rulemaking* (3rd ed.). American Bar Association.

Ma, J., Pender, M., & Welch, M. (2019). *Education pays 2019* (Trends in Higher Education Series). The College Board.

Maag, E., Mundel, D., Rice, L., & Rueben, K. (2007, May). Subsidizing higher education through tax and spending programs. *Tax Policy Issues & Options, 18*. Urban-Brookings Tax Policy Center.

Mangan, K. (2020, September 24). Trump bars federal grants for "divisive and harmful" racial- sensitivity training. *The Chronicle of Higher Education.* https://www.chronicle.com/article/trump-bars-federal-grants-for-divisive-and-harmful-racial-sensitivity-training

Marcus, J. (2014, September 8). College-rating proposal shines spotlight on powerful lobby. *The Hechinger Report.* https://hechingerreport.org/college-rating-proposal-shines-spotlight-powerful-lobby/

Margulies, P. (2018). Bans, borders, and sovereignty: Judicial review of immigration law in the Trump administration. *Michigan State Law Review*, 1–80.

Marshall, W. P. (2004). The limits on congress's authority to investigate the president. *University of Illinois Law Review (2004)*, 2, 781–828.

Marsicano, C. R. (2019). *Lobbying for Alma Mater: Higher education institutions as interest groups* [Doctoral dissertation]. Vanderbilt University.

Marsicano, C. R., & Brooks, C. (2020). Professor Smith goes to Washington: Educational interest group lobbying, 1998–2017. *Educational Researcher*, 49(6), 448–453.

Martin, M. V., & Hipp, J. S. (2016). Land grants: Back to the future. *Choices*, 31(3).

Matjie, M. (2018). Political appointees and career executives. In A. Farazmand (Ed.), *Global encyclopedia of public administration, public policy, and governance*. Springer. https://doi.org/10.1007/978-3-319-31816-5_1267-1

Matsudaira, J. (2017, September). *Federal efforts could improve the data available to drive improvement in higher education*. Urban Institute. https://eric.ed.gov/?id=ED578889

Matthews, C. M. (2008). *Federal research & development funding at Historically Black Colleges or Universities* (CRS Report No. RL34435). Library of Congress, Congressional Research Service.

Matthews, K. R., Evans, K. M., & Lane, N. F. (2017). Science advice in the Trump White House. *Science*, 355(6325), 574–576.

Mayer, K. R. (1999). Executive orders and presidential power. *The Journal of Politics*, 61(2), 445–466.

Mayer, K. (2002). *With the stroke of a pen: Executive orders and presidential power*. Princeton University Press.

Mayhew, M. J., Rockenbach, A. N., Bowman, N. A., Seifert, T. A., & Wolniak, G. C. (2016). *How college affects students: 21st century evidence that higher education works*. John Wiley & Sons.

McCann, L. A. (2017). The Age Discrimination in Employment Act at 50. *ABA Journal of Labor & Employment Law*, 33(1), 89–104.

McCann, C. (2018, September 13). *Letter to Ashley Higgins re: ED-2018-OPE-0042-0001*. New America. https://s3.amazonaws.com/newamericadotorg/documents/092018_New_America_Comments_on_GE_NPRM.pdf

McCann, C., & Laitinen, A. (2017, September 26). The Spellings Commission: Same story, different decade. *New America*. https://www.newamerica.org/education-policy/edcentral/spellings-commission-same-story-different-decade/

McCann, C., & Laitinen, A. (2019, November). *The Bermuda Triad: Where accountability goes to die* [Research report]. New America.

McCarthy, M. (2015). Judicial impact on education politics and policies. In B. S. Cooper, J. G. Cibulka, & L. D. Fusarelli (Eds), *Handbook of education politics and policy* (2nd ed.), pp. 148–165. Routledge.

McCarthy, M. A., Parton, B., Tesfai, L., & Prebil, M. (2018, May 11). CESNA's first reactions to recommendations from president's task force on apprenticeship expansion. *New America*. https://www.newamerica.org/education-policy/edcentral/first-reactions-apprenticeship-task-force/

McDonald, L. (2014). Think tanks and the media: How the conservative movement gained entry into the education policy arena. *Educational Policy*, 28(6), 845–880.

McDonnell, L. M., & Ellmore, R. F. (1987). Getting the job done: Alternative policy instruments. *Educational Evaluation & Policy Analysis*, 9(2), 133–152.

McGuinness, A. (2014, January 28). *Community college systems across the 50 states*. National Center for Higher Education Management Systems. https://www.leg.state.nv.us/Interim/77th2013/Exhibits/CommColleges/E012814J.pdf

McKee, G. (2008). Judicial review of agency guidance documents: Rethinking the finality doctrine. *Administrative Law Review*, 60, 371–408.

McKenzie, L. (2020, February 5). Key senators turn up heat on OPMs. *Inside Higher Education*. https://www.insidehighered.com/news/2020/02/05/online-program-management-companies-face-washington-microscope

McKenzie, L. (2021, March 8). ACICS on the ropes again. *Inside Higher Education*. https://www.insidehighered.com/news/2021/03/08/controversial-accreditor-acicss-federal-recognition-likely-be-revoked-again

McLaurin v. Oklahoma State Regents, 339 U.S. 637 (1950).

McLean, C., & Robin, L. (2017). Education policy think tank models and mission. *Policy Perspectives*, 24, 33–54.

McLean, D. (2020, June 11). Months after Congress sent emergency aid to college students, distribution remains spotty. *The Chronicle of Higher Education*. https://www.chronicle.com/article/months-after-congress-sent-emergency-aid-to-college-students-distribution-remains-spotty

McLendon, M. K., Hearn, J. C., & Deaton, R. (2006). Called to account: Analyzing the origins and spread of state performance-accountability policies for higher education. *Educational Evaluation & Policy Analysis*, 28(1), 1–24.

McMillon, B. J. (2018, June 27). *Supreme Court appointment process: President's selection of a nominee* (CRS No. R44235). Library of Congress, Congressional Research Service.

McMillon, B. J. (2019, March 21). *Judicial nomination statistics and analysis: U.S. District and Circuit Courts, 1977–2018* (CRS Report No. R45622). Library of Congress, Congressional Research Service.

Mercier, S. A., & Halbrook, S. A. (2020). *Agricultural policy of the United States: Historic foundations and 21st century issues*. Springer.

Messer, S. R. (2018). The parameters of trust: Public Service Loan Forgiveness and prioritizing reliable agency communications. *Administrative Law Review*, 70(1), 233–261.

Mettler, S. (2014). *Degrees of inequality: How the politics of higher education sabotaged the American dream*. Basic Books.

Mervin, D. (1995). The bully pulpit, II. *Presidential Studies Quarterly*, 25(1), 19–23.

Meyers, M., & Goman, C. (2017). Michelle Obama: Exploring the narrative. *Howard Journal of Communications*, 28(1), 20–35.

Meyers, M. K., Vorsanger, S., Peters, B. G., & Pierre, J. (2007). Street-level bureaucrats and the implementation of public policy. *The handbook of public administration*, 153–163.

Mikelson, K. S., Eyster, L., Durham, C., & Cohen, E. (2017, February). *TAACCCT goals, design, and evaluation: The Trade Adjustment Assistance Community College and Career Training Grant Program Brief 1*. Urban Institute.

Milakovich, M. E., & Gordon, G. J. (2013). *Public administration in America* (11th ed.). Wadsworth Cengage.

Military One Source. (n.d.). *About SECO*. https://myseco.militaryonesource.mil/portal/home/aboutseco

Miller, B. (2016, May 23). *Building a student-level data system*. Center for American Progress.

Miller, B., & Delisle, J. (2019, May). *Ensuring accountability and effectiveness at the Office of Federal Student Aid*. Center for American Progress.

Miller, B., & Flores, A. (2018, March 9). *ACICS should not regain its ability to grant access to federal financial aid*. Center for American Progress.

Miller, M. A. (2002). Editorial: The Fund for the Improvement of Postsecondary Education: 30 years of making a difference. *Change, 34*(5), 4.

Miller, G., & Moe, T. (1983). Bureaucrats, legislators, and the size of government. *American Political Science Review, 77*, 297–322.

Minnesota State Community & Technical College. (2020, August 31). *M State providing free laptops to eligible students*. https://www.minnesota.edu/news/m-state-providing-free-laptops-eligible-students

Mishkin, F. S., & White, E. N. (2002). *U.S. stock market crashes and their aftermath: implications for monetary policy* (NBER Working Paper No. 8992). National Bureau of Economic Research.

Mitchell, T. (2020, September 25). *Letter to The Honorable Nancy Pelosi & The Honorable Kevin McCarthy*. American Council on Education. https://www.acenet.edu/Documents/Letter-House-Fall-COVID-Supplemental-092520.pdf

Mitchell, T. (2021, February 8). *Letter to The Honorable Bobby Scott & The Honorable Virginia Foxx*. American Council on Education. https://www.acenet.edu/Documents/Letter-House-Committee-Education-Labor-Budget-Reconciliation-020821.pdf

Modan, N. (2019, October 11). DeVos pushes charter school growth through opportunity zone initiative. *Education Dive*. https://www.educationdive.com/news/devos-pushes-charter-school-growth-through-opportunity-zone-initiative/564812/

Moe, R. C. (2000, September 12). *The president's Cabinet: Evolution, alternatives, and proposals for change* (CRS Report No. RL30673). Library of Congress, Congressional Research Service.

Moe, T. M., & Howell, W. G. (1999). The presidential power of unilateral action. *The Journal of Law, Economics, and Organization, 15*(1), 132–179.

Monk, L. R. (2015). *The words we live by: Your annotated guide to the Constitution*. Hachette UK.

Moore, G. (2017a). The Smith-Hughes Act: The road to it and what it accomplished. *Techniques Magazine, 92*(1), 17–21.

Moore, G. E. (2017b). The status of agricultural education prior to the Smith-Hughes Act. *The Agricultural Education Magazine, 89*(4), 21–25.

Morgan, G. (1997). *Images of organization*. Sage Publications.

Morris, A. D. (1984). *The origins of the civil rights movement*. Simon and Schuster.

Mouat, L. (1981, January 20). Bell: Soft-spoken "good soldier." *The Christian Science Monitor*. Nexis Uni.

Mueller, D. C., & Murrell, P. (1986). Interest groups and the size of government. *Public Choice, 48*(2), 125–145.

Mullen, J., & Diamond, J. (2015, February 17). Obama vows to abide by immigration court order. *CNN Politics*. https://www.cnn.com/2015/02/17/politics/texas-obama-immigration-injunction/index.html

Mumper, M., Gladieux, L. E., King, J. E., & Corrigan, M. E. (2016). The federal government and higher education. In M. N. Bastedo, P. G. Altbach, & P. J. Gumport

(Eds.), *American higher education in the 21st Century* (4th ed.) (pp. 212–237). Johns Hopkins University Press.

Murakami, K. (2020a, January 10). Changing court attitudes on bankruptcies. *Inside Higher Education*. https://www.insidehighered.com/news/2020/01/10/recent-court-decisions-could-expand-bankruptcy-student-debt

Murakami, K. (2020b, February 11). Another Trump budget, likely DOA. *Inside Higher Education*. https://www.insidehighered.com/news/2020/02/11/trump-budget-would-boost-career-education-spending-cut-funds-college-aid-research

Murakami, K. (2020c, September 1). For-profits fear a Biden presidency. *Inside Higher Education*. https://www.insidehighered.com/news/2020/09/01/profits-see-lot-riding-elections

Murakami, K. (2021, January 18). More influence for science. *Inside Higher Education*. https://www.insidehighered.com/news/2021/01/18/biden-elevates-head-science-office-cabinet-level

Napolitano, J. (2012, June 15). *Exercising prosecutorial discretion with respect to individuals who came to the United States as children* [Memorandum]. U.S. Department of Homeland Security. https://www.templateroller.com/template/2083877/exercising-prosecutorial-discretion-with-respect-to-individuals-who-came-to-the-united-states-as-children-policy-memorandum.html

Nash, M. A. (2019). Entangled pasts: Land-grant colleges and American Indian dispossession. *History of Education Quarterly*, 59(4), 437–467.

NASPA. (n.d.). Background brief: HEA reauthorization. *NASPA Hill Days—Student Affairs Day of Action*. https://www.naspa.org/images/uploads/main/HEA_Background_Brief_FINAL.pdf

National Advisory Committee on Institutional Quality and Integrity. (2011, October 31). *National Advisory Committee on Institutional Quality and Integrity Charter*. U.S. Department of Education.

National Association of Student Financial Aid Administrators. (n.d.). *Federal budget and appropriations*. https://www.nasfaa.org/federal_budget_appropriations

National Association of Student Financial Aid Administrators. (2018, January 3). *Federal budget frequently asked questions*. https://www.nasfaa.org/budget_faqs

National Center for Education Statistics. (n.d.-a). *About IPEDS*. https://nces.ed.gov/ipeds/about-ipeds

National Center for Education Statistics. (n.d.-b). *About us*. https://nces.ed.gov/about/

National Commission on Excellence in Education. (1983). *A nation at risk: The imperative for educational reform* (a report to the nation and the secretary of education). United States Department of Education.

National Conference of State Legislatures. (n.d.). *The state role in education finance*. http://www.ncsl.org/research/education/state-role-in-education-finance.aspx

National Endowment for the Humanities. (2017). *Collaborative research grants*. https://www.neh.gov/sites/default/files/2018-06/collaborative-research-dec-6-2017-edit.pdf

National Immigration Forum. (2018, August 7). *Fact sheet: Immigration courts*. https://immigrationforum.org/article/fact-sheet-immigration-courts/

National Institutes of Health. (2021, April). *NIH grants policy statement: 11.1.2 Nondiscrimination*. https://grants.nih.gov/grants/policy/nihgps/html5/section_11/11.1.2_nondiscrimination.htm

National Institutes of Health. (2018, May). *The IACUC*. https://olaw.nih.gov/resources/tutorial/iacuc.htm

National Labor Relations Board. (n.d.). *The board*. https://www.nlrb.gov/about-nlrb/who-we-are/the-board

National Labor Relations Board v. Yeshiva University, 444 U.S. 672 (1980).

National Research Council. (1995). *Colleges of agriculture at the land grant universities: A profile*. National Academies Press.

National Research Council. (2004). *Science, medicine, and animals*. National Academy of Sciences.

National Research Council. (2012). *Review of disability and rehabilitation research: NIDRR grantmaking processes and products*. The National Academies Press.

Natow, R. S. (2015). From Capitol Hill to Dupont Circle and beyond: The influence of policy actors in the federal higher education rulemaking process. *The Journal of Higher Education, 86*(3), 360–386.

Natow, R. S. (2017). *Higher education rulemaking: The politics of creating regulatory policy*. Johns Hopkins University Press.

Natow, R. S. (2020). Research utilization in higher education rulemaking: A multi-case study of research prevalence, sources, and barriers. *Education Policy Analysis Archives, 28*, 95.

Natow, R. S. (2021a, January 4). The importance of congressional leadership for higher education policy. *Rockefeller Institute of Government Blog*. https://rockinst.org/blog/the-importance-of-congressional-leadership-for-higher-education-policy/

Natow, R. S. (2021b, April). *Understanding higher education bill success in the United States Congress*. Paper presented at the 2021 Annual Conference of the American Educational Research Association.

Natow, R. S. (2021c, May 4). Higher education policy implications of President Biden's first 100 days. *Rockefeller Institute of Government Blog*. https://rockinst.org/blog/higher-education-policy-implications-of-president-bidens-first-100-days/

Natow, R. S. (2021d, October). *A framework for understanding federal-state partnerships for higher education*. Rockefeller Institute of Government. https://rockinst.org/wp-content/uploads/2021/10/Fed-State-Partnerships-Higher-Ed.pdf

Natow, R. S., Reddy, V., & Ioannou, V. (2021). *How states respond to federal policy on state authorization for higher education: Findings from a multi-case study* (Final Report). State Higher Education Executive Officers Association.

NC-SARA. (n.d.). *Regional education compacts*. https://nc-sara.org/regional-education-compacts

Nebraska Legislature. (n.d.). *Unicam focus*. https://nebraskalegislature.gov/education/lesson3.php

Neiberg, M. S. (2000). *Making citizen-soldiers: ROTC and the ideology of American military service*. Harvard University Press.

Nelson, L. A. (2012, February 14). A symbolic, but pleasing, budget. *Inside Higher Education*. https://www.insidehighered.com/news/2012/02/14/obama-proposes-increase-education-spending

Nelson, L. (2018, June 21). Donald Trump's plan to (sort of) eliminate the Department of Education, briefly explained. *Vox*. https://www.vox.com/policy-and-politics/2018/6/21/17489456/education-workforce-department

Ness, E. C., & Gándara, D. (2014). Ideological think tanks in the states: An inventory of their prevalence, networks, and higher education policy activity. *Educational Policy, 28*(2), 258–280.
New America. (n.d.). *Student loan history*. https://www.newamerica.org/education-policy/topics/higher-education-funding-and-financial-aid/federal-student-aid/federal-student-loans/federal-student-loan-history/
New York State Department of State. (2018, November 16). *Local government handbook*. https://dos.ny.gov/system/files/documents/2019/05/pub.pdf
Nielson, A. (2014). In defense of formal rulemaking. *Ohio State Law Journal, 75*(2), 237–292.
Nienhusser, H. K. (2015). Undocumented immigrants and higher education policy: The policymaking environment of New York State. *The Review of Higher Education, 38*(2), 271–303.
Niskanen, W. A. (1968). The peculiar economics of bureaucracy. *The American Economic Review*, 293–305.
Niskanen, W. A. (1971). *Bureaucracy and representative government*. Aldine Atherton.
Nisenson, A. (2016). Constitutional due process and Title IX investigation and appeal procedures at colleges and universities. *Penn State Law Review, 120*(4), 963–976.
Nolan, A., & Glassman, M. E. (2016, November 28). The powers of Congress: A brief overview. *Congressional Research Service: In Focus* (CRS Report No. IF10518). Library of Congress, Congressional Research Service.
Obama, B. (2015, March 10). *Student Aid Bill of Rights* [Presidential Memorandum].
Obama White House. (n.d.). *About Vice President Biden's efforts to end violence against women*. https://obamawhitehouse.archives.gov/1is2many/about
O'Connell, A. J. (2019, July 22). *Acting leaders: Recent practices, consequences, and reforms* [Report]. Brookings Institution. https://www.brookings.edu/research/acting-leaders/
Office of Management & Budget. (2020). *A budget for America's future*. U.S. Government Publishing Office.
Office of the Under Secretary of Defense for Research & Engineering. (n.d.). *Today's research, tomorrow's breakthroughs*. https://basicresearch.defense.gov/
Olds, C. (2013, September). Assessing presidential agenda-setting capacity: Dynamic comparisons of presidential, mass media, and public attention to economic issues. *Congress & the Presidency, 40*(3), 255–284.
Oleszek, M. J. (2020, March 4). *Committee jurisdiction and referral in the House* (CRS Report No. R46251). Library of Congress, Congressional Research Service.
Oleszek, W. J. (2014). *Congressional procedures and the policy process* (9th ed.). CQ Press.
Oleszek, W. J., Oleszek, M. J., Rybicki, E., & Heniff, B. (2019). *Congressional procedures and the policy process* (11th ed.). CQ Press.
Oliver, R. W. (2002). Real-Time strategy: Instinctive strategy: Organic organizations rule. *Journal of Business Strategy* (September/October), 7–10.
Oliver, W. M., Hill, J., & Marion, N. E. (2011). When the president speaks . . . An analysis of presidential influence over public opinion concerning the war on drugs. *Criminal Justice Review, 36*(4), 456–469.
Olson, K. W. (1973). The GI Bill and higher education: Success and surprise. *American Quarterly, 25*(5), 596–610.

Onuf, P. S. (2019). *Statehood and union: A history of the Northwest Ordinance*. University of Notre Dame Press.
O'Reilly, J. T. (2006). *Federal preemption of state and local law: Legislation, regulation and litigation*. American Bar Association.
Orphan, C. M., Laderman, S., & Gildersleeve, R. E. (2021). Advocates or honest information brokers? Examining the higher education public policy agenda-setting processes of intermediary organizations. *The Review of Higher Education, 44*(3), 325–355.
Owen-Smith, A., & Coast, J. (2017). Understanding sampling and recruitment. In J. Coast (Ed.), *Qualitative methods in health economics* (pp. 42–58). Rowman & Littlefield Ltd.
Pardo, R. I., & Lacey, M. R. (2005). Undue hardship in the bankruptcy courts: An empirical assessment of the discharge of education debt. *University of Cincinnati Law Review, 74*, 405–529.
Park, S. (2015). State renewable energy governance: Policy instruments, markets, or citizens. *Review of Policy Research, 32*(3), 273–296.
Parker, D.C.W., & Dull, M. (2009). Divided we quarrel: The politics of congressional investigations, 1947–2004. *Legislative Studies Quarterly, 34*(3), 319–345.
Parker, J. E., & Wagner, D. J. (2016). From the USDA: Educating the next generation: Funding opportunities in food, agricultural, natural resources, and social sciences education. *CBE—Life Sciences Education, 15*(3), fe5, 1-fe5, 4.
Parks, C. (2017). Beyond compliance: Students and FERPA in the age of big data. *Journal of Intellectual Freedom and Privacy, 2*(2), 23–33.
Parrillo, N. R. (2019). Federal agency guidance and the power to bind: An empirical study of agencies and industries. *Yale Journal on Regulation, 36*, 165–271.
Parsons, M. D. (1997). *Power and politics: Federal higher education policymaking in the 1990s*. State University of New York Press.
Pasachoff, E. (2013). Conditional spending after *NFIB v. Sebelius*: The example of federal education law. *American University Law Review, 62*(3), 577–662.
Pasachoff, E. (2016). The president's budget as source of agency policy control. *Yale Law Journal, 125*(8), 2182–2291.
Pasachoff, E. (2020). The president's budget powers in the Trump era. In M. Bose & A. Rudalevige (Eds.), *Executive policymaking: The role of the OMB in the presidency* (pp. 69–98). Brookings Institution Press.
Pavela, G., & Pavela, G. (2012). The ethical and educational imperative of due process. *Journal of College & University Law, 38*, 567–627.
Pece, C. (2019, June). *NCSES Info Brief: Federal R&D obligations increase an estimated 2.7% in FY 2018* (NSF 19-321). National Science Foundation.
Pelesh, M. L. (1994). Regulations under the Higher Education Amendments of 1992: A case study in negotiated rulemaking. *Law & Contemporary Problems, 57*(4), 151–170.
Pelsue, B. (2017, Fall). When it comes to education, the federal government is in charge of . . . um, what? *Harvard Ed. Magazine*. https://www.gse.harvard.edu/news/ed/17/08/when-it-comes-education-federal-government-charge-um-what
Pepperdine University. (n.d.). *Wm. Matthew Byrne, Jr. Judicial Clerkship Institute*. https://law.pepperdine.edu/judicial-clerkship-institute/
Perna, L. W., & Leigh, E. W. (2018). Understanding the promise: A typology of state and local college promise programs. *Educational Researcher, 47*(3), 155–180.

Perry, A. M., & Hamilton, D. (2021, January 25). Just as we score policies' budget impact we should score for racial equity as well. *Brookings "The Avenue" Blog*. https://www.brookings.edu/blog/the-avenue/2021/01/25/just-as-we-score-policies-budget-impact-we-should-score-for-racial-equity-as-well/

Petracca, M. P. (2018). *The politics of interests: Interest groups transformed*. Routledge.

Pew Charitable Trusts. (2019, October). *Two decades of change in federal and state higher education funding*. https://www.pewtrusts.org/-/media/assets/2019/10/fedstatefundinghigheredu_chartbook_v1.pdf

Pfiffner, J. P. (2020). OMB, the presidency, and the federal budget. In M. Bose & A. Rudalevige (Eds), *Executive policymaking: The role of the OMB in the presidency* (pp. 11–40). Brookings Institution Press.

Pierce, R. J. (2009). What factors can an agency consider in making a decision? *Michigan State Law Review (2009)*, 67–88.

Pierce, C. & Siraco, J. (2018). Excelsior, New York state's "free" college scholarship. *Texas Education Review*, Fall 2018 Special Issue, 50–59. http://doi.org/10.15781/T20K26X27

Pilıos, D. N. (2005). Assuming maturity matters: The limited reach of the Establishment Clause at public universities. *Cornell Law Review*, 90, 1349–1376.

Pitre, C. C., & Pitre, P. (2009). Increasing underrepresented high school students' college transitions and achievements: TRIO educational opportunity programs. *NASSP Bulletin*, 93(2), 96–110.

Plott, E., & Nicholas, P. (2019, June 27). How a forgotten White House team gained power in the Trump era. *The Atlantic*. https://www.theatlantic.com/politics/archive/2019/06/trump-domestic-policy-council/592516/

Pogarcic, A. (2018, April 25). Out-of-date higher education laws persist amid congressional gridlock. *The Daily Tar Heel*. https://www.dailytarheel.com/article/2018/04/higher-ed-congress-0425

Porter, R. B. (1997). Presidents and economists: The Council of Economic Advisers. *The American Economic Review*, 87(2), 103–106.

Posner, P. (2007). The politics of coercive federalism in the Bush era. *Publius: The Journal of Federalism*, 37(3), 390–412.

Potter, R. A. (2020). Learning from failure: A "failure CV" for the Office of Information and Regulatory Affairs. In M. Bose & A. Rudalevige (Eds.), *Executive policymaking: The role of the OMB in the presidency* (pp. 145–171). Brookings Institution Press.

Prakash, S. (2006). Removal and tenure in office. *Virginia Law Review*, 92(8), 1779–1852.

Price, Z. S. (2018). Funding restrictions and separation of powers. *Vanderbilt Law Review*, 71(2), 357–464.

Proclamation No. 9172: National Historically Black Colleges and Universities Week, 2014. 79 Fed. Reg. 57427 (2014).

Proclamation No. 9203: National College Application Month, 2014. 79 Fed. Reg. 65863 (2014).

Proclamation No. 9326: National Historically Black Colleges and Universities Week, 2015. 80 Fed. Reg. 57507 (2015).

Proclamation No. 9356: National College Application Month, 2015. 80 Fed. Reg. 67619 (2015).

Proclamation No. 9527: National Historically Black Colleges and Universities Week, 2016. 81 Fed. Reg. 74653 (2016).
Proclamation No. 9642: National Historically Black Colleges and Universities Week, 2017. 82 Fed. Reg. 44295 (2017).
Proclamation No. 9786: National Historically Black Colleges and Universities Week, 2018. 83 Fed. Reg. 47541 (2018).
Proclamation No. 9922: National Historically Black Colleges and Universities Week, 2019. 84 Fed. Reg. 48223 (2019).
Proclamation No. 9986: Career and Technical Education Month, 2020, 85 Fed. Reg. 6717 (2020).
Program Integrity & Improvement: Notice of proposed rulemaking, 81 Fed. Reg. 48598 (2016).
Program Integrity: Gainful Employment: Notice of proposed rulemaking, 83 Fed. Reg. 40167 (2018).
Program Integrity: Gainful Employment, Final regulations. 84 Fed. Reg. 31392 (2019) (to be codified at 34 C.F.R. pts. 600 and 668).
ProPublica. (2021). *Bills similar to S.839 in other Congresses.* https://projects.propublica.org/represent/bills/117/s839/similar
Pullias Center for Higher Education. (2017, March). *Emerging issues in federal higher education law: A brief guide for administrators and faculty.* University of Southern California.
Putansu, S. (2020). *Politics and policy knowledge in federal education: Confronting the evidence-based proverb.* Palgrave Macmillan.
Rampell, C. (2020a, July 14). Even with the administration's about-face on international student visas, enrollment is still set to plummet. *Washington Post.*
Rampell, C. (2020b, October 29). Trump didn't build his border wall with steel. He built it out of paper. *Washington Post.*
Rauchway, E. (2008). *The Great Depression and the New Deal: A very short introduction.* Oxford University Press.
Rawson, J. M. (2006, March 20). *Agricultural research, education, and extension: Issues and background* (CRS Report No. RL33327). Library of Congress, Congressional Research Service.
Re, R. M. (2014). Narrowing precedent in the Supreme Court. *Columbia Law Review, 114*, 1861–1911.
Redden, E. (2019, November 13). Supreme Court takes up DACA. *Inside Higher Education.* https://www.insidehighered.com/news/2019/11/13/supreme-court-hears-arguments-daca
Redden, E. (2020, June 19). DACA lives for now. *Inside Higher Education.* https://www.insidehighered.com/news/2020/06/19/supreme-court-rules-trump-administration-cannot-immediately-end-daca
Redden, E. (2021, January 21). Biden makes immigration Day 1 priority. *Inside Higher Education.* https://www.insidehighered.com/news/2021/01/21/biden-takes-action-immigration-day-one
Reich, D., & Kogan, R. (2021, January 22). *Introduction to budget "reconciliation."* Center on Budget & Policy Priorities. https://www.cbpp.org/sites/default/files/atoms/files/1-22-15bud.pdf
Reichmann, D. (1996, October 29). Clinton, Dole clash on education. *Associated Press.* https://apnews.com/article/9d6e6546d8dbc58b7edf556aa892bac0

Regents of the University of California v. Bakke, 438 U.S. 265 (1978).
Relyea, H. C., & Tatelman, T. B. (2007, April 10). *Presidential advisers' testimony before congressional committees: An overview* (CRS Report No. RL 31351). Library of Congress, Congressional Research Service.
Resnik, J. (1998). The Federal courts and Congress: Additional sources, alternative texts, and altered aspirations. *Georgetown Law Journal, 86*, 2589–2636.
Reuben, J. A., & Perkins, L. (2007). Introduction: Commemorating the sixtieth anniversary of the President's Commission report, "Higher Education for Democracy." *History of Education Quarterly, 47*(3), 265–276.
Revilla-Garcia, N. J. (2019, December 10). *HACU joins HBCUs, TCUs and other MSIs pushing for prompt passage of the FUTURE Act to restore critical funding*. Hispanic Association of Colleges and Universities. https://www.hacu.net/NewsBot.asp?MODE=VIEW&ID=3143
Reynolds, M. E. (2020, September 9). What is the Senate filibuster, and what would it take to eliminate it? *Voter Vitals*. Brookings Institution. https://www.brookings.edu/policy2020/votervital/what-is-the-senate-filibuster-and-what-would-it-take-to-eliminate-it/
Rhoads, R. A. (2016). Student activism, diversity, and the struggle for a just society. *Journal of Diversity in Higher Education, 9*(3), 189–202.
Riley, R. W. (1997). The role of the federal government in education—Supporting a national desire for support for state and local education. *Saint Louis University Public Law Review, 17*(1), 29–54.
Ritvo, D. T. (2016, June). *Privacy and student data: An overview of federal laws impacting student information collected through networked technologies*. Cyberlaw Clinic, Berkman Center for Internet & Society at Harvard University.
Robert, A. (2021, January 4). What types of lawsuits were filed over COVID-19 in 2020? *ABA Journal*. https://www.abajournal.com/news/article/law-firms-schools-identify-lawsuits-filed-over-covid-19-in-2020
Roberts, A. (1997). Performance-based organizations: Assessing the Gore plan. *Public Administration Review, 465*–478.
Robinson, G. (2016). A federal role in education: Encouragement as a guiding philosophy for the advancement of learning in America. *University of Richmond Law Review, 50*, 919–949.
Rochelle, W. G. (1999). The literary presidency. *Presidential Studies Quarterly, 29*(2), 407–420.
Rockoff, H. (2004). *Until it's over, over there: the U.S. economy in World War I* (NBER Working Paper No. 10580). National Bureau of Economic Research.
Rooksby, J. H. (2016). Copyright in higher education: Review of modern scholarship. *Duquesne Law Review, 54*(1), 197–222.
Rooksby, J. H., & Collins, C. S. (2016). Trademark trends and brand activity in higher education. *The Review of Higher Education, 40*(1), 33–61.
Rooksby, J. H., & Hayter, C. S. (2019). Copyrights in higher education: Motivating a research agenda. *The Journal of Technology Transfer, 44*(1), 250–263.
Rose, A. D., & Stuckey, B. D. (2012). Funding innovative programs for adults: Searching for policy on the improvement of higher education. *Adult Education Research Conference*. https://newprairiepress.org/aerc/2012/papers/39
Rosenberg, C. E. (1964). The Adams Act: Politics and the cause of scientific research. *Agricultural History, 38*(1), 3–12.

Rottinghaus, B., & Lim, E. (2009). Proclaiming trade policy: "Delegated unilateral powers" and the limits on presidential unilateral enactment of trade policy. *American Politics Research*, 37(6), 1003–1023.

Rottinghaus, B., & Maier, J. (2007). The power of decree: Presidential use of executive proclamations, 1977–2005. *Political Research Quarterly*, 60(2), 338–343.

Rottinghaus, B., & Warber, A. L. (2015). Unilateral orders as constituency outreach: executive orders, proclamations, and the public presidency. *Presidential Studies Quarterly*, 45(2), 289–309.

Rudalevige, A. (2016). Old laws, new meanings: Obama's brand of presidential imperialism. *Syracuse Law Review*, 66, 1–39.

Ruhl, J. B., & Robisch, K. (2016). Agencies running from agency discretion. *William & Mary Law Review*, 58, 97–181.

Rybicki, E. (2019a, March 26). *Veto override procedure in the House and Senate*. Congressional Research Service (CRS Report No. RS22654). Library of Congress, Congressional Research Service.

Rybicki, E. (2019b, April 4). *Senate consideration of presidential nominations: Committee and floor procedure* (CRS Report No. RL31980). Library of Congress, Congressional Research Service.

Rybicki, E. (2021, January 11). *The Senate powersharing agreement of the 107th Congress (2001–2003): Key features* (CRS Report No. RS20785). Library of Congress, Congressional Research Service.

Sablan, J., & Hiestand, R. (2020). A primer on higher education, student aid, and the federal budget process. *Journal of Student Financial Aid*, 49(2), art. 5.

Sanger, J., & Bear, J. (2019, November). *Fall 2019 international student enrollment snapshot survey*. IIE Center for Academic Mobility Research & Impact.

Sargent, J. F. (2020, October 7). *Department of Defense research, development, test, and evaluation (RDT&E): Appropriations structure* (CRS Report No. R44711). Library of Congress, Congressional Research Service.

Sargent, J. F., & Shea, D. A. (2020, March 3). *Office of Science and Technology Policy (OSTP): History and Overview* (CRS Report No. R43935). Library of Congress, Congressional Research Service.

Sargent, J. F., Harris, L.A., Cowan, T., Lipiec, E., Esworthy, R., Morgan, D., Gallo, M. E., & Sekar, K. (2020, March 18). *Federal research and development (R&D) funding: FY2020* (CRS Report No. R45715). Library of Congress, Congressional Research Service.

Saturno, J. V. (2020, August 27). *Authorizations and the appropriations process* (CRS Report No. R46497). Library of Congress, Congressional Research Service.

Saturno, J. V., Heniff, B., & Lynch, M. S. (2016, November 30). *The congressional appropriations process: An introduction* (CRS Report No. R42388). Library of Congress, Congressional Research Service.

Saturno, J. V., & Yeh, B. T. (2016, November 30). *Authorization of appropriations: Procedural and legal issues* (CRS Report No. R42098). Library of Congress, Congressional Research Service.

Saxe, K. (2019, November 21). After a slow start, the Trump White House is ramping up its science policy activities. *AMS Blog*. https://blogs.ams.org/capitalcurrents/2019/11/21/after-a-slow-start-the-trump-white-house-is-ramping-up-its-science-policy-activities/

Scheb, J. M., & Stephens, O. H. (2017). Civil Rights Act of 1957. In K. E. Stooksbury, J. M. Scheb, & O. H. Stephens (Eds.), *Encyclopedia of American civil rights and liberties: Revised and expanded edition [4 volumes]* (p. 154). ABC-CLIO.
Scherer, N. (2017). Appointing federal judges. In L. Epstein & S. Lindquist (Eds.), *The Oxford Handbook of U.S. Judicial Behavior* (pp. 3–28). Oxford University Press.
Schmidt, C. W. (2018). Section 5's Forgotten Years: Congressional power to enforce the Fourteenth Amendment before *Katzenbach v. Morgan*. *Northwestern University Law Review, 113*(1), 47–108.
Schneider, J. (2006, November 3). *Committee assignment process in the U.S. Senate: Democratic and Republican party procedures* (CRS Report No. RL30743). Library of Congress, Congressional Research Service.
Schneider, J. (2009, October 14). *The committee system in the U.S. Congress* (CRS Report RS20794). Library of Congress, Congressional Research Service.
Schneider, J. (2016, September 8). *House standing committee chairs and ranking minority members; rules governing selection procedures* (CRS Report No. RS21165). Library of Congress, Congressional Research Service.
Schneider, J. (2018, December 10). *The committee markup process in the House of Representatives* (CRS Report No. RL30244). Library of Congress, Congressional Research Service.
Schuette v. Coalition to Defend Affirmative Action, 572 U.S. 291 (2014).
Scott-Clayton, J. (2017). *Undergraduate financial aid in the United States*. American Academy of Arts & Sciences. https://www.amacad.org/sites/default/files/publication/downloads/CFUE_Financial-Aid.pdf
Scott-Clayton, J. E., & Zhou, Y. (2017). *Does the Federal work-study program really work—and for whom?* Center for Analysis of Postsecondary Education & Employment Research Brief. Community College Research Center.
Selin, J. L., & Lewis, D. E. (2018). *Sourcebook of United States Executive Agencies* (2nd ed.). Administrative Conference of the United States.
Selko, A. (2021, March 3). National Skills Coalition forms workforce panels to advise Biden on recovery policies. *Industry Week*. https://www.industryweek.com/talent/article/21156858/national-skills-coalition-forms-workforce-panels-to-advise-biden-on-recovery-policies
Seltzer, R. (2019, January 2). Rural colleges' lender of last resort. *Inside Higher Education*. https://www.insidehighered.com/news/2019/01/02/under-radar-usda-lending-provides-big-boost-financially-pressed-colleges
Seltzer, R. (2020, November 25). What would a $435B loss mean for federal student loan portfolio? *Inside Higher Education*. https://www.insidehighered.com/news/2020/11/25/devos-education-department-estimates-large-student-loan-losses-figures-arent
Shaw, K. (2017). Beyond the bully pulpit: Presidential speech in the courts. *Texas Law Review, 96*, 71–140.
Sherman, M. (2016, June 23). Texas U. admissions can consider race, Supreme Court rules. *Star Tribune*. https://www.startribune.com/texas-affirmative-action-plan-survives-supreme-court-review/384113711/
Shobe, J. (2017). Agencies as legislators: An empirical study of the role of agencies in the legislative process. *George Washington Law Review, 85*, 451–535.

Shohfi, K. D. (2020, August 31). *School construction and renovation: A review of federal programs and legislation* (CRS Report No. R41142). Library of Congress, Congressional Research Service.

Shohfi, K. D., & Tollestrup, J. (2019, February 19). *Department of Education funding: Key concepts and FAQ* (CRS Report No. R44477). Library of Congress, Congressional Research Service.

Siddiqui, S. (2018, September 4). Brett Kavanaugh: Protests disrupt Senate supreme court hearing. *The Guardian.* https://readersupportednews.org/component/content/article/318/52117-brett-kavanaugh-protests-disrupt-senate-supreme-court-hearing

Siddiqui, S., & Andrews, N. (2020, December 3). Biden faces pressure from his party over cabinet picks. *Wall Street Journal.* https://www.wsj.com/articles/biden-faces-pressure-from-his-party-over-cabinet-picks-11607018376

Skrentny, J. D., & López, J. L. (2013). Obama's immigration reform: The triumph of executive action. *Indiana Journal of Law & Social Equality, 2*, 62–79.

Slaughter, S. A., & Rhoades, G. (2004). *Academic capitalism and the new economy: Markets, state, and higher education.* Johns Hopkins University Press.

Smith, A. A. (2015, September 9). Obama steps up push for free. *Inside Higher Education.* https://www.insidehighered.com/news/2015/09/09/obama-unveils-new-push-national-free-community-college

Smith, A. A. (2016, October 27). Bidens host event on free community college. *Inside Higher Education.* https://www.insidehighered.com/quicktakes/2016/10/27/bidens-host-event-free-community-college

Smith, A. A. (2019, February 1). For-profits and federal revenue. *Inside Higher Education.* https://www.insidehighered.com/news/2019/02/01/brookings-report-potential-impact-dropping-so-called-90-10-rule

Sopko, J. F., & O'Connor, C. D. (2009, October). A guide to congressional investigations. *Financial Fraud Law Report, 234–237.* https://www.akingump.com/a/web/4974/Sopko-OConnor-FFLR-Oct-2009.pdf

Spriggs, J. F., & Hansford, T. G. (2001). Explaining the overruling of U.S. Supreme Court precedent. *The Journal of Politics, 63*(4), 1091–1111.

Stallings, D. T. (2002). *A brief history of the United States Department of Education: 1979–2002.* Duke University Center for Child and Family Policy. https://childandfamilypolicy.duke.edu/pdfs/pubpres/BriefHistoryofUS_DOE.pdf

State Higher Education Executive Officers Association. (2018). *State higher education finance: Fiscal year 2017.* State Higher Education Executive Officers Association.

Stedman, J. B. (1998, October 7). *The Higher Education Act: Reauthorization by the 105th Congress* (CRS Report No. IB98004). Library of Congress, Congressional Research Service.

Stephens, G. R. (1996). Urban underrepresentation in the US Senate. *Urban Affairs Review, 31*(3), 404–418.

Stiglitz, J. (1997). Looking out for the national interest: The principles of the Council of Economic Advisers. *The American Economic Review, 87*(2), 109–113.

Stith, K. (1988). Congress' Power of the Purse. *Yale Law Journal, 97*, 1343–1396.

Stith, K., & Blumenthal, C. (2019). The *Dartmouth College* case and the founding of Historically Black Colleges. *University of New Hampshire Law Review, 18*(1), 27–40.

Stone, D. (2012). *Policy paradox: The art of political decision making* (3rd ed.). W. W. Norton & Company.

Stone, J. (2016). Awarding college credit for MOOCSs: The role of the American Council on Education. *Education Policy Analysis Archives, 24*(38), n38.

Stone, S. B. (2014). A more accurate measure of local public goods: Overlapping government combinations as units of analysis. *Urban Studies Research, 2014*, Article ID 963503. http://dx.doi.org/10.1155/2014/963503

Strach, P. (2009). Making higher education affordable: Policy design in postwar America. *The Journal of Policy History, 21*(1), 61–88.

Stratford, M. (2014, June 12). Loan bill blocked. *Inside Higher Education*. https://www.insidehighered.com/news/2014/06/12/senate-republicans-block-student-loan-reform-legislation

Stratford, M. (2015a, January 12). Federal Promise unveiled. *Inside Higher Education*. https://www.insidehighered.com/news/2015/01/12/obama-joined-republicans-unveiling-free-community-college-plan

Stratford, M. (2015b, January 21). Middle-class economics for tuition. *Inside Higher Education*. https://www.insidehighered.com/news/2015/01/21/obama-pitches-free-community-college-higher-education-tax-credits-state-union

Stratford, M. (2018, May 9). DeVos looks to ease rules on religious colleges. *Politico*. https://www.politico.com/newsletters/morning-education/2018/05/09/devos-looks-to-ease-rules-on-religious-colleges-208702

Strauss, D. A., & Sunstein, C. R. (1992). The Senate, the Constitution, and the confirmation process. *Yale Law Journal, 101*(7), 1491–1524.

Student Assistance General Provisions, Federal Family Education Loan Program, and William D. Ford Federal Direct Loan Program: Notice of proposed rulemaking, 80 Fed. Reg. 39608 (2015).

Student Assistance General Provisions, Federal Perkins Loan Program, Federal Family Education Loan Program, William D. Ford Federal Direct Loan Program, and Teacher Education Assistance for College and Higher Education Grant Program: Final regulations, 81 Fed. Reg. 75926 (2016).

Student Assistance General Provisions, Federal Family Education Loan Program, and William D. Ford Federal Direct Loan Program: Final regulations, 84 Fed. Reg. 49788 (2019).

Stuessy, M. M. (2019, July 18). *Regular vetoes and pocket vetoes: In brief* (CRS Report No. RS22188). Library of Congress, Congressional Research Service.

Sundquist, M. L. (2010). *Worcester v. Georgia*: A breakdown of the separation of powers. *American Indian Law Review, 35*(1), 239–255.

Sunstein, C. R. (2013). The Office of Information and Regulatory Affairs: Myths and realities. *Harvard Law Review, 126*, 1838–1878.

Sweatt v. Painter, 339 U.S. 629 (1950).

Sweezy v. New Hampshire, 354 U.S. 234 (1957).

Szlezinger, Z. (2021, February 3). *How to run a student lobby day*. Student PIRGs. https://studentpirgs.org/2021/02/03/how-to-run-a-student-lobby-day/

Tan, Y., & Weaver, D. H. (2007). Agenda-setting effects among the media, the public, and Congress, 1946–2004. *Journalism & Mass Communication Quarterly, 84*(4), 729–744.

Tandberg, D. A., Bruecker, E. M., & Weeden, D. D. (2019, July). *Improving state authorization: The state role in ensuring quality and consumer protection in higher education*. State Higher Education Executive Officers Association. https://sheeo.org/wp-content/uploads/2019/07/SHEEO_StateAuth.pdf

Tandberg, D. A., & Martin, R. R. (2019, May). *Quality assurance and improvement in higher education: The role of the states*. State Higher Education Executive Officers Association. http://nashonline.org/wp-content/uploads/2019/05/QUALITY-ASSURANCE-AND-IMPROVEMENT-IN-HE.pdf

Taylor, A. N. (2012). Undo undue hardship: An objective approach to discharging federal student loans in bankruptcy. *Journal of Legislation, 38*(2), 185–236.

Taylor, A., Fram, A., Kellman, L., & Superville, D. (2020, March 28). Trump signs $2.2T stimulus after swift congressional votes. *Associated Press*. https://apnews.com/article/donald-trump-financial-markets-ap-top-news-bills-virus-outbreak-2099a53bb8adf2def7ee7329ea322f9d

Taylor, T. E., Coleman, A. L., Little, B. M., & Saddler, A. N. (2016, September). *Getting our house in order: Clarifying the role of the states in higher education quality assurance*. Education Counsel. https://educationcounsel.com/?publication=getting-house-order-clarifying-role-state-higher-education-quality-assurance

Teter, M. J. (2011). Recusal legislating: Congress's answer to institutional stalemate. *Harvard Journal on Legislation, 48*, 1–48.

Thelin, J. (2011). *A history of American higher education* (2nd ed.). Johns Hopkins University Press.

Thompson, F. J. (2013). The rise of executive federalism: Implications for the picket fence and IGM. *The American Review of Public Administration, 43*(1), 3–25.

Thorning, M. (2019, January 11). The House has new rules. Now it needs bold leaders. *Bipartisan Policy Center Blog*. https://bipartisanpolicy.org/blog/the-house-has-new-rules-now-it-needs-bold-leaders/

Thornton, S. R., & Westcott, K. S. (2013). *The Family and Medical Leave Act: Questions and answers. An AAUP Handbook*. American Association of University Professors.

Thrower, S. (2017). To revoke or not revoke? The political determinants of executive order longevity. *American Journal of Political Science, 61*(3), 642–656.

Tollefson, T. A. (2009). Community college governance, funding, and accountability: A century of issues and trends. *Community College Journal of Research & Practice, 33*(3–4), 386–402.

Totenberg, N. (2020, June 18). Supreme Court rules for DREAMers, against Trump. *National Public Radio*. https://www.npr.org/2020/06/18/829858289/supreme-court-upholds-daca-in-blow-to-trump-administration

Treisman, R. (2020, July 24). ICE confirms new foreign students can't take online-only course loads in the U.S. *National Public Radio*. https://www.npr.org/sections/coronavirus-live-updates/2020/07/24/895223219/ice-confirms-new-foreign-students-cant-take-online-only-course-loads-in-the-u-s

Trow, M. (1988). American higher education: Past, present, and future. *Educational Researcher, 17*(3), 13–23.

Trow, M. (1993). Federalism in American higher education. In A. Levine (Ed.), *Higher learning in America: 1980–2000* (pp. 39–66). Johns Hopkins University Press.

Trump, D. (2019, August 21). *Presidential Memorandum on Discharging the Federal Student Loan Debt of Totally and Permanently Disabled Veterans* [Presidential Memorandum].
Trustees of Dartmouth College v. Woodward, 17. U.S. 518 (1819).
Tua, U. F. (2009). A Native's Call for Justice: The call for the establishment of a federal district court in American Samoa. *Asian-Pacific Law & Policy Journal*, 11(1), 246–292.
Turner, C. (2015, September 12). President Obama's new "College Scorecard" is a torrent of data. *National Public Radio*. https://www.npr.org/sections/ed/2015/09/12/439742485/president-obamas-new-college-scorecard-is-a-torrent-of-data
Turner, C., & Arnold, C. (2018a, March 28). Dept. of Education fail: Teachers lose grants, forced to repay thousands in loans. *National Public Radio*. https://www.npr.org/sections/ed/2018/03/28/596162853/dept-of-education-fail-teachers-lose-grants-forced-to-repay-thousands-in-loans
Turner, C., & Arnold, C. (2018b, July 2). Senators urge DeVos on TEACH Grant debacle: "Urgent that these mistakes are fixed." *National Public Radio*. https://www.npr.org/sections/ed/2018/07/02/624278514/senators-to-devos-on-teach-grant-debacle-urgent-that-these-mistakes-are-fixed
Turner, C., Arnold, C., Lombardo, C., & Wren, I. (2018, April 23). Teachers share anger, frustration over grants turned into loans. *National Public Radio*. https://www.npr.org/sections/ed/2018/04/23/600949682/teachers-share-anger-frustration-over-grants-turned-into-loans
Ujifusa, A. (2018, July 23). Trump priority gathers steam as Senate passes career-technical education bill. *Education Week Politics K–12 Blog*. http://blogs.edweek.org/edweek/campaign-k-12/2018/07/trump-education-priority-career-technical-bill-senate-passes.html
Unah, I., & Williams, R. (2019). The legacy of President Obama in the U.S. Supreme Court. In W. C. Rich (Ed.), *Looking back on President Barack Obama's legacy* (pp. 149–189). Palgrave.
United States v. Fordice, 505 U.S. 731 (1992).
United States v. Lopez, 514 U.S. 549 (1995).
U.S. Bureau of Labor Statistics. (2009, February 9). *Careers at BLS: What BLS does*. https://www.bls.gov/jobs/aboutbls.htm
U.S. Census Bureau. (n.d.). *Congressional apportionment*. https://www.census.gov/topics/public-sector/congressional-apportionment.html
U.S. Census Bureau. (2020, October 15). *New earnings and employment data for college graduates*. https://www.census.gov/newsroom/press-releases/2020/post-secondary-employment-outcomes.html
U.S. Chamber of Commerce. (2014, October 20). *Comments from the U.S. Chamber of Commerce regarding the pending release of the final rule to regulate "Gainful Employment" under the Higher Education Act*. https://www.uschamber.com/comment/comments-us-chamber-commerce-regarding-pending-release-final-rule-regulate-gainful
U.S. Citizenship & Immigration Services. (n.d.). *U.S. territories*. https://www.uscis.gov/tools/glossary
U.S. Citizenship & Immigration Services. (2020, April 22). *Students and exchange visitors*. https://www.uscis.gov/working-in-the-united-states/students-and-exchange-visitors

U.S. Courts. (n.d.). *Comparing federal and state courts*. https://www.uscourts.gov/about-federal-courts/court-role-and-structure/comparing-federal-state-courts

U.S. Department of Agriculture. (n.d.). *Hispanic Serving Institutions National Program*. https://www.usda.gov/partnerships/hispanic-serving-institutions

U.S. Department of Agriculture. (2012, March 2). *USDA and Rural Community College Alliance, sign Memorandum of Understanding to strengthen the rural economy*. https://www.usda.gov/media/press-releases/2012/03/02/usda-and-rural-community-college-alliance-sign-memorandum

U.S. Department of Agriculture. (2020). *Request for application: Higher Education Challenge (HEC) Grant Program*. https://nifa.usda.gov/sites/default/files/rfa/fy-2020-2021-higher-education-challenge-rfa-20190925.pdf

U.S. Department of Commerce. (n.d.-a). *About Commerce*. https://www.commerce.gov/about

U.S. Department of Commerce. (n.d.-b). *Bureaus and offices*. https://www.commerce.gov/bureaus-and-offices

U.S. Department of Education. (n.d.-a). *Campus Safety & Security*. https://ope.ed.gov/campussafety/#/

U.S. Department of Education. (n.d.-b). *Centers of Excellence for Veteran Student Success*. https://www2.ed.gov/programs/cevss/funding.html

U.S. Department of Education. (n.d.-c). *Fast facts: Expenditures*. National Center for Education Statistics. https://nces.ed.gov/fastfacts/display.asp?id=75

U.S. Department of Education. (n.d.-d). *Federal TRIO programs—Home page*. https://www2.ed.gov/about/offices/list/ope/trio/index.html

U.S. Department of Education. (2008). *A profile of the federal TRIO Programs and Child Care Access Means Parents in School Program*. U.S. Department of Education.

U.S. Department of Education. (2011a, March). *College completion toolkit*. https://www.ed.gov/sites/default/files/cc-toolkit.pdf

U.S. Department of Education. (2011b). *History of the federal TRIO programs*. Office of Postsecondary Education. https://www2.ed.gov/about/offices/list/ope/trio/triohistory.html

U.S. Department of Education. (2014a, January 24). *U.S. Departments of Education and Treasury announce collaboration with Intuit Inc. to raise awareness about income-driven repayment options for student loans*. https://fsapartners.ed.gov/knowledge-center/library/electronic-announcements/2014-01-24/general-subject-us-departments-treasury-and-education-collaborate-raise-awareness-about-income-driven-repayment-options

U.S. Department of Education. (2014b, June 9). *About the Office of Legislation and Congressional Affairs*. https://www2.ed.gov/about/offices/list/olca/index.html?src=oc

U.S. Department of Education. (2015). *Grantmaking at ED: Answers to your questions about the discretionary grants process* (5th ed.). https://www.unco.edu/research/pdf/grant-writing-websites-docs/agency-specific-proposal-writing/grantmaking.pdf

U.S. Department of Education. (2016a, November). *FY 2017 annual plan*. https://www2.ed.gov/about/offices/list/oig/misc/wp2017.pdf

References

U.S. Department of Education. (2016b). *The handbook for campus safety and security reporting*. Office of Postsecondary Education. https://www2.ed.gov/admins/lead/safety/handbook.pdf

U.S. Department of Education. (2017, January 19). *Budget process in the U.S. Department of Education*. https://www2.ed.gov/about/overview/budget/process.html?src=ct

U.S. Department of Education. Privacy Technical Assistance Center. (2019a, February). *School resource officers, school law enforcement units, and the Family Educational Rights and Privacy Act (FERPA)*. https://studentprivacy.ed.gov/sites/default/files/resource_document/file/SRO_FAQs_2-5-19_0.pdf

U.S. Department of Education. (2019b, May). *The condition of education 2019* (NCES 2019-144). https://nces.ed.gov/pubs2019/2019144.pdf

U.S. Department of Education. (2019c, September 17). *Operating structure*. https://www2.ed.gov/about/offices/or/index.html

U.S. Department of Education. (2019d, October 17). *Federal student aid*. https://www2.ed.gov/about/offices/list/fsa/index.html

U.S. Department of Education. (2020a, May). *Frequently asked questions on the maintenance-of-effort requirements applicable to the CARES Act programs*. https://oese.ed.gov/files/2020/06/CARES-Act-Programs-Maintenance-of-Effort-FAQ.pdf

U.S. Department of Education. (2020b). Sources of financial aid. In *The Condition of Education 2020* (NCES 2020-144). https://nces.ed.gov/fastfacts/display.asp?id=31

U.S. Department of Education. (2021a, March 18). *Department of Education announces action to streamline borrower defense relief process*. https://www.ed.gov/news/press-releases/department-education-announces-action-streamline-borrower-defense-relief-process

U.S. Department of Education. (2021b). *The condition of education 2021 at a glance*. https://nces.ed.gov/pubs2021/2021144_AtAGlance.pdf

U.S. Department of Justice. (n.d.-a). *About DOJ*. https://www.justice.gov/about

U.S. Department of Justice. (n.d.-b). *Title VI legal manual*. https://www.justice.gov/crt/book/file/1364106/download

U.S. Department of Justice. (2020, August 13). *Justice Department finds Yale illegally discriminates against Asians and whites in undergraduate admissions in violation of federal civil-rights laws*. https://www.justice.gov/opa/pr/justice-department-finds-yale-illegally-discriminates-against-asians-and-whites-undergraduate

U.S. Department of Labor. (n.d.-a). *Employment and training resources*. https://www.dol.gov/general/topic/youthlabor/youthemploymenttraining

U.S. Department of Labor. (n.d.-b). *History of Executive Order 12246*. https://www.dol.gov/agencies/ofccp/about/executive-order-11246-history

U.S. Department of State. (n.d.). *Building capacity for study abroad*. https://studyabroad.state.gov/building-capacity-study-abroad

U.S. Department of State. (2012, August). *Fulbright*. Bureau of Educational and Cultural Affairs. https://eca.state.gov/files/bureau/fulbright.pdf

U.S. Department of State. (2015). *EducationUSA global guide 2015*. https://educationusa.state.gov/sites/default/files/edusa_global_guide_2015.pdf

U.S. Department of the Interior Office of Civil Rights. (n.d.). *Minority Serving Institutions Program*. https://www.doi.gov/pmb/eeo/doi-minority-serving-institutions-program

U.S. Department of the Treasury. (2021, February). *Publication 557: Tax exempt status for your organization.* https://www.irs.gov/pub/irs-pdf/p557.pdf

U.S. Department of the Treasury & U.S. Department of Education. (1995, June). *A study of the feasibility of the IRS collecting repayments of federal student loans.* https://home.treasury.gov/system/files/131/Report-Student-Loan-Repayments-1995_0.pdf

U.S. Department of Veterans Affairs, Office of Research & Development. (2018, July 13). *Program guide 1200.15: Eligibility for VA research support.* https://www.research.va.gov/resources/policies/ProgramGuide-1200-15-Eligibility-for-VA-Research-Support.pdf

U.S. Department of Veterans Affairs. (2021). *Federal benefits for veterans, dependents and survivors.* https://www.va.gov/opa/publications/benefits_book/2021_Federal_Benefits_for_Veterans_Dependents_and_Survivors.pdf

U.S. Government Accountability Office. (2021, April 20). *COVID-19: Emergency financial aid for college students under the CARES Act* (GAO-21-312R). https://www.gao.gov/assets/720/713850.pdf

U.S. Government Printing Office. (n.d.). *U.S. Government Manual.* https://www.usgovernmentmanual.gov/

U.S. House Committee on Financial Services. (2020, March 27). *Committee Democrats at work: Rep. Dean introduces bill to provide relief to student loan borrowers.* https://financialservices.house.gov/news/documentsingle.aspx?DocumentID=406451

U.S. House of Representatives. (n.d.-a). *List of in-person annual message and State of the Union Addresses.* https://history.house.gov/Institution/SOTU/List/

U.S. House of Representatives. (n.d.-b). *Party divisions of the House of Representatives, 1789 to present.* https://history.house.gov/Institution/Party-Divisions/Party-Divisions/

U.S. House of Representatives Committee on the Budget. (2018, September 6). *Budget reconciliation: The basics.* https://budget.house.gov/sites/democrats.budget.house.gov/files/documents/Budget%20Reconciliation%20The%20Basics%209.6.2018%20FINAL.pdf

U.S. National Archives & Records Administration. (n.d.). *Transcript of Northwest Ordinance (1787).* https://www.ourdocuments.gov/doc.php?flash=false&doc=8&page=transcript

U.S. Office of Government Ethics. (2021, January 22). *Executive orders on ethics commitments by executive branch personnel.* https://www2.oge.gov/Web/oge.nsf/Resources/Political+Appointees

U.S. Patent & Trademark Office. (n.d.). *General information concerning patents.* https://www.uspto.gov/patents/basics/general-information-patents

U.S. Patent & Trademark Office. (2019, August). *Protecting your trademark: Enhancing your rights through federal legislation* [Handbook]. https://www.uspto.gov/sites/default/files/documents/BasicFacts.pdf.

U.S. Senate. (n.d.). *Party division.* https://www.senate.gov/history/partydiv.htm

U.S. Senate Committee on Health, Education, Labor, & Pensions. (n.d.). *About.* https://www.help.senate.gov/about

U.S. Senate Committee on Health, Education, Labor, & Pensions. (2012, July 30). *For profit higher education: The failure to safeguard the federal investment and ensure student success.* https://www.help.senate.gov/imo/media/for_profit_report/PartI.pdf

U.S. Senate Committee on Health, Education, Labor, & Pensions. (2018, February 6). *Reauthorizing the Higher Education Act: Improving college affordability.* https://www.help.senate.gov/hearings/reauthorizing-the-higher-education-act-improving-college-affordability

U.S. Senate Committee on Health, Education, Labor, & Pensions. (2019, April 10). *Reauthorizing the Higher Education Act: Strengthening Accountability to Protect Students and Taxpayers.* https://www.help.senate.gov/hearings/reauthorizing-the-higher-education-act-strengthening-accountability-to-protect-students-and-taxpayers

U.S. Senate Committee on Appropriations. (n.d.). *Labor, Health & Human Services, Education, & Related Agencies.* https://www.appropriations.senate.gov/subcommittees/labor-health-and-human-services-education-and-related-agencies

USA.gov. (2019, October 18). *Branches of the U.S. government.* https://www.usa.gov/branches-of-government

Valocchi, S. (1996). The emergence of the integrationist ideology in the civil rights movement. *Social Problems, 43*(1), 116–130.

Vetter, J. (1974). *Affirmative action in faculty employment under Executive Order 11246* (Report in Support of Recommendation 75-2). Administrative Conference of the United States. https://www.acus.gov/sites/default/files/documents/1975-02%20Affirmative%20Action%20for%20Equal%20Opportunity%20in%20Nonconstruction%20Employment.pdf

Vice President's Education Initiatives. (n.d.). https://clintonwhitehouse4.archives.gov/WH/EOP/OVP/initiatives/education.html

Volden, C. (2005). Intergovernmental political competition in American federalism. *American Journal of Political Science, 49*(2), 327–342.

Volkwein, J. F. (2010). The assessment context: Accreditation, accountability, and performance. *New Directions for Institutional Research, 2010*(S1), 3–12.

Walker, C. J. (2017). Lawmaking within federal agencies and without judicial review. *Journal of Land Use & Environmental Law, 32*(2), 551–566.

Walker, R. A., & Brechin, G. (2010). *The living New Deal: The unsung benefits of the New Deal for the United States and California* [Working Paper #220-10]. Institute for Research on Labor and Employment, University of California–Berkeley. https://escholarship.org/uc/item/6c1115sm

Wartell, S. R. (2009). National Economic Council. In M. Green & M. Jolin (Eds.), *Change for America*, pp. 15–22. Basic Books.

Washington, G. E., & Hitter, T. E. (2020). State of the agency: Internal developments at OMB. In M. Bose & A. Rudalevige (Eds.), *Executive policymaking: The role of the OMB in the presidency* (pp. 207–231). Brookings Institution Press.

Washington Higher Education Secretariat. (n.d.-a). *About.* https://www.whes.org/about/

Washington Higher Education Secretariat. (n.d.-b). *Member directory.* https://www.whes.org/member-directory/

Waterman, A. T. (1960). National Science Foundation: A ten-year résumé. *Science*, 1341–1354.

Watson, C. E. (2019). Federal financing of higher education at a crossroads: The evolution of the student loan debt crisis and the reauthorization of the Higher Education Act of 1965. *Michigan State Law Review, 2019*(4), 883–978.

Weeks, J. P. (1989). George Washington Atherton and the creation of the Hatch Act. *Pennsylvania History: A Journal of Mid-Atlantic Studies, 56*(4), 299–317.

Weiner, S. A. (2009). Tale of two databases: The history of federally funded information systems for education and medicine. *Government Information Quarterly, 26*(3), 450–458.

Werner, E. (2017, April 6). GOP ends Supreme Court filibuster, clearing way for Gorsuch. *Boston Globe*. https://www.bostonglobe.com/news/politics/2017/04/06/showdown-hand-trump-supreme-court-nominee/u1bG8sYQubg7O0MB87LZ4K/story.html

Werner, E., Kane, P., Bade, R., & DeBonis, M. (2020, March 24). Senate negotiators cite progress on coronavirus bill after day of drama and rancor. *Washington Post*.

Wheatle, K. I. (2019). Neither just nor equitable. *American Educational History Journal, 46*(2), 1–20.

Wheatle, K. I., & Commodore, F. (2019). Reaching back to move forward: The historic and contemporary role of student activism in the development and implementation of higher education policy. *The Review of Higher Education, 42*(5), 5–35.

Whistle, W., & West, E. B. (2020, September 24). Congress should help college students bridge the digital divide. *The Hill*. https://thehill.com/opinion/education/518068-congress-should-help-college-students-bridge-the-digital-divide

White House. (n.d.-a). *Our government: State and local government*. https://www.whitehouse.gov/about-the-white-house/state-local-government/

White House. (n.d.-b). *Our government: The executive branch*. https://www.whitehouse.gov/about-the-white-house/the-executive-branch/

White House Office of the Press Secretary. (2015, March 10). *FACT SHEET: A Student Aid Bill of Rights: Taking action to ensure strong consumer protections for student loan borrowers*. https://obamawhitehouse.archives.gov/the-press-office/2015/03/10/fact-sheet-student-aid-bill-rights-taking-action-ensure-strong-consumer-

White House Office of the Press Secretary. (2018, February 27). *FACT SHEET: President Donald J. Trump prioritizes Historically Black Colleges and Universities*. https://trumpwhitehouse.archives.gov/briefings-statements/remarks-president-trump-announcement-additional-leadership-historically-black-colleges-universities-initiative/

White House Rural Council. (2011, August). *Jobs and economic security for rural America*. White House.

Whittington, K. E. (2015). The power of judicial review. In M. Tushnet, M. A. Graber, & S. Levinson (Eds.), *The Oxford Handbook of the U.S. Constitution* (pp. 387–440). Oxford University Press.

Wice, S. (2020, August 9). Examining procedures for how the Senate filibuster could be eliminated. *Notice & Comment: A blog from the Yale Journal of Regulation and ABA Section of Administrative Law and Regulatory Practice*. https://www.yalejreg.com/nc/the-end-of-the-senate-filibuster/

Wiener, M. L. (2018, October 29). General rules for agency adjudications? *The Regulatory Review*. https://www.theregreview.org/2018/10/29/wiener-general-rules-agency-adjudications/

Williams, R. L. (1991). *The origins of federal support for higher education: George W. Atherton and the land-grant college movement*. The Pennsylvania State University Press.

Wilson, R. (2017, February 8). How a 20-page letter changed the way higher education handles sexual assault. *The Chronicle of Higher Education*. https://www.chronicle.com/article/how-a-20-page-letter-changed-the-way-higher-education-handles-sexual-assault/

Wilson, J. Q., Dilulio, J. J., & Bose, M. (2016). *American government: Institutions and policies, brief version* (12th ed.). Cengage Learning.

Wohlstetter, P., Houston, D. M., & Buck, B. (2015). Networks in New York City: Implementing the Common Core. *Educational Policy, 29*(1), 85–110.

Wolanin, T. R. (2003). The federal role in higher education. *The NEA Almanac of Higher Education, 39*–51.

Wood, B. D. (2009). Presidential saber rattling and the economy. *American Journal of Political Science, 53*(3), 695–709.

Wood, B. D., Owens, C. T., & Durham, B. M. (2005). Presidential rhetoric and the economy. *The Journal of Politics, 67*(3), 627–645.

Woolley, J. T., & Peters, G. (2017). The contemporary presidency: Do presidential memo orders substitute for executive orders? New data. *Presidential Studies Quarterly, 47*(2), 378–393.

Wysession, M. E., & Rowan, L. R. (2013). *Geoscience serving public policy*. Geological Society of America Special Papers (no. 501). Geological Society of America.

Yeh, B. T. (2007, July). *Intellectual Property Rights Violations: Federal Civil Remedies and Criminal Penalties Related to Copyrights, Trademarks, and Patents* (CRS Report No. RL34109). Library of Congress, Congressional Research Service.

Yinug, L. D., & Burgat, C. (2016, August 2). *The president's budget: Overview and timing of the mid-session review* (CRS Report No. RL32509). Library of Congress, Congressional Research Service.

Yoho, J. (1998). The evolution of a better definition of "interest group" and its synonyms. *The Social Science Journal, 35*(2), 231–243.

Yokoyama, K. (2011). Quality assurance and the changing meaning of autonomy and accountability between home and overseas campuses of the universities in New York state. *Journal of Studies in International Education, 15*(3), 261–278.

You, H. Y. (2017). Ex post lobbying. *The Journal of Politics, 79*(4), 1162–1176.

Yourish, K., & Stanton, L. (n.d.). A guide to the federal budget process. *Washington Post Online*. https://www.washingtonpost.com/wp-srv/special/politics/federal-budget-process/budgetprocess.pdf

Zehrt, L. R. (2019). Title IX and Title VII: Parallel remedies in combatting sex discrimination in educational employment. *Marquette Law Review, 102*(3), 701–745.

Zelizer, J. (2018, November 10). How Democrats can leverage the midterm results to win big in 2020. *CNN Opinion*. https://www.cnn.com/2018/11/10/opinions/how-dems-can-win-big-in-2020-zelizer/index.html

Ziegler, M. (2018). What is race: The new constitutional politics of affirmative action. *Connecticut Law Review, 50*, 279–338.

Zinth, K., & Smith, M. (2012, October). *Tuition-setting authority for public colleges and universities*. Education Commission of the States. https://www.ecs.org/clearinghouse/01/04/71/10471.pdf

Zornow, D. M., & Strauber, J. E. (2019, August 30). Government investigations in the USA. *Lexology*. https://www.lexology.com/library/detail.aspx?g=7313d656-a228-45a9-a228-20cf0054bc0d

Zumeta, W. M. (2005). Accountability and the private sector: State and federal perspectives. In J. C. Burke & Associates, *Achieving accountability in higher education: Balancing public, academic, and market demands* (pp. 25–54). Jossey-Bass.

Zumeta, W., & Kinne, A. (2011). The recession is not over for higher education. *The NEA 2011 Almanac of Higher Education*, 29–41.

Index

Abdul-Alim, J., 138
Abel, J. R., 48, 154
Abrams, J., 141
Accountability. *See* Higher education quality and accountability policy
Accreditation of higher education institutions, 5, 29, 49–50, 97, 103, 138–139
Accrediting Council for Independent Colleges and Schools (ACICS), 139
ACE (American Council on Education), 62, 64, 128–133, 144, 148–149
ACPA (American College Personnel Association), 38
Adams Act (1906), 37
Adams v. Pennsylvania Higher Education Assistance Agency (2016), 17
Adler, E. S., 62
Administrative agencies. *See* Federal administrative agencies and higher education
Administrative Conference of the United States, 110
Administrative Office of the U.S. Courts, 23, 44n4, 108, 114–117
Administrative Procedure Act (2018), 77–78, 92, 117–118
Affordable Care Act (ACA), 63–64
Age discrimination
 Age Discrimination Act (1975), 47–48, 121
 Age Discrimination in Employment Act (1967), 47, 121
Agricultural Adjustment Act (1933), 39
Ahtone, Tristan, 13, 33–35, 51, 153, 154, 161

Alcindor, Y., 79
Alexander, F. K., 20, 135–138, 148
Alexander, K., 11, 55
Alexander, K. W., 11, 55
Alexander, M. D., 11, 55
Alger, J. R., 7, 30, 109
Altikriti, S., 31
American Association of College Registrars, 57
American Association of Community Colleges (AACC), 128
American Association of Community College Trustees, 128
American Association of State Colleges and Universities (AASCU), 128
American Association of University Professors (AAUP), 122, 128, 133–134, 152
American Bar Association, 75–76
American College Personnel Association (ACPA), 38
American Council on Education (ACE), 62, 64, 128–133, 144, 148–149
American Enterprise Institute, 142
American Opportunity Credit, 107
American Recovery and Reinvestment Act (ARRA, 2009), 20, 136
American Rescue Plan (2021), 20
Americans with Disabilities Act, 4, 61, 121
AmeriCorps, 110
Ancheta, A., 44, 120
Anderson, G., 22, 47n8
Anderson, J. E., 95, 98–100, 127, 151
Anderson, T., 104
Andrews, N., 132
Anthony, A. M., 29

Anthony, S. W., 61
Apkarian, J., 125
Armstrong, C. J., 56n3
Arnett, A. A., 80
Arnold, C., 125–126, 140, 152, 156
Ashbee, E., 21
Asian Law Caucus, 99, 105
Asimow, M., 99
Associated Press, 79
Association of American Medical Colleges, 106, 128
Association of American Universities (AAU), 107, 128
Association of Community College Trustees, 19, 156
Association of Governing Boards of Universities and Colleges, 128–129
Association of Private Sector Colleges and Universities, 133
Association of Public and Land-Grant Universities (APLU), 35, 128, 141
Authorizing legislation, 62

Back, C. J., 121
Bade, R., 24
Bagenstos, S. R., 4, 27, 61–62, 118, 148
Bair, F. H., 39
Baker, D. J., 4, 29
Bankhead-Jones Act (1935), 39
Bankruptcy law, 124–126
Barab, J., 57
Barkowski, E., 140
Barnes, M. D., 140
Barnes, R., 113, 121, 152
Basic Educational Opportunity Grant (BEOG)/Pell Grant programs, 28, 46–49, 63n7, 64, 75, 88, 108
Basken, P., 138–139
Batalova, J., 78
Battle, S., 96
Bauer-Wolf, J., 89
Baum, S., 10
Bauman, D., 47n7, 50, 102, 103, 159
Baumgartner, F. R., 10
Baumgartner, Jody C., 71n1, 86, 87
Bayh-Dole Act (1980), 7, 30

Bear, J., 89
Beerkens, M., 25, 26, 29
Bell, Terrel, 49, 159
Bellante, D., 9, 159–160
Bengston, D. N., 25, 26
Bertrand Jones, T., 127
Beth, R. S., 58
Biden, Jill, 88, 150
Biden, Joseph R., 22, 25, 47n8, 74–76, 78, 81, 86–89, 110–111, 139, 143, 149, 150
"Big Six Associations," 128–129, 134, 144, 155
Black, R. C., 23, 79–80
Blair, J., 130–132, 134, 140, 160
Block, M., 85n6
Blumenstyk, G., 110
Blumenthal, Claire, 36–37, 153
Bok, D., 67, 118, 120
Bombardieri, M., 19
"Borrower Defense to Repayment" policy (USDOE), 73, 110–111
Bose, M., 21, 23, 64, 66, 71, 72, 74, 82, 84, 150
Boudreaux, P., 55n2
Bound, J., 40
Bowen, J., 135
Bowen, W. G., 67, 118, 120
Bowers, D. E., 39
Bowman, A. O., 16–18
Bowman, N. A., 154
Boylan, H. R., 61
Brannon, V. C., 78n4
Brass, C. T., 21, 53, 64–68, 84, 150
Brechin, G., 38–39, 153, 160
Breger, M. J., 21n4, 91, 92, 111
Brennan, G., 10
Brint, S., 1, 4, 6, 100, 160
Brookings Institution, 142
Brooks, C., 8, 130
Brower, R., 127
Brown, B., 36, 37n2, 46, 130–132, 134, 140
Brown, C., 79
Brown, P., 45, 46
Brown, Sherrod, 66
Brown v. Board of Education of Topeka (1954), 36, 44, 45, 118, 119, 151

Index   223

Brudnick, I. A., 21, 53, 64–68, 108
Bruecker, E. M., 5, 19, 136, 154, 157
Buchanan, James, 35
Buchanan, J. M., 10
Buck, B., 141
Budget reconciliation process, 63–64
Bui, Q., 50n10
"Bully pulpit"
  of Cabinet heads, 94
  Congressional, 67–68
  presidential, 80–81
Bur, J., 91
Bureau of Consumer Financial
    Protection, 109–110
Bureau of Indian Affairs, 110
Burgat, C., 74
Burke, J. C., 49
Burns, J., 57
Burum, S., 71, 72, 149, 162
Bush, George W., 25, 50, 71, 83, 97
Bush, Vannevar, 41
Byrd, Robert, 64
Byrd Rule, 64

Caldera, C. G., 104
Camera, L., 139
Cameron, C. M., 73
Cameron, M. A., 16, 21
Camp, M. J., 8, 130
Campbell, D. S., 39
Campus crime policy, Clery Act
    (Jeanne Clery Disclosure of
    Campus Security Policy and
    Campus Crime Statistics Act),
    5–6, 21, 28, 47, 61, 96, 102, 148
Capps, R., 78
Career and Technical Education
    Month, 77
Career and technical education
    programs, 61, 74–75, 77, 129, 133
Career Education Colleges and
    Universities, 129, 133
CARES (Coronavirus Aid, Relief, and
    Economic Security) Act (2020), 24,
    61, 69, 136–137
Carey, M. P., 21, 53, 55, 64–68, 73n2
Carl D. Perkins Career and Technical
    Education Act, 61

Carleton, D., 34, 153
Carmines, E. G., 71, 149, 162
Carp, R. A., 113, 117
Carter, Jimmy, 47, 102
Case, D. A., 116–117
Cash, D. W., 35
Cashin, Sheryll D., 43, 45, 149, 162
Cate, F. H., 7, 30
Caulfield, R., 53, 56
Cellini, S. R., 20
Center for American Progress, 142
Center on Budget and Policy Priorities,
    62n6, 74, 100, 142
Center on Education Policy, 3, 10–11,
    26, 29, 34, 153
Centers for Disease Control &
    Prevention (CDC), 110
Centers of Excellence for Veteran
    Student Success, 5
Century Foundation, 142
Cervantes, A., 12, 34, 36, 39n3, 40–43,
    46n6, 51, 153, 154, 160
Chan, R. Y., 154
Chemerinsky, Erwin, 23, 67, 116–117,
    118
Chen, M. H., 22, 75, 77, 78, 91, 96,
    150, 151
Chopra, R., 109–110
Christensen, M. D., 74, 84
Chronicle of Higher Education, 89, 140
Chu, V. S., 71, 75, 76
Civilian Conservation Corps (CCC),
    38–39
Civil Rights Act (1957), 45
Civil Rights Act (1960), 45
Civil Rights Act (1964), 45–46, 61, 103
  Title VI, 4, 28, 32, 47, 121, 148
  Title VII, 46, 121
Civil rights and nondiscrimination
    policy, 3–4
  civil rights movement, 42–48, 53–54,
    118, 119, 151
  executive branch and, 43–44, 46
  federal oversight of state government
    and, 137–138
  overview of federal rules regarding, 28
Civil Works Administration (CWA), 38,
    160

Clark, C. S., 84
Clery Act (Jeanne Clery Disclosure of Campus Security Policy and Campus Crime Statistics Act), 5–6, 21, 28, 47, 61, 96, 102, 148
Clery Center, 5–6, 28
Clinton, Bill, 50, 76, 82, 83, 85, 88
Clotfelter, C. T., 4, 6, 100
Cloture, 58–59
Coast, J., 163
Cohen, D. M., 94
Cohen, E., 104
Cohen, J. E., 71n1, 86
Cohen, M., 58
Cohen, P., 79
Cohen-Vogel, L., 28–29
Cold War, 9, 12, 40, 41, 48, 51, 153–154, 160
Cole, J. P., 99, 121
Coleman, A. L., 19, 20, 50, 136, 138, 154
Collective action problems, 56
The College Board, 48, 155
College Completion Toolkit, 87
College Scorecard, 50, 86
College Transparency Act (proposed), 60
Collins, C. S., 7, 109
Collins, F. S., 6
Collins, P. M., 113, 133, 134
Commission on Higher Education (Truman Commission), 43–44
Commission on Independent Colleges & Universities, 129n1
Commission on the Future of Higher Education (Spellings Commission), 50, 97, 143
Committee for a Responsible Federal Budget, 62–63
Commodore, F., 43
Conditional spending, 27, 28, 55, 74–75
Congressional Budget Office (CBO), 108, 110
Congressional Research Service, 65, 78n4, 106n1
Congressional Review Act (1996), 55, 73n2, 96
Congress's role in higher education. *See* U.S. Congress; U.S. House of Representatives; U.S. Senate

Connelly, V. J., 122
Consumer Financial Protection Bureau (CFPB), 109–110
Contrubis, J., 31, 75–77
Cook, Constance Ewing, 8, 10, 128, 129, 130–132, 134, 140, 144, 152, 160–162
Cook, T. M., 47
Cooper, P. J., 77
Cooperative Extension Service, 136, 152
Cope, K. L., 121, 122
Copyright Act, 61
Corley, P. C., 134
Coronavirus Aid, Relief, and Economic Security Act (CARES Act, 2020), 24, 61, 69, 136–137
Corporation for National and Community Service, 110
Corrigan, M. E., 1, 4–6, 26, 100
Couch, J., 39
Council for Higher Education Accreditation, 129, 138
Council of Economic Advisers (CEA), 85–86, 150
Council of Independent Colleges, 129, 132
Council of the Inspectors General, 98
Council on Foundations, 142
Counseling Borrowers (2020), 29
Court of Appeals for the Federal Circuit, 114–115
Coval, M. M., 59
Coven, M. B., 31, 81
COVID-19 pandemic, 51–52
  American Rescue Plan (2021), 20
  Centers for Disease Control & Prevention (CDC), 110
  Coronavirus Aid, Relief, and Economic Security Act (CARES Act, 2020), 24, 61, 69, 136–137
  emergency funding and, 129
Cowan, T., 6, 109
Cowley, S., 91, 110–111
Cramer, K., 110
Creusere, M., 12, 34, 36, 39n3, 40–43, 46n6, 51, 153, 154, 160
Croft, G. K., 19, 35n1, 36, 136, 152
Cross, C. T., 9, 25n6, 28, 42, 46, 47, 49, 102, 159–161

Cross, F. B., 118
Cuéllar, M. F., 102
Cullen, F. T., 6
Cunningham, A., 19
Custer, B. D., 6

Dahill-Brown, S. E., 127
Darolia, R., 8, 20
Darville, S., 86, 149
Datla, K., 92
Dauster, William G., 21, 54n1, 58, 59n4
Davidson, A., 104
Davis, C. M., 21, 53, 55, 56, 58, 60, 64–68, 72, 73n2, 94, 111
Davis, E. J., 141
Deaton, R., 25
DeBonis, M., 24
Deferred Action for Childhood Arrivals (DACA) program, 78, 88–89, 107, 124, 132, 150, 151–152
Delaney, J. A., 136
DeLauder, W. B., 37
Delisle, J., 87
DeMitchell, T. A., 122
DeMonte, E., 140
Department of Homeland Security v. Regents of the University of California (2020), 78
Desan, C., 61
Desjean, J., 135
De Veau, Laura A., 131
Devins, N., 55–56, 69–70
DeVos, Betsy, 22, 79, 83, 86, 139, 149
Diamond, J., 124
Dietz, L., 119–120
Dietz, N., 110
Dietz, R., 48, 154
DiGiovanni, N., 125
Dill, D. D., 4–5, 15, 25–29
Dilulio, J. J., 21, 23, 64, 66, 71, 72
Direct Loans, 74
Disability discrimination
 Americans with Disabilities Act, 4, 61, 121
 Rehabilitation Act (1973), 4, 28, 47, 121
Dodd, L. G., 44, 119

Dodson, M., 140
Dole, Bob, 102
Domestic Policy Council, 72, 82, 83, 92
Donahoo, S., 119–120, 151
Dortch, C., 4, 8, 40, 50, 62n5, 64, 74, 102, 149
Dote, L., 110
Dougherty, K. A., 122, 123
Dougherty, K. J., 25, 26, 31n8, 48n9, 49
Douglas-Gabriel, D., 2, 73
Doyle, W. R., 25
Drawbaugh, K., 74
DreamActivist.org, 99, 105
Drews, E., 98
Drug-Free Schools and Communities Act (1986), 6
Drutman, L., 54
Due Process Clause
 Fifth Amendment, 123
 Fourteenth Amendment, 123
Duke, E. C., 78
Dull, M., 23, 24, 149
Durham, B. M., 80
Durham, C., 104
Dutile, F. N., 123
Dvoskin, J. A., 133
Dynarski, S., 4

Eaton, J. S., 5, 29, 103, 138–139, 142, 143
Eccleston, M., 140
Eckman, S. J., 21, 53, 54, 56, 64–68
Edles, G. J., 21n4, 91, 92, 111
Education Amendments (1972), 46–47
 initial passage, 47
 Title IX, 4, 6, 21, 22, 28, 32, 47, 61, 83, 87, 103, 121, 148, 150, 151, 158
 Title IX Dear Colleague Letters, 96
Education Commission of the States, 19
Education USA, 107
Educators for Fair Consideration, 99, 105
Egar, W. T., 56
Eglit, H., 47–48
Eisenhower, Dwight, 42, 45
Ekman, R., 132
Elementary and Secondary Education Act (ESEA, 1965), 25n6, 46, 47, 61, 140

Ellmore, R. F., 25
Elving, R., 79, 113, 116
Engle, J., 19
Environmental health and safety policies, 8
Environmental Protection Agency (EPA), 6
  Office of Environmental Stewardship, 8
Epp, Charles R., 42–44, 119
Epperson, L., 4, 29
Epstein, D., 24
Equal Protection Clause, Fourteenth Amendment, 29–30, 36, 43, 44, 55, 118, 119–121, 151
Erickson, B. C., 140
Erlandson, J., 143
Eshbaugh-Soha, M., 80
Establishment Clause, First Amendment, 122–123, 151
Esworthy, R., 6, 109
Evans, K. M., 86
Evans, S. E., 105
Executive action, 75–80
  federal appointments, 23, 53, 66–67, 79–80, 115–116
  unilateral, 71, 75–77. *See also specific Executive Orders*
  via federal agencies, 77–78
Executive branch, 16, 21–22. *See also* President's roles in higher education
  accountability to Congress, 53, 64–65
  advisory role of administrative agencies and, 97
  civil rights movement and, 43–44, 46
  Executive Office of the President. *See* Executive Office of the President (EOP)
  federal agencies within, 93, 101–108, 109–110. *See also* Federal administrative agencies and higher education; *specific federal agencies*
  interest group strategies used with, 132–133
  overview, 72
  policymaking by, 81–88
  reexamining role in higher education, 149–150
  separating and sharing powers, 22–23, 53, 66–67
  Vice President, 56, 72, 86–88
Executive Office of the President (EOP), 76, 81–86, 92
  Council of Economic Advisers (CEA), 85–86, 150
  Office of Management & Budget (OMB), 72, 74, 75, 84–85, 95, 132–133, 144, 150
  Office of Science and Technology Policy (OSTP), 86, 150
  White House Office, 16–17, 79, 82–84, 149–150
Executive Order No. 11246: Equal Employment Opportunity (1965), 46, 76
Executive Order No. 12291: Federal Regulation (1981), 76
Executive Order No. 12835: Establishment of the National Economic Council (1993), 82
Executive Order No. 12859: Establishment of the Domestic Policy Council (1993), 82–83
Executive Order No. 12866: Regulatory Planning and Review (1993), 76, 84
Executive Order No. 13575: Establishment of White House Rural Council (2011), 77
Executive Order No. 13779: White House Initiative to Promote Excellence and Innovation at Historically Black Colleges and Universities (2017), 77, 149
Executive Order No. 13864: Improving Free Inquiry, Transparency, and Accountability at Colleges and Universities (2019), 76–77
Executive Order No. 13891: Promoting the Rule of Law Through Improved Agency Guidance Documents (2019), 78n5

Index 227

Executive Order No. 13988: Preventing and Combatting Discrimination on the Basis of Gender Identity or Sexual Orientation (2021), 47n8
Eyster, L., 104

Fain, P., 22, 25, 73–74, 129, 133, 139
Fair Labor Standards Act, 61
Falleti, T. G., 16, 21
Family Educational Rights and Privacy Act (FERPA, 1974), 7, 28, 47, 61, 148
Farrell, J., 46, 76
Fass, P., 38–39, 153, 160
Feder, J., 1, 28, 30, 121
Federal administrative agencies and higher education, 21–22, 91–112
  adjudication by, 99
  advisory role for the president and Congress, 97–98
  categories of agency employees, 94
  Congressional Review Act (1996) and, 55, 73n2, 96
  discretionary decision making by, 100–101
  executive action via, 77–78
  executive branch agencies, 93, 101–108, 109–110
  funding by, 99–100
  importance of, 91
  interest group strategies used with, 133
  investigations and inspections by, 98–99
  judicial branch agencies, 93, 108
  legislative branch agencies, 93, 108
  list, 93. *See also specific federal administrative agencies*
  overview, 92–94
  policy powers of federal agencies, 94–101
  reexamining role of, 150–151
  rulemaking by, 95–96
  Senate confirmation power and, 23, 53, 66–67, 79–80, 113, 115–116
  sub-regulatory guidance, 96
Federal Bar Association, 116–117
Federal Family Education Loan (FFEL) program, 74–75

Federal government role in higher education
  administrative agencies and, 91–112. *See also* Federal administrative agencies and higher education
  capacity-building, 26, 28–29
  conditional spending, 27, 28, 55, 74–75
  Congress and, 53–70, 148–149. *See also* U.S. Congress; U.S. House of Representatives; U.S. Senate
  Constitution and. *See* U.S. Constitution
  expansion over time, 2, 25, 51. *See also* History of federal government in higher education
  federal courts and, 113–126. *See also* Judicial branch
  history of, 12–13, 33–52. *See also* History of federal government in higher education
  incentives, 26–30, 32
  information, 26, 29–31
  overreach complaints, 2, 49
  partisan politics and, 2, 3, 22, 23–25, 49, 52, 53–54, 56, 59, 71, 113, 139
  policy areas in higher education, 3–8. *See also* Federal policy in higher education; Nonfederal actors' influence on federal higher education policy
  president and, 71–89, 149–150. *See also* President's roles in higher education
  reexamining, 147–162
  rules/regulations, 26–29, 30, 32, 57–59, 95–96
  self-regulation, 26, 29
  structure of federal government, 12, 15–32
Federalism, 15–20
  branches of government, 16, 20–22
  higher education policy and, 18–20
  levels of government, 15–18
  metaphors for, 18
  preemption, 17–18
  relative sovereignty, 17–18

Federalism *(continued)*
  separating and sharing powers, 22–23
  subnational government influence on higher education policy, 134–138
Federal Judicial Center, 23, 108, 117
Federal Perkins Loan Program, 9, 22, 42, 46n6
Federal policy in higher education, 3–8
  affordability, 155–156
  bankruptcy law, 124–126
  campus crime, 5–6. *See also* Campus crime policy
  civil rights and nondiscrimination, 3–4, 119–121. *See also* Civil rights and nondiscrimination policy
  due process rights, 123
  education quality and accountability, 5, 156–157. *See also* Higher education quality and accountability policy
  equity, 157–158
  executive branch appointments, 23, 53, 66–67, 79–80, 115–116
  executive branch policymaking and, 81–88
  federal judiciary and, 119–125
  federal structure and higher education policy, 12, 15–32
  First Amendment rights, 121–123
  funding for higher education institutions, 2
  intellectual property rights, 7. *See also* Intellectual property policy
  other federal policies, 7–8
  overview of policy instruments, 25–26
  policy powers of federal agencies, 94–101
  reexamining, 155–158
  research and development, 6–7. *See also* Research and development
  size of government and, 9–10, 159–161
  student financial aid, 4–5. *See also* Student financial aid
  student privacy, 7. *See also* Student privacy policy

Federal Register, 77, 95, 100
Federal Security Agency, 102
Federal structure and higher education policy, 12, 15–32
  branches of government, 16, 20–22
  Constitution and. *See* U.S. Constitution
  federalism, 15–20
  levels of government, 15–18
  political partisanship and, 2, 3, 22, 23–25, 49, 52, 53–54, 56, 59, 71, 113, 139
  separating and sharing powers, 22–23
Federal Student Aid, 4, 102, 156
Federal Supplemental Opportunity Grant, 47
Federal Trade Commission (FTC), 109–110
Fichtner, J., 122, 123
Field, K., 31, 81, 150
Filibuster, 58–59
Financial aid. *See* Student financial aid
Fischer, K., 81, 89
Fisher, B. S., 6
Fisher, L., 22–23, 72, 75
Fisher v. University of Texas (2016), 120–121, 151
Fiske, S. T., 6
Flaherty, C., 8, 104
Fletcher, J. O., 25, 26
Florer, J. H., 35
Flores, A., 49, 50, 139, 154
Ford, Gerald, 47–48
Fordham Institute, 142
For-profit higher education sector, 22, 25, 49–50, 65–66, 71–73, 75, 79, 89, 95, 110–111, 117–118, 127–129, 139, 143, 150, 154, 156–157
Forseth, R., 21n3
Foster, D., 70, 71
Foundations, 142–143
Fountain, J. H., 47
Fowler, M., 71, 149, 162
Fram, A., 69
Frandsen, F., 141
Frankenberg, E., 103

Frankfurter, Felix, 122
Fránquiz, M. E., 61
Free Application for Federal Student Aid (FAFSA), 108
Free Exercise Clause, First Amendment, 122–123
Friedman, E. M., 105
Friedman, Z., 73
Fulbright Grant programs, 107
Fuller, M. B., 2, 4, 24n5, 40, 43
Funding for higher education
  accreditation and, 5, 29, 49–50, 97, 103, 138–139
  administrative agency role in, 99–100
  denial for violations of civil rights, 4
  federalism and, 18–20
  importance of, 2
  local funding, 19
  market-oriented incentive programs, 25
  state funding, 19
  Taxing and Spending Clause, U.S. Constitution, 26–29
Furlong, S. R., 76–78, 91, 95, 96
Futrell, G. A., 35, 37, 39
FUTURE Act (2019), 107–108

Gainful Employment Rule (2019), 22, 50, 95–96, 117–118, 124, 143
Gallaudet University, 34
Gallo, M. E., 6, 109
Gallup, 162
Gamper, Anna, 15–16, 17
Gándara, D., 46, 53, 57, 59, 60, 70, 142
Garces, L. M., 103
Gardner, L., 21n3
Garland, Merrick, 113
Garrett, Thomas A., 10, 128, 160
Garvey, T., 21, 53, 64–68, 71, 75, 76
Gates, B., 142
Gavazzi, S. M., 35–37, 153
Gee, E. G., 35–37, 153
Geiger, R. L., 9, 12, 40–42, 160
Gelles, E., 55
Gender discrimination
  civil rights movement and, 43
  federal judiciary and, 121
  GI Bill and, 41

Title IX, Education Amendments (1972), 4, 6, 21, 22, 28, 32, 47, 61, 83, 87, 103, 121, 148, 150, 151, 158
Gersen, J. E., 96, 151
GI Bill of Rights (1944), 8, 40–41, 61, 105, 154
Gilbert, C. K., 43–44
Gildersleeve, R. E., 141
Gilfoyle, N., 133
Gilmour, J. B., 94
Gingrich, Newt, 129–130
Gladieux, L. E., 1, 4–6, 26, 100
Glassman, M. E., 55
Goldin, C., 15
Goldstein, D., 45
Goldstein, J. K., 71n1
Goldstein Hode, M., 120
Goman, C., 84, 150
Goodwin, D. K., 31, 67, 80, 149
Gordon, G. J., 15
Gore, Al, 50, 87, 88
Gorsuch, Neil, 134
Granovskiy, B., 61
Grassley, Charles, 113
Gratz v. Bollinger (2003), 120
Grawe, N. D., 162
Great Depression, 38–39, 153, 160
Great Recession 2007–2009, 20, 136
Great Society, 45–47, 60, 160
Green, E. L., 79
Greenberg, D., 31, 67, 80, 81, 149
Greene, M., 66, 72, 94, 111
Gregory, D. E., 21n3, 44, 120
Gresko, J., 116
Griffin, A., 62n5, 63n7, 135
Griffin, O. R., 122
Grimm, R., Jr., 110
Grissom, J. A., 16, 18n2, 61, 135
Grodzins, Morton, 18
Grove, T. L., 67–68
Grutter v. Bollinger (2003), 120, 151
Gulasekaram, P., 75
Gumport, P. J., 7, 30
Guynn, J., 76, 149

Haddad, N., 142
Haeder, S. F., 84

Halbrook, S. A., 35, 106
Hall, C. E., 142
Halstead, T. J., 75–77
Hamilton, C., 119–120
Hamilton, D., 157
Hamner, J., 134
Haney, P., 27, 61–62, 148
Hannah, S. B., 20, 21n3
Hansford, T. G., 118
Hanson, C. L., 140
Harbridge, Laurel, 3, 25, 52, 53, 56, 58, 149
Harden, J. D., 2
Harnisch, T., 19, 20, 50, 135–138, 148, 154
Harper, S. R., 2, 34, 36, 46, 69, 76, 161
Harris, A., 22, 81, 139, 149
Harris, C. M., 16n1
Harris, D. N., 10
Harris, Kamala, 87
Harris, L. A., 6, 92, 94, 109
Hartman, J. L., 6
Harvard Law Review, 99
Harvard University, 86
Harvey, O. L., 39
Hatch Act (Hatch Agricultural Experiment Station Act, 1887), 35
Hauser, R. K., 7, 30
Hauser, R. M., 6
Hawkins, B. D., 120
Hayter, C. S., 7, 30
Health Care and Education Reconciliation Act (2010), 63–64
Hearn, J. C., 6, 25, 26, 100
Hebert, J. G., 54
Hechinger Report, 140
Hegji, A., 5, 48, 60–61, 62n5, 94
Heilig, J. V., 119–120
Heisler, E. J., 62n5
Heitshusen, V., 53, 56–59
Helhoski, A., 125
Heller, D. E., 43–44
Henderson, L. J., 36, 119–120
Heniff, B., 53, 56–60, 62–64, 148
Henry, L. M., 110
Herbert, W. A., 125
Herbold, H., 41, 51
Herian, M. N., 18

Herrington, C. D., 16, 18n2, 61, 135
Hersch, J., 45, 46
Herszenhorn, D. M., 149
Hessick, F. A., 117
Hesson, T., 89
Hevel, M. S., 38
Hiers, R. H., 122
Hiestand, R., 62–64
Higgins, T., 98n1
Higher Ed Dive, 140
Higher Education Act (1965), 17, 20–22, 60–62, 69–70, 72, 133, 143–144, 157, 160
  Amendments (1998), 87
  Amendments (2018), 19, 95
  Centers of Excellence for Veteran Student Success, 5
  initial passage, 4, 24, 46, 47, 60
  major provisions, 60–61
  reauthorization dates, 2, 3, 24, 25, 46–47, 49–50, 56, 85
  Title III, 130
  Title IV programs, 5, 20, 23, 25, 28–29, 46, 61, 101, 136, 138, 151
Higher Education Challenge Grants, 106
Higher Education Compliance Alliance, 8
Higher Education for American Democracy (Truman Commission), 43
Higher Education Opportunity Act (2008), 2, 137
Higher education quality and accountability policy
  accreditation of institutions, 5, 29, 49–50, 97, 103, 138–139
  Gainful Employment Rule (2019), 22, 50, 95–96, 117–118, 124, 143
  National Advisory Committee on Institutional Quality and Integrity (NACIQI), 103, 138–139
  Program Integrity Triad, 5, 49–50, 136, 138
  student loan default rates, 5, 49–51, 108
  TRIO programs for student success, 5, 46, 61, 62
Hill, F., 91, 92
Hill, J., 31, 80, 81

Hill, M. A., 141
Hillison, J., 35
Hills, R. M., 18, 135
Hiltzik, M., 40
Hinrichs, P., 11, 137–138
Hipp, J. S., 35, 153, 154
Hispanic Association of Colleges and Universities, 129
Hispanic-Serving Institutions, 61, 106, 129
Hispanic Serving Institutions National Program, 106
Historically Black Colleges and Universities (HBCUs), 19, 28, 34–37, 60–61, 77, 83, 120, 129, 138, 158
History of federal government in higher education, 12–13, 33–52
civil rights movement and aftermath (1930s–1970s), 42–48
Civil War and aftermath, 29, 33, 34–35, 37, 55
consumerism and accountability era (1970s–2020s), 48–50
COVID-19 pandemic and. *See* COVID-19 pandemic
early expansion (1780s–1920s), 34–38, 153
Great Depression/New Deal, 38–39, 153, 160
national defense era (1940s–1950s), 39–42, 153–154
post-World War I era (1920s–1940s), 38–39, 153
reexamining, 153–154
World War I, 37–38
World War II/GI Bill, 40–41, 153–154
Hitter, T. E., 82, 84, 150
Hogue, H. B., 79–80, 94
Holcombe, R. G., 9, 159–160
Holzer, J., 86
Homans, C., 113, 116
Honig, M. I., 141
Hooker, S., 78
Hoover Institute, 142
Houston, D. M., 141
Howard University, 34

Howell, William G., 71, 75, 89, 91, 92
Hu, S., 127
Huang, W. C., 10
Hubler, S., 51, 69
Hudson, K. L., 6
Human resources policies, 7–8
Hurley, D., 20, 135–138, 148
Hutchens, N. H., 1–2, 4, 17, 18, 22, 27–30, 32, 60, 61, 67, 107, 119, 121–123, 125, 151
Hutchins, A., 46n6

Immigration and Customs Enforcement (ICE), 107
Immigration policies, 8, 81, 88–89, 99, 105, 107, 123–124
Inside Higher Education, 132, 140
Institute for Higher Education Policy, 10, 142
Institute of Education Sciences, 72, 103
Integrated Postsecondary Education Data System (IPEDS), 29, 103
Intellectual property policy, 7, 54
Copyright Act, 61
Patent and Copyright Clause, U.S. Constitution, 30
U.S. Patent & Trademark Office, 7, 30, 109
Interest groups, 128–134
associations, 128–130, 134, 144, 155
colleges and universities as, 130
in the federal policy space, 128–130
size of government and, 160–161
strategies used by, 130–134
Internal Revenue Service (IRS), 4–5, 26–29, 107–108
Ioannou, V., 5, 136, 137, 141, 152
Itzkowitz, M., 5
Iuliano, J., 125

Jackson, C., 50, 87, 96
Janosik, S. M., 21n3
Jaschik S., 74, 104–105, 125
Jeanne Clery Disclosure of Campus Security Policy and Campus Crime Statistics Act (Clery Act), 5–6, 21, 28, 47, 61, 96, 102, 148

Jenkins, M. K., 54
Jennings, J., 91–92
Johansen, W., 141
Johnson, C. H., 54, 55n2
Johnson, K. R., 78, 88–89, 113, 152
Johnson, L. K., 55
Johnson, Lyndon B., 39n3, 44n4, 45–47, 60, 76, 160
Johnson, T., 33, 46–48, 60, 154, 160
Johnstone, D. B., 48
Jones, D. R., 70
Jones, S., 36, 37n2, 46, 53, 57, 59, 60, 70, 130–132, 134, 140
Jones, S. M., 26, 31n8, 49
Judicial branch, 16, 21, 22, 113–126
 civil rights movement and, 36, 44, 45, 118, 119, 151
 education policy areas affected by the federal judiciary, 119–125
 federal agencies within, 93, 108. *See also specific federal agencies*
 interest group strategies used with, 133–134
 judicial review and, 23, 117, 126
 jurisdiction and powers of federal courts, 117–119
 overturning policy of federal administrative agencies, 95–96
 overview of federal court system, 114–117
 protection of institutional autonomy, 36–37
 reexamining role in higher education, 151–152
 Senate confirmation power and, 23, 53, 66–67, 79–80, 113, 115–116
 separating and sharing powers, 22–23
 U.S. Constitution, Article III, 22, 23, 114, 116, 117, 123–124
Julius, D. J., 125

Kagan, E., 76
Kahn, C., 89
Kaiser, F. M., 108
Kamensky, J. M., 87
Kane, P., 24
Kantor, H., 38, 43–45, 47, 154, 160
Kaplan, S., 86

Kaplin, W. A., 1–2, 4, 17, 18, 22, 27–30, 32, 60, 61, 67, 107, 119, 121–123, 125, 151
Karam, J., 21n3
Kay, S., 41, 42, 160
Keillor, J. B., 40
Kelchen, R., 1, 4–5, 12–13, 20, 28, 29, 34, 36–37, 41, 49–51, 103, 129, 138–139, 154, 157, 160, 161
Kelderman, E., 22, 139
Keller, R., 117, 124
Kellman, L., 69
Kelly, A., 10
Kennedy, John F., 45, 46
Kenney, M., 7, 30, 109
Kent, R. T., 6
Kerr, E., 108
Kerwin, C. M., 76–78, 91, 95, 96
Kesavan, V., 31
Keshner, A., 111
Kevles, D. J., 41
Kim, C. Y., 123–124
Kim, J. Y., 80
King, J. E., 1, 4–6, 26, 100
Kingdon, John W., 74, 80, 82
Kinne, A., 4
Kiousis, S., 80
Klein, A., 61
Kochhar, S., 80
Kogan, R., 63
Konur, O., 4
Korenman, S. G., 6
Koricich, A., 61
Koss, M. P., 6
Kreighbaum, A., 1–2, 22, 25, 47n8, 61, 70, 75–77, 80, 83, 95, 96, 110, 139, 150
Krent, Harold J., 21, 31, 73, 76, 78, 79, 150
Kriner, D. L., 23, 55, 64, 65, 68
Kuhn, D. P., 113, 152
Kumar, M. J., 83
Kuzenski, J. C., 55
Kyaw, A., 50

Labaree, David F., 9, 12–13, 36–37, 40–42, 48–49, 51, 53, 154, 160
Lacey, M. R., 124

Lacy, T. A., 6, 100
Laderman, S., 141
Lahr, H., 26, 31n8, 49
Laitinen, A., 5, 49, 50, 97, 154, 157
Lampe, J. R., 113, 114, 152
Land-grant institutions, 19, 34–36, 37, 39, 57, 61, 106, 128, 136, 141, 153
Lane, N. F., 86
Langford, C. L., 10
La Pira, T. M., 10
Laski, F. J., 47
Lavery, L., 127
Lax, J. R., 17
Leal, D. L., 37
Lebryk, D., 108
Lederman, D., 108
Lederman, L., 116–117
Lee, B. A., 1–2, 4, 17, 18, 22, 27–30, 32, 60, 61, 67, 107, 119, 121–123, 125, 151
Lee, E. A. S., 6
Lee, F. E., 21, 53, 56, 71
Lee, M. M., 123–124
Lee, P., 122
Lee, Robert, 13, 33–35, 51, 153, 154, 161
Lee, S., 78
Lee, V., 2
Leech, B. L., 10
Legislative branch, 16, 20. *See also* U.S. Congress; U.S. House of Representatives; U.S. Senate; *specific legislation*
 advisory role of administrative agencies and, 97–98
 civil rights movement and, 45–48, 53–54
 federal agencies within, 93, 108. *See also specific federal agencies*
 interest group strategies used with, 130–132
 president's roles in, 73–75
 reexamining role in higher education, 148–149
 separating and sharing powers, 22–23, 53, 64–67
Legrenzi, G., 9
Lehmuller, P., 44, 120

Leigh, E. W., 156
Lerner, J. Y., 30, 142
Levine-Brown, P., 61
Levinson, Daryl J., 24, 149
Levinson, R., 122
Lewis, David E., 21, 82, 84, 85, 91, 92–94, 108
Lewis, M. M., 103
Lewis-Beck, M. S., 10
Lieberman, J. I., 18n2
Lifetime Learning Credit, 107
Light, P., 31, 80, 81
Lim, E., 77
Lincoln, Abraham, 35
Lindquist, S. A., 118
Lingenfelter, P. E., 19
Lipiec, E., 6, 109
Liptak, A., 120, 121
Little B. M., 19, 20
Lobby day events, 131, 143
Local government, 16, 17–18, 19, 134–138
Lombardo, C., 140, 156
Longanecker, D. A., 15, 141
Looney, A., 2, 49, 102, 156
López, J. L., 78
Lopez, L., 48–49, 51, 154
Loss, Christopher P., 12, 20, 34, 37–44, 47, 48, 51, 106, 153, 154, 160, 161
Lowande, K. S., 77
Lowe, R., 38, 43–45, 47, 154, 160
Lowery, J. W., 122, 123
Lowry, R. C., 50, 97, 128, 129
Lu, J., 10, 160
Lubbers, J. S., 95, 96
Lumina Foundation, 142
Lynch, M. S., 23, 62, 63, 79–80

Ma, J., 154
Maag, E., 4–5, 27
Madison, James, 34
Madonna, A. J., 23, 79–80
Mahan, S. M., 4, 50, 64, 74, 102, 149
Maier, J., 77
Maintenance-of-effort (MOE) requirements, 20, 136–137
Mangan, K., 76, 100, 109
Manhattan Institute, 142

Manhattan Project, 40
Manning K. L., 113, 117
Marcus, J., 50n10, 152, 160
Margulies, P., 124
Marion, N. E., 31, 80, 81
MarketWatch, 111
Marshall, Thurgood, 44n4
Marshall, W. P., 64, 65
Marsicano, C. R., 8, 130
Martin, M. V., 35, 153, 154
Martin, R. R., 5, 136, 138
Massachusetts Institute of Technology, 86
 Radiation Laboratory, 40
Mathematica Policy Research Institute, 142
Matjie, M., 94
Matsudaira, J., 86
Matthews, C. M., 28–29
Matthews, K. R., 86
Mayer, K. R., 21, 75–76
Mayhew, M. J., 154
McCann, C., 5, 49, 50, 97, 142, 154, 157
McCann, L. A., 47
McCarthy, M., 21, 44, 113, 115, 117, 118
McCarthy, M. A., 109, 143
McConnell, Mitch, 113
McDonald, L., 142
McDonnell, G., 10
McDonnell, L. M., 25
McGuinness, A., 19
McIntyre, E., 140
McKee, G., 96
McKenzie, L., 66, 139
McLaurin v. Oklahoma State Regents (1950), 44
McLean, C., 142
McLean, D., 61, 69
McLendon, M. K., 6, 25, 100
McMillion, R., 12, 34, 36, 39n3, 40–43, 46n6, 51, 153, 154, 160
McMillon, B. J., 79–80, 115, 116n1, 134
McQueen, C., 12, 34, 36, 39n3, 40–43, 46n6, 51, 153, 154, 160
Meacham, A. T., 140
Meisenbach, R. J., 120

Mercier, S. A., 35, 106
Mervin, D., 71
Messer, S. R., 100
Methodology of study, 8–12, 148–158
 guiding questions, 8–9, 148–158
 perspectives, 9–11, 159–161
 sources, 11–12, 163–166
Mettler, S., 22
Meyers, M., 84, 150
Meyers, M. K., 127
Midwestern Higher Education Compact, 141
Mikelson, K. S., 104
Milakovich, M. E., 15
Milas, C., 9
Military One Source, 105
Miller, B., 60, 87, 137, 139
Miller, G., 9, 159
Miller, L. L., 105
Miller, M. A., 28–29
Minnesota State Community & Technical College, 69
Minority-Serving Institutions, 19, 46, 60, 106, 110, 129–130, 131, 158
Mishkin, F. S., 38
Mitchell, T., 10, 51, 129
Modan, N., 79
Moe, Ronald C., 97, 151
Moe, T. M., 9, 75, 159
Monahan, B., 140
Monk, L. R., 123
Moore, G., 35, 37
Moran, R., 20, 135–138, 148
Morgan, D., 6, 109
Morgan, G., 10, 161
Morrill, Justin, 35
Morrill Act (1890), 35, 36, 153
Morrill Land Grant Act (1862), 35–36, 106, 153
Morris, A. D., 43
Mouat, L., 49
Mueller, D. C., 10, 160
Mullen, J., 124
Mumper, M., 1, 4–6, 26, 100
Mundel, D., 4–5, 27
Murakami, K., 72, 75, 86, 124, 125
Murrell, P., 10, 160

Index 235

Nagel, J. C., 91–92
Napolitano, J., 78
Nash, Margaret A., 35, 36, 154, 161
NASPA (National Association of Student Personnel Administrators), 38, 61–63, 129, 131
Nassirian, B., 19, 20, 50, 136, 138, 154
National Advisory Committee on Institutional Quality and Integrity (NACIQI), 103, 138–139
National Aeronautic and Space Administration (NASA), 42, 109
National Association for Equal Opportunity, 129
National Association of College Admission Counseling (NACAC), 104–105, 129
National Association of College and University Business Officers, 129
National Association of Independent Colleges and Universities (NAICU), 128
National Association of Student Financial Aid Administrators, 62, 63, 129
National Association of Student Personnel Administrators (NASPA), 38, 61–63, 129, 131
National Board for Professional Teaching Standards, 85
National Center for Education Statistics (NCES), 103
National Center for Higher Education, 129
National College Application Month, 77
National Commission on Excellence in Education, 49, 159, 161
National Conference of State Legislatures, 19, 135
National Defense Education Act (NDEA, 1958), 9, 22, 42, 46n6
National Economic Council (NEC), 82, 150
National Endowment for the Humanities, 109
National Governors Association, 135
National Historically Black Colleges and Universities Week, 77

National Immigrant Youth Alliance, 99, 105
National Immigration Forum, 99
National Institutes of Health (NIH), 7, 27, 109, 150
National Labor Relations Act, 125
National Labor Relations Board (NLRB), 99, 104, 133–134
National Labor Relations Board v. Yeshiva University (1980), 104, 125
National Partnership for Reinventing Government, 87
National Public Radio (NPR), 85n6, 140–141, 152
National Research Council, 7, 35, 100n2
National Science Foundation (NSF), 6, 92, 94, 109
National Science Foundation (NSF) Act (1950), 41
National Youth Administration (NYA), 39
Nation at Risk, A (National Commission on Excellence in Education), 49, 159, 161
Native American peoples
  and federal government role in higher education, 35–36, 51
  Tribal Colleges and Universities, 35n1, 36, 110
Natow, Rebecca S., 1–2, 5, 8, 20, 22, 23, 25, 26, 28, 31n8, 48–52, 56, 60–61, 64n8, 69, 70, 71, 74n3, 75, 76, 78, 87, 91, 95–100, 103, 104, 118, 127–129, 131–145, 150–152, 154, 157, 159, 163–165
NC-SARA, 141
Nebraska Legislature, 17
Neiberg, M. S., 35, 37
Neil, J., 80
Nelson, K. C., 25, 26
Nelson, L. A., 75, 103
Ness, E. C., 25, 26, 142
New America, 4, 142
New Deal, 20, 38–39, 153, 160
New England Board of Higher Education, 141

News media
  interest groups influencing federal education policy and, 131–132, 134
  in methodology of study, 11, 165
  role in federal higher education policy, 140–141
New York State Department of State, 17
Nicholas, P., 82
Nielson, A., 95
Nielson, E., 140
Nienhusser, H. K., 8
Nisenson, A., 123
Niskanen, W. A., 9, 159
Nixon, Richard, 39n3, 47
Noel, H., 140
Nolan, A., 55
Nonfederal actors' influence on federal higher education policy, 127–145
  accreditors, 138–139
  business community members, 143
  foundations, 142–143
  general public, 144
  government size and, 160–161
  interest groups, 128–134
  lobby day events, 131, 143
  news media, 140–141
  in policy implementation stage, 127
  reexamining role of, 152–153
  regional higher education compacts, 141
  state and local governments, 134–138
  students in higher education, 143–144
  think tanks, 142
Northwest Ordinance (1787), 33, 34, 153
Notice of Proposed Rulemaking (NPRM), 95–96
Novilla, L. M., 140

Obama, Barack, 22, 25, 31, 46n5, 47n8, 50, 64n8, 73–75, 77, 79–81, 83, 84, 87–89, 96, 104, 106, 110–111, 113, 116–118, 124, 132, 133, 139, 142, 148–150
Obama, Michelle, 84, 150
Obama White House, 87

Occupational Safety and Health Administration, 110
O'Connell, A. J., 80
O'Connor, C. D., 53, 65
Office for Civil Rights (OCR), 72, 98, 101, 102–103, 138
Office of Communications, 83–84
Office of Digital Strategy, 84
Office of Information and Regulatory Affairs (OIRA), 84–85
Office of Management & Budget (OMB), 72, 74, 75, 84–85, 95, 132–133, 144, 150
Office of Science and Technology Policy (OSTP), 86, 150
Office of the First Lady, 84
Office of the Under Secretary of Defense for Research & Engineering, 106
Office of the Vice President, 150
O'Halloran, S., 24
Olds, C., 80
Oleszek, M. J., 21, 53, 56–60, 62–68, 148
Oleszek, Walter J., 21, 23, 53, 56–60, 62–68, 148
Oliver, R. W., 10, 161
Oliver, W. M., 31, 80, 81
Olson, K W., 40
Online program management (OPM), 66
Onuf, P. S., 34
O'Reilly, J. T., 17
Orphan, C. M., 141
Ortiz, A. A., 61
Owens, C. T., 80
Owens, R. J., 23, 79–80
Owen-Smith, A., 163

Page, L. C., 29
Pardo, R. I., 124
Park, E., 19
Park, S., 25, 26
Park, T., 127
Parker, D. C. W., 23, 24, 149
Parker, J. E., 106
Parks, C., 7
Parrillo, Nicholas R., 78, 96, 100, 151
Parsons, Michael D., 3, 8, 10, 24–25, 34, 35, 37, 42, 46, 47, 49, 56, 60–61, 128, 129, 144, 152, 154, 159, 160

Index

Parton, B., 109, 143
Pasachoff, E., 4, 74, 75, 81, 84, 113, 150, 152
Patton, D., 7, 30, 109
Patton, L. D., 2, 34, 36, 46, 76, 161
Pavela, Gary, 123
Pavela, Greg, 123
Pear, R., 149
Pece, C., 6
Peer, N. O., 61
Pelesh, M. L., 95, 133
Pell Grant programs, 28, 46–49, 63n7, 64, 75, 88, 108
Pelsue, B., 4
Pence, Mike, 86, 149
Pender, M., 154
Pepperdine University, 108
Performance-based organizations, 50
Perkins, Carl, 46n6
Perkins, L., 43–44
Perkins Loan program, 9, 22, 42, 46n6
Perna, L. W., 156
Perry, A. M., 157
Peters, B. G., 127
Peters, G., 71, 77, 89
Petersen, R. E., 21, 53, 64–68
Petracca, M. P., 128
Pew Charitable Trusts, 1, 27, 100
Pfiffner, J. P., 63
Pheatt, L., 26, 31n8, 49
Phillips, J. H., 17
Pierce, C., 156
Pierce, R. J., 101
Pierre, J., 127
Pihos, D. N., 123
Pildes, Richard H., 24, 149
Pitre, C. C., 5
Pitre, P., 5
Plessy v. Ferguson (1896), 36, 118
Plott, E., 82
Pogarcic, A., 53, 70
Porter, P., 9, 159–160
Porter, R. B., 85
Posner, P., 18
Potochnick, S., 8
Potter, R. A., 84, 96, 150

Power and Politics (Parsons), 3, 8, 10, 24–25, 34, 35, 37, 42, 46, 47, 49, 56, 60–61, 128, 129, 144, 152, 154, 159, 160
Prakash, S., 55
Prebil, M., 109, 143
President's roles in higher education, 71–89
  advisory role of administrative agencies and, 97
  "bully pulpit" and, 80–81
  executive action and, 71, 75–80. *See also specific Executive Orders and Proclamations*
  executive branch policymaking, 81–88
  federal appointments, 23, 53, 66–67, 79–80, 115–116
  immigration policy, 8, 81, 88–89
  legislative role and, 73–75
  overview, 72
  reexamining, 149–150
  "State of the Union" address, 31, 81, 84, 149–150
  U.S. Constitution, Article II, 21–23, 30–31, 64–65, 66, 71, 72, 79, 81, 86
Proclamation No. 9172 (2014), 77
Proclamation No. 9203 (2014), 77
Proclamation No. 9326 (2015), 77
Proclamation No. 9356 (2015), 77
Proclamation No 9527 (2016), 77
Proclamation No. 9642 (2017), 77
Proclamation No. 9786 (2018), 77
Proclamation No. 9922 (2019), 77
Proclamation No. 9986 (2020), 77
Program Integrity: Gainful Improvement, 22, 50, 95–96, 117–118, 124, 143
Program Integrity Triad, 5, 49–50, 136, 138
ProPublica, 60
Pullias Center for Higher Education, 121
Purnell Act (1925), 37
Putansu, S., 34, 37, 39, 42, 60, 153

Qualified Tuition Program, 107

Racial discrimination
  civil rights movement and, 42–48
  Equal Protection Clause, Fourteenth Amendment and, 29–30, 43, 44, 55, 118, 119–121, 151
  federal judiciary and, 119–121
  GI Bill and, 41
Ragas, M. W., 80
Ramakrishnan, S. K., 75
Rampell, C., 88–89
RAND Corporation, 142
Rauchway, E., 38
Rawson, J. M., 57
Re, R. M., 118
Read, B., 47n7, 102, 103, 159
Reagan, Ronald, 2, 49, 76, 82, 102
Reckhow, S., 142
Redden, E., 8, 78, 124, 150, 152
Reddick, R. J., 119–120
Reddy, V., 5, 26, 31n8, 49, 136, 137, 141, 152
Regents of the University of California v. Bakke (1978), 44, 120, 151
Rehabilitation Act (1973), 47
  Section 504, 4, 28, 121
Reich, D., 63
Reichmann, D., 102, 159
Reid, Harry, 54n1
Religious freedom, 122–123
Relyea, H. C., 21, 64, 82, 92, 97, 151
Research and development, 6–7. *See also* Intellectual property policy
  agricultural research, 106
  Department of Defense, 105–106
  ethics in research, 6–7
  funding sources, 6, 27
  Institute of Education Sciences, 72, 103
  intermediaries between research and policy, 142–143
  national defense policy and, 41–42
Research and Marketing Act (1946), 39
Resnik, J., 117
Reuben, J. A., 43–44
Revesz, R. L., 92
Revilla-Garcia, N. J., 129
Reynolds, M. E., 58, 59
Rhine, Russell M., 10, 128, 160
Rhoades, G., 48n9, 122, 123
Rhoads, R. A., 43
Riccard, T. N., 21, 53, 64–68
Rice, L., 4–5, 27
Rice, T. W., 10
Richardson, J. T., 7, 30
Riley, R. W., 33, 34, 102, 153, 159
Ritvo, D. T., 28
Robert, A., 51
Roberts, A., 87
Robin, L., 142
Robinson, G., 102, 159
Robisch, K., 101
Rochelle, W. G., 71
Rockenbach, A. N., 154
Rockoff, H., 37
Rooksby, J. H., 1–2, 4, 7, 17, 18, 22, 27–30, 32, 60, 61, 67, 107, 109, 119, 121–123, 125, 151
Roosevelt, Franklin Delano, 38, 40, 45, 149
Roosevelt, Theodore, 67, 80
Rose, A. D., 5
Rosenberg, C. E., 37
Rottinghaus, B., 75, 77
Rowan, L. R., 86
Rudalevige, A., 78
Rueben, K., 4–5, 27
Ruhl, J. B., 101
Rybicki, E., 53, 56–60, 62, 63, 66, 67, 73, 148

Sablan, J., 62–64
Saddler, A. N., 19, 20, 50, 136, 138, 154
Sanger, J., 89
Sargent, J. F., 6, 86, 100, 105–106, 109
Saturno, J. V., 55, 62, 63
Saxe, K., 86
Scheb, J. M., 45
Scherer, N., 44, 115, 116, 134
Schickler, E., 23, 55, 64, 65, 68
Schmidt, C. W., 55
Schneider, J., 56–57, 59, 65
Schuette v. Coalition to Defend Affirmative Action (2014), 120–121

Schweickart, T., 80
Scott-Clayton, J. E., 4–5, 27
Sea Grant College Program, 109
Seifert, T. A., 154
Sekar, K., 6, 109
Seldin, A., 29
Selin, J. L., 21, 82, 84, 85, 92–94, 108
Selko, A., 143
Seltzer, R., 106, 108
Semanko, N. A., 10
Seru, A., 30
Servicemen's Readjustment Act (GI Bill, 1944), 8, 40–41, 61, 105, 154
Shaw, K., 31, 67, 80, 149
Shea, D. A., 86
Sherman, M., 121
Shinall, J. B., 45, 46
Shobe, J., 97–98
Shohfi, K. D., 34, 62n5
Short, M., 12, 34, 36, 39n3, 40–43, 46n6, 51, 153, 154, 160
Sidak, J. G., 31
Siddiqui, S., 113, 132, 152
Simpson, L., 122, 123
Siraco, J., 156
Skrentny, J. D., 78
Slaughter, S. A., 48n9
Smith, A. A., 27, 31, 88
Smith, M., 19
Smith, M. F., 7, 30, 122, 123
Smith-Hughes Act (1917), 37
Smith-Lever Act (1914), 37
Smole, D. P., 4, 50, 62n5, 64, 74, 102, 149
Sobocinski, E. J., 21n3
Social media, 83–84, 89, 134, 144
Sonnenfeld, K., 140
Sopko, J. F., 53, 65
Southern Regional Education Board, 141
Soviet Union (former)
  Cold War and, 9, 12, 40, 41, 48, 51, 153–154, 160
  national defense policy, 41–42
  Sputnik (1957), 9, 42, 160
Spellings, Margaret, 50, 97, 143

Spellings Commission (Commission on the Future of Higher Education), 50, 97, 143
Spriggs, J. F., 118
Stallings, D. T., 2
Stanton, L., 62, 63
State Authorization Reciprocity Agreement, 141
State government, 16–17, 19, 20
  in the consumerism and accountability era of higher education, 48–49
  influence on federal higher education policy, 134–138
  property tax revolts, 48–49
  race-conscious admissions policy and, 120–121
  state-level accountability programs, 49
State Higher Education Executive Officers Association (SHEEO), 19, 129, 135, 141
Stedman, J. B., 85
Steiner, M., 12, 34, 36, 39n3, 40–43, 46n6, 51, 153, 154, 160
Stephens, G. R., 54
Stephens, O. H., 45
Stidham, R., 113, 117
Stiglitz, J., 85
Stith, Kate, 27, 36–37, 153
Stone, D., 25–28, 32
Stone, J., 128
Stone, S. B., 17
Stout, T. T., 35, 37, 39
Strach, P., 40, 41, 46–48, 154
Stratford, M., 31, 58, 79, 81, 150
Strauber, J. E., 98, 99
Straus, J. R., 21, 53, 64–68
Strauss, D. A., 79
Strömbäck, J., 80
Stuckey, B. D., 5
Student Aid Alliance, 129–130, 140
Student Aid and Fiscal Responsibility Act (SAFRA, 2009), 50, 63–64, 74, 80, 148–149
Student Aid Bill of Rights, 77
Student Army Training Corps programs, 37

Student Assistance General Provisions, 22, 135
Student financial aid, 4–5. *See also* Higher Education Act (1965)
  bankruptcy law and, 124–126
  Basic Educational Opportunity Grant (BEOG)/Pell Grant programs, 28, 46–49, 63n7, 64, 75, 88, 108
  "Borrower Defense to Repayment" policy (USDOE), 73, 110–111
  defaults on student loans, 5, 49–51, 108
  Department of Education as direct lender, 4, 50, 64, 74–75, 102, 156
  extent of federal financial aid, 1, 4
  Federal Family Education Loan (FFEL) program, 74–75
  federal sources of, 27
  forms of, 4
  GI Bills, 8, 40–41, 61, 105, 154
  impact of policies for, 2
  NDEA/Perkins Loans, 9, 22, 42, 46n6
  Student Aid Alliance, 129–130, 140
  Student Aid Bill of Rights, 77
  Student Assistance General Provisions, 22, 135
  tax benefits and, 4–5
  Teacher Education Assistance for College and Higher Education (TEACH) Grants, 140–141, 152
  Title IV programs, Higher Education Act (1965), 5, 20, 23, 25, 28–29, 46, 61, 101, 136, 138, 151
  work-study programs, 20, 38–39, 46, 160
Student privacy policy, Family Educational Rights and Privacy Act (FERPA, 1974), 7, 28, 47, 61, 148
Student Veterans Association, 143
Stuessy, M. M., 21, 53, 64–68, 73, 85
Sundquist, M. L., 21
Sunstein, C. R., 79, 132, 144, 152
Superville, D., 69
Sweatt v. Painter (1950), 44, 119–120, 151
Sweezy v. New Hampshire (1957), 122
Szlezinger, Z., 131, 143

Tan, Y., 140
Tandberg, D. A., 5, 19, 127, 136, 138, 154, 157
Tatelman, T. B., 21, 64, 82, 92, 97, 151
Taylor, A., 69
Taylor, A. N., 125
Taylor, T. E., 19, 20
Teacher Education Assistance for College and Higher Education (TEACH) Grants, 22, 140–141, 152
Tesfai, L., 109, 143
Teter, M. J., 56
Thelin, John R., 2, 12, 34–38, 40–41, 43, 51, 53, 153, 154, 161
Think tanks, 142
Thomason, A., 50
Thompson, F. J., 18, 135
Thorning, M., 58
Thornton, S. R., 8
Thrower, S., 75–76
Tollefson, T. A., 19
Tollestrup, J., 62n5
Totenberg, N., 124, 152
Trade Adjustment Assistance Community College and Career Training Grant, 104
Treisman, R., 96
Tribal Colleges and Universities, 35n1, 36, 110
TRIO programs, for historically underserved students, 5, 46, 61, 62
Trow, Martin, 18, 19, 36–37, 135, 153
Truman, Harry, 43, 45
Truman Commission (Commission on Higher Education), 43–44
Trump, Donald, 2, 22, 25, 47n8, 50, 59, 69, 71, 73–81, 83, 86, 88–89, 96, 98, 102–104, 110–111, 113, 116, 124, 132, 139, 149–152
Trump University, 79
Trustees of Dartmouth College v. Woodward (1819), 36–37, 153
Tua, U. F., 116–117
Tuition-free community college proposal, 31, 74, 81, 88, 149–150
Turner, C., 50, 140, 152, 156
Turner, L. J., 20

Turner, M. G., 6
Turner, S., 40

Ujifusa, A., 74–75
Unah, I., 79, 113, 115, 116
U.S. Army, 37
U.S. Bureau of Labor Statistics (BLS), 104
U.S. Census Bureau, 54, 109
U.S. Chamber of Commerce, 143
U.S. Citizenship & Immigration Services, 16n1, 107
U.S. Congress, 16, 21, 53–70. *See also* U.S. House of Representatives; U.S. Senate; *specific legislation*
  advisory role of administrative agencies and, 97–98
  budget reconciliation process, 63–64
  "bully pulpit," 67–68
  collective action problems, 56
  enumerated powers, 54–56
  executive branch accountability and, 53, 64–65
  interest group strategies used with, 130–132
  leadership and committees, 56–57
  legislative power, 59–64
  oversight powers, 64–66, 68
  power of the purse, 27, 53–54, 61–64, 70
  reexamining role of, 148–149
  rules of, 57–59
  structure of Congress, 54–59
  U.S. Constitution, Article I, 21, 22–23, 26–29, 30, 53–56, 60, 73, 74, 86, 148
U.S. Constitution, 16, 25–31, 51
  Amendment I, 121–123, 126, 151
  Amendment V, 123
  Amendment X, 1
  Amendment XII, 72
  Amendment XIII, 55, 72
  Amendment XIV, 29–30, 36, 43, 44, 55, 118, 119–120, 123, 151
  Amendment XV, 55
  Article I, 21, 22–23, 26–29, 30, 53–56, 60, 73, 74, 86, 148
  Article II, 21–23, 30–31, 64–65, 66, 71, 72, 79, 81, 86
  Article III, 22, 23, 114, 116, 117, 123–124
  Article IV, 117
  Equal Protection Clause, Fourteenth Amendment, 29–30, 36, 43, 44, 55, 118, 119–121, 151
  as "living" document, 10
  Patent and Copyright Clause, 30
  preamble, 39–40
  silence on education, 1, 2, 25
  Taxing and Spending Clause, 26–29
U.S. Courts, 16, 17
U.S. Department of Agriculture (USDA), 6, 19, 39, 77. *See also* Land-grant institutions
  extension programs, 19, 37, 39
  Hispanic Serving Institutions National Program, 106
  National Institute of Food and Agriculture (NIFA), 106
U.S. Department of Commerce, National Oceanic and Atmospheric Administration, 109
U.S. Department of Defense (DOD), 6, 105–106
  My Career Advancement Account Scholarship (MyCAA), 105
  Office of the Under Secretary of Defense for Research & Engineering, 106
  Spouse Education and Career Opportunities (SECO) programs, 105
U.S. Department of Education, 21–22, 25, 27, 84, 150–151, 159
  accountability standards, 91
  "Borrower Defense to Repayment" policy, 73, 110–111
  College Scorecard, 50, 86
  COVID-19 pandemic and, 136–137
  as direct lender of federal student loans, 4, 50, 64, 74–75, 102, 156
  executive action and, 77, 78, 80
  federal funding "priorities," 100
  funding sources for research and development, 6
  Gainful Employment Rule (2019), 22, 50, 95–96, 117–118, 124, 143

U.S. Department of Education (*continued*)
as independent agency, 47, 49, 102
interest group strategies used with, 133
mechanisms influencing higher
education, 102–103
National Institute on Disability and
Rehabilitation Research, 100n2
Office for Civil Rights (OCR), 72,
98, 101, 102–103, 138
Office of Career, Technical, and Adult
Education, 102
Office of Federal Student Aid, 50, 87,
102
Office of Hearings and Appeals, 23, 99
Office of Legislation and
Congressional Affairs, 98
Office of Postsecondary Education,
72, 95, 102
partnership with U.S. Department of
the Treasury, 4–5, 107–108
predecessor to, 39, 42
Program Integrity Triad, 5, 49–50,
136, 138
rulemaking, 1–2, 5–6, 7, 28
website, 76–77
U.S. Department of Education and the
Workforce (proposed), 103
U.S. Department of Energy, 6, 109
U.S. Department of Health, Education
and Welfare (HEW), 42, 102
U.S. Department of Health and Human
Services (HHS), 6, 110
U.S. Department of Homeland Security
(DHS)
Deferred Action for Childhood Arrivals
(DACA) program, 78, 88–89,
107, 124, 132, 150, 151–152
Immigration and Customs
Enforcement (ICE), 107
U.S. Department of the Interior, 102
Bureau of Indian Education, 110
Office of Civil Rights, 110
U.S. Department of Justice (DOJ), 28, 98
Executive Office for Immigration
Review, 99
mechanisms influencing higher
education, 104–105
"Varsity Blues" scandal (2019), 105

U.S. Department of Labor, 76, 149
antidiscrimination policies, 45, 46n5
Bureau of Labor Statistics (BLS), 104
mechanisms influencing higher
education, 103–104
unionization and collective bargaining
on college campuses and, 104
workforce education programs, 103–104
U.S. Department of State, Bureau of
Educational and Cultural Affairs,
107
U.S. Department of the Treasury, 4, 27
Internal Revenue Service (IRS), 4–5,
26–29, 107–108
partnership with U.S. Department of
Education, 4–5, 107–108
Taxing and Spending Clause, U.S.
Constitution, 26–29
U.S. Department of Veterans Affairs,
77, 105, 106
U.S. Government Accountability Office
(GAO), 61, 69, 98, 99, 108
U.S. Government Printing Office, 82,
92–93
U.S. House of Representatives, 16, 21,
24n5
Committee on Appropriations,
62–63, 66
Committee on Financial Services, 57
Committee on the Budget, 62–64,
63, 64
Education & Labor Committee, 57
Speaker of the House, 56
U.S. National Archives & Records
Administration, 33
U.S. Office of Education, 39, 42, 102
U.S. Office of Government Ethics, 94
U.S. Patent & Trademark Office, 7, 30, 109
U.S. Senate, 16, 21, 24n5
Committee on Appropriations,
62–63, 66
Committee on Health, Education,
Labor and Pensions (HELP), 57,
65–66, 135
Committee on the Budget, 62–64
confirmation power over presidential
appointments, 23, 53, 66–67,
79–80, 113, 115–116

filibuster and cloture, 58–59
Judiciary Committee, 113, 115–116
tie-breaking role of vice president, 86–87
U.S. Sentencing Commission, 108
United States Student Association, 129
U.S. Supreme Court, 36–37, 113–115, 118–121, 122, 125
United States v. Fordice (1992), 120
United States v. Lopez (1995), 55n2
University of California, 78
University of California–Davis, 44, 120, 151
University of California–Los Angeles, 143
University of Michigan, 120
University of Texas, 120–121, 151
Urban Institute, 142
USA.gov, 21n4, 92, 93

Valocchi, S., 42–43
Veterans, 104–105
 Centers of Excellence for Veteran Student Success, 5
 GI Bill of Rights (1944), 8, 40–41, 61, 105, 154
 Student Veterans Association, 143
Veto power
 Congressional overriding of presidential veto, 23, 35, 60, 73
 of the president, 21, 23, 31–32, 35, 60, 73
 Senate filibuster and cloture rules, 58–59
Vetter, J., 76, 109, 149
Vice President, 56, 72, 86–88
Vice President's Education Initiatives, 88
Volden, C., 18
Volkwein, J. F., 138
Vorsanger, S., 127

Wagner, D. J., 106
Walker, C. J., 95, 98
Walker, R. A., 38–39, 153, 160
Wallace, George, 45
Warber A. L., 75
Warren, Elizabeth, 66
Wartell, S. R., 82
Washington, G. E., 82, 84, 150

Washington, George, 34, 79
Washington Higher Education Secretariat, 129
Washington Post, 2
Waterman, A. T., 41
Watson, C. E., 109–110
Weaver, D. H., 140
Webster, J., 12, 34, 36, 39n3, 40–43, 46n6, 51, 153, 154, 160
Weeden, D. D., 5, 19, 136, 154, 157
Weeks, J. P., 35
Weiner, S. A., 6
Welch, M., 154
Werner, E., 24, 116
Wessel, D., 102, 156
West, E. B., 69
Westcott, K. S., 8
Western Interstate Commission for Higher Education, 141
Wexman, V., 7, 30
Wheatle, Katherine I., 13, 33–36, 43, 51, 153, 154, 161
Wheeler, T. E., 96
Whistle, W., 69
White, E. N., 38
White House Office, 16–17, 79, 82–84, 149–150
White House Office of the Press Secretary, 83
White House Rural Council, 77, 106
Whittington, K. E., 23, 117
Wice, S., 58, 59
Wiener, M. L., 99
Wilgus, J. K., 6
Wilhelm, B., 21, 53, 64–68
Wilkerson, J. D., 62
William D. Ford Federal Direct Loan program, 22, 50
Williams, R. L., 1, 25, 79, 113, 115, 116
Williamson, K. M., 6
Wilson, J. Q., 21, 23, 64, 66, 71, 72
Wilson, R., 87
Wohlstetter, P., 141
Wolanin, Thomas R., 1–3, 4–5, 6, 8, 10–11, 15, 19, 28–29, 40, 100
Wollstein, K., 141
Wolniak, G. C., 154
Wood, B. D., 80

Wooden, O. S., 2, 34, 36, 46, 76, 161
Woolley, J. T., 71, 77, 89
Wooten, T., 56n3
Workforce Innovation and Opportunity Act, 61, 104
Works Progress Administration (WPA), 39, 160
Work-study programs, 20, 38–39, 46, 160
Wren, I., 140, 156
Wysession, M. E., 86

Xu, C., 10, 160

Yackee, S. W., 84
Yale University, 98
Yannelis, C., 49

Ye C., 140
Yeh, B. T., 30, 62
Yeshiva University, 104, 125
Yilla, K., 102, 156
Yinug, L. D., 74
Yoho, J., 128
Yokoyama, K., 19
You, H. Y., 127
Yourish, K., 62, 63

Zehrt, L. R., 47, 121
Zelizer, J., 68
Zhou, Y., 4
Ziegler, M., 120–121
Zinth, K., 19
Zornow, D. M., 98, 99
Zumeta, W. M., 1, 4, 25

About the Author

Rebecca S. Natow is an assistant professor of educational leadership and policy at Hofstra University. Dr. Natow is an expert on higher education policy and has written extensively about the federal higher education rulemaking process in the U.S. Department of Education. She has also researched and written about performance-based funding policies for higher education, technology use in postsecondary developmental education, and research utilization in the creation of federal regulations. Dr. Natow received her EdD, EdM, and MA in higher and postsecondary education from Teachers College, Columbia University, and her JD from Georgetown University Law Center.